COMMON GROUND
ON COMMON CORE

COMMON GROUND ON COMMON CORE:

*Voices from across the Political Spectrum
Expose the Realities of the
Common Core State Standards*

Edited by

KIRSTEN LOMBARD

RESOUNDING BOOKS

Madison, Wisconsin

Resounding Books, Madison, WI 53704
© 2014 by Resounding Books

Published 2014, trade paperback, advance print version.
ISBN: 978-0-9908809-0-5

Printed in the United States of America
by The Book Patch, Scottsdale, AZ

This title may be purchased in bulk. For information, please email: orders@resoundingbooks.org.

For my nieces, Keagen and Callie,
because I am determined that they should
inherit something better.

For my parents, who helped me to know
what it means to be a woman of principle.

And for all children across these United States,
because they merit true education
and intellectual liberation,
not subjugation.

CONTENTS

ACKNOWLEDGEMENTS

This volume, with its unique array of voices and perspectives, quite literally could not have come to be without the assistance of a number of important people. Undoubtedly, I will fail to remember them all—for which forgiveness will almost certainly be necessary. However, I am keen to recognize certain individuals whose support has been nothing short of extraordinary—more than I could have hoped or imagined.

To Jeff Tallard, a true mentor, who believed in the vision of Resounding Books from the first moment I shared it with him and who materially assisted in birthing its identity and mission, I offer my deepest gratitude. To his wife Karen, who so graciously indulged her husband's belief in this dream, I render likewise my sincerest thanks. I hope that this first volume of essays will be but the first of many fruits to demonstrate that your mutual investment was not in vain.

Josh Tolley, too, served as a guide and sounding board, handing me some of the most powerful tools imaginable, insights that I could apply to literally every aspect of making Resounding Books, this publication, and many others to come a reality.

My farflung friend Rich Disney is also owed great thanks for the time he spent in helping me to develop a practical model for how Resounding Books could work. He quite literally worked out the operational foundation on which I could build and expand a very large and noble vision. In a similar vein, Beau G. Williams spent time looking over my plans, helping me to find holes, telling me when I was on the right track, and giving me all manner of other key advice and feedback.

Over the past year and a half, my parents, James and Andrea Lombard, have consistently encouraged me in the formation of my own publishing company. Moreover, they saw the value in its stated mission: to establish political common ground by fostering real dialogue. They brainstormed ideas with me, offered feedback, suggested possibilities, and prayed for me and the project. They never ceased to express interest in every detail of Resounding Books or its very first book projects, no matter how tiny. Not everyone is so fortunate as to list their parents among their best friends. I am. What a privilege to have their love and support on this adventure.

The idea to assemble a book of essays on Common Core, an issue on which we have both been engaged as grassroots activists, came from my friend and colleague Jeffrey D. Horn during one of our epic dinner conversations at a local Perkins. For that idea alone, I owe Jeff a great debt, though it only grew from there. Jeff facilitated an introduction to one of the book's first contributors, Kris Nielsen, and instantly agreed to pen an essay himself when asked. Moreover, he magnanimously stepped in to assist with literally every aspect of the technology involved in bringing the publishing company and *Common Ground* to fruition. At this juncture, I think my obligation to him stretches up somewhere beyond the stratosphere. When—not if, *when*—Jeff decides to pursue his own goals, I hope he knows that I will, with nary a complaint, return tenfold the time, energy, and painstaking effort he has so freely volunteered to advance mine.

The true-blue members of my Dane County grassroots group—my second family—didn't bat a collective eyelash when I said I needed to step back from my responsibilities for several months in order to realize the Resounding Books vision, particularly when they learned that my first book projects would be education-related. Brothers and sisters in arms, they told me to go do what I needed to do and just kept saying that they couldn't wait to see the outcome. Here, too, Jeff Horn has been a godsend, taking on the reins of leadership for the bulk of my absence.

Jennifer C. Johnson has been nothing short of a saint on the legal front. I render her my grateful thanks for looking out so keenly for Resounding Books and the aims of the *Common Ground* project. Her friendship and loyalty has blessed every step of this journey. As she works to forge a path toward her own remarkable aims, I look forward to repaying some of her many insights and kindnesses.

Ryn Bruce at Coloryn Studio has been stupendous on the design end of the equation. From the beginning, she listened carefully to my thoughts and vision, ultimately giving something close to literal wings to the identity I envisioned for Resounding Books. When the time came to design the *Common Ground* book cover, she shaped my ideas into something not just appealing and aesthically appropriate but also visually symbolic. Anyone looking for a friendly, approachable, and highly professional designer who will bring concepts to life in remarkable and unexpected ways could do no better than Ryn.

Tony Urso not only believed in *Common Ground* but has unceasingly used his networks on behalf of the project to make it a success. He began by introducing me to people who have since become contributors. He has finished by being pretty much the best unofficial publicity agent ever. Before advance copies were even available, he had people intrigued and asking if there was a way they could get hold of one. If this book gains real steam with the public, Tony will have had a great deal to do with it. He has planted seeds of interest anywhere and everywhere that he had opportunity to do so.

Most of all, I want to thank my essay contributors. I knew exactly three of you when I began this journey. Yet, in the last several months of working with each of you on these essays, I have gained truly valuable connections, remarkable friendships, and—the crux of what this project was always about—substantive dialogue, understanding, mutual respect, and partnership. When I came to most of you in the winter of 2014 with my plan for Common Ground, you opened your hearts and minds to the mission of a grassroots activist and first-time publisher. Then, with unmatched gestures of kindness and commitment, you got behind that mission with everything you had. I am proud of the work we have done together. Your essays are powerful. Gathering them into a single volume and helping to polish them is, to my mind, the most important and personally rewarding thing I have ever had the privilege to do. I could not be more proud than to be sallying forth to do battle with all of you in this way. I trust in the impact that our union will have. Alone each of us poses a significant threat to those who would force false education reforms on the citizenry. Together, I am convinced, we *are* downright dangerous. Thank you for your investment with me in finding and planting a flag in precious common ground—not just for ourselves but also, I trust, on behalf of many, many others.

This is just the beginning. Hold tight, everyone. Here we go...

CONTRIBUTORS

(in alphabetical order)

MARY CALAMIA, LCSW, CASAC, is a psychotherapist practicing in Stony Brook, New York. She treats children, adolescents, and adults from more than twenty different school districts on Long Island. Mary partners with Jack, a 100-pound Labrador retriever who uses his own "special skills" to make the therapeutic environment feel safe and enjoyable for her most vulnerable clients. After testifying before the New York State Assembly Forum on Education about the mental health consequences of the Common Core, Mary took on a leadership role in the grassroots fight against the controversial initiative. Co-founder of Long Islanders United Against the Common Core, Mary speaks at educational forums and advocates tirelessly with legislators to eliminate Common Core from New York State schools.

MARSHA FAMILARO ENRIGHT holds a Master of Arts in Psychology from the New School for Social Research as well as a Bachelor of Arts in Biology from Northwestern University. President of the Reason, Individualism, Freedom Institute, Marsha is a 40-year advocate of a free society. An education entrepreneur, writer, and speaker, she developed the Great Connections Seminars, an innovative educational program for high school and college students, implemented in Chicago, Buenos Aires, and San Jose; readers may learn more at: www.rifinst.org. In 1990 she co-founded Council Oak Montessori School for ages 3 to 15, named one of the best private schools in Chicago by *Chicago Magazine* in 2009 and 2011. Her writing, much of which is on view at the Fountainhead Institute website (fountainheadinstitute.com), includes research papers on neuropsychology, psychology, philosophy, and education, reviews of novelists, and political and historical commentary. She also served as editor of *Ayn Rand Explained: From Tyranny to Tea Party* (Open Court, 2013), which includes her own original material.

WILLIAM A. ESTRADA began working for the Home School Legal Defense Association (HSLDA, www.hslda.org) in January 2004 as a legal assistant. After obtaining his J.D. from Oak Brook College of Law, he began to direct HSLDA's Federal Relations department and to serve as its federal lobbyist. As HSLDA's representative on Capitol Hill, Will uses his passion for homeschooling to advocate for all homeschoolers before Congress and the federal departments. He has testified before Congress and met with senior officials from federal agencies and the executive branch. From October 2007 through December 2012, Will served as director of HSLDA's Generation Joshua division, where he worked with young people who are passionate about making a difference in politics. He oversaw a doubling of Generation Joshua's membership and an expansion of its reach and effectiveness. In July 2011, he also took on lobbying for ParentalRights.org as the organization's director of federal relations, where he advocates before Congress for the Parental Rights Amendment to the U.S. Constitution. He is a member of the U.S. Supreme Court bar and the California bar. Will and his wife Rachel, both homeschool graduates, reside with their son Dominic in northern Virginia.

JED HOPKINS is associate professor of education at Edgewood College in Madison, Wisconsin. He received his Ph.D. in the Department of Curriculum and Instruction at the University of Minnesota in 2009. Hopkins began his teaching career in London, England, as an elementary school teacher almost thirty years ago. Since then he has taught at numerous levels from elementary through middle school as well as teaching pre-service and in-service teachers at the undergraduate and graduate levels. His teaching and research interests straddle literacy, teacher education, drama in education, and philosophy of education. He is particularly interested in existentialist philosophies, social linguistics and integrating the arts into teaching.

JEFFREY D. HORN is a father of four children, a grassroots activist, and a data scientist. Earning his Bachelor of Science degree from Marquette University in Milwaukee, Wisconsin, he also holds a master's degree in mathematics and a Ph. D. in computer science from the University of Wisconsin – Madison. A professional programmer, he works daily to build infrastructure that can be used to leverage Big Data in improving advertising, medical decisions, investing, and more. Very conscious of the tension that exists between technology and personal freedom, he has been educating and advocating against Common Core and high-stakes testing in Wisconsin for several years. Over the course of 2013 and 2014, he spearheaded an initiative to unite a variety of organizations and individuals on Common Core related issues for the purpose of sending several open letters to state-level public officials in Wisconsin. The letters ultimately helped to ensure a series of public hearings on Common Core at locations around the state in late 2013.

KAREN LAMOREAUX is a married mother of three and a small-business owner in Maumelle, Arkansas. A member of Arkansas Against Common Core (www.arkansasagainstcommoncore.com), Karen's opposition to the controversial reform package, videorecorded before the Arkansas Board of Education in December 2013, went viral on the Internet. Since then, Karen has been given a voice on *Fox and Friends*, the *Willis Report* on Fox Business, the *Glenn Beck Show*, the *Pat & Stu Radio Show* as well as local television and radio networks in Arkansas. Together with her fellow coalition members, she travels statewide and regionally, educating other parents about the realities of Common Core and working toward its repeal by the Arkansas State Legislature. She advocates for the preservation of parental rights as well as state rights in education. She has recently started homeschooling her children.

MORNA MCDERMOTT has been working in, with, and around public schools for over twenty years. Currently she is an associate professor at Towson University in Maryland. Her scholarship and research interests focus on democracy, social justice, and arts-informed inquiry in Kindergarten through post-secondary educational settings as well as working with both beginning and experienced educators. Recent artwork and installations have emphasized the value of art as a "public pedagogy" in creating grassroots social-political-educational change. Tapping into this theme, Morna recently authored *The Left-Handed Curriculum: Creative Experiences for Empowering Teachers* (IAP, 2012). She is also one of the founding members of United Opt Out National, which has become a strong voice and conduit for advocacy against high-stakes testing. She currently lives in Baltimore with her husband and two children. For more of Morna's thoughts and work, visit her Educational Alchemy blog (www.educationalchemy.com).

BRIAN MEDVED ran for and won a seat on the Board of Education in Germantown, Wisconsin, in 2013. Since Brian's election, Germantown's board has become the first in the state to enthusiastically—and unanimously—reject the Common Core State Standards. The board is now working to develop its own Germantown Model Academic Standards, a process in which Brian is actively involved. Germantown's standards development process may be tracked on the Germantown School Board website (https://sites.google.com/a/germantownschools.org/germantown-standards-and-curriculum-development/), where the resulting standards will also be accessible to all. Brian continues to work to remove Common Core from the state of Wisconsin and across the country, believing that it is detrimental to learning. He maintains his own website to that end (www.brianmedved.com). In his personal life, Brian owns a construction business, as well as owning and managing rental properties. He is the father of four boys, two in college and two in high school. His wife is his high-school sweetheart, inspiration, and soul mate, and also happens to be an outstanding educator.

R. JAMES MILGRAM is professor of mathematics emeritus at Stanford University. An internationally recognized mathematician, he helped author the pre-Common Core California Standards, and was the math reviewer for the *Curriculum Focus Points* book series (National Council of Teachers of Mathematics, 2006 - 2011). Dr. Milgram is one of only three mathematicians in the last forty years to be awarded the Gauss Professorship (1989) at the University of Göttingen. In 2000, he was also awarded a Distinguished Visiting Professorship in the Chinese

Academy of Sciences, Beijing, rarely granted to mathematicians. In the United States, Dr. Milgram has held the prestigious Ordway Professorship at the University of Minnesota, the Regents Professorship at the University of New Mexico, and has given many named lectures at top American universities. Dr. Milgram served on the validation committee charged with overseeing the development and writing of the Common Core standards, the only member of that committee to hold a Ph.D. in mathematics. He has also served on the NASA Advisory Council and the National Board for Education Science, which oversees all research at the U.S. Department of Education. Dr. Milgram received his undergraduate and master's degrees in mathematics from the University of Chicago and his Ph.D. in mathematics from the University of Minnesota.

KRIS L. NIELSEN has worked in education for approximately a decade and is an expert on national education "reform." He holds a master's degree in education, with emphasis on child development and motivational learning. He is a dedicated activist against corporate education reform. Upon leaving a post as a science teacher at a school in North Carolina in 2012, Kris penned a resignation letter concerning the hidden and serious circumstances that daily plague students and teachers in the current education environment. The letter went viral globally in the space of a week. Kris has since written two books on issues within the education system and the need to find a better way, *Children of the Core* and *Uncommon* (both published through CreateSpace, 2013). He continues to work diligently to inform parents and citizens about the real dangers that are already resulting from the failure to create an environment in which teachers can authentically teach and students can truly learn. He has also helped lead parent and student opt-out movements in New York, Colorado, and New Mexico. Kris blogs at @ *the Chalkface* (www.atthechalkface.com).

JANE ROBBINS is an attorney and a senior fellow with the American Principles Project in Washington, D.C. (americanprinciplesproject.org). In that position she has crafted federal and state legislation designed to restore the constitutional autonomy of states and parents in education policy and to protect the rights of religious freedom and conscience. Her essays on these topics have been published in various print and online media. With Emmett McGroarty she co-authored the APP/Pioneer Institute report *Controlling Education From the Top: Why Common Core Is Bad for America* and, with Joy Pullmann and Emmett McGroarty, the Pioneer Institute report *Cogs in the Machine: Big Data, Common Core, and National Testing*. She has published numerous articles about the problems with Common Core, including those of intrusive data-collection and threats to student privacy, and has testified about these issues before the legislatures of nine states. She is a graduate of Clemson University and the Harvard Law School.

TIM SLEKAR began his career in education as a second grade teacher in Williamsburg, Virginia, and later taught fifth grade in York, Pennsylvania. He attended the University of Maryland at College Park where he earned his Ph. D. in social studies education. During his studies, he worked with seventh and eighth grade teachers in the city of Baltimore. He has published his research in some of the top educational research journals including *Teacher Education Quarterly*, *Theory and Research in Social Education*, and the *Journal of Thought*. He recently became the dean of the School of Education at Edgewood College in Madison, Wisconsin. Prior to accepting that position, Dr. Slekar was at Pennsylvania State-Altoona for ten years, where he was responsible for building an elementary education program and leading the Division of Education, Human Development, and Social Sciences. His wife, Michelle, is the CEO of the Slekar household. Together, Tim and Michelle are the parents of Luke and Lacey.

CERESTA SMITH is a twenty-six year veteran educator who has taught grades 6 through 12 in reading, language arts, and beginning and advanced television production. She earned her National Board Certification in adult/young adult English language arts in 2002 and now serves as a teacher leader and mentor. In September of 2008, Ceresta moved from a Florida school deemed "high performing" to serve as a teacher leader and literacy coach in a school deemed "low performing." While there, she became a 2009 – 2010 recipient of a Jordan

Fundamental Grant. The grant facilitated the implementation of Text Titans, a literacy-building initiative she designed, funded by basketball great Michael Jordan's philanthropic non-profit, which honors teachers who motivate and inspire students toward achieving excellence. As a committed educator and activist, Ceresta also founded the Concerned Teacher Coalition in 2009 to address the inequities in Miami-Dade County's predominantly African-American public schools. One of the original organizers of Save Our Schools March and National Call to Action and a sought after public speaker, she continues to champion public education in her roles as a Save Our Schools steering committee member and an administrator for United Opt Out National, an organization that advocates for an end to punitive high-stakes testing and on other key education issues.

SANDRA STOTSKY is professor of education emerita at the University of Arkansas, where she held the 21st Century Chair in Teacher Quality. She did her undergraduate work at the University of Michigan and holds a Ph.D. in reading research from the Harvard Graduate School of Education. From 1999-2003, she served as senior associate commissioner (a professional position) at the Massachusetts Department of Elementary and Secondary Education, where she was in charge of developing or revising all of that state's K-12 standards, teacher licensure tests, and teacher and administrator licensure regulations. She served on the Massachusetts Board of Elementary and Secondary Education from 2006-2010 (a citizen position) and on the National Mathematics Advisory Panel from 2006-2008. From 1991-1997, she also edited the premier research journal of the National Council of Teachers of English, Research in the Teaching of English. She has published extensively in professional journals and written several books. From 2009-2010, she also served on the Common Core Validation Committee, where she was one of five members who would not sign off on the standards as being internationally benchmarked, rigorous, or research-based.

CHRISTINE T. worked in special education for more than fifteen years, first as a teachers' aide and then as an applied behavior analysis specialist. When she started a family, she took time off to raise her two sons. After her boys had reached school age, she returned to school to study social work, aspiring to work with drug and alcohol addicts as a rehabilitation counselor. She has currently put her education on hold in order to homeschool her youngest son. She lives with her family and two dogs in New York State, where she is an avid reader and writer. In their spare time together, she and her family enjoy spending a great deal of time in active outdoor pursuits.

CHRISTOPHER H. TIENKEN, Ed.D., is an assistant professor at Seton Hall University. His research focuses on curriculum and assessment policies and practices. His latest book is *The School Reform Landscape: Fraud, Myth, and Lies* (Rowman and Littlefield, 2013). The international honor society Kappa Delta Pi awarded him the 2013 Truman Kelley Award for Outstanding Research. For more information on Chris and his work, visit his website: www.christienken.com.

SHANE VANDER HART is the founder and editor of the blog *Caffeinated Thoughts* (caffeinatedthoughts.com) and also writes extensively about the Common Core State Standards for Truth in American Education (truthinamericaneducation.com). He founded Iowans for Local Control (iowansforlocalcontrol.com) in order to fight against the Common Core and Next Generation Science Standards and to advocate for education liberty in his home state. Vander Hart has twenty-one years of youth ministry experience. As part of that experience he served as both dean of students and teacher in a private Christian school in Indiana. In 2012 he launched 4:15 Communications, LLC, a social media and communications consulting business. Vander Hart and his family reside just outside Des Moines, Iowa, where they homeschool their three teenage children.

S. WHARTON is the parent of two school-aged children in Florida. She holds a Bachelor of Science in mass communication from Emerson College as well as a Master of Science degree in counseling and college student development from Northeastern University. In 2010 she undertook graduate work at the University of South Florida to become a counselor in private practice, and is currently a registered mental health intern. Before moving to Florida, she worked as a personal counselor, career counselor, academic advisor, and freshman seminar instructor in university and community college settings in Massachusetts. Some of her career-exploration publication work has been presented professionally and distributed to guidance professionals nationwide. For three years she taught a course in success skills for college and life. Her students regularly rated her highly for lessons that they could apply practically. Ms. Wharton is committed to high standards in education but believes that such standards must remain under local control if K-12 students are to receive tailored instruction that benefits their learning needs.

ZE'EV WURMAN is currently a visiting scholar at the Hoover Institution, Stanford University. Between 1995 and 2007, he participated in developing California's education standards and state mathematics assessments. From 2007 to 2009 he served as a senior policy adviser with the Office of Planning, Evaluation and Policy Development at the U.S. Department of Education in Washington, D.C. Throughout the development of the Common Core standards in 2009-2010, Wurman analyzed the mathematics drafts, both for the Pioneer Institute and the State of California. In 2010 he served on the California Academic Content Standards Commission, which evaluated the suitability of the Common Core standards for California. He has authored evaluation reports on the Common Core for both the Pioneer and Pacific Research Institutes and professionally evaluated other state and national standards. Wurman has spent four decades in the electronic and semiconductor industries. Currently he is an executive with Monolithic 3D, a Silicon Valley semiconductor start up. He holds fifteen U.S. patents and is the recipient of the Israel Security Prize (E. Golomb). Wurman holds bachelor's and master's degrees in electrical engineering from the Technion – Israel Institute of Technology.

FOREWORD

Throughout my political career, I have worked in coalitions with others who, while they do not agree with libertarians on every issue, do agree with us on one or more important issues. Today, this approach is becoming increasingly common as a number of activists, intellectuals, and even some politicians look to build coalitions that cross party and ideological lines.

Coalitions between libertarians, constitutional conservatives, and progressives are reshaping the public debate on foreign policy, civil liberties, crony capitalism, and the Federal Reserve. Now principled conservatives, progressives, and libertarians have united to fight the so-called Common Core standards.

Common Ground on Common Core: Voices from across the Political Spectrum Expose the Realities of the Common Core State Standards is a result of this cross-ideological alliance. The essays in the book serve as both a good introduction to Common Core and as ammunition for those already involved in the fight.

The idea that education policy could unite liberals, conservatives, and libertarians seems counter-intuitive. After all, don't liberals believe bureaucrats, not parents, should control education? And aren't conservatives split between those that want to take over local school boards so they can impose a conservative curriculum on the public schools—complete with teaching creationism and other religiously-based doctrines—and those that want to dismantle public schools through taxpayer-funded voucher programs? How could conservatives and liberals work together, much less unite with libertarians who favor complete elimination of all public ("government") schools so that education can be provided by the market, just like life's other necessities?

But if we go beyond these caricatures of progressivism, conservativism, and libertarianism and look closely, we find good reasons why opposition to Common Core unites Americans of all ideological stripes. First of all, whatever their political ideology, all parents want their children to receive a quality education. As detailed in the essays in the book, Common Core does not provide anything close to a quality education. The grassroots movement against Common Core has been fueled by parents who do not care what ideological box opposition to the initiative falls in; they only care that it is hurting their children.

Secondly, conservatives, liberals, and libertarians all have a tradition of opposing centralized bureaucracies. For example, the "New Left" of the 1960s was motivated in part by the same distrust of centralization and large bureaucracies that fueled the Goldwater movement. Many such progressives recognized that concentrated power served the interests of big businesses and other entrenched interests to the detriment of small businesses, workers, and families. While today it is common for libertarians and free-market conservatives to explore and expose the ways Big Business promotes and benefits from taxes, regulations, and other government programs, much of the pioneering work in this area was done by socialist scholars such as historian Gabriel Kalko.

One of the most unreported tendencies in American politics is how many progressives have found common ground with libertarians and conservatives in supporting efforts to encourage state governments to fulfill their constitutional function as a check on federal abuses of liberty. Progressive activists have joined with libertarians and constitutional conservatives, for instance, in efforts to nullify parts of the National Defense Authorization Act and end police militarization. Now this coalition has a chance to reshape the national debate over education.

The Left-Right coalition opposing Common Core has its antithesis in the coalition of establishment Republicans and Democrats pushing the initiative. Many supposed conservative Republican governors have embraced this signature education initiative of the progressive Obama administration.

The ability of Common Core to unite establishment conservatives and establishment progressives may be explained by the enthusiasm

Big Business has shown. According to an article posted at *Politico* on March 14, 2014, "Big Business Takes on Tea Party on Common Core," two of the biggest business lobbies in the country, the Business Roundtable and the U.S. Chamber of Commerce, are spending millions to promote the initiative and defeat anti-Common Core efforts. Big Business says that dumbing down public education somehow improves its workforce. In the article, the president of the Business Council of Alabama inadvertently reveals Big Business' attitude toward education: "The business community is by far the biggest *consumer* of the product created by our education system." (emphasis mine) I wonder how many parents would agree that their children are a "product"?

In a free society the goal of education should be to produce well-rounded individuals capable of pursuing their own interests and dreams. While part of education should be to help students figure out and develop skills that will serve them in whatever career they choose, schools should never tailor their offerings to suit the perceived needs of established businesses. In fact, tailoring education to ensure that existing businesses have a good supply of workers is a form of central planning that, like all types of central planning, will eventually fail. School officials simply cannot know if the businesses dominating today's economy will even exist five or ten years from now; so why shape curriculum around preparing students for jobs that might not be available in the future?

The alignment between the supposedly progressive Obama administration and establishment Republicans to promote Common Core is not the first such alliance to increase federal control over education. In fact, Common Core builds on one of George W. Bush's major domestic polices, the No Child Left Behind Act (NCLB). Before the attacks of September 11, 2001, NCLB was Bush's major priority. He bragged about working with liberal icon Senator Ted Kennedy and other Democrats to pass the act.

Most notably, NCLB imposed student "assessments" in what were deemed core subjects. Those schools whose students did not perform up to a certain standard on the assessments faced reductions in federal funds.

Not long after passage, however, it became clear that No Child Left Behind should have been called Leave Every Child Behind.

NCLB's emphasis on so-called assessments pressured teachers to "teach to the test," robbing students of any true mastery. Subjects not assessed under NCLB were deemphasized, thus also depriving students of a well-rounded education.

In the years following NCLB, not one parent or teacher who came into my congressional office to discuss education policy had anything good to say about the act. While some complained that the government was not spending enough money on education (even though the Bush administration was spending record amounts on federal education programs), the main complaint was that NCLB was dumbing down education by forcing teachers to teach to the test. As NCLB's failure became more apparent, conservatives turned against it. Liberals, some of whom had initially supported the bill, were also vocal about the ways the act's testing mandates were harming education.

As bad as NCLB's national testing provisions were, they were a symptom of the problem, not the cause. American education will continue to suffer as long as education policy is dominated by the idea that politicians and bureaucrats can somehow develop an education system capable of meeting the needs of all children in the country. The failure to recognize that lesson is what leads the Obama administration to repeat in Common Core the mistakes made under NCLB. Obama could have fulfilled his campaign promises to be a "non-partisan" and transformational president by listening to the criticism of NCLB's mandates, criticism coming not just from the Right but from influential constituencies in his own party, including public school teachers. Had he repealed NCLB's testing and other mandates instead of doubling down on them, the education system might look quite different today.

Instead, the Obama administration went beyond NCLB. A group of supposed education experts developed Common Core to serve as a model curriculum for use in every school in the nation.

Common Core's defenders deny that it is any way a mandate on local schools since the federal government does not force any school to adopt the initiative. Instead, schools are merely "encouraged" to adopt

Common Core via the promise of receiving additional federal funds. But few states will turn down "free" federal money.

Of course, the money is not really free; the federal government gets its money from taxation or borrowing. One way the federal government finds its borrowed funds is through Federal Reserve monetization of the debt, which imposes the most insidious tax on the people, the inflation tax. So Common Core does not give any state free money. Rather, money is taken from the state's constituents, either directly or via inflation, and used to bribe the state into adopting Common Core.

While Common Core may appear to make sense in the abstract, in practice it has been a disaster. For example, the experts who developed the standards recommend replacing traditional math with reform math. Reform math turns traditional mathematics on its head by focusing on having children master "abstract thinking" instead of traditional mathematics concepts like addition and subtraction. Teaching children abstract thinking instead of skills may seem sensible in theory, but in practice it means children will no longer master *either* basic mathematical skills or analytical thinking. One positive of the Common Core's new math is that many parents have become involved in the fight against the initiative after struggling to help their children with their math homework.

Mathematics is not the only subject ruined by Common Core's standards. Reading and literature instruction have also been impacted by a misguided attempt to make them "relevant." Common Core's idea of relevancy is to replace traditional English literature with informational texts. Students will read such inspiring materials as studies by the Federal Reserve Bank of San Francisco, the EPA's "Recommended Levels of Insulation," and "Invasive Plant Inventory" by California's Invasive Plant Council. If you find it hard to believe that reading Federal Reserve Studies and EPA guidelines instead of classics like *Huckleberry Finn* will instill children with a lifetime love of reading, well, you are probably just a parent or a teacher, not a federally-funded education expert.

Replacing classic literature with government reports seems an unlikely way to achieve Common Core's stated goal of developing critical thinking skills. It certainly does not seem likely to encourage students to think critically of the government.

Examining Common Core shows why opposition to these latest federal schemes to "improve" education crosses party and ideological lines. Instead, the fault lines on Common Core lie between the establishment of both parties and Big Business, who side with education bureaucrats, and the grassroots activists who stand with parents, teachers, and children.

The fight against Common Core is one of the most important battles raging in American politics today, and *Common Ground on Common Core* is an important contribution to that battle. I am honored to be a part of this project, and I am pleased to recommend the essays in this book to anyone concerned about American education—which should be every American.

RON PAUL
Former U.S. Congressman
and Presidential Candidate
Lake Jackson, Texas
October 2014

A WORD FROM THE EDITOR:
Finding Common Ground

WARNING: There are no safe essays in this book. Standing alone, each essay herein exposes truth, provides insight, plants a flag, and takes a stand against false education reform. In so doing, each of the authors places hope in the possibility that others will hear and join with them. Their presence in this volume also signifies that each of these individuals envisions and is committed to realizing something better and more noble: true education. These realities make every essay in the collection a significant threat to those who have been pushing something else.

Together, the essays are a force—wholly subversive and dangerous.

We have all long assumed that there are those with whom we simply cannot have a dialogue. In fact, quite frequently, we've been plainly told that there are those with whom we should not—dare not—partner and work.

But what if the prohibitions against communicating with each other actually serve an agenda that isn't ours? What if we're not as far apart as we think? What if, instead, we've simply lacked reliable information about each other for far too long? What if the truth is that we're not necessarily enemies at all? And what if the information and perspective each of us holds is part of a larger picture that must be considered—a full picture without which it will be impossible to win the war against false education reform?

The Goal

This book is intended to challenge conventional wisdom concerning who our friends and enemies actually are in the fight for true education.

Many of *Common Ground on Common Core*'s contributors have, in fact, grown tired of respecting artificial political lines. We are consciously heading into uncharted territory, choosing to talk to all the "wrong" people, taking the time and making the effort to see each other not as depersonalized foes, but as thoughtful, engaged citizens—as potential, even necessary partners.

It is highly purposeful, then, that those who share their voices here cannot be slotted into any single or neat group. We cover a wide range along the political and ideological spectrum. Libertarian, radical leftist, constitutionalist, moderate, conservative, voluntarist, liberal progressive, objectivist: all of these and more are terms by which the contributors to *Common Ground* self-identify. We also represent a range of social roles and life paths: a couple of lawyers, some academics, a number of grassroots activists, a social worker, a school board member, and, most importantly, parents and educators. All of these individuals have done extensive homework on the facts surrounding false education reform such as the Common Core State Standards (Common Core) as well as the implications if we do not change course.

Under normal circumstances, seeing this diverse array of perspectives in a single volume might be unthinkable; but that's the whole point. Common Core has remarkably facilitated common ground. Not just a tiny patch, either; it's significant real estate. This reality makes us far more difficult to marginalize or dismiss—that, as a heterogeneous group of informed individuals, we demonstrate so much overlap in our respective concerns. Even in those areas where disagreement sometimes proves sticky, a growing willingness exists to reject shallow talking points, talk deeply, listen carefully, and understand.

It isn't that problems in education didn't exist before now. False education reform has been with us for decades. Rather, No Child Left Behind, Race to the Top, and Common Core have so accelerated a cycle of toxicity that many people are finally recognizing the need to reconsider and revise strategy and tactics. If we are to push back in a meaningful and lasting manner against what is poisoning first our children and ultimately our society, we will indeed need to leverage each other's insights, connections, research, and expertise—despite our differences.

The Challenges

To be clear, as the editor of this work, I'm not interested in advancing some unrealistic, utopian vision. Difficult discussions lie ahead in relationship to some of what has gone wrong in the realm of U.S. education. A number of *Common Ground's* essays respectfully point toward potential trouble spots. However, our discussions will inevitably be more productive—and viable solutions more likely—if we stand first on our places of agreement and, from there, work to comprehend each other's additional priorities and concerns. I say solutions (plural) very purposely. One of the most troubling aspects of Common Core and related initiatives is that they have made grand and impossible claims to being the one perfect solution for everyone. Meanwhile, they fail to take into consideration a host of needs pertinent to the realities of individual children, parents, teachers, and communities.

The process of engaging with each other is a risk. Opening our minds involves the uncomfortable possibility that we might have to *change* our minds. All of us are likely to find out we've been wrong about pieces of what we've believed to be true…maybe even wrong about everything. Willingness to face such possibilities, to lay all of the evidence out on the table and re-evaluate, takes tremendous courage.

Do we have it in us…?

Are we willing to acknowledge that, like the blind men describing the elephant, we've examined only those portions of the education debacle within our immediate experience, assuming them to be the whole? Are we honest enough to ask ourselves if we may have dismissed, ignored, or forgotten important considerations? Are we willing to re-examine instructional theories, operational approaches, structural models, and other possibilities that we've either embraced or rejected on political or ideological grounds—sometimes without actually closely evaluating their merit, workability, or likely results? Do we have the grace to acknowledge that we've perhaps stereotyped problems, concerns, ideas, and people in thinking about education?

In short: Are we open to doing ourselves what we want our children to learn to do—think and evaluate critically; develop solutions rooted in as much evidence and perspective as we can gather?

One thing is for certain: It is the people, the concerned citizens of this nation— with parents and teachers leading the way—who must drive the discussion around education going forward. As a whole, the credibility of the education establishment has crumbled; the chickens of their increasingly centralized and standardized vision have come home to roost with a vengeance. They have helped no one. Well, that's not quite true...

The Truth

The education establishment *has*, in fact, facilitated tremendous rewards for Big Government (Big Gov) and Big Business (Big Biz) alike.

While an oversimplification, it is at least useful to acknowledge that a specialization of concerns has developed along the political spectrum, contributing in many senses to our inability to address our education difficulties effectively. People who identify more closely with what is generally thought of as the political "Left" have primarily preoccupied themselves with the sins of Big Biz, often seeing government as the surest means of checking corruption. Those who identify on the traditional "Right" have instead tended to fixate on the corruption and wrongful infringements of Big Gov, in many cases uncritically regarding private business as the fix for overreaching government. The two ends of the continuum have spent untold time and energy sanctimoniously screaming at each other about our respective pet preferences.

What we've mostly failed to grasp, till now, is that we're all correct.

Public-private partnership, crony capitalism, elitism, corporatism, fascism—call it what you want. In truth, our problems almost all stem from Big Biz and Big Gov working hand-in-hand. Such arrangements always subvert the proper voice of the people, pick their pockets, and rob them of their natural and civil rights. The grossest corruptions of Big Biz would remain mostly impossible without assistance derived through public policy. Take, for instance, the relatively recent gutting of the Family Educational Rights and Privacy Act, or FERPA. Anyone who wants personal student data can now acquire it simply by saying they "need" it, not least large corporations who view the classroom as a captive market. Big Biz only achieved this travesty by leveraging the force of government; it enlisted the assistance of key elected officials for whom personal power, public status, and campaign dollars have often meant far more than principled duty toward the people they ostensibly serve.

Just as troubling is the cloak of legitimacy in which education's public-private partners have wrapped themselves. In fact, they have thoroughly co-opted familiar language on both Right and Left in order to mislead us about ourselves and each other, foment disagreement among us, and leverage the ensuing distraction to further their own aims. To begin with, we are told that that partnership between Big Gov and Big Biz amounts to more efficient government—quicker action, lower costs, and better results. Technically, public-private partnership *does*, in fact, result in more efficient government: Government is always more efficient when it can find ways to circumnavigate behind, around, under, or above the will of the people. However, under such circumstances, the likelihood of lower cost for the citizen is questionable at best, while a yield of better results must always cynically be followed with the question: "For whom...?"

We are further told that the partnership of Big Gov and Big Biz will provide us with "free market" solutions, all while helping to achieve what it terms "social justice." This amalgamation of co-opted terminology should be viewed as nothing less than the betrayal of the entire political and ideological spectrum. "*We've been framed!*" exclaims Morna McDermott in her essay, explaining that the concept of social justice has been hijacked in order to provide people on the Left with a reason to buy into questionable education reforms.[1] Her cry could just as easily have issued from my own [small "l"] libertarian typing fingers concerning free markets. Creating the illusion that public-private partnership is somehow interested in the free exchange of goods and services—or in justice of any kind—serves only to deceive well-intentioned people, all in the service of achieving market monopoly (or oligopoly) and political oligarchy.

Brilliant strategy, the co-option of language has, in fact, wrought untold havoc, dividing us superficially and falsely for quite some time. It is imperative that we finally see through such word games, use our dialogue as an opportunity to define terms for one another, and start to reclaim vocabulary from those who have used it to wrongful purpose. Once terms are defined, we may find we still do not agree with one another; but it's imperative that we at least know the truth about what we do and don't endorse—and why—so that we can no longer, in ignorance and under false pretenses, be duped, maneuvered, and pitted against one another.

The Book

In constructing this volume, it would have been impossible to cover every important angle of the Common Core debacle. I confess that I did not attempt to do so. Rather, I mapped out a series of general topic areas, bones that I saw as crucial to the book's basic structure, flow, and thrust. I worked to make each of these sections general enough that any contributor, regardless of background, could find a niche within them. Then, in reaching out to various authors, I began the process of mapping voices to those sections. In some cases, based on their particular expertise, I asked contributors to write within a specific section. In other cases, there was discussion about where people felt they could best direct their efforts and insights. The reader will, in fact, note that some of the essays could easily have slotted into more than one category.

As promised essays began to roll in, it quickly became clear that Shane Vander Hart would be best positioned to set the stage for readers. An education watchdog *par excellence*, Vander Hart reveals in plain terms—and demonstrates via carefully documented examples—the manner in which an unsuspecting public was wholly bypassed in the advancement of Common Core. While he doesn't label it as such, he paints a clear picture of what education researcher and author Beverly Eakman in 1998 identified as "inside-out," a strategy whereby an initiative is embraced by key players, embedded within various layers of infrastructure, and almost wholly implemented without public knowledge. Only after the program has been rooted to a degree that would make it extremely difficult to reverse or remove is a public relations campaign mounted to alert citizens to its existence and sell them on its "merits."

Just as deception has been perpetrated on the American people, it has been propagated among elected representatives, who have likely been among some of the biggest victims of the misleading information exposed by Christopher Tienken's essay. Tienken has written extensively elsewhere on the topic of how student performance on international assessments, such as TIMSS and PISA, has been used to manufacture a false perception that the United States is significantly lagging behind other nations academically and risks becoming irrelevant in the global economy. Here, he not only explains for the layman the means by which this false view was created, he also lays out how the perception of crisis has driven an incorrect conclusion that increased centralization and standardization of education are necessary in order to produce U.S. students able to compete with top-performing cohort groups around the world.

In focusing on the Common Core standards themselves, Sandra Stotsky was the most qualified person to cover two separate topics—which she graciously did, the only contributor in this book to do double duty. Her background as an expert in the development of academic standards, as well as instruction for English language arts (ELA), garnered her a position on the national validation committee for the Common Core standards. Ostensibly formed to ensure the quality of the standards, the committee, as it turns out, was only meant to rubber stamp them. Dr. Stotsky is able to speak very directly to the deep flaws in the validation process; her experience should raise the eyebrow of any citizen willing to consider the matter. She has also taken tremendous care in outlining for readers specific problems and concerns with the ELA standards, providing a solid refutation of their rigor.

Rounding out the book's section on the academic standards are R. James Milgram and Ze'ev Wurman, with an examination of the Common Core mathematics standards. The only other subject matter expert to sit on the national validation committee, Dr. Milgram's credentials as a mathematician are unassailable. Wurman, an engineer who formerly held a post with the U.S. Department of Education, reviewed the math standards for the State of California. Together, Milgram and Wurman detail numerous specific weaknesses with the standards. In addition, they stunningly demonstrate clear manipulation in how the rigor of those standards has been represented.

Three essays examine Common Core in relationship to the standardization of education, all from different angles. Like Christopher Tienken, William Estrada tackles the ubiquitous myth, propagated by the education establishment and its friendlies, that centralization and standardization offer a superior route to education. Noting an utter lack of evidence for either the value or success of centralized education, Estrada argues powerfully for decentralized learning models—homeschooling among them—for which plentiful and historic evidence of success does exist.

Pointing to current consumer conveniences that most of us likely take for granted, Jeffrey Horn reveals that they, in fact, possess a dark side. Drawing the reader back to industrial efficiency theory and application at the beginning of the twentieth century, Horn provides strong evidence for the increasing implementation of parallel structures and methods within American schools. The essay is, in its own way, a meditation: Under a regimen of tightly monitored instruction and standardized testing, is the schoolroom any longer a place of learning meant to set us free? Or has it instead been appropriated as a closely managed training center, intended to fulfill the needs of others?

In the third of the standardization-themed essays, Ceresta Smith pulls no punches. She effectively destroys the notion that centralization, standardization, and high-stakes testing work to create an equal playing field for minority students. Her direct experience, citation of assessment scores, and analysis of the practical effects of policy decimate Common Core's bold claims concerning equitable education and increased opportunity for underserved students. She exposes the reality that the situation in underserved minority communities is stagnant at best, but more likely devolving as the result of a long line of failed education reforms that have repeatedly shortchanged those who have been given little choice but to put their faith in them. In many senses, Smith's essay is one of the most dangerous in the book because it exposes lies that the education establishment desperately needs to keep up in an effort to maintain its credibility. It is also one of the most prophetic essays: While vulnerable black and brown communities have been most heavily impacted by false reform to date, the problems they experience will be on display far more broadly unless we change course.

This volume would not have been complete without an examination of data collection and data mining. The issue closely relates to standardization, since the flow of student data comes largely through formative and summative standardized assessments. While many have shrugged their shoulders over data collection, sighing that it is the way of things now, it becomes difficult to remain complacent in the face of the facts and implications Jane Robbins presents. She offers the reader a concise, no-nonsense view of the current lay of the land. The truth is disturbing. Federal policy has been deeply altered to make our children's personal data available to whoever wants it. Well, almost anyone. Strike off of that long list the people to whom the data should actually belong—students and parents. "Isn't this anonymous data?" the reader may wonder. It isn't, as Robbins makes abundantly clear. Our children are terribly vulnerable. Working to safeguard their data must be a central component of the fight against false education reform.

We will all be affected by Common Core and related policy in the end. However, three groups will experience immediate impact as full implementation goes into effect in most states this year. Teachers are on the front lines. It is they who are placed in the position of having to transmit Common Core's lessons and administer its standardized assessments—high-stakes enforcement mechanisms designed chiefly to ensure their own unwavering compliance. Kris Nielsen, an exceptional educator who cares deeply about his profession, explores the implications of Common Core, particularly as they relate to his professional colleagues. Teaching the Common Core is not, in fact, teaching, Nielsen asserts in the title of his essay, then lays out a candid view of the ways in which the craft of teaching is being undermined and destroyed. The good news is that many teachers already agree with him and are taking a stand. Let us hope that Nielsen's final exhortation inspires many more to rise up. Teachers are indispensable to winning the fight.

Students are the second link in the chain of vulnerability created by Common Core, standing at perhaps the greatest risk by virtue of their dependent status. Here again, three essays render some of the predicaments of students from different perspectives. Mary Calamia, a licensed social worker, describes the uptick in her practice after the full implementation of Common Core in New York State in 2012. The emotional and psychological states in which her young clients began to present as a result of the stresses Common Core appears to have placed them under are disturbing—and heartrending.

Christine T. allows us an unhindered view of the manifestation of such stress within the home and family, displaying several angles from which parents have become the third group most immediately vulnerable in the Common Core debacle. Christine felt utterly baffled and helpless for more than a year as she watched first one son and then another devolve emotionally under the pressure of triggers she could not at the time identify. She ended up stumbling into the answer almost by accident. The good news is that the trauma that Christine's family experienced, now transformed into an essay, can at last be other families' gain, perhaps even their salvation, by providing answers for them far more quickly.

The final essay in the section on students considers, in particular, the dilemma Common Core poses for students with learning differences. The mother of two children, one *with* learning differences, S. Wharton notes Common Core's lack of room for children who don't fit the particular learning styles to which the initiative is predisposed. What, Wharton rightly asks, is the result for these students? How are they to embrace the learning process—at all, much less with any joy. Honing in specifically on misapplications of constructivism and the difficulties with high-stakes testing, Wharton takes a dual approach to the topic, providing not only explanations, facts, and research, but also a personal window onto her family's direct experiences.

And what *of* parents...? As already indicated, by nature of Common Core's impact on their children, parents will likewise struggle. But there is another facet to consider when it comes to their particular dilemma. In an essay pulled largely from her own journals, Karen Lamoreaux takes the reader on a journey of personal experience and research. She first shows us the formation of troubling barriers in her ability to assist and relate to her children in regard to learning. Pursuing the fuller implications of that reality, Karen takes us through a developing process of awareness of the compromise of her parental rights. The reader becomes, in essence, a fly on the wall as she does her homework on Common Core, gradually becoming an activist out of both conviction and necessity. Helpfully, Karen discusses not just Common Core itself, but issues and technologies that dovetail with it in various ways, helping us to see that what lies at the initiative's periphery is not necessarily any less worthy of concern.

Several of Common Ground's authors became activists unexpectedly. Kris Nielsen and Karen Lamoreaux both certainly fit that category. In each case, something they had expressed went viral on the Internet, serving as a flashpoint and giving them a valuable platform to say far more. Brian Medved has a similar if somewhat quieter story. His essay describes his transformation from a parent into a concerned citizen willing to run for office—one who discovered that he wasn't quite as informed as he'd first believed—and ultimately into a full-fledged activist working diligently to inform and empower others. In Medved's case, his successful run for school board provided an exceptional platform from which he has helped to achieve the only significant local pushback to Common Core in Wisconsin to date. Helping us to understand how this seeming educational miracle occurred, Medved further provides practical advice for those wishing to make a similar difference where they live. His essay forms part of the final section of the book, devoted to avoiding false reform.

Morna McDermott's essay, also a natural fit for this last portion of *Common Ground*, is likely to shake a lot of trees...hard. McDermott is perhaps best known for video-recording a hand-drawn diagram of the numerous corporate interests involved in Common Core's development and advancement. So, perhaps it should come as no surprise that she begins her contribution with an exposé of public-private partnership in action. McDermott takes the reader straight to the text of model legislation developed within the American Legislative Exchange Council, an organization that brings legislators and special interests together to formulate state-level policy. The model bills McDermott cites would facilitate data collection and mining, allow for direct marketing to students in the classroom, and provide favorable conditions for the expansion of factory-style, for-profit charter schools—or McCharters, as McDermott aptly terms them. In the second portion of her essay, she looks openly and honestly at her hopes and reservations about Left-Right coalitions, ultimately coming down on the side of hope but giving us important food for thought.

As Kris Nielsen points out, Common Core and related measures place educators under threat, often making it extremely risky to speak out. As educators of educators, working within the school of education at a small college in Madison, Wisconsin, Jed Hopkins and Tim Slekar consider a slightly different angle of this same problem. Framing their essay as a brief dialogue, the two converse about the constrictive parameters that have been placed around not only education but, more particularly, how education is even permitted to be discussed today. With passion and forthrightness, they enjoin us to break out of these wrongly enforced limits, asserting the crucial nature of doing so if we are ever to find our way back to authentic teaching, substantive learning...and, hence, true education.

What might education look like if it were liberated? This is the question posed by the book's final essay. Marsha Familaro Enright first defines the concept of a voluntary cooperative society, then lithely considers with the reader a host of educational possibilities that such a society could yield—as well as the debacles that those possibilities could help us to overcome. It is a fitting place to end because brainstorming, envisioning, and dreaming in relationship to solid principle is, in fact, a huge part of what we will need to do together to crawl out of the ugly trench we're in; it is the path to building something better for ourselves and our children

It is time to do what those advancing the false reform of Common Core fear most: talk to and begin to understand one another; find ways to partner with each other in rejecting factory-style education; and work together to find alternative solutions.

If I might be granted one wish as an editor, let it be this: May this book be a clarion call...

Well, they blew the horn
And the walls came down
They'd all been warned
And the walls came down
They stood there laughing
They're not laughing anymore
The walls came down[2]

KIRSTEN LOMBARD
Madison, Wisconsin
September 2014

NOTES

1. See McDermott's essay in section 9, specifically, page 325.

2. Michael Been, from "The Walls Came Down," *Modern Romans*, 1983.

I. A PRE-PLANNED "SOLUTION":

Shafting the Public

COMMON CORE:

The Silent Revolution in Education Policy

SHANE VANDER HART

"The philosophy of the classroom today is the philosophy of government tomorrow." Questionably attributed to Abraham Lincoln, it is one of my favorite quotes when debating education policy. It encapsulates one of the primary reasons my wife Cheryl and I homeschool—to ensure that we are the main influencers of our children while they are in their formative years.

These words bring home why education policy is so important. It doesn't just impact an individual child, but eventually impacts us all. We must, as part of a constitutional republic, have a voice in the direction of education policy as it relates to all of us as parents and/or taxpayers.

"A State-Led Initiative"

The most prevalent myth that I have heard and read in my research of the Core is that the standards are a state-led initiative—a claim made by the Common Core State Standards Initiative (CCSSI) itself.[1]

The claim is hardly accurate.

The Common Core is *not* state-led. To be fair, I'm not saying that the U.S. Department of Education (DoED) wrote the Common Core. I'm not even saying it was their idea. It wasn't. Advocates of the Common Core who say it is state-led typically insist neither of these things is true.

On that we can agree.

It's always important to get past lingo and clarify what we mean. When I say something is "state-led," I mean it is initiated within state departments of education with the blessing of the state legislative and executive blessings, undergoes exacting analysis as well as a period of genuine public comment that solicits most particularly parents and educators, is approved by the state legislature, and is only then actually signed into law by the state's governor. From there states can and should start having discussions with one another about what works.

Why not look at Massachusetts' standards, Indiana's English Language Arts (ELA) standards, and say California's math standards (prior to Common Core alignment)? That would be common sense, and I'm for common sense.

That isn't what happened, however.

The Common Core standards process was seemingly initiated by the Center for Best Practices of the National Governors Association (NGA) and the Council of Chief State School Officers (CCSSO).[2] It began long before that, however.

The American Diploma Project

The standards and accountability movement began in the 1990s. States started to develop state standards in order to outline what students needed to know and be able to do in each grade level. States also implemented assessments designed to measure whether students were meeting the standards.[3]

In 1996 the NGA and a roster of business leaders founded Achieve, Inc., a bipartisan organization, in order to raise academic standards and graduation requirements, improve assessments, and strengthen accountability in all 50 states.[4]

In 2004, Achieve published a report titled *Ready or Not: Creating a High School Diploma That Counts*. The report framed the principle problem facing the American school system as a gap. Both employers and colleges were now demanding more of high school graduates, the report asserted, yet high school graduates were not being provided with the skills and knowledge they needed to succeed in either college or careers. The diploma itself had lost its value, Achieve maintained, because graduates could not compete successfully beyond high school: "While students and their parents may still believe that the diploma reflects adequate preparation for the intellectual demands of adult life, in reality it falls far short of this common-sense goal." The solution to this problem, the report asserted, was a common set of rigorous standards.[5]

This was the work of the American Diploma Project (ADP). From 2002-2004 Achieve Inc. partnered with the Education Trust, the Thomas B. Fordham Foundation, and the National Alliance of Business. Together, these organizations worked with representatives from K-12, postsecondary institutions, and business communities in Indiana, Kentucky, Massachusetts, Nevada, and Texas to identify the English and mathematics knowledge and skills that high school graduates would need for success in college and careers.[6]

As ADP's first step, "economists analyzed labor market projections to identify the most promising jobs—those that pay enough to support a family and provide real potential for career advancement" and "reviewed high school transcripts and other longitudinal education data to determine the preparation that workers in those occupations had received through high school."[7]

They then claim to have "partnered with postsecondary faculty from two- and four-year broad-access institutions in the five partner states to determine the prerequisite English and mathematics knowledge and skills required in entry-level, credit-bearing courses in English, mathematics, the physical sciences, the social sciences, and the humanities."[8]

In 2005, Achieve expanded ADP's mission into the American Diploma Network, comprised initially of thirteen states, "to help states close the significant gap between what students need to know for postsecondary success and what states require them to demonstrate in order to earn a high school diploma."[9] The following goals[10] were set forth to close this gap:

- Align high school standards with the demands of postsecondary education and the workplace;

- Require students to complete a college-and-career-ready curriculum to earn a high school diploma;

- Build college-and-career-ready measures into statewide high school assessment systems; and

- Hold high schools and postsecondary institutions accountable for student preparation and success.

By 2008 thirty-three states had signed on to the American Diploma Network.[11]

According to Achieve, the ADP college-and-career-ready benchmarks defined the knowledge and skills in English and mathematics that all students must acquire in high school in order to meet the challenges awaiting them on college campuses and in the workplace. "The ADP Core has become the 'common core' as a byproduct of the alignment work in each of the states," they wrote.[12]

The ADP was, for all practical purposes, a failure. That didn't stop it from being recycled as the CCSSI. On the surface it may have seemed that ADP was state-led; yet, just like the CCSSI, ADP was a public-private partnership with no legislative grant of approval. Our elected representatives were left out even then.

Purchasing Education Policy

We can pick up the money trail in 2007 with the Bill & Melinda Gates and Eli Broad Foundations pledging a total of $60 million to inject their education vision into the 2008 campaign cycle, including "uniform American standards."[13] Then, in May of 2008, the Gates Foundation awarded the Hunt Institute for Educational Leadership and Policy a $2.2 million grant to work with governors and other key stakeholders to promote the adoption of standards.[14] The following month the Hunt Institute and the NGA hosted a symposium to explore education strategies.

In fact, looking at total funding since 2008, some of the primary entities responsible for the Common Core—the NGA, the CCSSO, Achieve, and Student Achievement Partners—have accepted more than $147.9 million from the Gates Foundation alone.[15]

In December of 2008, the NGA, the CCSSO, and their Washington-based contractor, Achieve, laid out their education vision in *Bench-*

marking for Success: Ensuring U.S. Students Receive a World Class Education. In it they outline five reform steps:

- Upgrade state standards by adopting a common core of internationally benchmarked standards in math and language arts for grades K-12 to ensure that students are equipped with the necessary knowledge and skills to be globally competitive.[16]

- Leverage states' collective influence to ensure that textbooks, digital media, curricula, and assessments are aligned to internationally benchmarked standards and draw on lessons from high performing nations and states.[17]

- Revise state policies for recruiting, preparing, developing, and supporting teachers and school leaders to reflect the human capital practices of top performing nations and states around the world.[18]

- Hold schools and systems accountable through monitoring, interventions, and support to ensure consistently high performance, drawing upon international best practices.[19]

- Measure state-level education performance globally by examining student achievement and attainment in an international context to ensure that, over time, students are receiving the education they need to compete in the 21st century economy.[20]

Special-interest Led

With the NGA and the CCSSO at its helm, the CCSSI has been able to claim that it is a state-led effort.[21] Yet making this claim implies that the initiative had legislative grants of authority from individual states, which in most cases it did not. Through 2008 the CCSSI was, in fact, a plan of private groups being implemented through trade associations, albeit trade associations with official sounding names.

A first draft of the Common Core standards was not released for public comment until September 21, 2009.[22] However, subjecting the initiative to standard legislative process and public scrutiny in all fifty states would take years. State legislators and the general public would naturally want to read the standards and provide feedback. A way was needed to lock states into the standards quickly and avoid difficulties inherent in the democratic process. Common Core advocates found it in a program launched by the DoED.

Race to the Top

The American Recovery and Reinvestment Act enacted on February 17, 2009 provided the breakthrough that the CCSSI needed. The stimulus bill created a $4.35 billion earmark for states "that have made significant progress" in meeting four education reform objectives, including taking steps to improve state standards and enhancing the quality of academic assessments.[23]

The week following the bill's passage, Education Secretary Arne Duncan announced during a C-SPAN interview that the DoED would distribute this stimulus earmark to the states through a competitive grant program called Race to the Top (RttT).[24] Through that process, Duncan said, the department would identify a "set number of states" that would want to commit to very high common standards, "great assessments," and building a "great data system so you can track those students throughout their academic career."[25]

Secretary Duncan was asked during this same interview whether he envisioned "national standards for every kid across all subjects and national tests," he replied, "We want to get into this game…There are great outside partners—Achieve, the Gates Foundation, others—who are providing great leadership…I want to be the one to help it come to fruition."[26] Less than two weeks later, on March 7, 2009, the DoED did indeed announce the RttT national competition to distribute stimulus money through two rounds of grant awards.[27]

By June 1, 2009, the NGA and the CCSSO had formally launched the CCSSI to develop and implement national K-12 academic standards—in particular a set of learning standards, or benchmarks, in ELA and mathematics. Then-CCSSO President-elect Sue Gendron described the launch as "transforming the education of every child."[28] Considering her organization and others driving the initiative planned to "leverage states' collective influence to ensure that textbooks, digital media, curricula, and assessments"[29] would be part and parcel of the standards, the CCSSI would indeed transform education.

In its RttT request for applications,[30] the DoED actually changed the objectives set out in Congress' stimulus bill from general improvement of state standards and assessments to these specific federal dictates:[31]

- Adopting internationally benchmarked standards and assessments that prepare students for success in college and the workplace;

- Building data systems that measure students' success and inform teachers and principals about how they can improve their practices;

- Increasing teacher and principal effectiveness and achieving equity in their distribution; and

- Turning around the lowest-achieving schools.

With respect to its "standards and assessments" objectives, RttT coincided closely with the *Benchmarking for Success* action steps. It also designated these four reforms as "absolute priorities," meaning an applicant state had to address all four to be considered for funding.[32]

The DoED's clear intent was for all states to adopt the Common Core. Underscoring this understanding and intention in the RttT request for state applications, the agency defined "internationally benchmarked standards" as a "common set of K-12 standards" that is "substantially identical across all States in a consortium."[33] Moreover, the DoED directed peer reviewers of a state's RttT application to award a state high evaluation points in the funding consideration process if "the consortium includes a majority of the States in the country," but medium or low points if the consortium "includes one-half of the states or fewer."[34] The DoED took the view that "the larger the number of states in the consortium, the greater the benefits and potential impact."[35] The agency even admitted that the "goal of common K-12 standards is to replace the existing patchwork of State standards." It should be noted that in 2009, the CCSSI was the only game in town. No other consortium existed.

By tracking Common Core terminology in its grant requests for applications and by stating its intent to have one set of standards and one consortium, essentially the DoED discouraged other states from forming competing consortia. Though the DoED has said that this outcome wasn't intended, it was certainly the natural consequence of the application process.[36]

The release of the Common Core standards was "just the beginning of the effort," Secretary Duncan said. "As states move forward to implement the standards, they will need to translate standards into classroom teaching that will help all students master these new standards. The Department plans to support state implementation efforts by providing federal funds for high quality assessments, professional development to help teachers enhance the knowledge and skills needed to help students master the standards, and research to support continual improvement of the standards and assessments over time."[37]

The final draft of the standards was released on June 2, 2010. Forty-five states, the District of Columbia, four territories, and the Department of Defense Education Activity have adopted the Common Core since that date.[38] Most did so through the impetus of federal stimulus money in the form of RttT grants. In fact, simply applying for RttT funding committed states to adopt "college- and career-ready" standards and join an assessment consortium aligned to those standards by August 2, 2010.[39]

This high-pressure process, executed on an extremely short time line, led to a flawed adoption process. Political scientists Lorraine McDonnell and Stephen Weatherford found that, while "the Common Core's strongest supporters assumed it would take three years or more for a majority of states to adopt the standards," the RttT funding application deadlines shortened the process to "only a few months if not weeks." They also noted that the rollout was structured more like a well-staged political campaign, complete with a messaging toolkit provided by the NGA and the CCSSO—"answers to frequently asked questions, template letters to the editor, and a sample op-ed article—to aid in targeting "individuals and groups who had the potential to influence the [state board of education] vote."[40]

Only Alaska, Nebraska, Texas and Virginia never formally adopted the standards. Minnesota adopted only the ELA standards, excluding them from official standing as part of the CCSSI. When adopted by a state, the Common Core replaces existing state standards in ELA and math and can only be augmented by up to 15 percent.[41] How are those additional standards measured? Since it has become clear that they will not be covered by Common Core-aligned assessments, will they actually garner any focus in the classroom?

No Child Left Behind Conditional Waivers

On September 23, 2011 Secretary Duncan wrote a letter to chief state school officers inviting them to apply for flexibility under No Child Left Behind (NCLB) requirements.[42] As with RttT funding, just to apply for the waiver, state educational agencies (SEAs) had to agree to adopt "college- and career-ready standards in at least the reading/ language arts and mathematics" and to develop and administer "annual, statewide, aligned, *high-quality assessments*, and corresponding academic achievement standards, that measure *student growth* in at least grades 3-8 and at least once in high school."[43] (emphasis theirs)

Essentially states that hadn't already formally adopted the Common Core via the RttT funding application process had to show how their standards lined up to the Common Core in order to qualify for NCLB flexibility.

Lindsey Burke of the Heritage Foundation notes that the NCLB waivers illustrate a growing federal creep into education, being "granted only in exchange for implementing new executive branch priorities." She cites the DoED's initial denial of New Mexico's waiver when the state did not move quickly enough to embrace Common Core standards and assessments as well as the rejection of Iowa's request because, without legislative action, that state could not overcome local control to implement policies required to obtain the waiver.[44]

States such as Alaska, Texas, and Virginia who received waivers but were not a part of the CCSSI still ultimately made significant changes in their standards and/or joined testing consortia. Alaska rewrote its math and ELA standards, virtually plagiarizing the Common Core.[45] It also joined the Smarter Balanced Assessment Consortium (SBAC), but later pulled out in favor of developing its own assessment.[46] Virginia, in its waiver request, noted its involvement with the ADP and included an alignment study of its standards indicating strong parallels to the Common Core. Then-Governor Bob McDonnell also held conversations with Duncan regarding his state's standards.[47] Texas application for NCLB flexibility was a surprise, as it meant yielding concessions to the Feds.[48] Texas also had to demonstrate how the Texas Essential Knowledge and Skills lined up with the Common Core.[49]

States that have received waivers will think twice about pulling out of the Common Core. Those that have recently repealed the Common Core, such as Indiana, are still having to demonstrate how their standards align with the Common Core.[50] States that want to drop Common Core have to demonstrate that their standards are "college- and career- ready" in order to keep their NCLB waiver. The DoED sees the Common Core as the gold standard, so states may still end up with something similar to Common Core.

Common Core Assessments

The DoED leveraged its power to facilitate adoption not only of the Common Core standards but also the assessments designed to enforce them. States that joined an assessment consortium, such as SBAC or the Partnership for Assessment of Readiness for College and Careers (PARCC), signed memorandums of understanding prior to joining either as an advisory state or a governing state. Member states had to agree to remove barriers existing on their state's books to administration of the assessments. For example, the SBAC memorandum of understanding comprehensively required its member states to "identify and implement a plan to address barriers in State law, statute, regulation or policy to implementing the proposed assessment system and to address any such barriers prior to full implementation of the summative assessment components of the system."[51]

PARCC's memorandum of understanding contained similar language: "A Governing State must identify and address the legal, statutory, regulatory and policy barriers it must change in order for the State to adopt and implement the Consortium's assessment system components by the 2014-2015 school year."[52]

COMMON CORE: THE SILENT REVOLUTION   13

Ceding State Sovereignty over Education

One must ask how any state can maintain its sovereignty over education if it adopts these standards and joins either of the two assessment consortia. The answer is simple: They can't.

Emmett McGroarty and Jane Robbins of the American Principles Project write that "[t]he story of the Common Core Standards has been one of disdain for the American people" in which "the federal government and private organizations have imposed the Standards on the states...in a manner that denied the people and their elected legislators a meaningful chance to review the Standards and to consider the implications of participation...including assessments and data collection."[53]

State legislatures were entirely bypassed through the RttT funding application process. In fact, most state legislatures were not even in session during the short time frame provided for adoption in 2010.[54] No full state legislature voted on the Common Core prior to its state's adoption of the standards.[55]

McGroarty and Robbins note that Congress was bypassed as well: "The federal constitutional structure—a compound republic with a separation of powers—serves to protect our liberties and governance by the people. The Common Core Standards Initiative and [RttT] misused that structure by taking the people's money and forcing their elected representatives to decide whether to compete for a chance to get that money back, and did so without respecting the states' responsibility to put the issue to their people."[56]

At both the federal and state levels, the Common Core literally represents executive overreach off the chain.

Robert Scott, former commissioner of the Texas Education Agency, noted his skepticism of efforts to nationalize curriculum standards but waited to see if something would result out of CCSSI that could be incorporated into his state's curriculum frameworks. However, he says, "[o]nce we were told that states had to adopt the so-called Common Core State Standards in English and math with only a marginal opportunity for differentiation, it was clear that this was not about collaboration among the states. It was about control by the federal government and a few national organizations who believe they will be the ones to operate this new machinery."[57]

Scott also pointed out the flawed process in the states due to the timelines associated with the RttT grant competition, noting that most states that adopted the standards failed to subject them to "scrutiny by state education leaders, state board members, or even citizens and parents," relying instead on analyses funded directly or indirectly by the Gates Foundation.[58]

McDonnell and Weatherford, too, found that state education leaders, legislators, and staffers in many cases assumed that the NGA and the CCSSO "had used the [Common Core] validation committee and other mechanisms to ensure that the CCSSI had been adequately vetted and [was] grounded in relevant research."[59]

Had state lawmakers even known that five members of the Common Core Validation Committee did not sign off on the standards, perhaps they would have taken more time to contemplate adopting them. Unfortunately, the Common Core validation report did not include why five members did not sign-off. In fact, it neglected to mention that anyone had dissented at all.[60]

Iowa's Adoption of Common Core

It is a useful exercise to explore the process used to implement the Common Core at the state level. As a prominent example, one that I have explored in depth, I offer my own state of Iowa.

In 2005 the Iowa Legislature passed SF 245, which set voluntary standards for high school students in literacy, math, and science. These standards were known as "the Iowa Core." However, in 2008 the Iowa State Legislature gave the State Board of Education authority to "align the Iowa Core with any national or internationally recognized standards." That same year, with the state legislature's passage of SF 588, the Iowa Core not only expanded to include ELA, math, and science standards for grades K-8, but also incorporated social studies for grades K-12. SF 588 also made the expanded Iowa Core mandatory for public and accredited non-public schools.

On March 11, 2010, around the time that the first draft of the

Common Core was released, the Iowa State Board of Education held a meeting. The public agenda makes no mention of Common Core.[61] However, the minutes for that month's meeting contain evidence that Iowa Department of Education Director Judy Jeffrey mentioned them briefly during her report:

> Jeffrey indicated that the National Core Standards document is open for public input at www.corestandards.org. Department staff members have been continually providing comments to earlier drafts.
>
> Jeffrey mentioned there are concerns with the document. One concern deals with categorization by grade levels rather than age ranges or grade spans. *Another concern is the stipulation by the [CCSSO] and the NGA that states need to adopt the standards word for word.* Another concern deals with "skill and drill" in the language arts section.
>
> Jeffrey stated that the Department is extremely supportive of the movement and believes that National Core Standards are essential for all of the students in the nation. Jeffrey told State Board members that if they are in agreement with these concerns, they should weigh in during this time of public comment either as a Board or individually.[62] (emphasis mine)

The state board's May 13, 2010, meeting was held prior to the release of the final draft of the Common Core standards. Once again, there is no mention of the Common Core on the agenda.[63] Yet the minutes mention its discussion during Acting Director Kevin Fangman's report on the status of Iowa's RttT grant application. Fangman noted the impending deadline for the RttT application and that seventy of 361 school districts had already signed memorandums of understanding to meet the application's requirements, with approximately 200 anticipated. He also stated that the State Board would need to take action at its July meeting in order to ensure compliance with the stipulation to adopt Common Core by August 2, 2010. He further related information concerning funding competition for the two assessment consortia and provided details about SBAC, to which Iowa belongs.

The May minutes mention two additional items related to Common Core that should have been troubling:

[I]nstitutes of higher education are now being asked to sign on and say they will accept certain scores for summative [high school] assessments that…measure college and career readiness. As a result, students would not be required to take remedial classes in math and reading.

There was discussion about whether there are alignment issues, concerns that the Common Core Standards and assessment model are so complex that they won't produce the desired end results, how information will be reported to the general public, the role of Board members to communicate this information in plain English, and how the department can manage these initiatives with limited staff.[64]

Not only were the standards clearly controversial, they were already beginning to reach well beyond the K-12 system and into higher education.

The minutes discuss no concerted public relations push to inform the public about the Common Core. The original Iowa Core had been debated and discussed; it made the news. This set of standards instead flew under the radar. The Common Core and RttT were listed on the public agenda for the board's retreat on June 23-24, 2010, as an hourlong presentation given by Fangman;[65] but there are *no minutes* for that meeting available on the department's website. So we can't verify what was actually discussed during this "transparent" process of adoption.

Common Core was listed on the agenda for the state board's next meeting on July 29, 2010.[66] However, according to the minutes, no public comment was given.[67] In attendance were three reporters: Staci Hupp of the *Des Moines Register*, who is now the communications director at the Iowa Department of Education; Patrick Hogan of the *Cedar Rapids Gazette*; and Lee Rouse of WHO-TV. Did media coverage go beyond a news cycle?

Here is what the minutes record:

The Governor urged the Board to adopt the Common Core Standards. He stated that he feels good about the fact that the State Board, school districts, educators, and the Department have worked collaboratively in trying to find the best pathway to excellence in education for the future.…

Kevin Fangman introduced Rita Martens and Judith Spitzli, Department Program Consultants. Fangman indicated that an in-depth comparison was done comparing the Common Core Standards and the Iowa Core. He recapped the development of the Common Core Standards and future plans. *If the Common Core is adopted, it would become part of the Iowa Core and not a separate document.*

Martens described the process used in the alignment. She indicated that the Achieve organization created an online tool for states to compare their state standards with the Common Core Standards. *With the help of Brad Niebling, an [Area Education Agency] alignment specialist, it was decided to use Achieve to conduct the study. Work teams were convened in English language arts and mathematics. Martens explained the make-up of the work teams and the process used with the Achieve tool.* She also reviewed the research questions used during the alignment process and the results of the English language arts questions.

Judith Spitzli reviewed the results of research questions that related to mathematics. *She reminded the Board that states are allowed to add 15 percent of their own standards in addition to the Common Core.* She indicated that the Department was very pleased with the results and now has a process to fall back on.

There was discussion clarifying information on the additional content that will need to be added to the Iowa Core, difference in specificity between the Iowa Core and the Common Core Standards, clarification of inclusion of instructional strategies, and the types of delivery mechanisms other states that have adopted the Common Core are using to help equip teachers.[68] (emphasis mine).

I have a few observations about the process of adoption in Iowa.

First I have personally heard at least two proponents of the Common Core from the Iowa Department of Education mention the "alignment study," showing that the Iowa Core was almost aligned to the Common Core. As their logic goes it is not a big deal that Iowa adopted the Common Core. Yet, this study was done by Achieve, Inc., the same organization that developed the Common Core standards—an obvious conflict of interest.[69]

Second, the board's minutes clearly show that the Common Core is part of the Iowa Core. This fact is often repeated in Iowa and is part of a larger narrative—that because the Common Core is just a part of the much broader Iowa Core, the state doesn't actually have the Common Core. It does. This misleading narrative has mainly sprung from an executive order issued by Governor Terry Branstad on October 16, 2013.[70] The executive order asserts that there has been no federal overreach in the adoption of standards in Iowa. There has. The executive order similarly asserts that the State of Iowa maintains control of its standards. It doesn't. In addition, the governor's campaign claims that he has rejected the Common Core. He hasn't.[71]

Third, the minutes of July 29 reinforce that the 15 percent rule was discussed: "[S]tates are allowed to add 15 percent of their own standards." I would ask the reader: Does it sound to you like the state has control over the Common Core?

Fourth, it is obvious from the speed with which this process transpired and the fact that no contrary testimony was provided that the adoption of the Common Core State Standards was an initiative directed by the Iowa Department of Education. The board was simply a rubber stamp. Troublingly, it seems like the process may repeat itself with the Next Generation Science Standards.[72]

Fifth, there was not any public comment given—none. There is no mention in the board minutes of a forum being held to solicit public comment from Iowans. Nor do the minutes reflect that any dissent was offered. It appears that Iowa has an echo chamber within its educational establishment and bureaucracy.

Finally, in the March minutes, the board expressed a concern that the standards would need to be adopted word for word. They do. The board adopted them anyway.

For good measure, I wanted to look at another state in order to determine whether Iowa was unique in the way it adopted the Common Core. Sadly, it wasn't.

South Dakota's Adoption of the Common Core

While South Dakota wasn't as fast to adopt the Common Core, its claim to a public, transparent process should raise eyebrows. During a public forum in Sioux Falls on September 17, 2013, South Dakota Secretary of Education Dr. Melody Schopp declared that the process of adopting the Common Core included hiring teachers to review the standards in their draft and final forms, but I could not find any records or minutes of those work groups.

According to the South Dakota Department of Education website the Board of Education didn't first discuss the Common Core until its meeting of September 28, 2010.[73] The Common Core was both listed on the agenda for that meeting and reflected in the minutes, which were recorded as follows:

11.0 First Reading Common Core Standards

[DoED] is in support of moving forward with the Common Core State Standards Initiative. [DoED] is in support of "adopting" the Common Core Standards. However, the "implementation" of the Common Core is not determined. A proposed timeline of content standards and "implementation" timeline will be proposed at the November 2010 [Board of Education] meeting.

The [CCSSI] is a state-led effort to establish a shared set of clear educational standards for English language arts and mathematics that states can voluntarily adopt. The...[CCSSO] and the National Governors Association Center for Best Practices (NGA Center) led the effort to develop common core state standards.

The Common Core State Standards are designed to be robust and relevant to the real world, reflecting the knowledge and skills that our young people need for success in college and careers.

Common core state standards will enable participating states to work together to:

- Make expectations for students clear to parents, teachers, and the general public;

- Encourage the development of textbooks, digital media, and other teaching materials aligned to the standards;

- Develop and implement comprehensive assessment systems to measure student performance against the common core state standards that will replace the existing testing systems that too often are inconsistent, burdensome and confusing.

RECOMMENDED ACTION:

Approve and move to November BOE meeting for a Public Hearing to "adopt" the Common Core State Standards.

Motion: A motion by Marilyn Hoyt and seconded by Dick Gowen to approve moving the adoption of the Common Core State Standards to a Public Hearing at the November Board of Education meeting.

Conclusion: The motion carried.[74]

Here is how the official minutes described the South Dakota board's adoption of the Common Core on November 29, 2010:

10.0 Public Hearing – Adoption of Common Core Standards for English language arts, and math 1:03 p.m.

President Duncan asked for any Proponents to the adoption. Written comments that were submitted through e-mail were provided to board members. Becky Nelson from Dept. spoke in favor of adopting the common core and Fred Aderhold from the Sioux Falls school district shared his approval for the adoption on behalf of the Sioux Falls school district. Having no other proponents come forward Duncan asked for opponents. Steve S_____ from Mitchell came forward to express his disapproval of adopting the Common Core Standards and why. No other proponents came forward at this time and President Duncan asked for a motion.

Motion: Motion by Richard Gowen and seconded by Phyllis Heineman to approve the proposed adoption of Common Core Standards.

Conclusion: The motion carried.[75]

Two meetings: At one meeting the standards are introduced, and during the second, after a brief "public" forum, they are adopted. Does it seem like the South Dakota board gave the standards the scrutiny they deserved; or, just like the Iowa board, did they act as a rubber stamp?

Conclusion

It is clear that at both the state and federal levels "We the People" were not given a voice through our elected representatives when it came to Common Core and aligned assessments. The Obama administration used RttT money in a manner not stipulated by Congress. There were no state legislative grants of authority for the adoption of the state level. The separation of powers and natural checks and balances provided in our federal and state constitutions were ignored.

Through RttT grant applications, NCLB waivers, and contractual agreements with their respective assessment consortia, states ceded control of education over to the federal government and third parties—and they did it wholesale.

Action is required.

In far too many states, unelected boards of education are acting as if they are both the executive and legislative branches. Governors have been acting unilaterally, as well, approving decisions made by the boards that they have substantial, if not complete, control in appointing. It is clear to me that the only remedy is a legislative one. State legislatures must provide a check on their state boards of education, and citizens should be organizing to demand that they do so.

At the federal level, Congress must act to prevent federal funding of testing consortia, conditional NCLB waivers, and grants that push states into particular decisions such as the adoption of particular standards or assessments. Recently, two bills along such lines were filed in the U.S. Senate,[76] along with one in the U.S. House.[77] So Congress is at last starting to take note of grassroots opposition. But only with sustained pressure can we expect to see passage of such legislation or fruit from its implementation.

It is encouraging to see anti-Common Core legislation active in thirty states as of spring 2014, the time of this writing.[78] State legislatures must act. Time is of the essence. The longer the standards have to take root in our nation's classrooms, the harder they will be to repeal.

NOTES

1. "About the Standards," Common Core State Standards Initiative (CCSSI), 2014, http://www.corestandards.org/about-the-standards.

2. Ibid.

3. Thomas J. Gibbs and Aimee Howley, "'World-Class Standards' and Local Pedagogies: Can We Do Both?" *Thresholds in Education*, Aug./Nov. 2001, 51–55.

4. "About Us," Achieve, Inc., 2014, http://www.achieve.org/about-us.

5. The American Diploma Project, *Ready or Not: Creating a High School Diploma That Counts* (Washington, D.C.: Achieve, 2004), http://www.achieve.org/files/ReadyorNot.pdf.

6. Achieve, Inc., *Out of Many One: Toward Rigorous Common Core Standards from the Ground Up* (Washington, D.C.: Achieve, 2008), http://www.achieve.org/OutofManyOne.

7. Ibid., 4.

8. Ibid.

9. Ibid., 3.

10. Ibid.

11. Ibid.

12. Ibid., 16.

13. David Herszenhorn, "Billionaires Start $60 Million School Effort, *New York Times*, Apr. 25, 2007, http://www.nytimes.com/2007/04/25/education/25schools.html?_r=0.

14. The grant to the Hunt Foundation is easily searchable via the Gates Foundation's grant database, .

15. Mercedes Schneider, "A Brief Audit of Bill Gates' Common Core Spending," *Deutsch29: Mercedes Schneider's EduBlog*, Aug. 27, 2013, http://deutsch29.wordpress.com/2013/08/27/a-brief-audit-of-bill-gates-common-core-spending/.

16. Achieve, Inc., the National Governors Association (NGA), and the Council of Chief State School Officers (CCSSO), *Benchmarking for Success: Ensuring U.S. Students Receive a World Class Education*. Report prepared by Craig D. Jerald (Washington, D.C.: Authors, 2008), 24,

http://www.corestandards.org/assets/0812BENCHMARKING.pdf.

17. Ibid., 26.

18. Ibid., 27.

19. Ibid., 30.

20. Ibid., 31.

21. "About the Standards," CCSSI, http://www.corestandards.org/about-the-standards.

22. NGA, "Common Core State Standards Available for Comment." Press release, Sept. 21, 2009, http://www.nga.org/cms/home/news-room/news-releases/page_2009/col2-content/main-content-list/title_common-core-state-standards-available-for-comment.html.

23. American Recovery and Reinvestment Act, PL 111-5, Sec. 14005-06.

24. *News Makers*, CSPAN, Feb. 22, 2009.

25. Ibid.

26. Ibid.

27. U.S. Dept. of Education (DoED), "Education Department to Distribute $44 Billion in Stimulus Funds in 30 to 45 Days." Press release, Mar. 7, 2009, http://www.ed.gov/news/press-releases/education-department-distribute-44-billion-stimulus-funds-30-45-days.

28. NGA, "Forty-nine States and Territories Join Common Core State Standards Initiative." Press release, June 1, 2009, http://www.nga.org/cms/home/news-room/news-releases/page_2009/col2-content/main-content-list/title_forty-nine-states-and-territories-join-common-core-standards-initiative.html.

29. Achieve, *Benchmarking for Success*, 26. See note 16 for link.

30. *Federal Register* 74, no. 221, Nov. 18, 2009, 59836, http://www.gpo.gov/fdsys/pkg/FR-2009-11-18/pdf/E9-27427.pdf.

31. Ibid., 59688, http://www.gpo.gov/fdsys/pkg/FR-2009-11-18/pdf/E9-27426.pdf. Compare with Achieve, *Benchmarking for Success*, 24.

32. Ibid., 59836. See note 30 for link.

33. Ibid., 59838, http://www.gpo.gov/fdsys/pkg/FR-2009-11-18/pdf/E9-27427.pdf.

34. Ibid., 59689, http://www.gpo.gov/fdsys/pkg/FR-2009-11-18/pdf/

E9-27426.pdf.

35. Ibid., 59773, http://www.gpo.gov/fdsys/pkg/FR-2009-11-18/pdf/ E9-27426.pdf.

36. Ibid.

37. DoED, "Statement on National Governors Association and State Education Chiefs Common Core Standards." Press release, June 2, 2010, http://www.ed.gov/news/press-releases/statement-national-governors-association-and-state-education-chiefs-common-core-

38. "Standards in Your State" CCSSI, accessed July 6, 2014, http://www.corestandards.org/in-the-states. The site currently reflects the forty-three states still signed on to the standards.

39. "States Applications, Scores and Comments for Phase 1," DoED, Feb. 15, 2012, http://www2.ed.gov/programs/racetothetop/phase1-applications/index.html.

40. Lorraine McDonnell and Stephen Weatherford, "Evidence Use and Stages of the Common Core Standards Movement." Unpublished paper presented at the annual meeting of the American Educational Research Association, Vancouver, BC, Apr. 16, 2012.

41. NGA, "Fifty-One States and Territories Join Common Core State Standards Initiative." Press release, Sept. 1, 2009, http://www.nga.org/cms/home/news-room/news-releases/page_2009/col2-content/main-content-list/title_fifty-one-states-and-territories-join-common-core-state-standards-initiative.html. The release notes that "[s]tates may choose to include additional standards beyond the common core as long as the common core represents at least 85 percent of the state's standards in English language arts and mathematics."

42. "Letters from the Secretary of Education or Deputy Secretary," DoED, Sept. 23, 2011, http://www2.ed.gov/policy/gen/guid/secletter/110923.html.

43. DoED, "ESEA Flexibility Document," updated June 7, 2012. The document is downloadable as a Word document at the link in note 42.

44. Lindsey Burke, "No Child Left Behind Waivers: Bogus Relief, Genuine Overreach," Issue Brief #3718, Heritage Foundation, Sept. 5, 2012, http://www.heritage.org/research/reports/2012/09/no-child-left-behind-waivers-bogus-relief-genuine-overreach.

45. See page 26 of Alaska's approved ESEA waiver request,

http://www2.ed.gov/policy/eseaflex/approved-requests/ak1.pdf. The request was originally submitted in June 2012. It was revised in April 2013 and received approval on May 15. Also see Shane Vander Hart, "Alaska Is Bringing Common Core through the Back Door," Truth in American Education, May 13, 2013, http://truthinamericaneducation.com/common-core-state-standards/alaska-is-bringing-common-core-through-the-back-door/.

46. Weston Marrow, "Alaska Changes School Testing Consortium," *Fairbanks News-Miner*, Jan. 15, 2014, http://www.newsminer.com/news/education/alaska-changes-school-testing-consortium/article_05509298-7d77-11e3-9606-001a4bcf6878.html.

47. Virginia's approved ESEA flexibility request, Feb. 12, 2012, 16-17, http://www2.ed.gov/policy/eseaflex/approved-requests/vaamend31513.pdf. Also note Appendices 4 and 5, which outline the hoops Virginia had to jump through to demonstrate their standards were "college and career ready." Part of this hoop-jumping involved demonstrating full alignment to the Common Core State Standards.

48. Caitlin Emma, "Texas No Child Left Behind Waiver Means Concessions to the Feds," *Politico*, Oct. 29, 2013, http://www.politico.com/story/2013/10/texas-no-child-left-behind-waiver-means-concessions-to-feds-98964.html.

49. Texas' approved ESEA flexibility request, Oct. 16, 2013, 15-16, http://www2.ed.gov/policy/eseaflex/approved-requests/txrequestltr092613.pdf. See also appendix 4.

50. Brittany Corona, "Indiana Faces Consequences from Federal Government for Exiting Common Core," *The Daily Signal*, May 6, 2014, http://dailysignal.com/2014/05/06/indiana-faces-consequences-federal-government-exiting-common-core/.

51. Iowa's memorandum of understanding with the Smarter Balanced Assessment Consortium (SBAC), signed June 2010, http://iowansforlocalcontrol.com/wp-content/uploads/2013/09/Iowa-SBAC-MOU.pdf.

52. Ohio's memorandum of understanding with the Partnership for Assessment of Readiness for College and Careers (PARCC), signed June 2010, http://educationfreedomohio.org/wp-content/uploads/2013/06/MOUOhio.pdf.

53. Emmett McGroarty and Jane Robbins, *Controlling Education from the Top: Why the Common Core Is Bad for America* (Boston, MA: Pioneer

Institute for Public Policy, 2012), 20, http://pioneerinstitute.org/download/controlling-education-from-the-top/.

54. "2010 Legislative Session Calendar," National Conference of State Legislatures (NCSL), http://www.ncsl.org/research/about-state-legislatures/2010-legislative-session-calendar.aspx.

55. NCSL College & Career Readiness State Standards State Legislation Update, updated Sept. 2014, https://sites.google.com/site/ncslccssupdate/home/adopting-agency.

56. McGroarty and Robbins, *Controlling Education*, 20.

57. Robert Scott, *A Republic of Republics: How Common Core Undermines State and Local Autonomy over K-12 Education* (Boston, MA: Pioneer Institute for Public Policy Research, 2013), 1, http://pioneerinstitute.org/download/a-republic-of-republics-how-common-core-undermines-state-and-local-autonomy-over-k-12-education/.

58. Ibid., 10.

59. McDonnell and Weatherford, *Evidence, Use, and Stages*, 13.

60. CCSSI, *Reaching Higher: Common Core State Standards Validation Committee* (Washington, D.C.: NGA and CCSSO, 2010), http://www.corestandards.org/assets/CommonCoreReport_6.10.pdf. For more about the problematic nature of the validation process, see Dr. Sandra Stotsky's essay, "An Invalid Validation of Common Core's Standards."

61. Iowa State Board of Education, Public Agenda, Mar. 2010, https://www.educateiowa.gov/march-2010-state-board-meeting-agenda.

62. Iowa State Board of Education, Minutes, Mar. 11, 2010, https://www.educateiowa.gov/sites/files/ed/documents/March%202010%20Minutes.pdf.

63. Iowa State Board of Education, Public Agenda, May 2010, https://www.educateiowa.gov/may-2010-state-board-meeting-agenda.

64. Iowa State Board of Education, Minutes, May 13, 2010, https://www.educateiowa.gov/sites/files/ed/documents/May%202010%20Minutes.pdf.

65. Iowa State Board of Education, Public Agenda, June 23-24, 2010, https://www.educateiowa.gov/june-2010-state-board-annual-retreat-agenda.

66. Iowa State Board of Education, Public Agenda, July 2010, https://www.educateiowa.gov/july-2010-state-board-meeting-agenda.

67. Iowa State Board of Education, Minutes, July 29, 2010, https://www.educateiowa.gov/sites/files/ed/documents/July%202010%20 Minutes.pdf.

68. Ibid.

69. "Examining the Alignment of the Iowa Core to the Common Core: English Language Arts and Mathematics: Summary Report for the Iowa State Board of Education," Iowa State Board of Education, n.d., https://www.educateiowa.gov/sites/files/ed/documents/Examining%20 the%20Alignment%20of%20the%20Iowa%20Core%20to%20the%20 Common%20Core%20English%20Language%20Arts%20and%20 Mathematics.pdf.

70. Shane Vander Hart, "Branstad Signs Executive Order Addressing Common Core Concerns," *Caffeinated Thoughts*, Oct. 16, 2013, http://caffeinatedthoughts.com/2013/10/branstad-signs-executive-order-addressing-common-core-concerns/.

71. Shane Vander Hart, "No Governor Branstad Did Not Reject the Common Core," Iowans for Local Control, Jan. 23, 2014, http://iowansforlocalcontrol.com/2014/01/no-governor-branstad-did-not-reject-the-common-core/.

72. Emily Rouse, "One Parent's Perspective on the Next Generation Science Standards Task Force Meeting," Iowans for Local Control, Oct. 22, 2013, http://iowansforlocalcontrol.com/2013/10/one-parents-perspective-next-generation-science-standards-task-force-meeting/.

73. "Common Core Standards on agenda," South Dakota Dept. of Education, 2010, http://doe.sd.gov/pressroom/educationonline/2010/Sept/art_2.asp.

74. South Dakota Board of Education, Minutes, Sept. 28, 2010, http://doe.sd.gov/board/packets/documents/Sept10/Sept10min.pdf.

75. South Dakota Board of Education, Minutes, Nov. 29, 2010, http://doe.sd.gov/board/packets/documents/Nov10/Nov10MinA.pdf.

76. S.R. 345 introduced by Senator Lindsey Graham (R-SC), Feb. 6, 2014, http://beta.congress.gov/bill/113th-congress/senate-resolution/345/ text and S. 1974 introduced by Senator Pat Roberts (R-KS), Jan. 30, 2014, http://beta.congress.gov/bill/113th-congress/senate-bill/1974/text.

77. H.R. 4008 introduced by Congressman Phil Gingrey (R-GA), Feb. 6, 2014, http://beta.congress.gov/bill/113th-congress/house-bill/4008/text.

78. Shane Vander Hart, "2014 Common Core Legislation Round-up," Truth in American Education, updated Mar. 27, 2014, http://truthinamericaneducation.com/common-core-state-standards/2014-common-core-legislation-round-up/.

II. A "MANUFACTURED CRISIS":

Manipulating the Public

CHALLENGING CORE ASSUMPTIONS:

What Does U.S. Performance on International Assessments Tell Us

CHRISTOPHER H. TIENKEN

Fraudulent Claims

U.S. Secretary of Education Arne Duncan recently warned the nation that the entire U.S. public education system is in a state of dangerous stagnation and needs to follow the path of standardization set out by policies and programs associated with the Race to the Top (RttT) grant program. That path includes the Common Core State Standards (Common Core). Just after the December 3, 2013, release of the results of the Programme for International Student Assessment, or PISA, Duncan asserted: "The PISA is an important, comparative snapshot of U.S. performance because the assessment is taken by 15-year-olds in high schools around the globe. The big picture of U.S. performance on the 2012 PISA is straightforward and stark: It is a picture of educational stagnation. That brutal truth, that urgent reality, must serve as a wake-up call against educational complacency and low expectations."[1]

In making this statement, Duncan advanced three empirically unsupportable claims: (1) the results from over sixty nations and cities are comparable; (2) those results accurately describe the quality of the U.S. education system and the education systems in other countries; and

(3) the results relate directly to the economic strength and future of countries who took the PISA. In fact, Duncan and others are advancing these fraudulent assertions, and thereby indiscriminately peddling international test rankings, in order to bolster the implementation of policies that seek to standardize and centralize curriculum and testing in public schools.

The Push for Standardization

Implementation of the policies and programs that attempt to standardize, centralize, and homogenize public education in the United States continue to accelerate. The Common Core standards, published in 2010, are the most recent example of a program created from the ideology that standardization and centralization can effectively improve student achievement on state, national, and international assessments and improve global economic competitiveness.

Proponents of Common Core impose strong claims that the standardization program will make U.S. students better able to compete with their peers abroad. They most often point to ranks and scores on international tests to argue that American students are lagging behind their peers worldwide in academic achievement and warn that this lag is weakening overall competitiveness.

I would instead argue that the need to implement Common Core in all public schools does not exist, nor does any evidence for its effectiveness. In fact, data suggest not only that the achievement of American students on international tests is quite robust but also that the United States is one of the most competitive nations on the planet as evidenced by the output of its workforce, which was largely educated prior to the standards-based era.

Privately Developed Standards

Two private trade organizations, the National Governors Association (NGA) and the Council of Chief State School Officers (CCSSO) facilitated the proliferation of state adoption of these standards for mathematics and English Language Arts, without input or approval from parents or taxpayers. Representatives from these organizations claim, with great hubris, that the standards will prepare all 50 million public school students for the approximately 4,400 American colleges and universities and, further, make them globally competitive in any one of tens-of-thousands of careers, some of which have not been invented yet. The NGA and CCSSO proclaim on the CoreStandards.org website that the standards are: (a) [r]esearch- and evidence-based, (b) [c]lear, understandable, and consistent, (c) [a]ligned with college and career expectations, (d) [b]ased on rigorous content and application of knowledge through higher-order thinking skills, (e) [b]uilt upon the strengths and lessons of current state standards, and (f) [i]nformed by other top performing countries in order to prepare all students for success in our global economy and society.[2] They also assert that "[f]or years, the academic progress of our nation's students has been stagnant, and we have lost ground to our international peers."[3]

The NGA and CCSSO spokespeople insinuate not only that the empirical evidence supports the standards' claimed effectiveness, but also that American students are unprepared to compete globally, lagging behind their international peers academically in ways that will impact the U.S. economy. To bolster their claims of lagging achievement, they cite results from international mathematics tests: "Findings from the Trends in International Mathematics and Science (TIMSS) and other studies [such as PISA] concluded that the traditional U.S. mathematics curriculum must become substantially more coherent and focused in order to improve student achievement."[4]

The NGA and the CCSSO also claim that the Common Core mathematics standards will improve academic competitiveness on international tests: "What is important to keep in mind is that the progression in the Common Core State Standards is mathematically coherent and leads to college and career readiness at an internationally competitive level."[5]

In essence, then, the NGA and CCSSO identify the need to implement the Common Core due, in part, to low U.S. student achievement on international tests of mathematics and an overall lag in global economic competitiveness. Yet, U.S. student achievement on international tests of mathematics is not as woefully inadequate as vendors of the Common Core might want us to believe. Moreover, U.S. workers educated prior to the standards-based era are some of the most competitive workers on the planet. Evidence drawn from work I have previously published on this topic, allows me to provide a counter-narrative to the public education "crises" pandering in which vendors and supporters of the Common Core regularly engage.

International Achievement in Mathematics

Any discussion about student achievement on international tests of mathematics needs to be prefaced by the fact that the vendors of these exams state clearly that the results should not be used to make sweeping judgments about the quality of a country's education system.[6] For example, the researchers associated with the TIMSS warn that 33 percent of the questions on the grade 8 mathematics section contained algebra concepts such as functions and solving equations.[7] U.S. stakeholders must consider that not all U.S. students complete Algebra I by the end of grade 8, but that most do complete it by the time they graduate high school. Therefore, a portion of the TIMSS score tells us more about curriculum alignment among nations and less about overall education quality.

Based on comments from the authors of the PISA, there is even more reason to be cautious when drawing conclusions about U.S. achievement based on the results of that test. Mathematics results from the latest PISA were released on December 3, 2013. The assessment involved 15-year-olds from over 60 countries, cities, and provinces. The Organisation of Economic Co-operation and Development (OECD), the private group that develops and vends the PISA, cautioned that policy makers should not use the results from the test to draw important conclusions about education systems or to make important education policy decisions.[8] The OECD authors, in fact, alert readers that a combination of factors contribute to the results of the PISA tests, including total years of schooling, life experiences, poverty, and access to early childhood programs: "If a country's scale scores in reading, scientific or mathematical literacy are significantly higher than those in another country, it cannot automatically be inferred that the schools or particular parts of the education system in the first country are more effective than those in the second. However, one can legitimately conclude that the cumulative impact of learning experiences in the first country, starting in early childhood and up to the age of 15, and embracing experiences both in school, home and beyond, have resulted in higher outcomes in the literacy domains that PISA measures."[9]

Poverty Still Matters

As I have written elsewhere, PISA results are not only influenced by the experiences children have "in the home and beyond," but there exists a strong relationship between the level of child poverty in a country and PISA results.[10] The child poverty rate in a country explains up to 46 percent of the PISA scores in the thirty major industrialized countries in the world and it has a similar influence on TIMSS results.[11] As a country's percentage of childhood poverty increases, its rank on the PISA and TIMSS tests decreases.

Unfortunately, the United States has the highest level of childhood poverty in the industrialized world except for Romania and Bulgaria, a ranking that affects its performance and rankings on international tests of academic achievement.[12] There are multiple methods to calculate poverty, but regardless of the method, the results are similar. The OECD calculates childhood poverty using a harmonized international method. According to the OECD researchers, "People are classified as poor when their equivalised household income is less than half of the median prevailing in each country…The poverty rate is a headcount of how many people fall below the poverty line."[13] Using the OECD harmonized definition of poverty, approximately 23 percent of U.S. public school children lived in poverty in 2012.

The poverty threshold for a U.S. family of four during the 2011-2012 school year was $22,811 according to the National Center for Education Statistics (NCES), based on the official U.S. Census Bureau calculations. According to the NCES, more than 22 percent of U.S. public school children lived in poverty in 2012 when the PISA was administered compared to 15.6 percent in 2000.[14]

Moreover, in 2010, almost 48 percent of U.S. public school children qualified for either free or reduced priced school lunches.[15] No other democratic OECD country boasts childhood poverty statistics like those. Consider that Finland and Denmark have less than 5 percent childhood poverty and Norway and Germany have less than 10 percent.

Furthermore, according to UNICEF, the United States ranks twenty-sixth out of twenty-nine industrialized countries in overall well-being of children, just ahead of Lithuania, Latvia, and Romania, but behind countries like Estonia, Hungary, and Slovakia; all countries that outranked the U.S. on PISA 2012 mathematics.[16]

Regardless of which organization calculates the poverty rate, the United States ranks near the bottom of the industrialized world in terms of the percentage of its children living in poverty. During the period beginning with the administration of the 2011 TIMSS through the completion of the 2012 PISA testing, the U.S. child poverty rate ranged from 20-23 percent. Poverty exerts a negative influence on international tests scores, and test scores in general, in a variety of ways. But how?

Math Confidence

I use mathematics as an example of how poverty pervades learning and output on international standardized tests. In mathematics the answer lies in part with mathematics self-efficacy, which in essence serves as an indicator of math confidence, or how well a student believes he or she performs at mathematics. Some students believe they are good at math, while others do not. Belief in one's ability to perform mathematics influences student achievement. Analysis reveals that approximately 28 percent of the variance, or difference, on PISA mathematics test results is explained by student math self-efficacy in the OECD countries.[17] Self-efficacy has a .50 correlation to mathematics achievement on the PISA.[18] A correlation that size means there is a noticeable relationship between self-efficacy and math achievement. As self-efficacy rises, so too does mathematics PISA achievement. Countries where children had higher levels of self-efficacy also had higher PISA scores.

However, digging a little deeper, it's important to realize that poverty demonstrably relates to mathematical self-efficacy via anxiety. Math anxiety is related to math self-efficacy, and poorer students have more anxiety about math. Math anxiety accounted for an average of 14 percent of the variance in math scores.[19]

As already discussed, the United States has a high rate of child poverty. Consequently, the influence of self-efficacy on PISA mathematics is stronger in the United States compared to other nations with lower child poverty. The U.S. score-difference between students with high and low self-efficacy levels was approximately 50 scale score points on the PISA 2012 math test.[20] That difference would propel the U.S. students' score from 481 to 531, into ninth place on PISA math, tied with Switzerland. The strong correlation between mathematical self-efficacy and mathematics achievement helps explain the strong relationship between poverty and mathematics achievement on the PISA.

It starts to become clear, then, that Common Core advocates have been leveraging U.S. scores on the PISA in a manner that fails to reflect the deeper meaning of those scores.

National Standards No Guarantee

Even without bringing poverty into the equation, U.S. students score higher than most nations that have a nationally standardized curriculum. Statistically, U.S. eighth-grade students were significantly outranked on the 2011 TIMSS mathematics test only by students in Korea, Taiwan, Singapore, Russia, Japan, and the city of Hong Kong.[21] However, thirty-two countries with national standards ranked lower than the United States on grade 8 TIMSS math.[22] The results for the 2012 PISA were similar in that more countries with national standards ranked lower than the United States.[23]

The Power of Poverty

In 2013, I modeled the power that poverty had on the PISA 2012 mathematics and the TIMSS 2011 mathematics results.[24] I used the U.S. states that participated in the TIMSS and PISA tests and their child poverty percentages to model the results for a less poor America. The best model is based on the 2012 PISA mathematics results for students from Massachusetts because they represent the least poor group of children that took the test, with a state average of 15 percent child poverty. The results from the Massachusetts students provide a view of a less poor America compared to the U.S. average of more than 23 percent child poverty.[25]

Massachusetts eighth-grade students achieved a scale score of 561 on the TIMSS mathematics test compared to the U.S. average of 509, a difference of 52 scale score points. The difference moves the U.S. ranking to fifth place and puts it on par with the selective populations of Japan and Hong Kong.[26] Korea ranked first with a score of 613. I found strikingly similar results for the PISA 2012 mathematics test, where students in Massachusetts scored 520 on the mathematics test, launching them from the U.S. average rank of twenty-ninth to twelfth place, one point behind Estonia.[27]

The testing populations of Hong Kong, Macao, and Shanghai are included in the Chinese rank average; however they do not actually generalize to the country of China, making them nonrepresentational. If one ignores these three Chinese testing populations—my own justification for doing so is provided below—the Massachusetts students move even higher, into ninth place. The other countries that outrank the students in Massachusetts—including Switzerland, Lichtenstein, Netherlands, Japan, Korea, and Singapore—all have reported child poverty levels below 15 percent, and their economies and populations do not mirror those of the United States.

My results align with earlier studies of the PISA 2009 test where Executive Director of the National Association of Secondary School Principals Gerald N. Tirozzi modeled the results from the PISA 2009 tests using poverty bands.[28] The U.S. rankings and scores skyrocketed when he separated the scores by poverty rates. Students in U.S. schools that had less than 10 percent of the children in poverty ranked and scored at the top of the world.

Choosing Your Team in China

Some pundits or opponents of a vibrant, non-standardized public school system might question why I do not include the Chinese cities that participate in TIMSS and PISA in my analyses of international test results. Hong Kong and Macao are special administrative regions of the People's Republic of China. I remove them both from my analyses of international testing because their samples of students tested do not represent the general population of students from China. The schools in Hong Kong and Macao do not follow all of the curriculum standardization and testing requirements of the general Chinese system.[29] Moreover, parents there must pay large sums of money to the principals of the top high schools in order to enroll their children, and more of those selective high schools participate in the international tests than average high schools, significantly skewing the testing samples in those cities.[30]

I similarly remove Shanghai from my analyses of international test ranks and scores because its student population does not represent that of China as a whole. Shanghai has more than 140 thousand millionaires in a city with a total population of almost 23 million people. The city has the third highest concentration of wealth in China, and the population is internationalized and more highly educated than the general Chinese population.[31] For example, almost 84 percent of the high school seniors in Shanghai go on to attend college.[32] That rate is more than three times the rate of high school students across China who pursue college.[33]

The wealth and family demographics of Shanghai are likewise radically different than those of the country of China, where 29 percent of the total population, more than 392 million people, live on $2 a day or less.[34] This percentage represents more people than the entire population of the United States.

Pundits who cite China as an education powerhouse and attempt to compare the achievement of Shanghai students to those in the United States are nothing more than shamen selling snake oil to the American public.

The Price of China

For the most part, high school is not free in China. Although regulations now prohibit charging for high school, the practice continues. Only the students whose parents can afford to pay are in school at age 15 and only the ones that can pay handsomely are in quality schools. These realities limit the testing pool for the PISA tests in China severely. Also, not all children are allowed to attend high school in the cities in which they live. Shanghai is a prime example of the selection policy some Chinese high school bureaucrats impose on their citizens.

Some of the poorer children who live in Shanghai, Hong Kong, and other major cities in China are required to attend high school in their ancestral provinces.[35] Therefore, many students who might score lower on the PISA are not included in the calculations. Also, there are not many students with special education needs in Shanghai, Hong Kong, or regular Chinese high schools. Indeed, the enrollment rates for students with special needs in Chinese schools are lower than those in the United States, and many are not enrolled in school by age 15 when the PISA tests are given.[36]

The use of China to scare the American public into reforms that standardize and centralize education is even more egregious when one considers that the majority of children in China never graduate high school. The opportunities to receive a quality education are limited in the cities and even more reduced in the rural areas.

Some statistics about education opportunities in the rural provinces in China provide more evidence as to why the results from Shanghai and other Chinese cities should be disregarded and not used to drive U.S. reform policies. According to Stanford University's Rural Education Action Program (REAP), only about 40 percent of rural children attend high school in China, and only 35-45 percent of those students go on to graduate high school.[37] In addition, approximately 25 percent of middle school students drop out of school before entering high school.[38] When the country of "China" starts reporting their real results on the PISA, then I will include "China" in the testing samples for calculating ranks. PISA collects the data but they are not allowed to report it. Right now, however, the richest, least standardized cities in China are the only ones taking the PISA test, with their results masquerading as the overall nation of China.

Dissent

Perhaps stakeholders in the U.S. public education system might rebut fraudulent claims about the need for more standardization and homogenization of curriculum, testing, and thought if they knew the truth about international test results. Perhaps they might question more deeply policies that attempt to centralize and standardize the U.S. education system in the pursuit of being "#1" on international tests if they knew that the main causes of the claimed underachievement for U.S. students were child poverty and selective testing on the part of top-scoring nations. Maybe stakeholders would hold their state legislators more accountable for appropriate education policies if they knew their loss of local control resulted from frauds, myths, and lies about public education in crisis, when, in fact, U.S. students who do not live in poverty score at or near the top of the world on international tests.[39] Dissent in relationship to this deceptive push for standardization is both necessary and warranted.

Global Competitiveness

More than a score or rank on an international standardized test, global competitiveness relates far more to creativity, entrepreneurship, and innovation. I am not alone in these assertions. IBM Corporation, The Institute for Management Development, Daniel Pink, Ken Robinson, The United States Council on Competitiveness, and Yong Zhao, to name just a few, argue that it is the skills that are hard to measure on standardized test that matter most.[40] The skills of creativity, entrepreneurship, and innovation are hard to outsource, and those are the skills that are valued in the innovation economy.[41] These skills are nurtured through a spirit of exploration, risk-taking, collaboration, and experimentation.

Those hard-to-measure competencies do not derive from standardization and a centralized curricula and testing system based on conformity of results. They are fostered from a belief in diversity, divergence, open-ended critical-thinking—and dissent. It is not by accident that the United States has an established history as one of most competitive nations on Earth in the areas of creativity, entrepreneurship, and innovation, and for its adult population.

Creatively Advanced

In 2011, the Martin Prosperity Institute (MPI) produced a Global Creativity Index, providing an indicator of adult creativity as it relates to economics. The MPI researchers ranked overall economic creativity for eighty-two countries, including the thirty most industrialized nations. To perform their analysis, they assembled data about each country for the period from 2000-2009, covering three areas of creativity: economic, social, and cultural.[42] MPI's findings rank the United States second, behind Sweden and ahead of countries like Finland, Denmark, Australia, Norway, Japan, Germany, and Singapore. China, on the other hand, ranked fifty-eighth.

The United States also ranks near the top of the world in entrepreneurship. Based on results from the 2013 Global Entrepreneurship and Development Index (GEDI), the United States ranked third in a group of 121 countries on overall global entrepreneurship, behind the smaller countries of Denmark and Canada and ahead of countries like Japan, China, Singapore, and Finland.[43] The United States ranked first in the world on the Entrepreneurial Aspirations Index and sixth on turning those aspirations into reality, sub-measures of the overall GEDI reflected in the Entrepreneurial Activities Index. Here again, the United States came in ahead of Japan, Germany, Singapore, and Finland. It's interesting to note that the tiny nation of Denmark ranked first, while China ranked near the bottom third of the world.[44]

Global Innovation Index researchers ranked the United States fifth in the world out of 142 countries, behind only Switzerland, Sweden, the United Kingdom, and the Netherlands.[45] China, by contrast, ranked thirty-fifth. In fact, the United States consistently ranks as one of the most innovative countries in the world on all areas of the Global Innovation Index.

All of the surveys mentioned above were conducted on adults between the ages of 24-35. They represent some of the last populations of children to be educated before the standards-based era in the United States.

Competitive Outcomes

Some outcomes of entrepreneurship, innovation, and creativity include utility patents and Nobel Prizes in the sciences and medicine. The U.S. Patent and Trademark Office reported that the United States was granted 121,026 utility patents in 2012.[46] According to the same office, utility patents are "issued for the invention of a new and useful process, machine, manufacture, or composition of matter, or a new and useful improvement thereof."[47] The remaining 195 countries of the world produced only 132,129 utility patents. Japan produced the second most patents in 2012 with 50,677, almost 40 percent of the rest of the world's output.[48]

The Nobel Committee has issued 915 prizes in Chemistry, Economics, Literature, Medicine, Peace, and Physics since 1901. Out of the total number of Nobel Laureates, the United States has been home to more recipients than any other nation. Looking more specifically, it has outperformed the world in Nobel Prizes in the sciences and medicine with 305 awards. The next closest countries are the United Kingdom and Germany with 94 and 87 awards respectively.

Some pundits might try to claim that the United States' large accumulation of Nobel Prizes in the sciences was a result of the space race and that the numbers do not reflect current output. The data suggest otherwise. Since 2000, U.S.-based scientists received twenty of the thirty-three awards in physics, twenty-one of the thirty awards in chemistry, and twenty-one of the thirty-five awards in medicine. Furthermore, since 2003, 60 percent of the award winners were products of U.S. public schools.[49] All recipients were educated before the standards-based era in the United States.

Although some might not view scientific accomplishments as creative, entrepreneurial, or innovative, scientific output relates at least indirectly to those competencies. The number of scientific papers published by a nation's scientists is one leading indicator of creativity and innovation.[50] U.S. scientists ranked first in the world in terms of scientific papers published, with 3,049,662; whereas Chinese scientists published only 836,255 papers.[51]

Publication numbers by themselves do not provide a complete picture of the innovativeness, creativity, or quality of the science in those papers.[52] However, one gauge of quality or innovativeness for scientific publications is how many times papers are cited. Citations provide an indicator of the level of acceptance of scientific ideas and also of how well those ideas have been vetted and determined to be worth pursuing.[53] Papers from U.S. scientists garnered 48,862,100 citations. The country with the next closest number of citations was Germany with 10,518,133. Papers from Chinese scientists garnered only 5,191,358 citations.[54]

Non-standardized Education

All of the aforementioned accomplishments are "downstream" outcomes of a vibrant and powerful public education system. Those accomplishments become even more impressive when one considers that the more than ninety U.S. Nobel Prize winners since 2000, thousands of utility patent holders recorded for 2012, authors of millions of scientific papers, and all the other adults aged 25 or older currently in our workforce were educated in an era of limited or no state curriculum standards. The United States had, approximately, a 150-year history of locally developed and customized curriculum standards and testing prior to the No Child Left Behind Act, Common Core State Standards, and national testing; and we have been one of the most economically competitive, creative, innovative, and entrepreneurial countries in the world.

Select students from countries like Singapore, China, Korea, Estonia, Slovenia, Slovak Republic, Poland, and even Latvia outrank U.S. students on PISA math tests. So what? What is the per-capita GDP or per capita adjusted income in those countries? It is not near that of United States.[55] How many Nobel Prizes have their citizens been awarded? How many utility patents have they produced? Countries that "outcompete" the United States on international tests do not outpace it in the creative, innovative, and entrepreneurial areas that produce economic success. The pursuit of a centralized and standardized curriculum is a fool's errand.

Standards for Standards

I oppose education reforms that seek to standardize curriculum and testing for the children in the U.S. public school system. There is no empirical evidence to support the effectiveness of such reforms. Programs and policies that cause mass standardization of Pk-12 student outcomes and outputs through rote imitation, compliance testing, knowledge regurgitation, and conformity of thinking have no place in the U.S. public school system. Convergent education should not take the place of creation, passion, interest, diversity of talents, and innovation. As I have written elsewhere:

> A system of standardization and centralization limits the pursuit
> of dreams and aspirations to those defined by state bureaucrats as
> important. Mimicking the convergent practices of totalitarian and
> authoritarian governments such as China and Singapore that constrict
> human thought and freedoms is not the way to foster the growth of
> an innovation economy or strengthen a democracy. The attempt to
> limit diversity will not promote the entrepreneurial spirit. Limiting
> original thinking via a constricted set of curriculum possibilities will
> not lead to cognitive risk taking.[56]

Local Control for Competitiveness

I advocate for a return to local control of curriculum and testing guided by evidence-informed practices customized to the students in each locale. Locally developed curriculum, customized to the needs of the students, has a long history of producing superior results.[57] "Twentieth-century skills," such as imitation and regurgitation of information, measured by international tests and embedded in the Common Core, will not help our children to remain the most economically competitive in the world. We must return to our locally controlled roots of curriculum and assessment to go beyond the routine skills of compliance, conformity, and convergence.

There are many ways to pursue creativity, innovation, and entrepreneurship to remain globally competitive. Those ways should be decided locally. Local school district personnel, along with all interested community stakeholders, can develop comprehensive strategic plans for their districts. They can democratically debate which examples and non-binding guidance to use with their children—from national academic subject-matter organizations and universities to professional organizations dedicated to the healthy development of the whole child. Communities could decide, for instance, to access assistance in helping to guide and structure a customized local curriculum that would be both comprehensive and creative.

American workers will not be able to compete for routine manufacturing jobs that pay $10 a day in China or $2 in Bangladesh.[58] We must capitalize on our strengths of resilience, persistence, creativity, collaboration, cooperation, cultural literacy, strategic thinking, empathy, courage, innovation, entrepreneurship, and divergent thinking. Those are skills that cannot be outsourced or developed by authoritarian governments, but they are necessary for an innovation economy.[59]

Conclusion

Large-scale education interventions should derive from a verified need as well as a foundation of demonstrated effectiveness. Common Core has neither. In fact, the claims made by Common Core proponents as a justification for standardizing the education of 50 million public school children and additional millions of private school and homeschooled children do not hold up well to scrutiny. Would you give your child an untested prescription medication for no reason?

The available evidence about U.S. student performance on international tests and overall global economic competitiveness of U.S. adults suggests that the Common Core is unnecessary and built upon frauds, myths, and lies. U.S. students do achieve at the highest levels of the world on international tests. The problem is not one of curriculum standards. One problem is caused by the policy-making that entrenches immense child poverty; another is the peddling of misleading and fraudulent information that standardization and centralization will improve education. A standardized system of education will not fix any of our problems and it will likely make them worse.

NOTES

1. Arne Duncan, "The Threat of Educational Stagnation and Complacency." Official remarks, Dec. 3, 2013, http://www.ed.gov/news/speeches/threat-educational-stagnation-and-complacency.

2. "About the Common Core State Standards," Common Core State Standards Initiative (CCSSI), 2014, http://www.corestandards.org/about-the-standards/.

3. Ibid.

4. "Frequently Asked Questions," CCSSI, 2014. http://www.corestandards.org/about-the-standards/frequently-asked-questions/.

5. Ibid.

6. See Ina V.S. Mullis, Michael O. Martin, Pierre Foy, and Alka Arora, *TIMSS 2011 International Results in Mathematics* (Chestnut Hill, MA: International Association for the Evaluation of Educational Achievement, 2012); Svein Sjøberg, "PISA: Politics, Fundamental Problems and Intriguing Results" [English trans.]. *La Revue, Recherches en Education* 14 (2012), 1–21, http://www.uhr.no/documents/6b_Sjoberg_PISA_English_La_Revue_no_20.03..pdf; and Organisation of Economic Co-operation and Development (OECD), *PISA 2012 Results. What Students Know and Can Do: Student Performance in Mathematics, Reading and Science*, Vol. I (Paris: OECD Publishing, 2013), with complete PDF file for download at http://www.oecd.org/pisa/keyfindings/pisa-2012-results-volume-i.htm.

7. Mullis et al., *TIMSS 2011 International Results*, 476.

8. See both OECD, *PISA 2012 Results*, Vol. I and Christopher H. Tienken, "PISA Problems," *AASA Journal of Scholarship and Practice* 10, no. 4 (Winter 2014), 4-14.

9. OECD, *PISA 2012 Results*, Vol. I, 265.

10. Tienken, "PISA Problems," 4-14; Christopher H. Tienken, "Conclusions from TIMSS and PISA Testing," *Kappa Delta Pi Record 49*, no. 2 (2013), 56-58; and Christopher H. Tienken and Donald C. Orlich, *The School Reform Landscape: Fraud, Myth, and Lies* (New York: Rowman and Littlefield, 2013).

11. Mullis et al., *International Results in Mathematics* and OECD, *PISA 2012 Results*, Vol. I, 35-36.

12. OECD, *PISA 2012 Results*, Vol. I and OECD, *PISA 2012 Results: Ready to Learn – Students' Engagement, Drive and Self-beliefs*, Vol. III, PISA (Paris: OECD Publishing, 2013), http://www.oecd.org/pisa/keyfindings/pisa-2012-results-volume-iii.htm.

13. OECD, *Society at a Glance* (Paris: OECD Publishing, 2009), 90, http://www.oecd-ilibrary.org/social-issues-migration-health/society-at-a-glance-2009_soc_glance-2008-en.

14. U.S. Dept. of Education (DoED), National Center for Education Statistics, *Digest of Education Statistics 2011* (NCES 2012-001), compiled by Thomas D. Snyder and Sally A. Dillow (Washington, D.C.: U.S. Government Printing Office, 2012), table 27.

15. Ibid., table 45.

16. Peter Adamson, *Child Well-being in Rich Countries: A Comparative Overview*, Innocenti Report Card 11 (Florence, IT: UNICEF Office of Research, 2013), 2, http://www.unicef-irc.org/publications/pdf/rc11_eng.pdf; and OECD, *PISA 2012 Results*, Vol. 1, 21.

17. OECD, *PISA 2012 Results*, Vol. III, 83-86.

18. Ibid., 83.

19. Ibid., 87.

20. Ibid., 86.

21. Mullis et al., *International Results*, 6.

22. Ibid., 6.

23. OECD, *PISA 2012 Results*, Vol. I.

24. Tienken, "Conclusions."

25. "Kids Count Data Center: Children in Poverty," Annie E. Casey Foundation, accessed Sept. 20, 2014, http://datacenter.kidscount.org/data/tables/43-children-in-poverty?loc=1#detailed/1/any/false/868,867,13,12,11/any/321,322.

26. Tienken, "Conclusions," 58.

27. Tienken, "PISA Problems."

28. Tirozzi's work was extensively cited by Mel Riddle in "It's Poverty Not Stupid" National Association of Secondary School Principals, *The Principal Difference*, Dec. 15, 2010. Riddle recently updated the post as "PISA: It's Still Poverty Not Stupid," Feb. 12, 2014, http://nasspblogs.org/principaldifference/2014/02/pisa-its-still-poverty-not-stupid/.

29. Dan Levin, "A Chinese education, for a Price," *The New York Times*, Nov. 12, 2012, http://www.nytimes.com/2012/11/22/world/asia/in-china-schools-a-culture-of-bribery-spreads.html?_r=0.

30. Tienken, "PISA Problems."

31. Ibid., 7.

32. "Regular Education," Shanghai Government, accessed July 6, 2014, http://www.shanghai.gov.cn/shanghai/node17256/node17432/node17446/userobject22ai22041.html.

33. Tom Loveless, "PISA's China Problem," Brookings, *The Brown Center Chalkboard*, Oct. 9, 2013, http://www.brookings.edu/blogs/brown-center-chalkboard/posts/2013/10/09-pisa-china-problem-loveless.

34. World Bank, "Poverty headcount ratio at $2 a day (PPP)," World Bank, 2014, http://data.worldbank.org/indicator/SI.POV.2DAY.

35. Loveless, "PISA's China Problem."

36. Saga Ringmar, "Here's the Truth about Shanghai Schools: They're Terrible," *The Guardian*, Dec. 28, 2013, http://www.theguardian.com/commentisfree/2013/dec/28/shanghai-china-schools-terrible-not-ideal.

37. Rural Education Action Program (REAP), "Keeping Kids in School," The Freeman Spogli Institute for International Studies, Stanford University, accessed July 6, 2014, http://reap.fsi.stanford.edu/research/keeping_kids_in_school___migration; and REAP, *Money for Matriculation*, REAP Brief #114 (Stanford, CA: REAP, 2013), http://iis-db.stanford.edu/pubs/23435/REAP114-EN.pdf.

38. REAP, "Keeping Kids in School."

39. Tienken and Orlich, *The School Reform Landscape*.

40. IBM Corporation, *Leading through Connections: Insights from the Global Chief Executive Officer Study*, CEO C-Suite Studies (Somers, NY: IBM Corporation, 2012); The Institute for Management Development (IMD), *World Competitiveness Handbook* (Lausanne, Switzerland: IMD, 2012); Daniel H. Pink, *A Whole New Mind* (New York: Riverhead Press, 2006); Ken Robinson, *Out of Our Minds: Learning to Be Creative* (Mankato, MN: Capstone Press, 2011); U.S. Council on Competitiveness (USCOC), *Clarion Call. A Look Back and a Path Forward* (Washington, D.C.: Council on Competitiveness, 2012), http://www.compete.org/images/uploads/File/PDF%20Files/CoC_2013_Clarion_FINAL.pdf; and Yong Zhao, *World Class Learners: Educating Creative and Entrepreneurial Students* (Thousand Oaks, CA: Corwin Press, 2012).

41. Christopher H. Tienken, "International Comparisons of Creativity and Innovation," *Kappa Delta Pi Record* 49, 153-155.

42. Martin Prosperity Institute (MPI), *Creativity and Prosperity: The 2010 Global Creativity Index* (Toronto, ON: MPI, 2011), http://martin-prosperity.org/2011/10/01/creativity-and-prosperity-the-global-creativity-index/.

43. Zoltan J. Acs, Laszlo Szerb, and Erkko Auitio, *Global Entrepreneurship and Development Index 2013* (Northhampton, MA: Edward Elgar Publishing, 2013).

44. Tienken, "International Comparisons," 154.

45. Cornell University, INSEAD, and the World Intellectual Property Organization, *The Global Innovation Index 2013: The Local Dynamics of Innovation*, edited by Soumitra Doutta and Bruno Lanvin (Geneva, Switzerland: World Intellectual Property Organization, 2013), http://www.wipo.int/export/sites/www/freepublications/en/economics/gii/gii_2013.pdf.

46. "Patents by Country, State, and Year: Utility Patents," 2012, U.S. Patent and Trademark Office, http://www.uspto.gov/web/offices/ac/ido/oeip/taf/cst_utl.htm.

47. "Types of Patents," U.S. Patent and Trademark Office, 2013, http://www.uspto.gov/web/offices/ac/ido/oeip/taf/patdesc.htm.

48. Tienken, "International Comparisons," 154.

49. National Association of Secondary School Principals, "What's Right about U.S. Public Schools," Principal.org, 2013, http://www.principalspr.org/whatsright.html.

50. Tienken, "International Comparisons," 155.

51. Thomson Reuters, "Top 20 Countries in All Fields, 2001- August 31, 2011," *Science Watch*, 2011, http://archive.sciencewatch.com/dr/cou/2011/11decALL.

52. Tienken, "International Comparisons," 155.

53. Ibid.

54. Thomson Reuters, "Top 20 Countries."

55. "World Fact Book: Country Comparison. GDP per Capita," Central Intelligence Agency, 2013, https://www.cia.gov/library/publications/the-world-factbook/rankorder/2004rank.html.

56. Christopher H. Tienken, "Non-standardized Standards," *Kappa Delta Pi Record* 50 (2014), 58.

57. John Dewey, *The School and Society* (Chicago: Illinois: The University of Chicago Press, 1900); Jacob W. Wrightstone, *Appraisal of Newer Practices in Selected Public Schools* (New York, New York: Teachers College Press, 1935); Wilford M. Aikin, *The Story of the Eight-Year Study* (New York: Harper and Brothers, 1942); John I. Goodlad, *School, Curriculum, and the Individual* (Waltham, Massachusetts: Blaisdell Publishing Company, 1966); and Margaret C. Wang, Geneva D. Haertel, and Herbert J. Walberg, "Toward a Knowledge Base for School Learning," *Review of Educational Research* 63, no. 3 (1993), 249-294.

58. "Wages in China," China Labour Bulletin, June 10, 2013, http://www.clb.org.hk/en/content/wages-china.

59. Zhao, *World Class Learners*.

III. AN ACADEMIC FRAUD

Pretending at Rigor

AN INVALID VALIDATION OF COMMON CORE'S STANDARDS

SANDRA STOTSKY

M ajor flaws exist in the mathematics and English language arts (ELA) standards of the Common Core State Standards (Common Core). To understand why, state legislators, teachers, local school boards, and parents need background information on several aspects of the Common Core State Standards Initiative (CCSSI). A close look at Common Core's Validation Committee (VC) is crucial because it was supposed to be the mechanism for assuring the public that Common Core's standards were in fact research-based, internationally benchmarked, and rigorous. The fact that they are not is largely due to the limitations of the membership of this committee and to the deliberate subversion of its ostensible functions by the private organizations that developed the standards.

Who Developed the Standards and Funded Their Development?

Education is constitutionally the responsibility of state and local governments, explicitly on matters of curriculum and instruction. To bypass the statutes forbidding the federal government to develop national standards and related curriculum material, Common Core's standards were developed by two non-governmental organizations—the National Governors Association (NGA) and the Council of Chief State School Officers (CCSSO)—in coordination with Achieve, Inc. Achieve is, in fact, another non-governmental organization established by the NGA and business officials in 1996 to evaluate state standards and to develop common tests across states. Where Common Core was concerned, the U.S. Department of Education (DoED), lurking behind the scenes, supplied financial incentives to the states via the Race to the Top (RttT) grant competition. RttT funds, then, were a carrot meant to grease the skids for adoption of the standards developed by these three unaccountable private organizations. Expenses for managing the project were defrayed by large grants from the Bill and Melinda Gates Foundation.

Who Chose the Standards Writers, and What Were Their Qualifications?

In the absence, to date, of official information from these three private organizations, it seems likely that Achieve, Inc. and the Gates Foundation selected most of the key personnel to write and review the standards. The CCSSI was officially launched in the spring of 2009.[1] In July of that same year, the names of the twenty-four members of the Standards Development Work Group (Work Group), designated as developing the two sets of high school-level "college-and career-readiness standards," were revealed publicly in response to complaints about the CCSSI's lack of transparency.[2] Almost all the members, it turned out, were on the staff of Achieve, Inc., and three other test/curriculum development companies—American College Testing (ACT); College Board (CB); and America's Choice, a for-profit project of the National Center on Education and the Economy, or NCEE. The Work Group also included four of the six grade-level standards writers: Jason Zimba and David Coleman, both identified as partners in a business enterprise called Student Achievement Partners; Susan Pimentel, identified as a consultant to Achieve, Inc., as well as a founder of StandardsWork; and William McCallum, a mathematics professor at the University of Arizona, also identified as a consultant to Achieve.

Not only did the Work Group fail to include any high school mathematics teachers, it failed to include any English professors or high-school English teachers. How could legitimate standards in either subject be created without the two groups of educators who know the most about what students should and could be learning in secondary mathematics and English/reading classes? Because the twenty-four members of the Work Group labored in secret—without open meetings, sunshine-law meeting minutes, or accessible public comment—their reasons for making the decisions they did are lost to history.

The names of individuals in a much larger Feedback Group did include an English professor, one high school English teacher, and one mathematics teacher. But it was made clear that the members of the Feedback Group would have only an advisory role—final decisions would be made for English language arts (ELA) by the English-teacher-bereft Standards Development Work Group. Indeed, Feedback Group members' suggestions were frequently ignored without explanation, according to the English professor in the Feedback Group.

The absence of relevant professional credentials in each standards-writing team helps to explain the flaws in the grade-level standards. The "lead" writers for the grade-level ELA standards, Coleman and Pimentel, had never taught reading or English in K-12 or at the college level. Neither has a doctorate in English or reading, nor had either of them ever published serious work on K-12 curriculum and instruction.[3] Neither had engaged in literary scholarship or research in education; they were virtually unknown to English language arts and reading educators and to higher education faculty in rhetoric, speech, composition, or literary study. A third ELA standards writer originally listed as part of the three-person grade-level standards-writing team—James Patterson, a staff member at ACT—dropped out of the limelight early on. What role he played is unknown.

Two of the lead grade-level standards-writers in mathematics had relevant academic credentials for the subject. Zimba was a physics professor at Bennington College (now retired), while McCallum was, and remains, a mathematics professor at the University of Arizona. However, Phil Daro, the only member of this three-person team with K-12 teaching experience (middle school mathematics) had been an undergraduate English major; he was also on the staff of NCEE. None of the three had ever developed K-12 mathematics standards before.

Who recommended these people as standards-writers and why, we still do not know. No one in the media commented on their lack of credentials for the task they had been assigned. Indeed, no one in the media showed the slightest interest in the qualifications of the grade-level standards-writers or the members of the Work Group, even though it was obvious that most of the latter group were connected to test/curriculum development companies.

What Are the Chief Qualities and Goals of Common Core's Standards?

According to the CCSSI in 2013,[4] the standards:

- are aligned with college and work expectations;
- are clear, understandable, and consistent;
- include rigorous content and application of knowledge through high-order skills;
- build upon strengths and lessons of current state standards;
- are informed by other top performing countries, so that all students are prepared to succeed in our global economy; and
- are evidence based.

Common Core also claims that "[t]hese standards define the knowledge and skills students should have within their K-12 education careers so that they will graduate from high school able to succeed in entry-level, credit-bearing academic college courses and in workforce training programs." However, Zimba further elucidated this abstract goal in comments to the Massachusetts Board of Elementary and Secondary Education at a public meeting in March 2010. After being asked to clarify the concept of college readiness, he is reported in the official minutes of the meeting as saying that "the concept of college readiness is minimal and focuses on non-selective colleges." The official videotape of the meeting clarifies the context for this statement.[5] At this meeting, Zimba clarified this statement in many ways, stating, for example, that "the minimally college-ready student is a student who passed Algebra II," and "[Common Core's document is] "not only not for STEM, it's also not for selective colleges."

Zimba was truthful. There is nothing in Common Core's mathematics standards to prepare high school students for the beginning college-level mathematics coursework taken by mathematics-intensive majors in a STEM field.

In contrast, Coleman and Pimentel have never explained in public how they defined college and career readiness in ELA. Neither have they indicated how they would exemplify its practical meaning with respect to the level of reading difficulty or specific texts of which students would have to demonstrate understanding. Nor has anyone in the media asked them, to our knowledge. It is true that Appendix B in Common Core's ELA document offers a range of titles in grades 11 to 12, indicating the "quality and complexity" of texts that students should be able to read. But the titles span a wide range of reading levels so that it is not clear what level constitutes college and career readiness. For instance, titles mapped to these two highest grade levels include *Dreaming in Cuban*, a novel with a low middle school reading level according to a recognized readability formula (ATOS for Books, developed by Renaissance Learning, Inc.), and Thomas Paine's *Common Sense*, which is generally understood to be at an adult reading level.

Who Owns Common Core's Standards?

In order to sit on the VC, members had to sign a confidentiality agreement that included the following language: "Ownership of the Common Core State Standards, including all drafts, copies, reviews, comments, and non-final versions (collectively, Common Core State Standards), shall reside solely and exclusively with the Council of Chief State School Officers ('CCSSO') and the National Governors Association Center for Best Practices ('NGA Center')."

The terms of use provided on Common Core's website also make it clear that two private organizations own the standards.[6] Because Common Core's standards are privately developed, its producers are not subject to freedom of information requests. It is not at all clear whether or how these standards and the tests based on them are subject to public control or change if parents and teachers suspect they are damaging public education. Furthermore, unless states participate regularly as independent countries in Trends in International Mathematics and Science Surveys (TIMSS)—a well-known international assessment of mathematics and science knowledge—states will not be able to obtain information from independent sources, free of control by the DoED and the Bill and Melinda Gates Foundation, on the effects of Common Core's standards on the mathematics and science curriculum in their public schools.

What Attempts Were Made to Remedy the Flaws in the ELA Standards?

As a member of the VC from August 2009 to August 2010, I wrote up a detailed critique of the draft college and career readiness standards in English language arts in September 2009 and other critiques of draft grade-level standards in ELA as they were made available to the VC in subsequent months. I always sent my comments to the three lead ELA standards writers, other members of the VC (until the VC was directed to send comments only to the Common Core staff for distribution to other VC members), and, because I am a fellow member of the Massachusetts Board of Education, also to Massachusetts Education Commissioner Mitchell Chester. At no time did I receive queries, never mind replies, to my comments, from the CCSSI staff, the standards writers, or Commissioner Chester and fellow board members. Most of my critiques were subsequently published as Pioneer Institute white papers, some co-authored with either Ze'ev Wurman or R. James Milgram, in order to address flaws in Common Core's mathematics standards.

In a private conversation at the end of November 2009, Chris Minnich, a CCSSI staff member at the time, asked me if I would be willing to work on the standards during December with Susan Pimentel. Pimentel and I had worked together under contract to StandardsWork on the 2008 Texas English language arts standards and, earlier, on other standards projects. I thus agreed to spend about two weeks in Washington, D.C. working pro bono on the ELA standards, after Minnich assured me that Pimentel was the decision-making ELA standards writer.

On the first Sunday in December, I called Pimentel to discuss the kind of changes I thought the November 2009 draft needed before we began to work together. I also wanted to clarify that agreed-upon revisions would not be changed by unknown others before going out for comment to other members of the VC and, eventually, the public. After our telephone conversation, I sent Minnich an e-mail with the list of the possible changes I would propose and asked for support for Pimentel because she had indicated in our conversation that she was not, in fact, the final decision-maker for ELA standards. She did not specify who exactly was the final authority, but she made it clear to me that it was not her. A week later, I received a cursory e-mail reply from Minnich, thanking me for my comments, indicating that my suggestions would be considered along with those from the fifty states, and that I would hear from the staff sometime in January—in effect, a dismissal.

In the second week of January 2010, CCSSI sent out a "confidential draft" to state departments of education, in advance of the January 19 cut-off for states to submit applications for RttT funds. It should be noted that more than fifteen state applications, including the one submitted by the Commonwealth of Massachusetts where I reside, were prepared by professional grant writers chosen and paid for by the Bill and Melinda Gates Foundation—for roughly $250,000 each. A few states included the watermarked confidential draft in their application material and posted the whole application on their department of education's website as required by their respective laws. Consequently, the draft was no longer confidential. I could now critique it openly, which I did. It contained none of the kinds of revisions I had proposed in my December e-mail to Minnich and Pimentel.

Over the next six months, as the Pioneer Institute published my analyses of the January 2010 "confidential" draft and succeeding drafts, including the final June 2 version, I repeatedly pointed out the serious flaws in the document. At no time did the lead ELA standards writers, including Pimentel, communicate with me, despite my requests for a private discussion with David Coleman. Nor did anyone provide an explanation of the organizing categories for the standards and their focus on skills, rather than literary/historical content, in the literature standards.

Coleman was apparently responsible for the division of reading standards, at every grade level, into ten standards for informational text and nine standards for literary texts. Despite the consistent criticisms I sent to the standards writers, those in charge of the VC, the Massachusetts Board of Elementary and Secondary Education, the Massachusetts commissioner of education, the media, and the public at large, one aspect of the ELA standards that remained untouchable was David Coleman's idea that at least half of the readings in every English class should consist of nonfiction or informational texts, to the detriment of classic literature and of literary study more broadly speaking. His idea was clearly set in stone and could not even be discussed privately, even though all of the historical and empirical evidence weighed against such a division. In fact, there was nothing supporting it. Coleman has repeatedly stated in public that literary study is to remain the focus of the English class, that 30 percent of what students read across the curriculum should be literary, and that 70 percent should be informational. But he has never explained how 30 percent of what students read across the curriculum can be literary when—due to his idiosyncratic division of ELA reading standards into ten for informational texts and nine for literary texts—students have to read informational texts for 50 percent of their reading instructional time and literary texts for less than 50 percent of their reading instructional time in English or reading classes. The arithmetic doesn't add up. But then, Coleman has never pretended he was a mathematics expert, too.

The original deadline for producing a complete draft of the college-readiness and grade-level ELA and mathematics standards had been planned prior to January 19, 2010—again, the date the DoED had set for state RttT grant applications. To even qualify for RttT funds, these applications had to indicate a commitment to adopt the Common Core standards. But the confidential draft sent to state departments of education in early January was so poorly written and content-deficient that CCSSI had to delay releasing a public comment draft until March 2010. While the language in the March version was cleaner than that in the January draft, the March version was not much better in organization or substance—the result of unqualified drafters working with undue haste and untouchable premises.

None of the public feedback to the March draft has ever been made available. The final version of Common Core's ELA standards, released in June 2010, contained most of the problems apparent in the first draft: lack of rigor (especially in the secondary standards) and minimal indications of literary content. Moreover, like the mathematics standards, they continued to lack international benchmarking and research support.

How Were the Standards to Be Validated?

The federal government could have funded an independent group of experts to evaluate the soundness and validity of the standards it was incentivizing the states to adopt. But it did not do so. This is an important point that seems to have been lost on the media, public officials, and the public at large. Instead of an independent evaluation, the NGA and CCSSO created their own validation committee— eventually numbering twenty-nine members—to exercise this function. Some were *ex officio*, others were recommended by the governor or commissioner of education of an individual state. No more is known officially about the rationale for the individuals chosen for the CCSSI-formed VC.

Similar to the composition of the Standards Development Work Group and the standards-writing teams, the VC contained very few academic experts on ELA and mathematics standards. Most were education professors or associated with testing companies, from here and abroad.[7] R. James Milgram was the only mathematician on the VC, although there were several mathematics educators—people with doctorates in mathematics education and/or appointments in a school of education, but who do not teach mathematics courses in higher education. I was the only nationally recognized expert on ELA standards by virtue of my work in Massachusetts as well as on Achieve,

Inc.'s high school ELA exit standards through the American Diploma Project, and on that same organization's backmapped ELA standards at earlier grade levels.

The VC's charge was threefold, as set forth in the papers we received:

- Review the process used to develop the college- and career-readiness standards and recommend improvements in that process. These recommendations will be used to inform the K-12 development process.

- Validate the sufficiency of the evidence supporting each college- and career-readiness standard. Each member is asked to determine whether each standard has sufficient evidence to warrant its inclusion.

- Add any standard that is not now included in the common core state standards that they feel should be included and provide the following evidence to support its inclusion: 1) evidence that the standard is essential to college and career success; and 2) evidence that the standard is internationally comparable.

Problematically, the VC was to address this charge simultaneous to the standards' development, from 2009 to 2010. Just as troublingly, by the time we were asked to sign off on the standards, the original charge to the VC had been reduced in an unclear manner and by unidentified individuals to just the first two—and least important—of the three bullets above.

Culmination of the VC's participation was reduced to signing or not signing a letter by the end of May 2010 asserting that the not-yet-finalized standards[8] were:

1. reflective of the core knowledge and skills in ELA and mathematics that students need to be college- and career-ready;

2. appropriate in terms of their level of clarity and specificity;

3. comparable to the expectations of other leading nations;

4. informed by available research or evidence;

5. the result of processes that reflect best practices for standards development;

6. a solid starting point for adoption of cross-state common core standards; and

7. a sound basis for eventual development of standards-based assessments.

The VC members who signed the letter are listed in the very brief official report on the VC. Since all members had been asked prior to their first meeting to sign an agreement that made all committee work confidential, there was little on which the *rapporteur* could report. The five members who did not sign off were not listed as such in the official report, nor were their reasons mentioned or letters shared. My own letter explaining why I could not sign off was posted on several online venues,[9] as was Professor Milgram's.[10] However, the *rapporteur*, as I found out later, never even received copies of our letters from CCSSI staff.

So far as Milgram and I could determine, the VC was intended to function as a rubber stamp, despite the charge to validate the standards. Even though we made repeated requests, we did not get the names of high-achieving countries whose standards were supposedly used as benchmarks.

It is now clear why we did not get any names. Regardless of CCSSI claims, Common Core's standards were not internationally benchmarked or made comparable to the most demanding standards elsewhere. Common Core has since revised its claims, stating only that it was "informed by" documents in other countries. It has never clarified the meaning of that verb and, to my knowledge, has never corrected any source claiming that its standards were internationally benchmarked.

Nor did Common Core offer any research evidence to support its stress on writing over reading; its division of reading texts into "information" and "literature"; its experimental approach to Euclidean geometry; its deferral of the completion of Algebra I to grade 9 or 10; or its claim about the value of informational reading instruction in the English classes. It couldn't, because there is no evidence to support Common Core's revision of the K-12 curriculum. Nor did Common Core offer evidence that its standards meet entrance requirements for most colleges and universities in this country or elsewhere—or for a high school diploma in many states.

How Were the Standards Supposedly Evaluated?

In addition to funding the development and promotion of the Common Core standards, the Bill and Melinda Gates Foundation has funded several studies—directly or indirectly, partially or wholly—in a post hoc attempt to validate Common Core's standards. These efforts include, for example the 2011 report by David Conley at the University of Oregon.[11] It is not completely clear if they include the 2012 report by William Schmidt at Michigan State University.[12] Conley's 2011 report contradicted the findings in his 2003 pre-Common Core report on college-readiness standards,[13] while Schmidt's 2012 report has been severely criticized on methodological grounds.[14]

The Gates Foundation also gave grants to the Thomas B. Fordham Institute and Achieve, Inc., to evaluate state standards and promote Common Core's standards. The reviews they released in 2010 at the time that most states were considering adoption of the standards showered praise on both the ELA and the mathematics standards. In fact, Fordham's "grades" for Common Core's standards were much higher than those it gave to the existing standards in most states, despite the many negative reviewer comments on Common Core's ELA standards, and the Fordham reviewer's failure to note the absence of preparatory STEM standards in its mathematics standards. However, Fordham did give California's standards higher grades than it gave Common Core's standards, in both mathematics and ELA.

In contrast, Achieve, Inc., concluded that Common Core's standards were superior to even the best sets of state standards (California's, for example). It found that Common Core's ELA standards were "more coherent and focused" than the ELA standards in top-performing states such as California and Massachusetts.[15] It also asserted that Common Core's mathematics standards "provide more precision about the importance, progression, and underlying concepts of content across the grades" than the mathematics standards in California and Massachusetts.

While little attention has been paid to Achieve's obviously-biased evaluation, Fordham's grades—if not necessarily their reviewers' comments—have been highly influential, especially its "bottom line" that a particular state's standards were "among the worst in the country." This boilerplate bottom line was used in its review of many states' standards (Wyoming, Wisconsin, and South Carolina among many others). Apparently, no reporter or state board member noticed the repetition of that line across state reviews or the additional statement that Common Core's standards were far superior to those in these benighted states. Yet both of these repeated phrases loudly hinted that the so-called bottom line was little more than a piece of propaganda added at the end of the reviewer's comments to get state boards of education to stampede to replace their "among the worst in the country" standards with Common Core's. It is not clear why the media were so completely taken in by Fordham's grades—and its subsequent claim that Common Core's standards were rigorous and far superior to those in most other states.

What Lies Are Regularly Told to the Public about Common Core's Standards?

As one example, the Foundation for Excellence in Education hits readers in the face with two bald-faced lies as soon as one looks at the material on Common Core on its website: "[The standards] were developed by experienced educators, leaders and experts nationwide and are benchmarked to top performing schools around the world."[16] As we know, Common Core's standards were not developed by nationwide leaders and experts; the names of David Coleman, Susan Pimentel, and James Patterson were as unknown to English educators and scholars, never mind the rest of the country, as were the names of Jason Zimba, William McCallum, and Phil Daro to mathematics teachers in the nation's schools. Moreover, Common Core's standards were not benchmarked with the standards of any top-performing schools or countries. We have never been given the names of the countries with which Common Core's standards were supposedly benchmarked; we have been given only the names of countries whose documents were "consulted" or "reviewed," or by which they were "informed."

As another example, the U.S. Chamber of Commerce—which endorses Common Core's standards because "businesses all across the country depend on a highly qualified workforce prepared for jobs in the 21st century"—claims Common Core's standards were "developed by a group of experts including teachers and school administrators."[17] The Chamber is simply repeating what it was told to say about who wrote Common Core's standards. Since the Gates Foundation also gave some money to the Chamber, it is possible that it advised the Chamber on wording.

Concluding Remarks

Common Core standards were created by people who wanted a "Validation Committee" in name only. An invalid process, with participation by an invalid validation committee, resulted not surprisingly in invalid standards.

States need to reconsider their hasty decisions to adopt this pig in an academic poke for more-than-substantive reasons. First, there has been no validation of Common Core's standards by a legitimate public process, nor any validation of its college-readiness level in either mathematics or ELA by the relevant higher education faculty in this country. State standards typically go out for a lengthy and timely public comment period—not usually during the summer when teachers and administrators are not in their schools—and then for revisions before approval by a board of education.

Second, state boards of education, which exist in most states, generally have no statutory authority to decide on college-readiness levels for credit-bearing, post-secondary courses. Such decisions are, rather, the prerogative of a board of higher education or a board of regents or trustees. State legislators seeking to explore the legitimacy of the votes taken by their boards of education in 2010 might request an investigation by the inspector general in their attorney general's office. Inspector generals are, by statute, allowed to determine whether the process followed by a state agency, committee, or board in making a policy decision abided by statutory authority and followed appropriate procedures.

Third, there is nothing in the history and membership of the VC to suggest that the public should place confidence in the willingness or interest of the CCSSI or the DoED to convene committees of experts from the relevant disciplines in higher education in this country and elsewhere to validate Common Core's college-readiness level.

It is possible to consider the original vote by state boards of education to adopt Common Core's standards null and void, regardless of whether a state board of education now chooses to recall its earlier vote. Any tests based on these invalid standards are, by definition, also invalid.

NOTES

1. See, for example, Laura Bruno, "NJ Joins Effort to Draft US Math Regs: National Math Standard Doesn't Add Up, Groups Say," *Daily Record*, June 3, 2009, http://www.dailyrecord.com/apps/pbcs.dll/article?AID=2009906020335.

2. National Governors Association (NGA), "Common Core State Standards Development Work Group and Feedback Group Announced." Press release, July 1, 2009, http://www.nga.org/cms/home/news-room/news-releases/page_2009/col2-content/main-content-list/title_common-core-state-standards-development-work-group-and-feedback-group-announced.html.

3. Nor is it clear in what subject Coleman received a degree from his studies in England as a Rhodes Scholar. No curriculum vitae has ever been attached to any biographical information offered by Common Core State Standards Initiative (CCSSI) or the College Board, which hired him as president in 2012. It should be noted that the CB has received large grants from the Gates Foundation in recent years.

4. See CCSSI's "About the Standards," web page, http://www.corestandards.org/about-the-standards/. These claims were widely disseminated with only insignificant variations in order and wording. The version cited here is pulled from "History of the Common Core Standards" on the ShareMyLesson website (2013), http://www.sharemylesson.com/article.aspx?storyCode=50000149.

5. The meeting was video-recorded and is available to view on the Pioneer Institute's website, http://pioneerinstitute.org/news/video-common-core-lead-writer-jason-zimba/.

6. Those terms include the following language: "Copyright: This website and all content on this website, including in particular the Common Core State Standards, are the property of NGA Center and CCSSO, and NGA Center and CCSSO retain all right, title, and interest in and to the same....

"Disclaimer: NGA Center and CCSSO do not warrant, endorse, approve or certify the information on this site, nor do they make any representation as to the accuracy, completeness, efficacy, or timeliness of such information. Use of such information is voluntary on your part...The information, products and services offered on or through the Website are provided 'as is' and without warranties of any kind either express or implied. To the fullest extent permissible pursuant to applicable law, we disclaim all warranties, express or implied, including, but not limited to, implied warranties of merchantability and fitness for a particular purpose.

"NGA Center and CCSSO assume no responsibility for consequences resulting from use of the information contained herein, or from use of the information obtained at linked sites, or in any respect for the content of such information. NGA Center and CCSSO are not responsible for, and expressly disclaim all liability for, damages of any kind arising out of use, reference to, reliance on, or performance of such information, as well as for any damages or injury caused by any failure of performance, error, omission, interruption, deletion, defect, delay in operation or transmission, computer virus, communication line failure, theft or destruction or unauthorized access to, alteration of, or use of any record."

The language can be viewed in full on the "Terms of Use" page of the CCSSI website, http://www.corestandards.org/terms-of-use/.

7. NGA, "Common Core State Standards Initiative Validation Committee Members Announced," Press release, Sept. 24, 2009, http://www.nga.org/cms/home/news-room/news-releases/page_2009/col2-content/main-content-list/title_common-core-state-standards-initiative-validation-committee-announced.html.

8. Keep in mind that the final version was not released until June 2, 2010, and that many changes were made behind the scenes to the public comment draft released in March 2010.

9. For example, a letter explaining my reasons for not signing off on the standards—addressed to Gene Wilhoit (CCSSO) and Dane Linn,

(NGA)—appeared in full on *NYCEye* blog, Aug. 25, 2013, http://nyceye. blogspot.com/2013/08/mass-standards-czar-stotskys-letter-on.html.

10. Dr. Milgram made his final report publicly available for download, ftp://math.stanford.edu/pub/papers/milgram/final-report-for-validation-committee.pdf.

11. David T. Conley, Kathryn V. Drummond, Alicia de Gonzalez, Mary Seburn, Odile Stout, and Jennifer Rooseboom, *Lining Up: The Relationship between Common Core State Standards and Five Other Sets of Comparison Standards* (Eugene, OR: Educational Policy Improvement Center, 2011), http://www.epiconline.org/publications/documents/LiningUp-Full-Report_2011.pdf. The report acknowledges that it was based on research funded at least in part by the Gates Foundation.

12. An abstract for the Schmidt paper, which he co-authored with Richard T. Houang, is available at the Sage Journals website, http://edr.sagepub.com/content/41/8/294.abstract. Schmidt's research findings were presented at a press conference sponsored by Achieve, Inc., Chiefs for Change, and the Foundation for Excellence in Education on May 3, 2012. Achieve had received a $375,000 grant for advocacy from the Gates Foundation, the Foundation for Excellence in Education had received a $1,000,000 grant for advocacy from the Gates Foundation, and Chiefs for Change is funded by the Foundation for Excellence in Education. Those who have helped to fund a seemingly important piece of research are typically among those who sponsor the press conference for the release of the final report.

13. David T. Conley, *Understanding University Success*. Report from Standards for Success, a joint project of the Association of American Universities and the Pew Charitable Trusts (Eugene, OR: University of Oregon, 2003).

14. Ze'ev Wurman, "Why Common Core's Math Standards Don't Add Up," *Pioneer Institute Blog*, June 24, 2013, http://pioneerinstitute.org/news/why-common-cores-math-standards-dont-measure-up-by-guest-blogger-zeev-wurman/.

15. "Common Core State Standards Comparison Briefs," Achieve, accessed July 6, 2014, http://www.achieve.org/CCSS-comparison-briefs. All of the papers Achieve uses to support its claims are dated 2010.

16. "Common Core State Standards," Foundation for Excellence in Education, copyright 2010-2014, accessed July 6, 2014, http://excelined. org/common-core-toolkit/.

17. U.S. Chamber of Commerce, "U.S. Chamber Applauds the Issuance of Common Academic Standards." Press release, Mar. 9, 2010, http://www.uschamber.com/press/releases/2010/march/us-chamber-applauds-issuance-common-academic-standards.

THE COMMON CORE MATHEMATICS STANDARDS

R. James Milgram and Ze'ev Wurman

The Common Core State Standards (Common Core) were rolled out in 2010, accompanied by a sea of support. Paid for largely by the Bill and Melinda Gates Foundation, the standards were praised as being "research and evidence based," "rigorous," "internationally competitive," and it was asserted that they would dramatically strengthen our science, technology, engineering, and mathematics (STEM) pipeline. To support those claims, Common Core's copyright holders, the Common Core State Standards Initiative (CCSSI)—comprised of the National Governors Association (NGA) and the Council of Chief State School Officers (CCSSO)—convened a validation committee (VC) in 2009 to review the standards. The VC's report was published together with Common Core's rollout in order to attest to the verity of those soaring claims.

Despite the lofty rhetoric, questions were raised. Critics found the research that supposedly backed Common Core to be unfocused and unspecific. The standards' international competitiveness was questioned. Careful reading, in fact, uncovered a large amount of missing content in many areas together with experimental approaches with a clear track record of failure in others. Moreover, after all that has been said about Common Core preparing American students to compete at the level of the world's highest achieving countries,[1] it actually turns out that the Common Core does not even start to prepare American students for college degrees in STEM areas.[2]

Common Core proponents were not idle in the face of the gathering evidence. After initially hoping to ignore their critics, and then refusing to engage with them,[3] two VC members, David Conley and William Schmidt, published new research attempting to substantiate Common Core's notion of college-readiness, and demonstrate the standards' alignment with high achieving countries. Unfortunately, carefully reading their research exposes even more clearly both the paucity of evidence behind the Common Core Mathematic Standards (CCMS) and their lack of coherence and rigor.[4]

What is the available evidence for Common Core's rigor, and how do Common Core's expectations align with those of high-achieving countries? Considering the fact that Common Core is in the process of being fully implemented across most of the United States and will affect not just the educations of millions of school children but all our futures, it is well worth investigating the answers to these two questions.

Common Core's Promise

The first major public call for a common core of standards came in a 2008 report *Benchmarking for Success* published jointly by the NGA, the CCSSO, and Achieve Inc.[5] The report cited four items in justifying the need for "a common core of internationally benchmarked standards":

1. We live in a global, competitive, skill-driven economy.

2. Strong education promotes economic growth.

3. Equity considerations for students from disadvantaged backgrounds require monitoring and uniform courses across schools and states.

4. Our international competitors are all gaining on us, and some are starting to outstrip us in key areas.

Following from this justification, *Benchmarking* offered five specific actions, beginning with "Action 1: Upgrade state standards by adopting a common core of internationally benchmarked standards in math and language arts for grades K-12 to ensure that students are equipped with the necessary knowledge and skills to be globally competitive."[6]

The report then went on to describe the rigor needed in the proposed standards:

> By the eighth grade, students in top performing nations are studying algebra and geometry, while in the U.S., most eighth-grade math courses focus on arithmetic. In science, American eighth-graders are memorizing the parts of the eye, while students in top-performing nations are learning about how the eye actually works by capturing photons that are translated into images by the brain. In fact, the curriculum studied by the typical American eighth-grader is two full years behind the curriculum being studied by eighth-graders in high performing countries.[7]

Maintaining American competitiveness was, indeed, a (if not *the*) major theme appearing throughout the publication of *Benchmarking* and the development of the Common Core State Standards Initiative (CCSSI).

In June 2009 NGA and CCSSO jointly formed the CCSSI to develop "research and evidence-based, internationally benchmarked" standards "aligned with college and work expectations" and including "rigorous content and skills."[8]

To ascertain that the standards would meet their promise, the CCSSI then established the Common Core VC, charged with monitoring and validating the standards' development process and content. Yet, when the standards were published, VC members were only asked to attest to a much-weakened set of assertions[9]—differing markedly from the original Common Core commitment—that they were:

- [r]eflective of the core knowledge and skills in ELA and mathematics that students need to be college- and career-ready; (originally: *aligned to* rather than *reflective of*)

- [a]ppropriate in terms of their level of clarity and specificity;

- [c]omparable to the expectations of other leading nations; (originally: *benchmarked* rather than the vacuous *comparable*)

- [i]nformed by available research or evidence; (originally: *research and evidence-based* rather than the, again, vacuous *informed by*)

- [t]he result of...best practices for standards development;

- A solid starting point for adoption of cross-state common core standards; (note the weak "starting point" rather than ready for prime time standards, which is the way they are promoted today) and

- A sound basis for eventual development of standards-based assessments.

These changes all have the effect of backing down on the promised quality of the standards, while maintaining the outside perception that they are still evidence-based and similar to international expectations. Even with these lower standards of certification, the VC's report does not mention that five out of its twenty-nine members—two of them being the only content-experts to sit on the VC—were not ready to sign off on the Common Core standards. Nor does it mention that at least three of those five individuals notified CCSSI of substantive reasons for their dissent, mostly around the standards' international benchmarking and evidence base.[10]

Validation Committee Process

When the VC was formed, it was given a strong three-point charter, charging its members to:

- Review the process used to develop the college- and career-readiness standards and recommend improvements in that process. These recommendations will be used to inform the K-12 development process.

- Validate the sufficiency of the evidence supporting each college- and career-readiness standard. Each member is asked to determine whether each standard has sufficient evidence to warrant its inclusion.

- Add any standard that is not now included in the common core state standards that they feel should be included and provide the following evidence to support its inclusion: 1) evidence that the standard is essential to college and career success; and 2) evidence that the standard is internationally comparable.[11]

The charter was far-reaching, allowing each individual member a strong voice in shaping the standards-writing process, challenging standards without sufficient evidence, and adding missing content. So how did the quality of the standards end up much lower than promised?

A key reason was that the first and third charges were quietly eliminated, effectively removing the oversight the VC was supposed to have. It was done out of the public view, and VC members, bound by confidentiality agreements, could not disclose the full details behind these changes. There is every indication that, when the VC and CCSSI leadership discovered that certain members of the committee fully intended to use their authority rather than go along to get along, the new and narrower charge was unilaterally imposed from the highest level.

College Readiness

The standards promised to define what it means to be college- and career-ready for American students. But even more, the standards promised that students who followed the requirements would be college- and career-ready by the time they graduated high school. Doubling down on this promise, the U.S. Department of Education (DoED) required adoption of "career- and college-ready standards" in its Race to the Top (RttT) grants program and its No Child Left Behind (NCLB) flexibility waiver applications. Nearly every state embraced Common Core standards via one or both of these avenues. When they did so, states also were required to ensure that high school graduation would no longer indicate only that students had achieved an academic level worthy of high school graduation, but instead that the graduating students were "college ready," with high school graduation made equivalent to college-readiness.

Such promises are difficult to reconcile with reality. Today over two-thirds of high school graduates continue on to a two- or four-year college. Yet, only about half of them—roughly one third of high school graduates—complete either a two-year degree within three years or a four-year degree within six years after entering college. A 2009 survey indicates that less than one-third of teachers believe that "we should expect all students to...graduate with the skills to do college-level work."[12] Using a true college-readiness as a criterion for high school graduation would imply that about two-thirds of our K-12 students should not graduate high school currently. Such attrition is clearly politically untenable and does not compare well with the over 90 percent high school graduation rate in most of the high-achieving countries. As a result, Common Core promoters quickly had to face this hard reality.

The chosen alternative was to redefine what college readiness means. Indeed, Common Core's September 2009 definition of College and Career Readiness Standards (CCRS) required little more than the content of a standard Algebra 1 course.[13] This low bar would have served the purpose of allowing most of the high school cohort to graduate, yet was such a ridiculously low "college-readiness" standard that even the leadership of the Common Core project had to raise it—but not by a lot.

In the final version of the standards released in June 2010, the implicit definition of college-readiness in mathematics was passing a weak Algebra 2 course and understanding geometry but only to a level considerably below the level expected in the high achieving countries. It is only implied, because CCSSI leadership never explicitly retracted its 2009 low-level definition. Instead, the final version suggests that all students should take three years of high school mathematics, comprising Algebra 1 and weak Algebra 2 and Geometry courses.

How good is this level of preparation for college? Some relevant data from California sheds light on this question. Since 2006, eleventh-graders in California could take a test to pre-qualify for non-remedial entry into the California State University system under the Early Assessment Program (EAP). These juniors must have taken at least a full Algebra 2 class in order to qualify for the EAP. Yet among those whose highest high school math class was just Algebra 2, only 28 percent tested college-ready on the EAP. By contrast 88 percent of those who had taken at least one math course beyond Algebra 2 tested college-ready.[14] Clearly, even a full Algebra 2 class is marginal for college readiness, yet the Common Core now declares its weak Algebra 2 and Geometry courses to be sufficient. Further data from the National Center for Education Statistics (NCES) shows that in 1992 only 39 percent of high school graduates whose highest math course was Algebra 2 obtained a four-year college degree.[15]

What may be even worse, many states have given this low-level of college-readiness the force of law and require that their public colleges and universities accept such students directly into non-remedial credit-bearing courses (which was a requirement to apply for RttT funds). One can only imagine the damage this will impose on those states' colleges and universities.

Science, Technology, Engineering and Mathematics (STEM) Readiness

The leadership of the writing team for the Common Core Math Standards consisted of three people, Mr. Phil Daro, Dr. William McCallum, and Dr. Jason Zimba. The last two were professors of mathematics at the university level,[16] but Daro has no academic background in the subject at all. Nevertheless, to put it in perspective, Daro was one of the leaders in the writing of the 1992 California math standards, which were so bad that they led to what are now known as the Math Wars.[17] More recently, he headed up the writing group for the Georgia math standards, where he created a draft with so many issues that it was necessary to bring in a group of mathematicians and math educators to rewrite those standards entirely. Also, it is worth noting that, prior to Common Core, neither McCallum nor Zimba had ever written K-12 state mathematics standards that were actually used.

As noted above, Algebra 1 was CCSSI's initial definition of the mathematics needed for college readiness. But it appears that both McCallum and Zimba knew that this standard would be far too low. Indeed, in referring to this first draft in a presentation at the national meeting of the joint national mathematics societies in January 2010, McCallum explained that "[i]t's not what we aspire to for our children, it's not what we as a nation want to set as a final deliverable. I completely agree with that. And we should go beyond that...We expect it to absolutely go beyond that level...K-12 standards will go beyond the level set by the college and career-ready document. It will include standards about permutations, for example, it already does."[18]

Upon questioning, McCallum continued: "[CCMS] will include standards describing what kids need to know if they are going to go into certain careers. So I completely agree this is not a level that we should aspire to. The level that was set at the [September 2009] college and career ready document was not based on university admission requirements but rather on data about what students actually do, how well they succeed if they go to a certain level of mathematics."

We now understand that this so-called body of data "about what students actually do" originally came from a 2009 report developed by Marc Tucker's organization, National Center on Education and the Economy (NCEE).[19] Phil Daro chaired the mathematics committee for that report, which claimed that all the mathematics most students need for college work is Algebra 1. However, an actual reading of the report shows that this level of mathematics is only the absolute minimum amount needed to take courses at a typical community college. From the beginning, it seems that, for Daro, the Algebra 1 standard for college readiness meant only being weakly prepared for attending a community college!

McCallum went on to say that "college admission requirements, I completely agree, are not in sync with that. So I just want to say that I'm not saying that is an aspiration level for our country, and it's not going to be the exit requirements of the final college ready standards." Actually, at this point McCallum was referring to the next CCMS draft, which appeared as a public draft in March 2010. That draft could have led to reasonable high school standards containing a natural path to calculus. In the final document in June 2010, however, virtually all of the more demanding content indicated in the March 2010 draft was gone. The only additions were in Geometry and Algebra 2 and were not nearly enough for students interested in technical areas or STEM majors.

Finally, Jason Zimba testified before the Massachusetts Board of Elementary and Secondary Education in March of 2010. Responding to a question about the definition of college readiness as passing an Algebra 2 course, he answered "I think it's a fair critique that [CCMS implies] a minimal definition of college readiness." When prodded further, Zimba added that this college-readiness standard is "[n]ot only not for STEM, it's also not for selective colleges."[20]

In sum, by all three of its authors' own admissions, the low level of Common Core's notion of college-readiness in mathematics is sufficient only for community colleges and non-selective four-year colleges. It is insufficient for today's typical four-year state colleges and universities, where virtually all of our students obtain their bachelor degrees, and it is at least two years below what students need to successfully major in STEM disciplines.

The data in table 1 is taken from a recent College Board study that looked into the freshmen mathematics course-taking in four-year, post-secondary institutions and it shows that fully 50 percent of first-year students who take any mathematics at all start college with at least calculus as their first math course.[21] This should give a clear picture of how far out of touch with reality Common Core's Algebra 2 definition of college-readiness is.

Equally concerning is the corruption of the meaning of being college-ready in the public mind, because parents are likely to be satisfied as long as their children's schools tell them their kids are on track to be college-ready when they graduate. Further, the requirements forcing

Table 1. Mathematics taken by college freshmen.

FIRST YEAR COLLEGE MATHEMATICS CONTENT AREA	PERCENT TAKING
Calculus	44
Analysis	2
Linear Algebra	2
Differential Equations	2
Elementary Functions	2
Discrete/Finite Math	4
Less than Calculus	44

colleges to accept unprepared students into credit-bearing courses will necessarily lower the academic expectations in public post-secondary institutions. At the same time, it will have no effect on the hiring requirements for higher-end jobs that, consequently, are likely to go—at an even higher rate than currently—to non-U.S. citizens.

Rigor of Content

ELEMENTARY AND MIDDLE GRADES

Common Core inappropriately expects too much rigor and abstraction in Kindergarten and grade1. For example, Kindergarteners are expected to decompose into pairs numbers up to ten and record such decomposition in the form of an equation.[22] Such abstract notation is beyond what most young children can comprehend and well beyond what high-achieving countries expect. Counting to 100 by ones and tens is probably possible for Kindergarteners but has little value as a skill this early, as children this young frequently simply treat the numbers as if they were letters of the alphabet. Insisting on it in the standards is inappropriate. Similarly, insistence in grade 1 on multiple specific strategies for addition and subtraction seems totally unnecessary, completely confusing and, again, inappropriate. Here is that standard:

> 1.OA.6 Add and subtract within 20, demonstrating fluency for addition and subtraction within 10. Use strategies such as counting on; making ten (e.g., $8 + 6 = 8 + 2 + 4 = 10 + 4 = 14$); decomposing a number leading to a ten (e.g., $13 - 4 = 13 - 3 - 1 = 10 - 1 = 9$); using the relationship between addition and subtraction (e.g., knowing that $8 + 4 = 12$, one knows $12 - 8 = 4$); and creating equivalent but easier or known sums (e.g., adding $6 + 7$ by creating the known equivalent $6 + 6 + 1 = 12 + 1 = 13$).

Looking closely at this standard, it is actually the concatenation of seven separate standards, two of which, all by themselves, form almost the totality of the content of the first half of typical first-grade courses in the high-achieving countries. Yet that is only one of twenty-one first-grade "standards" in Common Core. Likewise, expecting first-graders to be familiar with and compose 3D shapes such as cubes, prisms, cones and cylinders is unnecessarily pushing young children for no good mathematical reason.

In contrast to the dramatically inappropriate Kindergarten and first-grade standards, Common Core slows down significantly from second grade onward. It is slow to expect fluency with addition and subtraction using standard algorithms, a fourth-grade standard in Common Core that appears much earlier in the top performing countries. It is delayed by fully one to two years or even more by not expecting fluency with multiplication until grade 5 and division until grade 6. It is delayed by two years or more by expecting students to know the sum of the three interior angles in a triangle only in eighth grade. It is delayed by a year or more in discussing the use of parentheses, percents, circles, angles, and the area of a triangle. Moreover, Common Core has inexplicable holes such as failing to require prime decomposition[23] or converting among the three fractional representations: fractions, decimals, and percents. Actually, this is an astounding lack. One of the most crucial parts of students' preparation for more advanced mathematics is understanding how and why decimals are just a compressed way of writing certain fractions. Moreover, prime decomposition and its uniqueness is commonly called the *fundamental theorem of arithmetic*.

The standards repeatedly return—ad nauseam one might say—to instructing students to use "concrete models or drawings and strategies based on place value, properties of operations, and/or the relationships" throughout the grades, rarely allowing students to internalize past knowledge and simply build on it to move forward. Consequently, by the end of eighth grade, Common Core standards are, overall, between one and two years or even more behind what students in top-performing countries are expected and able to do, not only in the content being studied but, even more crucially, in the students' mathematical sophistication.

ALGEBRA 1

"By the eighth grade, students in top performing nations are studying algebra and geometry, while in the United States, most eighth-grade math courses focus on arithmetic," writes *Benchmarking for Success* in its call for action and the Common Core. Similarly, the presidential National Mathematics Advisory Panel in 2008 called on all school districts to "ensure that all prepared students have access to an authentic algebra course—and [to] prepare more students than at present to enroll in such a course by Grade 8."[24]

This push – to prepare more students for taking an algebra class in grade 8 similar to their peers overseas, has been one of the strongest positive driving forces in American math education since the first TIMSS[25] test in 1995 exposed the extent to which our math education has fallen behind. Actually, the United States had made major progress in that direction. The number of students taking an Algebra 1 course in the eighth grade increased by 50 percent across the nation between 1995 and 2011. In California, by 2011, two-thirds of students were taking Algebra 1 in eighth grade, and 7 percent even took a Geometry course by the end of grade 8. Maryland, Minnesota, Utah, and Virginia were not far behind. Indeed, U.S. results both on the NAEP,[26] and on TIMSS had risen significantly, too—roughly a quarter of a standard deviation on TIMSS and about one and a half years equivalent on the NAEP—for both fourth- and eighth-graders.

Yet the Common Core, despite its rhetoric about expecting American students to study content similar to their peers overseas, silently abandoned this goal and placed the first algebra course firmly at the high school level. In other words, it fully retreated from attempting to match up with international expectations. Instead, it went back to what had been the situation in the early 1990s when it became obvious that we were severely falling behind.

Defenders of Common Core frequently excuse this obvious indication of severely reduced rigor by arguing that Common Core expects students to perform "algebraic tasks" and engage in "algebraic thinking" in grades 7 and 8.[27]

But this assertion is specious. The reason algebra is so crucial in so many areas is that it provides a very powerful structure that can be applied in a great many situations to solve mathematics problems. An actual mathematician will talk about using the tools algebra provides to solve problems rather than the fuzzy term "algebraic thinking."

Let us look at how a student's understanding of these tools and their usage evolves. From the earliest grades, students using a good curriculum (including all of the students in the high-achieving countries) will explore linear problems that involve finding solutions to equations of the form $ax + b = c$ for arbitrary constants a, b, and c. The following story problem would be typical: "Suppose a bus, traveling from Minneapolis to Duluth at a constant 50 miles per hour passes through Clear Lake at noon, and Clear Lake is 27 miles from Minneapolis. If the distance from Minneapolis to Duluth is 154 miles, when, to the nearest quarter hour, will it arrive in Duluth?" Such problems are done more or less routinely in the high achieving countries in fifth grade. However, in Common Core, such problems are likely to be thought too difficult even in the seventh or eighth grade.

In the high-achieving countries, students start early to solve simpler problems such as: "The distance from Minneapolis to Duluth is 150 miles by train. Suppose the train is traveling at a constant speed of 50 miles per hour. How long will it take to travel by train from Minneapolis to Duluth?" A problem of this nature would be entirely appropriate in third grade as would a problem like: "Suppose the time it takes a train to travel from Minneapolis to Duluth is three hours and the train travels 50 miles per hour. How far is Duluth from Minneapolis by train?" With extensive practice on such problems from third through fifth grades, the students in the high-achieving countries are entirely ready for the abstraction to the algebraic problem "Solve for x if $3x + 5 = 27$," and then, in full generality, if a is non-zero and $ax + b = c$, solve for x in terms of a, b, and c. Common Core standards hint at this progression, but it occurs much later. Moreover, far too much other material is covered at the same time (and, of course, that material is far less important). Thus, students learning from Common Core aligned curricula will continue to have huge difficulties with basic algebra. In spite of claims to the contrary, Common Core remains fully as non-focused and superficial as virtually all state standards it has replaced.

Another element that Common Core glosses over is the radical change it makes in what is taught in a Common Core algebra class. Traditionally, the first algebra class develops fluency with *handling basic equations*. First, students master solving linear equations, inequalities, and systems of linear equations. Then they are introduced to quadratic equations and inequalities, and finally to polynomials and rational expressions. These skills serve them well both as steppingstones to quantitative sciences such as chemistry or physics, as well as more advanced mathematics. In contrast, in Common Core the focus of both Algebra 1 and Algebra 2 is on students' understanding of "functional relationships"—largely in the form of graphing functions and discussing their behavior[28]—rather than developing the ability to quantitatively and analytically manipulate those functions, particularly since many of the functions suggested by Common Core, such as tables, exponential functions, step and piecewise-linear functions,[29] are not yet amenable to analytical and quantitative handling by eighth or ninth grade students. Consequently, much of what will happen in such classrooms will be "talking the talk" rather than "walking the walk"; students will not develop the crucial technical skills they need actually to use such functions in more advanced math and science courses as well as further courses in areas such as economics or robotics.

In other words, not only is algebra under Common Core delayed when compared to top-performing nations, but the traditional content of the course is silently replaced by a so-called "Functional Algebra" that for decades tried to find its place in the K-12 curriculum, was found lacking, and was rejected. Common Core now stealthily introduces that same, failed, experimental set of topics into most classrooms in the nation under the guise of covering "algebra."[30]

GEOMETRY

When it comes to geometry, Common Core is guilty both of sins of commission and sins of omission. Sins of commission occurred when Common Core insisted on teaching triangle congruence via rigid transformations—slides, flips, and rotations—instead of via the traditional Euclidean approach. Had Common Core been true content standards—as it claims it is—it would have simply specified that students needed to learn triangle congruence and left the method to teachers. Instead, it chose to impose its own "cute" mathematical way to teach it, a method that is well beyond the capability of both high school students and too many high school teachers. This method was actually tried in the Soviet Union in the 1970s, failed even with gifted student prodigies, and was quickly abandoned.[31] That Common Core's authors imposed this experimental method on this country in one fell swoop, despite its failing track record, speaks not only to the inexperience of Common Core's architects and authors but also to their arrogance. Sins of omission are of a more typical nature. The geometry standards are not sufficiently clear about the depth to which students are expected to learn the material, but the examples given in the standards tend to be extremely elementary. This scenario leads to the conclusion that no deep study of geometry is expected. Here is an example:

> G.CO.10 Prove theorems about triangles. Theorems include: measures of interior angles of a triangle sum to 180°; base angles of isosceles triangles are congruent; the segment joining midpoints of two sides of a triangle is parallel to the third side and half the length; the medians of a triangle meet at a point.

The standard lists four specific theorems, three of them rather trivial. But there are probably more than fifty worthwhile theorems relating to triangles, and any serious geometry course would easily touch on a dozen or more. How is one to choose? How is one to know what the teacher (or the textbook writer) would choose? Would some choose just those four and nothing more? In fact, it's certain that some will, since the PARCC and SBAC Common Core assessments will be entirely keyed to the core standards; *if a topic is not mentioned in the standards, then it will not appear in the assessments.*

The problems with the following geometry standard are similar:

> G-C.2 Identify and describe relationships among inscribed angles, radii, and chords. Include the relationship between central, inscribed, and circumscribed angles; inscribed angles on a diameter are right angles; the radius of a circle is perpendicular to the tangent where the radius intersects the circle.

Here, too, the standard talks about "relationships" among angles, radii, and chords in a general and non-specific way, with all of the examples being on the trivial end of the spectrum. It virtually guarantees shallow coverage by most textbooks and curricula, particularly since the standard, in contrast with the previous one, doesn't even speak of proofs but rather uses the term "identify and describe." Here, again, the standards encourage talking the talk rather than walking the walk.

The examples above only begin to describe the lack of standard content in Common Core geometry and the difficulties that will subsequently arise from it.

HIGH SCHOOL CONTENT

It is clear that McCallum and Zimba made an effort to include standards for as much key K-12 mathematics as possible, given the constraints under which they were working. Given these constraints, they did an adequate but hardly outstanding job. As both authors indicated, there were limits on how far they could go; between January and March of 2010, it appears that they only had authorization to develop weak Geometry and Algebra 2 courses but that they were trying to add further content, including a path to calculus, before releasing the final version in June 2010. However, the new material hinted at in the March 2010 draft was not present in the final standards.

When we look at the content mandated in the Common Core math standards in Algebra 2 and beyond, we see that, while exponential functions and logarithmic functions appear at various points there is no discussion of logarithms themselves and how to work with them. Similarly, exponential functions are introduced but there is no substantive indication that they exist besides the fact that calculators graph them. In fact, on page 60 of the final document, there is a basically incorrect standard that attempts to justify them.[32] For that matter, another functions-related standard, F-BF.5, is also incorrect as written in that it indicates the relationship between exponentials and logarithms is inverse. In fact, this relationship is not inverse; while logarithms are inverse to exponentials, exponentials are not inverse to logarithms. To even make sense of this standard involves much more advanced material than is typically accessible to high school students.[33]

Conic sections, which are absolutely essential preparation for any STEM area, are extremely poorly handled. For example, there is barely any mention of the focus or directrix for given conic sections. Moreover, the fundamental intrinsic properties of parabolas and ellipses, all tied to the positions of the foci and the directrix, are never even mentioned, let alone developed and applied.[34]

Trigonometry is spread out between "functions" and "geometry" and is quite incomplete. The subject is addressed mainly in two groups of the high school standards, neither of which include any indication of how one uses trigonometric functions to solve problems in areas such as surveying.[35] As another example, there is no requirement that students even know the critical fact for applications—when T is the angle that a line makes with the x-axis, then tan(T), is exactly the slope of the line. Likewise, there is no indication except in a single (+) standard that students should know the addition and subtraction formulas for sine and cosine or how to use them—for example, to find sin(2x), sin(3x), or sin(x/2). There is no mention of polar coordinates (except for an oblique reference to "polar form" for complex numbers). Nor is there any mention of transforming between rectangular and polar coordinates. All this material is essential when students take college-level physics, chemistry, and even more so, engineering courses, to say nothing of calculus or more advanced math courses. Without it, students in these courses and areas flounder.

When it comes to pre-calculus, Common Core contains no discussion of mathematical induction except in a single footnote on page 60 of the final document. Aside from this single footnote, Common Core just talks about "inductive reasoning," an entirely different and non-mathematical animal. There is no mention of the fundamental theorem of algebra except in a single (+) standard; no discussion of parametric equations; and, except for a single mention of "informal limits," no discussion of limits at all. Yet, these topics are perhaps even more critical than conic sections for all technical majors since they are the key pre-calculus material students must have to handle calculus. While limits will generally be reviewed in calculus (the dreaded epsilons and deltas), we know that students who have not seen the basic ideas previously will struggle with the entire first calculus course.

International Benchmarking

Rigor was supposed to be a defining attribute of the Common Core standards. To that end the standards were supposed to be benchmarked at the level of the high-achieving nations. Jonathan Goodman, a mathematics professor at the Courant Institute of Mathematical Sciences at New York University reviewed and compared them to the expectations of East Asian high-achieving countries. In summarizing his findings, Goodman pointed out that the "Common Core standard [document] is similar in earlier grades but has significantly lower expectations with respect to algebra and geometry than the published standards of other countries I examined. The Common Core standards document is prepared with less care and is less useful to teachers and math ed administrators than the other standards I examined."[36]

Andrew Porter, dean of the Graduate School of Education at the University of Pennsylvania, and his colleagues also compared Common Core with high-achieving Asian countries. Their summary:

> The Common Core standards are also different from the standards of countries with higher student achievement....
> We also used international benchmarking to judge the quality of the Common Core standards, and the results are surprising both for mathematics and for [English Language Arts and Reading]. Top-achieving countries for which we had content standards put a greater emphasis on 'perform procedures'[37] than do the U.S. Common Core standards. High-performing countries' emphasis on 'perform procedures' runs counter to the widespread call in the United States for a greater emphasis on higher order cognitive demand.[38]

Stotsky and Wurman studied the question of whether the standards represent more rigorous expectations than those of Massachusetts or California. Their conclusions:

> Our analysis of Common Core's mathematics...and the evidence we provide, do not support the conclusion...that Common Core's standards provide a stronger and more challenging framework for the mathematics...curriculum than California's and Massachusetts' standards have provided. Common Core's standards will not prepare more high school students for authentic college-level work than standards in these states have prepared. To the contrary, they may lead to fewer high school students prepared for authentic college-level work.[39]

James Milgram, emeritus professor of mathematics at Stanford University, testified before the California Academic Standards

Commission as to Common Core's rigor and its comparison with high-achieving countries. Milgram concluded that among the difficulties with the standards "a large number of the arithmetic and operations, as well as the place value standards are one, two or even more years behind the corresponding standards for many if not all the high achieving countries." He continued, "Consequently, I was not able to certify that the Core Mathematics Standards are benchmarked at the same level as the standards of the high achieving countries in mathematics."[40]

William Schmidt, an educational statistician at Michigan State University and a former VC member, together with a colleague carried out a study to explore whether the CCMS are comparable to the expectations of leading nations and what reasonable outcomes might be expected after adoption of the Common Core. In contrast with all the other studies, he found that "[i]t is important to note the consistency between the Common Core State Standards for Mathematics and the internationally developed A+ standards. The measure of congruence on which this conclusion is based suggests that the CCMS are both coherent and focused. They were also found to be rigorous as indicated by the consistency in topic coverage between the two sets of standards especially at eighth grade."[41]

Yet a closer look at his study raises serious questions. In order to answer the question of comparative rigor, Schmidt and Houang used the methodology they developed to map mathematics curriculum content in grades 1-8 in the six highest-achieving countries as reflected on the 1995 TIMSS and reported in 2005.

Figure 1, from the 2005 study, shows what topics at least four of the six highest-achieving, or A+ countries, taught at each of these grade levels. The profile has a distinct triangular shape. The shape of the topic-by-grade profile conveys information on coherence and focus. A few things should be noted:

- The descending order of the rows reflects *a logical and coherent progression* of topics in terms of complexity, which is carefully followed in the high-achieving countries. So, for example, 3D geometry is introduced after 2D geometry.

- Only very few topics span more than half the grades. Most topics

Figure 1. Mathematics standards intended by at least four of six TIMSS A+ countries.

TOPIC	1	2	3	4	5	6	7	8
				GRADE				
Whole Number: Meaning	•	•	•	•	•			
Whole Number: Operations	•	•	•	•	•			
Measurement Units	•	•	•	•	•	•	•	
Common Fractions			•	•	•	•		
Equations and Formulas			•	•	•	•	•	•
Data Representation and Analysis			•	•	•	•		•
2D Geometry: Basics			•	•	•	•	•	•
2D Geometry: Polygons and Circles				•	•	•	•	•
Measurement: Permieter, Area, and Volume				•	•	•	•	•
Rounding and Significant Figures				•	•			
Estimating Computations				•	•	•		
Whole Numbers: Properties of Operations				•	•			
Estimating Quantity and Size				•	•			
Decimal Fractions				•	•	•		
Relation of Common and Decimal Fractions				•	•	•		
Properties of Common and Decimal Fractions					•	•		
Percentages					•	•		
Proportionality Concepts					•	•	•	•
Proportionality Problems					•	•	•	•
2D Geometry: Coordinate Geometry					•	•	•	•
Geometry: Transformations						•	•	•
Negative Numbers, Integers, and Their Properties						•	•	
Number Theory							•	•
Exponents, Roots, and Radicals							•	•
Exponents and Orders of Magnitude							•	•
Measurement: Estimation and Errors							•	
Constructions Using Straightedge and Compass							•	•
3D Geometry							•	•
Geometry: Congruence and Similarity								•
Rational Numbers and Their Properties								•
Patterns, Relations, and Functions								•
Proportionality: Slope and Trigonometry								•

Figure 2. The Common Core standards as presented by Schmidt and Houang.

TOPIC	1	2	3	4	5	6	7	8
Whole Number: Meaning	•	•	•	•	•			
Whole Number: Operations	•	•	•	•	•			
Whole Numbers: Properties of Operations	•	•	•	•	•	•		
Common Fractions	•	•	•	•	•	•		
Measurement Units	•	•	•	•	•	•	•	•
2D Geometry: Polygons and Circles	•	•	•	•	•	•	•	•
Data Representation and Analysis	•	•	•	•	•	•	•	•
3D Geometry	•	•			•	•	•	•
Measurement: Estimation and Errors		•	•					
Number Theory		•		•	•	•		
2D Geometry Basics		•		•	•	•	•	•
Rounding and Significant Figures			•	•	•			
Relation of Common and Decimal Fractions			•	•	•	•		
Estimating Computations			•	•	•		•	•
Measurements: Perimeter, Area, and Volume			•	•	•	•	•	•
Equations and Formulas			•	•	•	•	•	•
Decimal Fractions				•	•	•		
Patterns, Relations and Functions				•	•	•	•	•
Geometry: Transformations				•		•	•	•
Properties of Common and Decimal Fractions					•	•		
Exponents and Orders of Magnitude					•			•
2D Geometry: Coordinate Geometry					•	•	•	•
Exponents, Roots, and Radicals					•	•		•
Percentages						•	•	
Negative Numbers, Integers, and Their Properties						•	•	
Proportionality Concepts						•	•	•
Proportionality Problems						•	•	•
Rational Numbers and Their Properties						•	•	•
Constructions Using Straightedge and Compass							•	
Systematic Counting							•	
Uncertainty and Probability							•	
Real Numbers and Their Properties								•
Geometry: Congruence and Similarity								•
Proportionality: Slope and Trigonometry								•
Validation and Justification								•

Figure 3. Figures 1 and 2 side by side, showing differences between the original

		GRADE							
#	TOPIC	1	2	3	4	5	6	7	8
1	Whole Number: Meaning	•	•	•	•	•			
2	Whole Number: Operations	•	•	•	•	•			
3	Measurement Units	•	•	•	•	•	•	•	
4	Common Fractions			•	•	•	•		
5	Equations and Formulas			•	•	•	•	•	•
6	Data Representation and Analysis			•	•	•	•		
7	2D Geometry: Basics			•	•	•	•	•	•
8	2D Geometry: Polygons and Circles				•	•	•	•	•
9	Measurement: Permieter, Area, and Volume				•	•	•	•	•
10	Rounding and Significant Figures				•	•			
11	Estimating Computations				•	•	•		
12	Whole Numbers: Properties of Operations				•	•			
13	Estimating Quantity and Size				•	•			
14	Decimal Fractions				•	•	•		
15	Relation of Common and Decimal Fractions				•	•	•		
16	Properties of Common and Decimal Fractions					•	•		
17	Percentages					•	•		
18	Proportionality Concepts					•	•	•	•
19	Proportionality Problems					•	•	•	•
20	2D Geometry: Coordinate Geometry					•	•	•	•
21	Geometry: Transformations						•	•	•
22	Negative Numbers, Integers, and Their Properties						•	•	
23	Number Theory							•	•
24	Exponents, Roots, and Radicals							•	•
25	Exponents and Orders of Magnitude							•	•
26	Measurement: Estimation and Errors							•	
27	Constructions Using Straightedge and Compass							•	•
28	3D Geometry							•	•
29	Geometry: Congruence and Similarity								•
30	Rational Numbers and Their Properties								•
31	Patterns, Relations, and Functions								•
32	Proportionality: Slope, and Trigonometry								•
33	Systematic Counting								
34	Uncertainty and Probability								
35	Real Numbers and Their Properties								
36	Validation and Justification								

topic order and the revised order in Schmidt and Houang (2012).

1	2	3	4	5	6	7	8	#	TOPIC
•	•	•	•	•				1	Whole Number: Meaning
•	•	•	•	•				2	Whole Number: Operations
•	•	•	•	•	•			12	Whole Numbers: Properties of Operations
•	•	•	•	•	•			4	Common Fractions
•	•	•	•	•	•	•	•	3	Measurement Units
•	•	•	•	•	•	•	•	8	2D Geometry: Polygons and Circles
•	•	•	•	•	•	•	•	6	Data Representation and Analysis
•	•			•	•	•	•	28	3D Geometry
	•	•						26	Measurement: Estimation and Errors
	•		•	•	•			23	Number Theory
	•		•	•	•	•	•	7	2D Geometry Basics
		•	•	•				10	Rounding and Significant Figures
		•	•	•	•			15	Relation of Common and Decimal Fractions
		•	•	•		•	•	11	Estimating Computations
		•	•	•	•	•	•	9	Measurements: Perimeter, Area, and Volume
		•	•	•	•	•	•	5	Equations and Formulas
			•	•	•	•		14	Decimal Fractions
			•	•	•	•	•	31	Patterns, Relations and Functions
			•		•	•	•	21	Geometry: Transformations
				•	•			16	Properties of Common and Decimal Fractions
				•			•	25	Exponents and Orders of Magnitude
				•	•	•	•	20	2D Geometry: Coordinate Geometry
				•	•		•	24	Exponents, Roots, and Radicals
					•	•		17	Percentages
					•	•		22	Negative Numbers, Integers, and Their Properties
					•	•	•	18	Proportionality Concepts
					•	•	•	19	Proportionality Problems
					•	•	•	30	Rational Numbers and Their Properties
						•		27	Constructions Using Straightedge and Compass
						•		33	Systematic Counting
						•		34	Uncertainty and Probability
							•	35	Real Numbers and Their Properties
							•	29	Geometry: Congruence and Similarity
							•	32	Proportionality: Slope and Trigonometry
							•	36	Validation and Justification
								13	Estimating Quantity and Size

are taught to mastery, after which they are no longer taught but are instead applied in more advanced situations, reflecting the *focused* nature of the progression.

• The number of topic per grade (the number of topics in a vertical column) is limited. This allows for *depth* in instruction.

The profile in figure 2 in Schmidt and Houang's 2012 paper does resemble the overall shape of the curriculum profile of the A+ countries in figure 1. Figure 1 reflects only the topics in at least four of the six highest- achieving countries on the 1995 TIMSS test. Figure 2 instead reflects all of the standards in a complete set of standards, making it somewhat fuller.

Based on the seeming similarity in overall shape, Schmidt and Houang declare that because CCMS "bears a strong resemblance to Figure 1 (A+ model), at least in terms of its general shape....[f]rom that point of view, it can be suggested that the [CCMS] are coherent and focused."[42]

Schmidt and Houang conclude this part of their paper by asserting that "[t]here being no major differences between the two sets of standards, this provides further evidence that the [CCMS] are coherent and very consistent with the international benchmark."[43]

However, the order of the rows in figure 2 *differs from the order of rows in figure 1*. Figure 3 starkly shows these differences. Also note how the original sequence of standards 1-36 in the leftmost column is scrambled in the second column from the right.

Apparently, Schmidt and Houang rearranged the original coherent and hierarchical order of topics to achieve the desired triangular shape, ignoring notions of coherence and hierarchy. Consequently, in their figure 2, "3D Geometry" comes before "2D Geometry Basics," and "Relations of Common and Decimal Fractions" comes before students even study the more basic "Decimal Fractions." Their figure 2, then, is an artificially-produced shape that leads to their desired visual conclusion of "coherence" and "consistency" with the 2005 A+ curriculum profile, *despite lacking actual internal coherence and logical sequencing.*

Schmidt and Houang apply additional creative statistical tools to discover superb correlation between Common Core and high-achieving countries. They then go on to uncover a correlation, supposedly never previously noticed, between achievement and the similarity of a state's standards to the Common Core. Recalling that Schmidt already attested earlier in 2010, when he was a member of the VC, that the Common Core standards are "[c]omparable to the expectations of other leading nations," his efforts at *post facto* demonstration of his earlier attestation are quite remarkable.[44]

Before we leave this section, we should remind the reader of the original call for the Common Core in *Benchmarking for Success* yet again: "By the eighth grade, students in top performing nations are studying algebra and geometry, while in the U.S., most eighth-grade math courses focus on arithmetic...In fact, the curriculum studied by the typical American eighth-grader is two full years behind the curriculum being studied by eighth-graders in high performing countries."

One can try and find rigor in the Common Core for as long as one desires, but, after all is said and done, the indisputable fact remains that the Common Core firmly placed its first algebra course not in the eighth grade as top-performing nations do, but in high school. There can't be stronger evidence than this one simple fact for the lowered level of these mathematics standards.

Summary

What we have shown in this essay are three distinct things. First, despite its professed goal to improve American competitiveness, Common Core aimed from the beginning to redefine college-readiness much below where true college-readiness is. Second, the validation process was a sham; the Validation Committee was quickly and silently emasculated from any meaningful authority, and no real validation of the standards actually took place. Finally, the resulting standards in mathematics are far from rigorous; are not internationally benchmarked; and are infused with pedagogy and curricular directives, some of which are experimental or have already failed but none of which will prepare students for STEM careers.

NOTES

1.   See, for example, Governor Jim Douglas of Vermont at the Common Core initial rollout. NGA, "Fifty-One States And Territories Join Common Core State Standards Initiative." Press release, Sept. 1, 2009, http://www.nga.org/cms/home/news-room/news-releases/page_2009/col2-content/main-content-list/title_fifty-one-states-and-territories-join-common-core-state-standards-initiative.html; or Gene Wilhoit testimony at the U.S. House Committee on Education and Labor, Dec. 8, 2009, http://www.gpo.gov/fdsys/pkg/CHRG-111hhrg53732/html/CHRG-111hhrg53732.htm.

2.   R. James Milgram and Sandra Stotsky, *Lowering the Bar: How Common Core Math Fails to Prepare High School Students for STEM* (Boston, MA: Pioneer Institute, 2013), http://pioneerinstitute.org/?wpdmdl=381&.

3.   Rick Hess, "Is Anybody Up for Defending the Common Core Math Standards," *Education Week*, Sep. 6, 2011, http://blogs.edweek.org/edweek/rick_hess_straight_up/2011/09/is_anybody_up_for_defending_the_common_core_math_standards.html.

4.   In this chapter we will focus only on the Common Core Mathematics Standards, and only on the research of William Schmidt. A fuller discussion can be found in Ze'ev Wurman, *Common Core's Validation: A Weak Foundation for a Crooked House.* (Boston, MA: Pioneer Institute, 2014), http://pioneerinstitute.org/download/common-cores-validation-a-weak-foundation-for-a-crooked-house/.

5.   National Governors Association (NGA), the Council of Chief State School Officers (CCSSO), and Achieve, Inc., *Benchmarking for Success: Ensuring U.S. Students Receive a World-Class Education.* Report researched and prepared by Craig D. Jerald (Washington D.C.: Authors, 2008), http://www.corestandards.org/assets/0812BENCHMARKING.pdf.

6.   Ibid., 6.

7.   Ibid., 24.

8.   NGA, "Forty-Nine States and Territories Join Common Core Standards Initiative." Press release, June 1, 2009, http://www.nga.org/cms/home/news-room/news-releases/page_2009/col2-content/main-content-list/title_forty-nine-states-and-territories-join-common-core-standards-initiative.html.

9. Common Core State Standards Initiative (CCSSI), *Reaching Higher: The Common Core Validation Committee* (Washington D.C.: NGA and CCSSO, June 2010), http://www.corestandards.org/assets/CommonCoreReport_6.10.pdf.

10. A large number of people have maintained that there were at least seven other "mathematicians" on the Validation Committee besides Milgram, but this assertion is incorrect. All seven of these people were either *educational statisticians or math educators*, and all of them had their Ph.D.'s in education rather than in mathematics. It is worth noting that it is possible to obtain a math education Ph.D. without ever taking a single college mathematics course, and people with math education degrees work on issues in mathematics pedagogy or teacher training rather than mathematics. The other content expert on the committee, in English language arts, was Dr. Sandra Stotsky. See also: Wurman, *Common Core's Validation*.

11. NGA, "Common Core State Standards Initiative Validation Committee Announced." Press release, Sep. 24, 2009, http://www.nga.org/cms/home/news-room/news-releases/page_2009/col2-content/main-content-list/title_common-core-state-standards-initiative-validation-committee-announced.html.

12. John M. Bridgeland, John J. Dilulio Jr., and Robert Balfanz, *On the Front Lines of Schools: Perspectives of Teachers and Principals on the High School Dropout Problem.* Report by Civic Enterprises in association with Peter D. Hart Research Associates for the AT&T Foundation and the America's Promise Alliance (Washington, D.C.: Civic Enterprises, June 2009), http://www.civicenterprises.net/MediaLibrary/Docs/ED%20-%20on%20the%20front%20lines%20of%20schools.pdf.

13. "Common Core State Standards Initiative," archived informational page from the CCSSI site, captured Oct. 19, 2009, https://web.archive.org/web/20091019070946/http://www.corestandards.org/.

14. The 2013 data shows 6 percent ready and 22 percent conditionally ready after Algebra 2; with 22 percent ready and 66 percent conditionally ready after taking a post-Algebra 2 course. See http://eap2013.ets.org/ViewReport.asp.

15. See table 5 in Clifford Adelman, *Toolbox Revisited. Paths to Degree Completion from High School through College* (Washington, DC: U.S. Dept. of Education, 2006).

16. Currently, McCallum remains a professor at the University of Arizona, but Zimba appears to have resigned his position and currently works

full time on implementation issues for Common Core.

17. The Math Wars were a statewide rebellion led by parents and college professors against the mathematics texts and teaching techniques that had been imposed in California by their then new 1992 mathematics standards and framework. It is likely that the rebellion would have had no effect except that, due to the fact that they were having difficulties finding qualified people for entry-level jobs, top-level industry leaders also pressured the state government. The results were completely new standards in both math and ELA, as well as stringent requirements on the school texts that could be used in California.

18. Audio of this portion of the meeting can be accessed at http://pioneerinstitute.org/video/audio-lead-mathematics-standards-writer-william-mccallum/. The final version of the Common Core contains only a single mention of permutations as an advanced Statistics and Probability Standard. So much for that promise.

19. The report and associated summaries are available on the NCEE website, http://www.ncee.org/college-and-work-ready/.

20. Milgram and Stotsky, *Lowering the Bar,* 5.

21. See table 5 in Emily J. Shaw and Brian F. Patterson, *What Should Students Be Ready for in College? A Look at First-Year Course Work in Four-Year Postsecondary Institutions in the U.S.* (New York: The College Board, 2010).

22. Kindergartners are expected to understand and write equations of the form $3 + 7 = 10$, $7 + 3 = 10$, $4 + 6 = 10$, $6 + 4 = 10$ and so on when they barely understand the numbers involved let alone the use of the equal sign.

23. Prime decomposition, or "factorization," breaks a number down into the prime numbers that, when multiplied together, equal that same number. For instance, 12 factored into prime numbers is $2 \times 2 \times 3$. Prime decomposition becomes valuable in dealing with much larger numbers and is crucial in adding and subtracting fractions with different denominators.

24. National Mathematics Advisory Panel, *Foundations for Success: The Final Report of the National Mathematics Advisory Panel* (Washington, D.C.: US Department of Education, 2008).

25. Third International Mathematics and Science Study. It has since been renamed as Trends in International Mathematics and Science Study. An international assessment of mathematics and science of fourth- and eighth-graders given every four years since 1995.

26. National Assessment of Educational Progress, the so-called Nation's Report Card. See http://nces.ed.gov/nationsreportcard/.

27. We have no idea what the term "algebraic thinking" means. Moreover, when looking for definitions using Google, we found quite a number of them—no two alike.

28. As an example consider all the Common Core high school standards that ask for empirically discovering "that a quantity increasing exponentially eventually exceeds a quantity increasing linearly, quadratically, or (more generally) as a polynomial function" and similar tasks. Such tasks are wildly inappropriate at this stage. K-12 students are simply unequipped even to understand the significance of such a property, let alone discover it, and such properties lie entirely within the area of functional relationships.

29. Functions that graph a union of straight line segments, such as the top of a picket fence.

30. Dating from at least the 1989 National Council of Teachers of Mathematics (NCTM) Standards.

31. V.M. Tihomirov, "Andrei Nikolaevich Kolmogorov (1903--1987), the Great Russian Scientist," *The Teaching of Mathematics* vi, no. 1 (2003), 33-35, http://elib.mi.sanu.ac.rs/files/journals/tm/10/tm612.pdf.

32. Standard N-RN.1 attempts to explain exponential functions (abx) by looking at a single example of a rational exponent (1/3), but the main difficulty here revolves around the fact that for a > 0, ax needs to have a meaning for every real number x. The argument in N-RN.1 simply does not extend to such numbers.

33. It is virtually unique to Common Core that what are basically the national standards for a country contain serious mathematical errors, and is probably the clearest indication of how deep our difficulties really are.

34. Standard G-GPE.2 and the (+) standard G-GPE.3 are the only places that address the focus or directrix for conic sections.

35. Trigonometry is addressed in Common Core standards F-TF and G-SRT.

36. Jonathan Goodman, "A Comparison of Proposed U.S. Common Core Math Standard to Standards of Selected Asian Countries," *EducationNews*, July 9, 2010, http://www.educationnews.org/ed_reports/94979.html.

37. "Perform procedures" refers to the ability of students to fluently and

correctly perform routine mathematical operations appropriate to the grade level such as: addition in grades 2-3; multi-digit multiplication and long division in grade 4; or addition, subtraction, multiplication, and division of polynomials, or factoring of polynomials, in high school. "Higher order cognitive demand" tasks, in contrast, would typically refer to understanding why those procedures work.

38. Andrew Porter, Jennifer McMaken, Jun Hwang, and Rui Yang, "Common Core Standards: The New U.S. Intended Curriculum," *Educational Researcher* 40, no. 3 (2011), 103-116.

39. Sandra Stotsky and Ze'ev Wurman, *Common Core's Standards Still Don't Make the Grade: Why Massachusetts and California Must Regain Control over Their Academic Destinies* (Boston, MA: Pioneer Institute, 2010), http://pioneerinstitute.org/download/common-cores-standards-still-dont-make-the-grade/.

40. Ibid., appendix B.

41. William H. Schmidt and Richard T. Houang, "Curricular Coherence and the Common Core State Standards for Mathematics," *Educational Researcher* 41, no. 8, (2012), 294-308.

42. Ibid., 297-298.

43. Ibid., 299.

44. Wurman, *Common Core's Validation*.

HOW DID CHARLATANS EVER GET TO DESIGN NATIONAL ENGLISH LANGUAGE ARTS STANDARDS, AND WHY WOULD WE LISTEN TO THEM?

SANDRA STOTSKY

To answer the first part of this question, it's important to know that the Common Core standards were developed by the National Governors Association (NGA) and the Council of Chief State School Officers (CCSSO)—two private trade organizations—in collaboration with Achieve, Inc., another non-governmental organization established by the NGA and business officials in 1996. Their collaboration in developing the standards enabled the U.S. Department of Education (DoED) to bypass federal statutes forbidding it from developing national standards. Expenses for managing the project were defrayed by large grants from the Bill and Melinda Gates Foundation. In the absence of official information from all of these organizations, it seems likely that Achieve, Inc., and the Gates Foundation selected most of the key personnel to write the standards. On what basis we still do not know.

The "lead" writers for the grade-level ELA standards, David Coleman and Susan Pimentel, had never taught reading or English in K-12 or at the college level. Neither has a doctorate in language or literature. Neither has ever published serious work on K-12 curriculum and instruction.[1] Neither has engaged in literary scholarship or research in education. At the time they wrote the ELA standards, they were unknown to the entire field of English and reading educators, as well as to higher-education faculty in rhetoric, speech, composition, and literary study. The absence of relevant professional credentials in the "chief architects," then, helps to explain the major flaws in Common Core's grade-level ELA standards. And there are many.

Major Flaws in Common Core's ELA Standards

MOST COMMON CORE COLLEGE-READINESS AND GRADE-LEVEL READING STANDARDS ARE CONTENT-FREE SKILLS

Most of the statements presented as vocabulary, reading, and literature standards—where content would be indicated if it is indicated anywhere—point to no particular level of reading difficulty, little cultural knowledge, and few intellectual objectives. These statements are best described as skills or strategies when they can be understood at all. They therefore cannot be described as rigorous standards. Take the example of the following Common Core "anchor standard," a general standard intended to generate specific grade-level standards across the grades: "Analyze how and why individuals, events, and ideas develop and interact over the course of a text." The grades 11/12 standard "clarifying" this anchor standard is: "Analyze a complex set of ideas or sequence of events and explain how specific individuals, ideas, or events interact and develop over the course of the text." This anchor standard, along with the grade-level standard that supposedly clarifies it, is clearly a free-floating skill and can be applied to anything from "The Three Little Pigs" to *Moby-Dick*.

Skills training alone doesn't prepare students for college. They need a fund of content knowledge. But neither Common Core's ELA standards nor its literacy standards for other subjects specify the literary/historical knowledge that students need. The document provides no list of recommended authors or works, just examples of "quality and complexity." The standards require no British literature aside from Shakespeare. They require no authors from the ancient world or selected pieces from the Bible as literature so that students can learn about their influence on English and American literature. They do not require study of the history of the English language. Without requirements in these areas, students are not prepared for college coursework. They are also not prepared for a career—or active citizenship—in an English-speaking country.

COMMON CORE ELA STANDARDS STRESS WRITING MORE THAN READING AT EVERY GRADE LEVEL—TO THE DETRIMENT OF EVERY SUBJECT IN THE CURRICULUM

There are more writing than reading standards at almost every grade level in Common Core, a serious imbalance—the opposite of what an academically sound reading/English curriculum should contain, as suggested by a large body of research on the development of reading and writing skills.[2] The foundation for good writing is good reading. Students should spend far more time in and outside of school on reading than on writing if they are to improve both reading and writing in every subject of the curriculum.

COMMON CORE WRITING STANDARDS ARE DEVELOPMENTALLY INAPPROPRIATE AT MANY GRADE LEVELS

Adults have a much better idea of what "claims," "relevant evidence," and academic "arguments" are. Yet, beginning in grade 6, children are to "[w]rite arguments to support claims with clear reasons and relevant evidence." Most elementary children have a limited understanding of these concepts and find it difficult to compose an argument with claims and evidence. It would be difficult for children to do so even if Common Core's writing standards were linked to appropriate reading standards and prose models. But they are not.

Worse yet, Common Core's writing standards stress opinion-based writing in the elementary grades. From Kindergarten to grade 5, the very first writing standard expects children to "Write opinion pieces on topics or texts, supporting a point of view with reasons." A steady diet of opinion-based writing does not help to develop analytical thinking, and it establishes a very bad habit in very young children. There is no research evidence to support this kind of pedagogy.

AT EVERY GRADE LEVEL, COMMON CORE EXPECTS ENGLISH TEACHERS TO SPEND AT LEAST HALF OF THEIR READING INSTRUCTIONAL TIME ON INFORMATIONAL TEXTS

Students simply cannot benefit intellectually from this percentage. Common Core lists ten reading standards for informational texts and nine standards for literary texts at every grade level, reducing literary study in the English class to less than 50 percent. However, unlike science teachers, for instance, who are charged with teaching information about science, English teachers are not responsible to teach a particular body of information; so, it is not at all clear what Common Core wants systematically taught in the English class. College English departments and teacher preparation programs train English teachers to teach the four major literary genres (i.e., poetry, drama, fiction, and nonfiction) and the elements of rhetoric, not a large body of fragmented information on a variety of contemporary or historical topics.

COMMON CORE REDUCES OPPORTUNITIES FOR STUDENTS TO DEVELOP CRITICAL THINKING

Critical thinking develops in the English class when teachers teach students how to read analytically, between the lines of complex literary works. Such thinking is facilitated by knowledge that students acquire in other ways and via other subjects. In fact, it cannot take place in an intellectual vacuum. A 2006 ACT report, *Reading Between the Lines*, observes that complexity is laden with literary features in that it involves literary devices, tone, ambiguity, elaborate structure, intricate language, and unclear intentions.[3] Critical thinking applied to low-complexity texts, the report concludes, is inferior to critical thinking applied to high-complexity texts. Thus, reducing literary study in the English class in order to increase informational reading not only reduces the opportunity for students to learn how to do critical or analytical thinking but also, in effect, retards college readiness.

CONTRARY TO CLAIMS, COMMON CORE'S STANDARDS ARE NOT "FEWER, CLEARER, AND DEEPER"

They may appear to be fewer in number than the standards in many states because very different objectives or activities are often bundled incoherently into one so-called standard. It is frequently the case that these bundled statements posing as standards are not easy to interpret, and many are poorly written. For example, a literature standard for grades 9/10 asks students to: "determine a theme or central idea of a text and analyze in detail its development over the course of the text, including how it emerges and is shaped and refined by specific details; provide an objective summary of the text." This wretched sentence is a jumble of at least three different activities: determining a theme, analyzing its development, and summarizing a complete text.

Ratings of Common Core's ELA Standards

In organizing the strands and in writing the ELA standards, both David Coleman, now president of the College Board, and Susan Pimentel were assisted in unknown ways by dozens of reviewers, some from the schools, some from state departments of education, and many from schools of education. For an evaluation of their results, I offer ratings of Common Core's ELA standards, drawing on the criteria as well as the rubrics for a 0 to 4 rating scale that I had developed and used in reviews of state ELA standards for the Thomas B. Fordham Institute in 1997, 2000, and 2005.[4] The review form is located in appendix A. Where the abbreviation CC is used, it signifies Common Core.

A. READING PEDAGOGY AND INDEPENDENT READING

1. *The document expects explicit and systematic instruction in decoding skills in the primary grades as well as use of meaningful reading materials and an emphasis on comprehension.*

Rating: 3

Research in reading is clearly used to inform the acquisition of decoding skills. There is good coverage of key comprehension skills across subject areas, as well as use of meaningful reading materials. However, not one of the objectives on phonics and word analysis skills in grades K-3 expects students to apply these skills *both in context and independent of context* to ensure mastery of decoding skills. Only in grades 4 and 5 are students expected to read accurately unfamiliar words "in context and out of context." The placement of this standard at only grades 4 and 5 badly misinforms primary grade teachers.

2. *The document makes clear that interpretations of written texts should be supported by logical reasoning, accurate facts, and adequate evidence.*

Rating: 4

The standards indicate evidence is required for interpretations or claims for all texts.

3. *The document expects students to read independently through the grades and provides guidance on quality and difficulty.*

Rating: 3

Students are expected to read independently, and a list of exemplars of quality and difficulty is provided through the grades. However, we do not know if the titles in grades K-8 were independently vetted by literary experts or who those experts may have been. Moreover, CC suggests that teachers use a cumbersome set of factors to determine "complexity."

B. VALUE OF LITERARY STUDY

1. *The document expects and enables teachers to stress literary study in the ELA class.*

Rating: 1

Nonfiction or informational reading has been weighted almost equally to imaginative literature in ELA at all grade levels—with ten standards for the former and nine for the latter at each grade level. This balance augurs drastic decline in literary study in grades 6-12. English teachers are explicitly told to increase the number of informational or nonfiction texts they teach.

2. *The document and the standards indicate that assigned texts should be chosen on the basis of literary quality and cultural and historical significance.*

Rating: 1

For selection on the basis of quality and significance, a sidebar on page 35 and an appendix contain excellent advice. But most standards contain nothing to ensure that teachers or test-makers follow it. There are also no criteria for selecting informational or literary texts, nor recommended authors or titles. Just exemplars of "complexity" and "quality" at each grade level.

3. *The standards promote study of American literature.*

Rating: 1

They do so only in two standards in grades 11/12. American literature is not mentioned in earlier grades where it would be appropriate (e.g., for American folktales or tall tales), and there is no standard on studying authors who were born in or wrote about the state or region.

C. ORGANIZATION AND DISCIPLINARY COVERAGE OF THE STANDARDS

1. *The standards are grouped in categories and subcategories reflecting coherent bodies of scholarship or research in reading and the English language arts.*

Rating: 1

The organization of the ten anchor standards for reading does not reflect scholarship or research. The grade-level standards are mostly organized according to language processes, but major subcategories do not reflect coherent bodies of scholarship or research in the secondary grades. The writing standards are misleadingly organized as argument, narrative, or informational, even though academic arguments are not identical to persuasive writings, and practical or personal writing is not necessarily informational or narrative in nature (e.g., diaries).

The standards clearly address listening and speaking. They include use of various discussion purposes and roles, how to participate in discussion, desirable qualities in formal speaking, and use of established as well as peer-generated criteria for evaluating formal and informal speech.

2. *The standards clearly address listening and speaking. They include use of various discussion purposes and roles, how to participate in discussion, desirable qualities in formal speaking, and use of established as well as peer-generated criteria for evaluating formal and informal speech.*

Rating: 3

They address most of these elements but do not address the use of established criteria for evaluating formal and informal talks, presentations, or speeches.

3. *The standards clearly address reading to understand and use information through the grades. They include progressive development of reading skills, knowledge, and use of a variety of textual features, genres, and reading strategies for academic, occupational, and civic purposes.*

Rating: 2

The standards clearly ask for reading to understand and use information through the grades. However, they do not clearly distinguish modes of organization (e.g., chronology) from structural, or textual, elements of an expository text (e.g., introduction, conclusion); do not progressively develop informational reading skills from grade to grade; and omit such important concepts as identifying topic sentences.

4. *The standards clearly seek to develop strong vocabulary knowledge and dictionary skills.*

Rating: 1

Although the vocabulary standards highlight specific figures of speech and rhetorical devices, they do not teach use of glossaries for discipline-specific terms, or words that must be taught (e.g., foreign words used in written English that do not appear in an English language dictionary). CC leans heavily, and incorrectly in many cases, on use of context to determine the meaning of unknown words. For example, it is difficult for students to interpret correctly a literary, biblical, or mythological allusion "in context," as specified in the grade 7 literacy standards—"Interpret figures of speech (e.g., literary, biblical, and mythological allusions) in context"—if they have no knowledge of the texts that have served as the basis for these allusions and if the reading standards do not point to some of these significant texts, authors, or events.

5. *The standards clearly address the reading, interpretation, and critical evaluation of literature. They include knowledge of diverse literary elements and genres, use of different kinds of literary responses, and use of a variety of interpretive and critical lenses. They also specify those key authors, works, and literary traditions in American literature and in the literary and civic heritage of English-speaking people that should be studied because of their literary quality and cultural significance.*

Rating: 1

Most of the above areas are covered but very unsystematically. Most CC literature standards lack examples of authors, works, literary traditions, and literary periods and only sporadically address the major genres and their characteristics. Only a few high school level standards indicate specific cultural content. Even a reference to mythology in the elementary literary standards asks for identification only of mythological characters.

6. *The standards clearly address writing for communication and expression. They include use of writing processes, established as well as peer-generated criteria, and various rhetorical elements, strategies, genres, and modes of organization.*

Rating: 1

While there are a great many standards on writing, the substrand on "argument" confuses argument with expression of opinion in the elementary grades and with persuasive writing throughout. There is no scholarship to support the three "types" of writing proposed by Common Core and thus this strand badly misinforms English and reading teachers throughout the grades. There is also nothing on the use of established or peer-generated criteria for evaluating writing or written presentations.

7. *The standards clearly address oral and written language conventions. They include Standard English conventions for sentence structure, spelling, usage, penmanship, capitalization, and punctuation.*

Rating: 1

Oral and written language conventions are addressed, but the vertical progressions don't always make sense, many standards are placed at inappropriate grade levels, and much of the linguistic terminology is inappropriate at the grade level it appears. For example, grade 2: "Use adjectives and adverbs, and choose between them depending on what is to be modified." Or grade 4: "Use modal auxiliaries to convey various conditions." And what is a grade-8 teacher to make of: "Use verbs in the active and passive voice and in the conditional and subjunctive moods to achieve particular effects"?

8. *The standards clearly address the nature, dynamics, and history of the English language. They include the nature of its vocabulary, its structure (grammar), the evolution of its oral and written forms, and the distinction between the variability of its oral forms and the relative permanence of its written form today.*

Rating: 3

Common Core's standards on word origins and etymologies

are useful. But there is nothing on the distinctions among oral dialects or between oral and written forms of English, or on the history of the English language at the secondary level. In grade 5, we find a highly inappropriate standard: "Compare and contrast the varieties of English (e.g., dialects, registers) used in stories, dramas, or poems." This is graduate-level work.

9. *The standards clearly address research processes, including developing questions and locating, understanding, evaluating, synthesizing, and using various sources of information for reading, writing, and speaking assignments. These sources include dictionaries, thesauruses, other reference materials, observations of empirical phenomena, interviews with informants, and computer data bases.*

Rating: 3

All of the above areas seem adequately covered, including the research processes. But students are expected to apply the same reading standards ("Apply grades 9–10 Reading standards") to literary and informational texts at each grade level "to support analysis, reflection, and research," as if the same set of reading skills is applicable to both literary and informational texts.

D. QUALITY OF THE STANDARDS

1. *The standards are clear, specific, and measurable (i.e., they can lead to observable, comparable results across students and schools).*

Rating: 1

There are many vague standards with unclear meanings and inconsistently interpretable meanings. For example: "Compare and contrast the structure of two or more texts and analyze how the differing structure of each text contributes to its meaning and style." What kind of texts does the writer have in mind? What will be learned if the texts address different topics? Or another example: "Analyze a particular point of view or cultural experience reflected in a work of literature from outside the United States, drawing on a wide reading of world

literature." How much and what kind of reading of world
literature must precede the reading of a specific work that is
to be analyzed for the author's point of view? Thus, only some
standards are measurable as is.

There are also many standards with inappropriate or misleading examples. For example, informational reading standard
9 for grade 6: "Compare and contrast one author's presentation of events with that of another (e.g., a memoir written by
and a biography on the same person)." This standard needs a
sensible example.

Moreover, in the primary grades, many standards require
teachers to prompt or give guidance and support. There is no
specification of what would constitute meeting the standard
independently.

2. *The standards are of increasing intellectual difficulty at each higher
educational level and cover all important aspects of learning in the
area they address.*

Rating: 1

Most standards do not show meaningful increases in intellectual difficulty over the grades, because they are generic skills.
In addition, many grade-level standards are simply paraphrases
or repetitions of the governing anchor standard, especially
in grades 6-8. Primary grade standards are weak because of
overuse of prompting; prompted learning leaves unclear the
level of independence required for student performance. In the
secondary grades, the standards show no meaningful increases
in difficulty and/or complexity through the grades related to
skill development.

3. *The standards index or illustrate growth through the grades for
reading by referring to specific reading levels, to titles of specific
literary or academic works as examples of a reading level, or to
advanced content.*

Rating: 3

While the reading and literature standards only occasionally provide examples of specific texts or authors, one appendix contains a long list of illustrative titles for each grade for the main genres. However, each grade contains too wide a range of reading levels to establish a meaningful reading level for assessment purposes, especially in grades 9, 10, 11, and 12.

4. *The standards illustrate growth expected through the grades for writing with reference to examples and rating criteria, in the standards document or in other documents.*

Rating: 1

One appendix in the CC document is a collection of annotated student writing samples at all grade levels. However, no rating criteria, say, on a 1 to 6 scale, are offered by grade level—a serious and puzzling omission. Based on the annotations and the compositions themselves, it is clear what the best and least developed compositions are. But it is not at all clear how teachers are to develop common expectations for where most students will be at a particular grade level: above grade-level, about grade-level, or below grade-level performance.

5. *The standards' overall contents are sufficiently specific, comprehensive, and demanding to lead to a common core of high academic expectations for all students in the state.*

Rating: 1

CC's relatively content-empty reading standards cannot by themselves lead to a common core of high academic expectations, because they cannot frame an academic curriculum. Although the proponents of CC claim that the development of the school curriculum will take place at the local level, it is more likely that curriculum development and decision-making at the local level will be pre-empted by the nature of the content in the test items developed by the two testing consortia for the application of the ELA skills.

EVALUATION SUMMARY

CATEGORIES FOR RATING COMMON CORE'S ELA STANDARDS	0-4 SCALE
Reading Pedagogy and Independent Reading	3.3
Value of Literary Study	1
Organization and Disciplinary Coverage of Standards	1.7
Quality of the Standards	1.4
Total Average	**1.85**

Table 1. Average points per scoring section and total average.

INDEPENDENT CONFIRMATION

As table 1 suggests, Common Core's English language arts standards are well below the average of 2.5 on a five-point scale in four of the five categories of criteria. The question that may be raised at this point is how valid are my ratings. An independent corroboration of the thrust of my analysis can be found in comments by Fordham Institute reviewers in a 2010 review of state standards.[5]

The Fordham reviewers' comments, excerpted directly below from different sections of the report, address Common Core's ELA standards. They clearly point out the standards' deficiencies:

Overview:....[T]hey would be more helpful to teachers if they attended as systematically to content as they do to skills, especially in the area of reading.[6]

Clarity and Specificity:....The organization of the reading standards is hard to follow. They are organized into four categories...Since many kinds of texts, genres, sub-genres, and their characteristics are discussed in each category, it is also difficult to determine whether a logical sequence covering all of this important content has been achieved....

[T]he organization of the reading strand, as well as the instances of vague and unmeasurable language, mean that the standards do not ultimately provide sufficient clarity and detail to guide teachers and curriculum and assessment developers effectively.[7]

Content and Rigor–Reading:....[T]he reading standards for both literature and informational text fail to address the specific text types, genres, and sub-genres in a systematic intersection with the skills they target. As written, the standards often address skills as they might apply to a number of genres and sub-genres. As a result, some essential content goes missing....

The...standards for grades 6-12 [exhibit] only minor distinctions across the grades, such as citing evidence "to support analysis of what the text says explicitly as well as inferences from the text."

Several problems surface here. First, these standards don't properly scaffold skills from grade to grade. For example, quoting from text is arguably easier than paraphrasing, but the standards require mastery of paraphrasing first.

Second, these standards are also repeated verbatim in the informational text strand, thus making no distinction between applying this skill to literary and informational text....

What's more, while some genres are mentioned occasionally in the standards, others, such as speeches, essays, and many forms of poetry, are rarely if ever mentioned by name. Similarly, many sub-genres, such as satires or epic poems, are never addressed....

Many defining characteristics of the various genres are also rarely, if ever, mentioned....

Where literary elements *are* mentioned, their treatment is spotty.[8]

Content and Rigor–Writing:....[T]he Writing standards include too many expectations that begin with the phrase, "With guidance and support from adults"...Such standards are problematic because they fail to adequately scaffold or clearly delineate what *students* should be able to do....

One troublesome aspect of the writing standards is the persistently blurry line between an "argument" and an "informative/explanatory essay."[9]

Content and Rigor–Bottom Line:....[There is an] overwhelming focus on skills over content in reading combined with confusion about the writing standards, the lack of detail about oral presentations, and the sporadic rigor of the media standards.[10]

Given the huge deficiencies in Common Core's ELA standards as indicated by Fordham's own reviewers, it is a remarkable exercise of the imagination to believe that Common Core's ELA standards *earned* a B+ from Fordham. Yet Fordham often repeats this verb, "earned," in the "Bottom Line" section of its 2010 reviews for each of the 50 states. The phrase "among the worst in the country" also appears in many a Bottom Line (e.g., for the ELA standards in Mississippi, Missouri, North Dakota, West Virginia, Wisconsin, and Wyoming). It is not unreasonable to conclude that these Bottom Lines were boilerplates added *after* the reviewers' comments were written in order to provide a quotable phrase for state media to use, as well as to get governors, state boards of education, and departments of education to vote in Common Core as fast as possible.

Why Such Widespread Uncritical Acceptance?

Why did reporters, state boards of education, and state departments of education themselves not notice the many problems and deficiencies in Common Core's ELA standards? Is it because they don't know how to analyze a set of ELA standards and must depend on the arbitrary "grades" given by the one organization in the country grading state standards? Were they oblivious to the implications of the fact that, in this case, the organization was funded by the Gates Foundation to promote Common Core?

Is it because they may also depend on "crosswalks" prepared by education researchers and state departments of education? A crosswalk is a comparison by grade level that tries to match up the content in one set of standards with the content in another. As I have commented in a blog post on the Pioneer Institute website, crosswalks are probably the least useful way to compare sets of ELA standards.[11] Crosswalks not only fail to indicate that both sets may be weak, they also do not capture all the features of a set of ELA standards that determine rigor and coherence (such as how its strands are organized and how coherently the standards in a strand are developed through the grades). I point out the features that crosswalks fail to capture in that blog post.

Is it because few thought that K-12 ELA standards actually matter? To this day no professional organizations with expertise in the K-12 English language arts, literary study, and reading—such as the National Council of Teachers of English or the International Reading Association—have evaluated Common Core's standards. Nor have organizations for discipline-based college or university faculty or independent scholars—such as the American Academy of Arts and Sciences and the Modern Language Association.

Because most reporters, education researchers, business leaders, state boards of education, and state departments of education cannot appropriately evaluate either standards documents or the standards themselves, they would serve the public better by not offering their own limited judgments on how demanding Common Core's standards are and by seeking the advice of independent content experts. The criteria for judging a set of standards differ greatly from subject to subject. One evaluates a set of K-12 mathematics standards very differently from the way a set of K-12 ELA standards should be evaluated. The level and type of expertise required for such evaluations likewise vary significantly. How many reporters, state board members, and business leaders can evaluate a set of high school mathematics standards? Unless they actually possess such expertise, they should refrain from repeating, in parrot-like fashion, outlandish and unproven claims made by those who have reasons, often financial, for promoting these standards.

By outlandish claims, I refer specifically to the repetition of such wild assertions as the notion that Common Core's standards promote "critical thinking" or "deeper learning." By regularly describing or alluding to Common Core's standards as rigorous, demanding, and more difficult than a state's previous standards, those who repeat such unfounded claims legitimize the mountebanks who wrote Common Core's ELA standards, the many unsupported and unsupportable teaching practices they promote,[12] and the high consultant fees they extract from cash-starved schools that are attempting in good faith to abide by the policies adopted by their uninformed state boards and commissioners of education.*

---

* EDITORS' NOTE: To delve more extensively into academic standards, the lack of rigor in the Common Core standards, in particular and the implications of that lack, the reader will find helpful additional work Dr. Stotsky

Local school board members and school superintendents could profitably benefit from memorizing the following generalizations:

- Common Core's ELA standards are *not* rigorous.

- Common Core's standards are *not* internationally benchmarked and will not make any of our students competitive.

- There is *no* research to support Common Core's stress on writing instead of reading.

- There is *no* research to support Common Core's stress on informational reading instead of literary study in the English class.

- Available research suggests exactly the opposite of what Common Core's document and standards promote in the ELA classroom.

Recommendations

First, all states should return to, revise, and strengthen their own ELA standards. The adoption and implementation of Common Core's

---

has authored or co-authored, in some cases with other contributors to this volume. Much of this work is easily available online. See, for example: Mark Bauerlein and Sandra Stotsky, *How Common Core's ELA Standards Place College Readiness at Risk*, Pioneer Institute White Paper #89 (Boston, MA: Pioneer Institute, 2012), http://pioneerinstitute.org/download/how-common-cores-ela-standards-place-college-readiness-at-risk/; Sandra Stotsky, "Literature or Technical Manuals: Who Should Be Teaching What, Where, and Why?" *Nonpartisan Education Review/Essays* 9, no. 1 (2013), http://nonpartisaneducation.org/Review/Essays/v9n1.htm; Sandra Stotsky and Ze'ev Wurman, *Common Core's Standards Still Don't Make the Grade*, Pioneer Institute White Paper #65 (2010), http://pioneerinstitute.org/education/common-core-standards-still-dont-make-the-grade/; Sandra Stotsky and Ze'ev Wurman, *The Emperor's New Clothes: National Assessments Based on Weak "College and Career Readiness Standards,"* Pioneer Institute White Paper #61 (2010), http://pioneerinstitute.org/download/the-emperors-new-clothes/; and Sandra Stotsky, "An English Language Arts Curriculum Framework for American Schools," *ALSCW News*, May 1, 2013, http://alscw.org/news/?p=524.

ELA standards does not improve the academic education of any state's children, especially its neediest students.

Second, no state should base expensive state assessments in reading on Common Core's ELA standards. It would be a waste of taxpayers' money to base assessments on standards that need drastic revision if not total abandonment.

Third, state legislators should enlist humanities scholars at their own colleges and universities to work with well-trained high school English teachers to design a readiness test in reading for admission to their own institutions. Instead of federal education policy-makers, those who teach college freshmen in each state should decide on admission standards for their own institutions and the contents of credit-bearing courses for freshmen.

NOTES

1. Nor is it clear in what subject Coleman received a degree from his studies in England as a Rhodes Scholar. No curriculum vitae has ever been attached to any biographical information offered by CCSSI or the College Board, which hired him as president in 2012. It should be noted that the College Board has received large grants from the Gates Foundation in recent years.

2. See, for example, Sandra Stotsky, "Research on Reading /Writing Relationships: A Synthesis and Suggested Directions." *Language Arts* 60, no. 5 (May 1983), 627-642.

3. ACT, *Reading Between the Lines: What the ACT Reveals about College Readiness in Reading* (Iowa City, IA: ACT, 2006), http://www.act.org/research/policymakers/pdf/reading_report.pdf.

4. These ratings for Common Core's English language arts standards appear in a report on Georgia's previous standards for State Senator William Ligon and in a report on South Carolina's previous standards for State Senator Michael Fair. Copies of these reports can be obtained from their respec-

tive offices or from my University of Arkansas home page, http://www.uacdreform.org/sandra-stotsky/.

5. Sheila Byrd Carmichael, W. Stephen Wilson, Kathleen Porter-Magee, and Gabrielle Martino, *The State of State Standards—and the Common Core—in 2010* (Washington, D.C.: The Thomas B. Fordham Institute, 2010), http://www.edexcellence.net/publications/the-state-of-state-of-standards-and-the-common-core-in-2010.html.

6. Ibid., 22.

7. Ibid., 23-24.

8. Ibid., 24-25.

9. Ibid., 26.

10. Ibid., 27.

11. Sandra Stotsky, "9 Signs of Rigor in English Standards," *Pioneer Institute Blogsite*, Aug. 7, 2013, http://pioneerinstitute.org/blog/9-signs-of-academic-rigor-in-english-standards-by-sandra-stotsky/.

12. One prominent example of such dubious pedagogy is David Coleman's advice to teachers to ask students to read historical documents "cold," and to refrain from providing or eliciting relevant contextual information for interpreting these documents on the grounds that such a practice "levels the playing field."

IV. AN EDUCATION BOONDOGGLE
Standardizing Teaching and Learning

MARCHING TO THE BEAT OF A DIFFERENT DRUM:

Home School Success versus Standardization in the Common Core

WILLIAM A. ESTRADA

In the 1980s, Tennessee Governor Lamar Alexander instituted Basic Skills First. The program micromanaged public school curricula and required that Tennessee homeschoolers take the same annual assessment as public school students. After two years, homeschoolers had outperformed public students so dramatically that the state stopped administering the same standardized test to the homeschooled students. The triumph of homeschooling over Tennessee's centralized educational system is but one proof of an increasingly evident principle: decentralizing education is the surest way to improve American schools.[1]

And yet, three decades later, citizens across the United States are now facing down the latest push to nationalize education: the Common Core State Standards (Common Core). Already, we have begun to see the negative impacts of this push not just on public education, but also on alternatives such as homeschooling and private education. If left unchecked, homogenization will be the result, leaving no escape routes for those who want something different than centralized education has to offer.

America rose to greatness when education was utterly decentralized and widely considered to be beyond the competence of government.

One might, then, reasonably wonder why educational planners in recent years have failed to consider a return to that which has proven successful in the past rather than continue to pursue a failing trend of their own making. This question becomes particularly difficult to answer in light of the contemporary success of the homeschooling movement, which is both entirely individualistic and dominated by more traditional approaches to educational goals and content.

The Dubious Results of Centralized Education Reform

In the United States, extensive experimentation with centralized reform has done almost nothing to improve the performance of students. From 1971 to 2008, American students' scores on the National Assessment of Education Progress (NAEP) mathematics assessments have improved only 3.4 percent, despite the billions of dollars the federal government has poured into education. The data on reading is even more disconcerting: NAEP reading scores have not changed since 1992 and have improved just 1 percent since 1971.[2] Indeed, it appears that the more money the federal government invests in education, the smaller the return. In 2011, Andrew J. Coulson, director of the Education Center for Freedom at the CATO Institute, found that the achievement gap between students of different socioeconomic backgrounds has not improved since the beginning of federal education spending in 1958.[3]

Noting that several countries that consistently outperform America on the Programme for International Student Assessment (PISA) tests have nationalized education systems, U.S. reformers continue to argue for centralizing the American education system.* However, PISA results are inconclusive as to the effectiveness of centralized systems. In 2006, twenty-seven countries ranked higher than the United States on the PISA science exam; seventeen of them had nationalized systems. However, twelve nations ranking *below* the United States also had cen-

---

* EDITOR'S NOTE: For an exposé of the specious ways in which international testing has been used to justify standardization and high-stakes testing, see Christopher Tienken's essay, pp. 30-49.

tralized systems. Regardless, centralizing education has been ineffective in the United States. Professor Jay P. Greene offers a possible explanation saying, "We are a large and diverse country. Teaching everyone the same material at the same time and in the same way may work in small homogenous countries...but it cannot work in the United States. There is no single best way that would be appropriate for all students in all circumstances."[4]

Aside from the fact that the effectiveness of centralized reforms is questionable, such schemes ignore two of the most foundational concepts upon which our nation was established, individualism and self-determination—the idea that each person has unique value and the right to determine his or her own course in life. Professor Charles Glenn of Boston University writes with keen insight into the goals of centralized education schemes:

> How can the pluralism that we claim to value, the liberty that we prize, be reconciled with a "state pedagogy" designed to serve state purposes? Is there not wisdom in John Stuart Mill's remark that "all that has been said of the importance of individuality of character, and diversity of opinions and modes of conduct, involves, as of the same unspeakable importance, diversity of education. A general state education is a mere contrivance for molding people to be exactly like one another...in proportion as it is efficient and successful, it establishes a despotism over the mind.[5]

Perhaps the only thing missing from Glenn's observations is the partnership between government and corporations that has increasingly come to dominate the education scene and how common it has become in centralized reform initiatives such as the currently touted Common Core.

The Proven Record of Decentralized Education

Though evidence on the efficacy of centralized education systems is inconclusive, the benefits of a decentralized approach are documented both internationally and domestically. Finland's students topped the PISA charts in 2000 and 2006 and ranked in the top echelon in 2003 and 2009.[6] Finland has rejected heavy standardized testing since the national assessment movement swept through the world in the 1990s. It refuses to rank its teachers according to the test results of their students; its National Board of Education even closed its inspectorate in 1991. Finnish teachers design their own courses and spend about 80 percent more time teaching classes than American teachers.[7] Deliberate decentralization of education in Finland has produced one of the foremost systems in the world.

The benefits of a decentralized approach to education have also been proven in America. Since 2004, the U.S. Department of Education (DoED) has provided $7,500 scholarships to low-income residents of the District of Columbia (D.C.) for the purpose of allowing children to attend private schools.[8] In 2008–09, students attending private schools through this program performed equal to or better than children in public schools on standardized tests. The graduation rate of these private school students was also significantly higher than that of their public school counterparts. This decentralized approach yielded better results at a fourth of the cost of the average public school education in D.C. in 2008–09.[9]

The success of homeschooling in America offers further domestic proof of the benefits of decentralized education. In 2013, Robert Kunzman of Indiana University and Milton Gaither of Messiah College evaluated multiple studies and showed that homeschool students score above average in reading and English arts. They also noted that homeschool students transition into postsecondary life much more successfully than public school students.[10] Kunzman and Gaither cited ten independent studies indicating that homeschoolers outrank their traditionally schooled counterparts in collegiate grade-point average, agreeableness, conscientiousness, and strength of religious and political views. They also observed that homeschoolers soar far above their peers in leadership ability.[11]

The evidence indicates that if the designers of the Common Core are truly seeking to make students "college- and career-ready," they have chosen the worst possible approach. A one-size-fits-all, centralized system directed by bureaucrats and corporate interests far-removed from individual students, their families, and their teachers, is not the antidote for current troubles in American education. Again, only the individuality and innovation found in a decentralized approach can revive our failing system.

The Common Core as a Centralized Education Scheme

The Common Core standards require students to master a checklist of skills every year. While state education departments may add a limited number of learning objectives, classroom teachers are required to teach to these composite standards as the prime goal of their instruction.[12] Teachers must teach from the prescribed list and at the prescribed pace. This one-size-fits-all approach that supposedly makes children "college- and career-ready" will undoubtedly produce a generation that has been trained to think about the same things in the same way as all of their peers. How does such standardization in any way respect human individuality? Moreover, it is reasonable to question whether a regimented approach to learning will produce young men and women capable of careers that call for genuinely independent analysis and creative problem solving. In May 2013, a 15-year teaching veteran from Chicago expressed her frustration in a *YouTube* video, lamenting that "raising students' test scores on standardized tests is now the only goal, and in order to achieve it, the creativity, flexibility, and spontaneity…have been eliminated."[13]

Proponents of the Common Core respond that the combination of the new assessment techniques and the growing stockpile of educational data will enable computers and teachers to tailor lessons and tests to suit the learning needs of individual students. The use of computers, however, does not mitigate the rigid standards that refuse to bend to the needs of individual students.

The development of standardized curricula further destroys the chance for individualization. Supporters say that the Common Core individualizes education, but they seek to have every child in American read the same books, learn at the same rate, and be ready to assimilate into similar colleges and careers. The Common Core is the antithesis of an individualized approach; it is a uniform education for the 59 million schoolchildren in the United States.

The imposition of fixed standards and curricula are only the first blows to individualized education. Increasing emphasis on computer-assisted learning further eliminates the possibility for individualization. The DoED has praised the Common Core for its focus on "computer adaptive testing" to supply teachers with data so that they can adjust their teaching styles and provide their students with individualized instruction.[14] Individualized instruction is widely regarded as an ideal way to teach. But in practice, the Common Core's rigid and technology-laden approach to learning makes individualized education almost impossible. Moreover, the initiative's required expansion of statewide longitudinal data systems to include assessment and homework scores necessitates that students spend more time using computer-assisted learning programs and less time interacting with their teachers. The diminution of human interaction is accelerated by teachers using printed-off data analyses to make pedagogical decisions.

True individualized education comes from a teacher identifying a child's strengths and weaknesses and helping him or her to learn in light of those attributes and circumstances. It does not come from computers that are programmed to change questions based on certain inputs, because the computer will never know that a child may have decided to simply click "C" no matter how many ways the test question is asked. Nor will it know if the child's personal circumstances—illness, injury, hunger, trouble at home, trouble with peers, or any number of other possibilities—may be impacting his or her performance. Individualized education is not fostered when a teacher receives a dismal report about her students' progress, but she is given no time to help struggling students. Instead, she must rush to the next concept in order to cover this year's prescribed standards.

The rigid, dehumanized method necessitated by the Common Core's requirements also threatens quality of education. Whether incidentally or by design, the Common Core endangers the idea of a liberal education and jeopardizes the goal of preparing children to be good citizens by sacrificing on the altar of "college- and career-readiness" the pursuits of literacy, future curiosity, and loving what is objectively true. Aiming to teach "what students need to know and be able to do to be successful in college and careers" mass-produces humans who will obediently serve in the workforce.[15]

The beauty of a decentralized approach to education is that if teachers have the opportunity to teach small enough classes, they can more easily and accurately gauge when they should introduce particular concepts and where they should focus based on the interests and comprehension of their students. Students can be taught as individual human beings—not machines to be analyzed and responded to by a computer program. But tragically, there is no room for this kind of individualized education in the unbending, computerized Common Core.

Alignment of Standardized Assessments with the Common Core

The DoED's continued emphasis on comparing students across state lines is clearly aimed at implementing a scheme of national standardized testing controlled, at least in a *de facto* fashion. Since March 2009, Secretary of Education Arne Duncan has stressed the need for a new kind of assessment test to "set a consistent, high bar for success nationwide."[16] And indeed, states have flattened proficiency standards over the past decade, attempting to fulfill the steep proficiency requirements of the No Child Left Behind Act. Analysts at the Fordham Institute observed that students can get fewer than 50 percent of items correct and score "proficient." The exposure of this reality spurred the federal government to fund a set of nationalized assessments, or "tests," that measure student progress through open-ended and research-based questions.[17] Forty-two states committed to administer these tests beginning in the fall of 2014.

After states applied for Race to the Top (RttT) grants and promised to implement common academic standards and assessments, Secretary Duncan announced that consortia of states boasting at least fifteen members could receive part of $362 million to craft standardized assessments based on the Common Core.[18] To be considered, consortia had to submit assurances from each of their member states, agreeing to:

1. adopt a common set of college- and career-ready standards "substantially identical across all States in a consortium" by Decem-

ber 31, 2011, and implement the standards by the 2014–15 school year;

2. administer the new assessments beginning in the 2014–15 school year; and

3. collect student achievement and growth data that "will be available on an ongoing basis for research, including for prospective linking...that can be used to determine whether individual students are college- and career-ready."[19]

Two consortia—the Partnership for Assessment of Readiness for College and Careers, or PARCC, with 26 member states and the Smarter Balanced Assessment Consortium, or SBAC, with 31 member states—received $170 million and $160 million respectively from the DoED. Just as it had done with the RttT competition for individual states, the federal government successfully bound forty-five states to the Common Core, nearly identical national assessments, and newly expanded data systems.[20] Alabama, Florida, Georgia, Indiana, Kansas, Kentucky, Oklahoma, and Utah have since withdrawn from their respective consortia, but each of these states is still committed to administering standardized tests aligned to the Common Core.[21] Kentucky and New York have developed their own assessment tests that align with the Common Core.[22]

Secretary Duncan has persistently emphasized that the new tests are "designed and developed by the States," but the DoED quietly asserted even more authority over the assessments in March 2013 when it established a technical review board. The board has been charged with analyzing the consortia's adherence to RttT requirements and "identifying how [the DoED] can better partner with the consortia during this critical development phase."[23]

In 2011, the National Governors Association (NGA)—one of two organizations who hold the copyright on the Common Core standards—offered national testing as a goal by encouraging "Governors and other state leaders [to] keep pressure on the two assessment consortia to build assessment systems that will allow comparability across states regardless of which consortia a state has joined."[24] Mandatory national testing would be detrimental to parental rights and educational freedom.

Common Core's Role in the Establishment of National Curricula

"To make standards meaningful, they have to be integrated with changes in curriculum, assessment, and pedagogy."[25] The words of Jay P. Greene, professor of education reform at the University of Arkansas, regarding the Common Core are proving prophetic because implementing the Common Core is requiring states to alter their curricula substantially.

School officials have recognized the need for massive curriculum changes since 2011 when 64 percent of the officials surveyed by the Council of Chief School Superintendents Officials (CCSSO)—the second of the Common Core copyright holders—said that their states would need completely new or significantly revised math curriculum in order to implement the Common Core. Fifty-six percent responded identically concerning their English language arts curriculum.[26] As of 2012, twenty-nine states had developed new curriculum aligned to the Common Core.[27]

Though the implementation of the Common Core is supposed to be "state-led," the continued involvement of the federal government, the authors of the standards, and a handful of major investors indicates that the Common Core is intended to realize a national curriculum. Though the federal government is prohibited by three sets of laws from prescribing a national curriculum, the DoED has paid other organizations to do what it cannot.*

The same two consortia receiving millions from the federal government to write standardized assessments are also being paid to produce curriculum guides for their forty-two member-states. PARCC stressed in its application for a supplemental RttT award that it would develop

---

* EDITOR'S NOTE: Several essays in this volume touch on the circumvention, even the gutting, of federal education law, approaching it from different angles. See, for example, Shane Vander Hart on the standards' advancement (pp. 3-28) and Jane Robbins on student privacy (pp. 197-206).

"model instructional units" for teachers. It received $15.9 million to fund these efforts.[28] U.S. Secretary of Education Arne Duncan affirmed that "PARCC...will be developing curriculum frameworks."[29] Similarly, SBAC promised to build "curriculum materials...to support states' transition to the Common Core State Standards" and was rewarded with $15.9 million.[30] The efforts of the federal government to develop curriculum models confirm the analysis of two members of the Common Core Validation Committee who ultimately refused to sign off on the standards: the Common Core is "a laudable effort to shape a national curriculum."[31]

The groundwork for a national curriculum is also being laid by groups of states and private organizations collaborating to develop common curricula. In an effort funded by the Gates Foundation, the states of New York, Illinois, Massachusetts, North Carolina, and Colorado have started creating an open-source "platform" that will allow teachers to download and share resources aligned to the Common Core. The platform will be available to all states in 2014.[32] Additionally, Achieve, Inc., one of the organizations that advised the NGA and the CCSSO during the drafting of the Common Core, has partnered with those same groups to produce model curricula for the states.[33]

Implementation instructions for the states written by the authors of the Common Core suggest that the standards aim at a national curriculum. The NGA recommends that "States and districts...share the costs of developing new curricula and instructional tools and not each develop their own at greater expense for each."[34] The Common Core, Inc., calls for cooperation between the states to ensure that math standards are "translated into textbooks, workbooks, diagnostic tests for teacher use, and other classroom materials that enable teachers to bring the curriculum into the classroom in a relatively *consistent*, effective way"[35] (emphasis mine).

The DoED acknowledged in its announcement of RttT that standards are supposed to affect curriculum.[36] Those who support the Common Core also recognize that standards are intended to mold curriculum. Kathleen Porter-Magee, a fervent supporter of the Common Core, explains, "While one could choose to pit those two policy advancements against each other (standards versus curriculum), a much more logical way to view it is that while strong standards provide a solid foundation, you still need to build the schoolhouse."[37]

One of the frequently repeated arguments for implementation of the Common Core is that it will increase the ability of families to move from one state to another without interrupting their child's education. But completely uninterrupted education is only possible if the *same* material is taught at the *same* time across the entire country.

Academic standards are meaningless if they do not shape the curriculum used. If this movement to nationalize curriculum continues, again, it will not only endanger freedom within public schools but also increasingly strip away the ability of home schools and private schools to choose their own curriculum.

Former DoED Deputy General Counsel Robert S. Eitel and former General Counsel Kent D. Talbert warn, "Left unchallenged by Congress, these standards and assessments will ultimately direct the course of elementary and secondary study in most states across the nation, running the risk that states will become little more than administrative agents for a nationalized K-12 program of instruction and raising a fundamental question about whether the Department is exceeding its statutory boundaries."[38]

Dangers of Common Core to Home Schools and Private Schools

For now, the Common Core applies only to public schools in the forty-five states that have adopted it. Federal law, under 20 U.S.C. § 7886, prohibits any federal education mandates from applying to private schools that do not receive federal funds or home schools.

However, there is no such protection for families who have enrolled their children in programs that receive federal funds, especially those who are using virtual charter schools that are run through the local public school for their home education.

Though the specific provisions of the Common Core only directly bind public schools, it is reasonably predictable that private schools that accept federal funding (through the Individuals with Disabilities Education Act, for example) may face a decision between foregoing federal funding and accepting the Common Core standards in the near future. Moreover, President Obama intends to condition funding from Title I of the Elementary and Secondary Education Act on states' agreement to follow common standards "developed by a state-led consortium."[39] There is no reason to expect that private schools receiving Title I funding would not have to agree to this mandate.

The current impact of the Common Core on home and private education is revealed in the expanding state longitudinal databases, shifting college admissions expectations, newly updated curricula, and revised standardized tests. All of these trends are fulfilling education historian Diane Ravitch's prediction that "no one will escape [the Common Core's] reach, whether they attend public or private school."[40]

Perhaps the most immediate threat to home school and private school students is the expansion of statewide longitudinal databases. The designers of the new systems fully intend for home school and private school students to be part of the massive data collection. At the National Conference on Student Assessment in 2011, officials from Oklahoma explained to the CCSSO how the challenge of meeting the data requirements of federal and state education policies are motivating them to "Include student groups not now included (e.g., home-schooled) in the data system."[41]

In light of the growing revelations that the federal government is engaging in massive invasion of privacy in spheres other than education, it is utterly impossible to believe that these databases will not be mined and misused to serve the ulterior purposes of a centralized government intent on growing its own power.[42]

Apart from the databases, my own organization, the Home School Legal Defense Association, fears that the Common Core will eventually impact students in both home school and private school by affecting college admissions standards. Institutions of higher education are being pressured to adapt their own standards for college readiness to the Common Core standards. A guide compiled by the NGA for states to use while implementing the Common Core emphasizes that the Common Core standards for college readiness will be used by institutions of higher learning to determine whether a student is ready to enroll in a postsecondary course.[43] Achieve, Inc., even exhorts institutions of higher education to revise their curricula to create "seamless transitions" from K-12 to postsecondary schools.[44]

This concern is being realized in multiple states, including Illinois. In a 2012 policy brief, the Illinois State Board of Education emphasized the need to seamlessly connect high school and college education by streamlining the curriculum taught to high school seniors and college freshmen according to the Common Core.[45] Though Illinois encouraged state universities to share with state high schools what kind of material students will be expected to know in their first year of college, nothing indicates that home schools or private schools would be privy to the same information. This movement to standardize post-secondary academic standards reveals that the Common Core's emphases and methods will permeate American education beyond elementary and secondary public schools.

The final area of concern for homeschoolers is that national and other popular standardized tests across the country are being rewritten to align to the Common Core.[46] College Board President David Coleman, one of the primary authors of the Common Core English language arts standards, is overseeing the renovation of both the PSAT and the SAT to fully implement the Common Core.[47] The redesigned PSAT will be used in 2015; the new SAT will debut in 2016.[48] Questions are being added to the ACT to reflect the Common Core's emphasis on tracing ideas through multiple texts and increased focus on statistics. The ACT will also contain optional open-ended questions to assess students' ability to explain and support their claims.[49] The latest version of the Iowa Test of Basic Skills is based on the Common Core.[50] The GED has been redesigned for the first time since 2002 to incorporate "practices and skills from the Common Core State Standards for Mathematical Practice."[51] Writers of the GED explain that they decided to revise the test now because "[t]he shift to the Common Core standards is happening nationwide at the current time."[52]

The alignment of standardized tests with the Common Core may not seem alarming, because home school students consistently score much higher on standardized assessments than public school students.

However, as information about the content of newly designed curriculum begins to surface, it is becoming clear that the Common Core's focus on informational texts makes it easy to accentuate particular schools of thought. For example, English language arts curriculum in Utah inculcates the welfare-state mentality and characterizes a parent's directions as "nagging."[53] Students taking the SAT, ACT, or the Iowa Tests could soon encounter clear examples of social engineering, including the advancement of alternative family lifestyles and sexual practices. While such concerns may sound outmoded or prejudiced to some, it is important to consider that social engineering could be used just as wrongly to convey ideas, beliefs, or ideologies they might find objectionable. Social engineering efforts not only violate parental rights over what their children should and shouldn't learn, it also undermines the right of the child to make informed personal choices as he or she matures.

Conclusion: A Brief Look at the Common Core's Philosophical Underpinnings

The philosophical foundations of the Common Core deserve a much longer essay. However, in summarizing this essay and pointing the reader toward further avenues of inquiry, the subject must be at least briefly broached, particularly because Common Core proponents have been so quick to dismiss such concerns. In the face of such dismissal, those opposed to the Common Core have often been left without an answer, sometimes even doubting the legitimacy of their own objections.

To be clear, the philosophy and aims of the Common Core are not revealed in the individual standards. Common Core proponents, in fact, frequently point to the standards as an exoneration, insisting that there is little of concern to be found there. Indeed, many education initiatives of whatever form would likely result in guidelines specifying the acquisition of similar individual items of knowledge and skill. Instead, the philosophy of any educational program can manifest itself in either its overall construct or the details of its curricula—sometimes both. The philosophy of the Common Core that is antithetical to many is revealed in its broader purposes and coercive uniformity. The most important philosophical features of the Common Core, then, are exposed by observing its fundamental orientation, rather than by parsing the details of mathematics and language learning objectives. These philosophical underpinnings are revealed both by what the initiative proclaims and what it omits.

As demonstrated above, one of the chief threads that runs throughout the Common Core is centralized control. It is not the only thread, but it is perhaps the most obvious. The lockstep uniformity that serves as the overriding thesis of the program implicitly embodies statist goals. All children in all states will learn the same content in the same manner. As already discussed, this not only violates the right of parents to determine the educational course of the children entrusted to their care but also erodes the natural right of the child to think independently and chart his or her own course in life. The overall result of the rigid standardization of education that Common Core engenders cannot be diversity of thought and life, deep and critical thinkers, positive risk takers, or aware and engaged citizens. The structure and philosophy are designed for precisely the opposite outcome: uniformity, the mass production of useful workers, and achievement of unquestioning subjects.

As a society, we have allowed ourselves to be fooled over the last several decades. We have increasingly come to believe that the sole purpose of education is to ensure the attainment of a good job, a career. This deception has been used to advance most of the false and failed reforms of the past several decades—including the Common Core, with its promises of "college- and career-ready." Moreover, it has become the lynchpin in the lie that standardization can solve our every problem by identifying and providing the proper slot for everyone. But do we want to make up a machine that denies the uniqueness of its parts? Can a machine like that even work? Historical evidence suggests that it cannot and that pursuing such an aim is not only folly but dangerous.

Education must be about something higher, and it must honor the individual rather than seeking to create interchangeable cogs in someone else's machine. The idea that the purpose of education is merely for all students to study a specific set of material, show growth by typing narrative answers on assessments, and grow up to be productive members of the workforce must, at last, be refuted.

NOTES

1. Michael P. Farris, "Will a 'Five-Year-Plan' Save the Public Schools?" *The Home School Court Report* VII, no. 6 (Nov./Dec. 1991), http://www.hslda.org/courtreport/V7N6/V7N602.asp.

2. See the long-term trend analysis tool provided on the National Center for Education Statistics website, http://nces.ed.gov/nationsreportcard/lttdata/. The analysis specified reflects the test scores of 13-year-old students.

3. Andrew J. Coulson, "The Impact of Federal Involvement in America's Classrooms," *CATO Institute Blogsite*, Feb. 10, 2011, http://www.cato.org/publications/congressional-testimony/impact-federal-involvement-americas-classrooms.

4. Jay P. Greene, "Testimony before the United States House of Representatives Education and Workforce Committee," U.S. House of Representatives, Sept. 21, 2011, http://edworkforce.house.gov/uploadedfiles/09.21.11_greene.pdf.

5. Charles Leslie Glenn, Jr., *The Myth of the Common School* (Oakland, CA: ICS Press, 2002), 12.

6. See Samuel E. Abrams, "The Children Must Play," *New Republic*, Jan. 28, 2011, http://www.newrepublic.com/article/politics/82329/education-reform-Finland-US#; Organisation for Economic Cooperation and Development (OECD) and UNESCO-UIC, *The Programme for International Student Assessment (PISA), 2000* (Paris: OECD Publishing, 2003), 69, http://www.oecd.org/edu/school/programmeforinternationalstudentassessmentpisa/33690591.pdf; and *OECD, PISA 2009 Results, Executive Summary* (Paris: OECD Publishing, 2010), 14, http://www.oecd.org/pisa/pisaproducts/46619703.pdf.

7. Abrams, "The Children Must Play."

8. National Association for Educational Evaluation and Research Assistance of the Institute of Education Sciences, *Evaluation of the D.C. Opportunity Scholarship Program: Final Report* [NCEE 2010-4018] (Alexandria, VA: U.S. Dept. of Education, 2010), http://ies.ed.gov/ncee/pubs/20104018/pdf/20104018.pdf.

9. Coulson, "Impact of Federal Involvement."

10. See Robert Kunzman and Milton Gaither, "Homeschooling: A Comprehensive Survey of the Research," *The Journal of Educational Alternatives* 2, no. 1 (2013), 17.

11. Ibid., 29–30.

12. States may supplement the entirety of the Common Core with 15 percent of their own standards. See *Federal Register* 74, no. 221(Nov.18, 2009), 59836, http://www.gpo.gov/fdsys/pkg/FR-2009-11-18/pdf/E9-27427.pdf.

13. "Teacher Resigns in Video, Targets Standardized Education: 'Everything I Love about Teaching Extinct.'" *YouTube*, May 26, 2013, http://www.youtube.com/watch?v=66K4e8qjRmY.

14. Arne Duncan, "Beyond the Bubble Tests: The Next Generation of Assessments," U.S. Dept. of Education (DoED), Sept. 2, 2010, http://www.ed.gov/news/speeches/beyond-bubble-tests-next-generation-assessments-secretary-arne-duncans-remarks-state-l.

15. "Frequently Asked Questions," Common Core State Standards Initiative (CCSSI), 2014, http://www.corestandards.org/resources/frequently-asked-questions.

16. Duncan, "Beyond the Bubble Tests."

17. Ibid.

18. *Federal Register* 75, no. 68 (Apr. 9, 2010), 18171, http://www.gpo.gov/fdsys/pkg/FR-2010-04-09/pdf/2010-8176.pdf.

19. Ibid.

20. "Transition to High-Quality, College- and Career-Ready Assessments: Principles to Guide State Leadership and Federal Requirements," Council of Chief State School Officers, May 23, 2013, http://www.ccsso.org/Resources/Publications/Transition_to_High-Quality_College-_and_Career-Ready_Assessments_Principles_to_Guide_State_Leadership_and_Federal_Requirements.html.

21. Evelyn B. Stacey, "Alabama Exits National Common Core Tests,"

Heartland Institute, Feb. 13, 2013, http://news.heartland.org/newspaper-article/2013/02/13/alabama-exits-national-common-core-tests; "Governor Rick Scott Announces Path Forward for High Education Standards," Rick Scott 45th Governor of Florida, Sept. 23, 2013, http://www.flgov.com/2013/09/23/governor-rick-scott-announces-path-forward-for-high-education-standards-decision-to-withdraw-from-parcc/; "Georgia Withdrawing from the Partnership for Assessment of Readiness of College and Careers (PARCC) Consortium," DoED, July 22, 2013, http://www.doe.k12.ga.us/External-Affairs-and-Policy/communications/Pages/PressReleaseDetails.aspx?PressView=default&pid=123; Jim Stergios, "The Implosion of the PARCC Assessments," *Pioneer Institute Blogsite*, July 29, 2013, http://pioneerinstitute.org/common_core/the-implosion-of-the-parcc-assessments/; Celia Llopis-Jepsen, "Kansas Opts to Create Its Own Common Core Tests," *Topeka Capital Journal*, Dec. 10, 2013, http://cjonline.com/news/2013-12-10/kansas-opts-create-its-own-common-core-tests; Andrew Ulifusa, "PARCC Common Core Testing Consortium Loses Kentucky as Member," *Education Week*, Jan. 31, 2014, http://blogs.edweek.org/edweek/state_edwatch/2014/01/parcc_common-core_testing_consortium_loses_kentucky_as_member.html; "Utah Withdraws from Smarter Balanced Assessment Consortium Developing Common Core Tests," *Huffington Post*, Aug. 7, 2012, http://www.huffingtonpost.com/2012/08/07/utah-withdraws-from-smart_n_1752261.html.

22. Chester E. Finn, Jr., "Will the Assessment Consortia Wither Away?" Thomas B. Fordham Institute, *Flypaper Blog*, Apr. 18, 2013, http://www.edexcellence.net/commentary/education-gadfly-weekly/2013/april-18/will-the-assessment-consortia-wither-away.html.

23. "Performance—Race to the Top Technical Review," DoED, Mar. 2013, http://www2.ed.gov/programs/racetothetop-assessment/performance.html; "Race to the Top Assessment Program: Technical Review Process," DoED, Apr. 2013, http://www2.ed.gov/programs/racetothetop-assessment/technical-review-process.pdf.

24. Tabitha Grossman, Ryan Reyna, and Stephanie Shipton, *Realizing the Potential: How Governors Can Lead Effective Implementation of the Common Core State Standards* (Washington, D.C.: National Governors Association, 2011), 7, http://www.nga.org/files/live/sites/NGA/files/pdf/1110CCSSIIMPLEMENTATIONGUIDE.PDF.

25. Lindsey Burke, "Publicizing the Hidden Costs of the National Standards Push," Heritage Foundation, *Education Notebook*, Sept. 12, 2011, http://links.heritage.org/hostedemail/email.htm?h=ec4d3bd2a208dbd8242

88c7fa9ecb9c4&CID=9795639416&ch=2E03C8C87B70F318B54BE93A 9A394F60.

26. Nancy Kober and Diane Stark Rentner, *Common Core State Standards: Progress and Challenges in School Districts' Implementation*, Center on Education Policy (Washington, D.C.: Center on Education Policy, 2011).

27. Education First and Editorial Projects in Education, Inc., *Moving Forward: A National Perspective on States' Progress in Common Core State Standards Implementation Planning* (Seattle, WA and Bethesda, MD: Authors, 2013), 7, http://www.edweek.org/media/movingforward_ef_epe_020413.pdf.

28. PARCC, "PARCC Proposal for Supplemental Race to the Top Assessment Award," Dec. 23, 2010, http://www.edweek.org/media/parccsupplementalproposal12-23achievefinal.pdf; DoED, Race to the Top: SBAC Award Letter to Washington State, Sept. 28, 2010, http://www2.ed.gov/programs/racetothetop-assessment/sbac-award-letter.pdf.

29. Duncan, "Beyond the Bubble Tests."

30. Smarter Balanced Assessment Consortium (SBAC), "Supplemental Funding Scope: Overview Table," Jan. 16, 2011, http://www.smarterbalanced.org/wordpress/wp-content/uploads/2011/12/Smarter-Balanced-Supplemental-Funds.pdf; DoED, SBAC Award Letter to Washington State.

31. Sandra Stotsky and Ze'ev Wurman, *Common Core's Standards Still Don't Make the Grade: Why Massachusetts and California Must Regain Control over Their Academic Destinies*, Pioneer Institute White Paper no. 65 (Boston, MA: Pioneer Institute, 2010), iii, http://pioneerinstitute.org/download/common-cores-standards-still-dont-make-the-grade/.

32. Grossman, Reyna, and Shipton, *Realizing the Potential*, 24.

33. "Model Course Pathways in Mathematics," CCSSI, Aug. 2010, http://www.achieve.org/mathpathways.

34. Grossman, Reyna and Shipton, *Realizing the Potential*, 25.

35. Achieve, Inc., the National Governors Association (NGA), and the Council of Chief State School Officers (CCSSO), *Benchmarking for Success: Ensuring U.S. Students Receive a World Class Education*. Report prepared by Craig D. Jerald (Washington, D.C.: Authors, 2008), 26, http://www.achieve.org/files/BenchmarkingforSuccess.pdf.

36. See *Federal Register* 74, no. 221 (Nov. 18, 2009), 59836,

http://www2.ed.gov/legislation/FedRegister/finrule/2009-4/111809a.html.

37. Kathleen Porter-Magee, "No Love for Common Core? Why Tom Misses the Mark with His Critique," Thomas B. Fordham Institute, *Gadfly Blog* (now *Common Core Watch*), Feb. 17, 2012, http://www.edexcellence. net/commentary/education-gadfly-daily/common-core-watch/2012/no-love-for-common-core.html.

38. Robert S. Eitel and Kent D. Talbert, *The Road to a National Curriculum: The Legal Aspects of the Common Core Standards, Race the Top, and Conditional Waivers*, Pioneer Institute White Paper no. 81 (Boston, MA: Pioneer Institute, 2012), 15, http://pioneerinstitute.org/download/the-road-to-a-national-curriculum/.

39. "Preparing Students for College and the Workforce," White House, 2010, http://www.whitehouse.gov/sites/default/files/rss_viewer/education_standard_factsheet.pdf. See also "Improving Basic Programs Operated by Local Educational Agencies (Title I, Part A)," DoED, June 4, 2014, http://www2.ed.gov/programs/titleiparta/index.html.

40. Diane Ravitch, "Why I Oppose the Common Core Standards," *Washington Post*, Feb. 26, 2013, http://www.washingtonpost.com/blogs/answer-sheet/wp/2013/02/26/why-i-oppose-common-core-standards-ravitch/.

41. Sunny Becker et al., "Data, Data Everywhere: Progress, Challenges, and Recommendations for State Data Systems." Presentation of the Human Resources Research Organization at the National Conference on Student Assessment of the Council of the CCSSO, Orlando, FL, June 20, 2011, http://www.scribd.com/doc/110361334/Data-Data-Everywhere-CCSSO-Presentation-at-National-Conference-on-Student-Assessment.

42. For more information on the growing possibility of a national database, please see Will Estrada and Katie Tipton, "The Dawning Database: Does the Common Core Lead to National Data Collection?" HSLDA, Sept. 10, 2013, http://www.hslda.org/docs/news/2013/201309100.asp.

43. Grossman, Reyna and Shipton, *Realizing the Potential*, 19.

44. Jacqueline E. King, *Implementing the Common Core State Standards: An Action Agenda for Higher Education* (Washington, D.C.: American Council on Education, 2011), 5, http://www.acenet.edu/news-room/Documents/Implementing-the-Common-Core-State-Standards-2011.pdf. The document was produced in conjunction with Achieve and the State Higher Education Executive Officers Association (SHEEO).

45. Charis, McGaughy, Adrienne van der Valk, Jamila Singleton, Teresa Zalewski and Rachel Farkas, *Bridging the Gap: An Illinois Toolkit for Using the Common Core for Secondary and Postsecondary Alignment*. Report prepared for the Illinois Community College Board, the Illinois Board of Higher Education, and the Illinois State Board of Education, (Eugene, OR: Educational Policy Improvement Center, 2012), 11, http://www.epiconline. org/publications/document-detail.dot?id=fe40a824-dd0e-455b-a605-c14c8de1eabb.

46. For more information on the alignment of national standardized tests to the Common Core, please see HSLDA, "Common Core Issue 7: Will the Common Core Affect Home Schools and Private Schools," Common Core Issues, updated June 13, 2014, http://www.hslda.org/commoncore/topic7.aspx.

47. Tamar Lewin, "Backer of Common Core School Curriculum Is Chosen to Lead College Board," *The New York Times*, May 16, 2012, http://www.nytimes.com/2012/05/16/education/david-coleman-to-lead-college-board.html?_r=0; Jason Tomassini, "New College Board President to Seek Common Core–SAT Link," *Education Week*, May 16, 2012, http://blogs.edweek.org/edweek/marketplacek12/2012/05/new_college_board_president_has_common_core_background.html.http://blogs.edweek.org/edweek/marketplacek12/2012/05/new_college_board_president_has_common_core_background.html.

48. Scott Jaschik, "Delay for New SAT," *Inside Higher Ed*, Dec. 3, 2013, http://www.insidehighered.com/news/2013/12/03/college-board-pushes-back-revised-sat-one-year.

49. "Continuous Improvement Announcements at ACT – May 2013," ACT, Inc., May 2013, http://www.act.org/announce/improvements/index.html#act.

50. "Monitor the Growth and Achievement of Today's Students," Houghton Mifflin Harcourt, Mar. 2014, http://www.riversidepublishing.com/products/ia/.

51. GED Testing Service, *The GED Test: A Content Comparison* (Washington, D.C. and Bloomington, MN: Author, 2012), http://www.gedtestingservice.com/uploads/files/2487f6e1ca5659684cbe1f8b16f564d0.pdf.

52. "2014 GED Test FAQs," GED Testing Service, July 10, 2013, http://www.gedtestingservice.com/educators/2014-faqs#about.

53. Oak Norton, "USOE Recommends Social Justice Curriculum Materials for 1st Grade," *Utahns Against Common Core*, May 11, 2013, http://www.utahnsagainstcommoncore.com/usoe-recommends-social-justice-curriculum-materials-for-1st-grade/.

LEARNING WITH LEVIATHAN:
Objectification, Surveillance, and Control in a Concealed Command Economy

Jeffrey D. Horn

I f technology can improve so many areas of our lives, why can't we employ it to improve our children's education? Why can't the miracles of this Internet age remove, or at least minimize, the doubt about our children's futures?

Wishes Granted

> Destiny has two ways of crushing us—by refusing our wishes and by fulfilling them.
>
> – Henri-Frédéric Amiel[1]

The last two decades have witnessed tremendous advances in consumer delivery systems. Americans today have unprecedented access to a veritable cornucopia of products and services. As consumers, it's hard to imagine anything better, for example, than the instant gratification made possible by Amazon's recommendation engines and efficient delivery of merchandise. The company anticipates customers' needs, providing suggestions and even products within mere moments or hours of a click. Technology now allows us to go from not knowing about a product to wishing for it to wish granted in a span of time that would have seemed nothing short of miraculous less than a generation ago.

Technology has also provided consumers with unprecedented access to low-cost products. Well before the Internet age, Walmart was using technology to improve the efficiency of its supply chain. Today many people can afford the products they need on a daily basis precisely because Walmart found a way to leverage technology to drive down the cost of bringing products to the consumer. Americans are now quite used to getting what they want and to paying as little as possible to get it. Consumers' preoccupation with speed, cost, and efficiency has naturally been transferred to almost every aspect of our service-dominated economy. Frequently quite realistically, we expect our wishes to be granted quickly and cheaply in a range of industries from insurance and health care to financial and legal services.

When it comes to our hopes for our children, in many senses our wishes become needs. We want the best for them, *and* we feel it should be affordable. Americans fully expect that the same types of technology that have wrought such unbelievable advancements for us as consumers can and should be leveraged to provide our children with a world-class education at a reasonable cost. Yet, every year it seems the cost of educating our children rises. We're consistently confronted with news that our children are falling behind those of other nations. We fear our children will not be better off than we were—and that they are not being prepared for the "jobs of the future." In challenging economic times, we fear that they may not be able to find gainful employment at all.

The desire to dispel such doubts causes many parents to breathe a sigh of relief when they hear that schools will provide students with access to school-issued iPads or laptop computers. That standardized assessments will now be taken on touch screen devices gives parents a sense that schools are finally moving into the twenty-first century. The idea of "personalized learning environments" and "efficient classrooms" suggests to the worried parent that the future has finally arrived. Using Big Data and data mining to deliver children ready to work in the jobs of the future sounds like a fantastic guarantee to many. It is the wave of the future, after all. We're ready for our wishes to be granted. Add the bonus of technology that promises to weed out the bad teachers and reward the good…and parents are sold, right along with taxpayers. Common standards and streamlining education? Absolutely, if they will make education more efficient and drive down costs.

Careful what you wish for.

"Fewer, Clearer, Higher"…or Cheaper, Faster, More Efficient?

> Modern technology has become a total phenomenon
> for civilization, the defining force of a new social order
> in which efficiency is no longer an option but a
> necessity imposed on all human activity.
>
> – Jacques Ellul[2]

As consumers, most of us only see the upside of practices at companies like Walmart and Amazon. A downside does exist. For instance, after significantly reducing its workforce in an effort to cut costs and compensate for stagnating sales, Walmart subsequently, began an effort in 2010 to extract an increasing amount of work from its remaining workforce via a technology-supported management initiative known as Task Manager. Employees swipe their employee ID into a Task Manager enabled device, prompting Walmart's workforce management system to tell each specific employee what tasks to complete, how long they have to complete those tasks, and whether they have met their target time for each task. The system singles out employees who miss their target times for spoken reprimands, or "coachings," as well as decision-making days, "d-days," where employees must explain why they should not be fired. Using Task Manager technology allows Walmart consistently to ratchet up the pressure on its employees to produce. Since the technology's introduction, many former managers have reported a "big increase in coachings and more terminations." Simon Head, fellow at New York University's Institute for Public Knowledge, writes:

> The Walmart case provides a spectacular firm-level example of the
> role of information technology in driving the wages-productivity
> gap. On the production side, IT supports a global system of logistics
> that coordinates very efficiently the movements of tens of millions of

goods from factories to warehouses and to stores; on the labor side, it promulgates rules that govern the movement and actions of more than a million employees, incorporating the monitoring systems that ensure these actions are performed according to the rules and within the designated time frames.[3]

For all the instant gratification Amazon delivers to consumers, its employees labor under an oppressive, state-of-the-art computer business system (CBS) that tracks their minute-by-minute movements and performance. A CBS essentially functions as an amalgam of systems:

- Providing control and monitoring of businesses and their employees;

- Facilitating the ability to mine giant data warehouses in order to compare performance against historical patterns; and

- Incorporating expert systems that simulate human intelligence, thereby replacing cognitive tasks important to the business.

For instance, Amazon's scientific managers have determined through time and motion studies the "one best way" to perform each task; their CBS ensures, among other things, that employees conform to these tasks precisely. Amazon tags many of its employees with personal satellite-navigation computers that tell employees the exact path they must take to shelve or retrieve items. These computers also set target times for trips through the warehouse and record whether or not these target times are met.[4] Many global companies have instituted similar practices.

Companies like IBM, SAP, and Oracle offer CBS solutions that allow for easy configuration modeling of work processes that employees must follow.

CBSs are now being put into place to achieve such efficiencies in educational settings.

Dirty Little Secrets

The secret of American schooling is that it doesn't teach the way children learn, and it isn't supposed to; school was engineered to serve a concealed command economy and a deliberately restratified social order. It wasn't made for the benefit of kids and families as those individuals and institutions would define their own needs. School is the first impression children get of organized society; like most first impressions, it is the lasting one. Life according to school is *dull* and *stupid*, only consumption promises relief: Coke, Big Macs, fashion jeans, that's where the real meaning is found, that is the classroom's lesson, however indirectly delivered.

– John Taylor Gatto[5]

How does the use of CBS systems relate to education "reform"?

In order to produce students ready for the "jobs of the future," teachers and school administrators are increasingly subject to the same high stakes scrutiny that employees at companies such as Walmart and Amazon endure. This reality is far from accidental.

In 2008 Achieve, Inc., the National Governors Association (NGA), and the Council of Chief State School Officers (CCSSO) published *Benchmarking for Success: Ensuring U.S. Students Receive a World-Class Education*. The report not only calls for the adoption of Common Core standards but also for "[holding] schools and systems accountable through monitoring, interventions, and support to ensure consistently high performance."[6] We have increasingly seen the implementation of this vision. Value-added measures (VAM) rate teachers' performance by monitoring their classroom activities and aggregating their students' test scores. With compensation and retention of teaching staff tied directly to classroom surveillance and the telemetry provided by the results of standardized assessments, "interventions" and "support" bear a striking similarity to Walmart's coachings and d-days. The telemetry is continuous. The Internet provides an immediate mechanism for evaluation of formative assessment results, down to a specific classroom, determining whether a given teacher has met performance targets. Teachers can be compared and ranked on their performance in real time by school management. Principles, in turn, are compared and ranked in real time, based on the performance of the teachers in their school.

Moreover, many states are now using performance on assessments aligned to the Common Core State Standards (Common Core), combined with adherence to similarly aligned curricula, to create single letter grades that indicate whether teachers, schools, and districts measure up. If they don't, sanctions guarantee intervention or elimination. Letter grades also facilitate public buy-in to accountability measures. A simple label assigned to teacher, school, or district—something familiar that most people think they understand—signals a merited reward or sanction. If a teacher receives a poor grade, most people will assume the teacher to be a problem and not examine other factors—for example, the system within which the teacher must operate. These grades essentially become scarlet letters, borne first and foremost by educators. Not that it stops with them. Common standards permit schools, districts, and even states to be monitored, compared ...and "corrected."

Think this approach doesn't affect students? Race to the Top (RttT) grants have paved the way for states to create longitudinal databases for student data—tracking individuals from pre-school through post-graduation (P-20).[7] Achieve's brief on RttT and P-20 data systems asserts that "[a] seamlessly integrated, accessible P-20 longitudinal data system with college and career readiness as its central driver should be a linchpin of any state's effort to maximize the impact of its RTTT strategy."[8]

Nothing New Under The Sun

> What I demand of the worker is not to produce any
> longer by his own *initiative*, but to execute punctiliously
> *the orders given* down to their minutest detail.
>
> – Frederick Winslow Taylor[9]

What is happening today under education reforms such as No Child Left Behind (NCLB), RttT, and Common Core is not, in fact, isolated. Historically, a current has run through American education, favoring the application of industrial advances in efficiency to schools. Around the turn of the last century, Frederick W. Taylor introduced and effectively advanced the concept of scientific management for industry. Taylor suggested that factory managers gather all relevant information about the work in their shops, analyze it via "scientific" methods, determine the most efficient methods for workers to perform individual tasks, then instruct and incentivize workers to conform precisely to those methods. Popularly known as "Taylorism," this approach revolutionized industry in the early twentieth century. The modern assembly line, popularized by Henry Ford, has its roots in Taylor's ideas.

Prior to the rise of Taylorism, workers were craftsmen working toward a common goal. After Taylorism, with just a small amount of training, workers were largely interchangeable or replaceable. One end result of this operational and organizational shift was to give management vastly more control over how work got done in industrial settings.

In 1912, University of Chicago Professor John Franklin Bobbitt published a seminal paper, "The Elimination of Waste in Education," in which he argued that Taylor's ideas were directly applicable to primary and secondary education. The preferred way of achieving education goals, Bobbitt asserted, "was to create a thoroughly modern school plant, equipped with every modern necessity; then to operate it according to recently developed principles of scientific management, so as to get a maximum of service from a school plant and teaching staff of minimum size."[10] He later underscored this theme, focusing on objectives, or in today's vocabulary, outcomes:

> It is the objectives and the objectives alone...that dictate the pupil-experiences that make up the curriculum. It is then these in their turn that dictate the specific methods to be employed by the teachers and specific material helps and appliances and opportunities to be provided. These in their turn dictate the supervision, the nature of the supervisory organization, the quantity of finance, and the various other functions involved in attaining the desired results. And, finally, it is the specific objectives that provide standards to be employed in the measurement of results.[11]

Following Taylor's lead, Bobbitt puts the design and control of school processes in the hands of administrators. Teachers, seen as incapable of determining content and curriculum on their own, are relegated merely to following the dictates of administration:

> The new and revolutionary doctrine of scientific management states in
> no uncertain terms that the management, the supervisory staff, has the
> largest share of the work in the determination of proper methods...Under scientific management, the supervisory staff, whose primary duty
> is direction and guidance, must therefore specialize in those matters
> that have most to do with direction and guidance, namely, the science
> relating to the processes. The burden of finding the best methods is
> too large and too complicated to be laid on the shoulders of the teachers...The ultimate worker, the teacher in our case, must be a specialist
> in the performance of the labour that will produce the product.[12]

Bobbitt was, in fact, one of the first advocates of using standardized testing to rank teachers, maintaining that a teacher's retention, promotion, and compensation should be tied to the performance of that teacher's students on such measures.

By the 1920s scientific management of public schools had become the norm, though there were significant opponents to the accountability and efficiency regime. Chief among them was educational icon John Dewey: "We have yielded to the arrogance of 'big business men' and have accepted their criteria of efficiency at their own valuation, without question. We have consented to measure the results of educational efforts in terms of price and product—the terms that prevail in the factory and the department store. But education, since it deals in the first place with human organisms, and in the second place with individualities, is not analogous to a standardizable manufacturing process."[13]

While Dewey's definition of efficiency had its own drawbacks, he deserves credit for recognizing that Bobbitt's merited strong critique.[14]

Expanded Conformity and Surveillance

> In the past the man has been first; in the future the system
> must be first. This in no sense, however, implies that great
> men are not needed. On the contrary, the first object of any
> good system must be that of developing first-class men;

and under systematic management the best man rises to the
top more certainly and more rapidly than ever before.

– Frederick Winslow Taylor[15]

Even as Dewey's ideas began to make their way into classrooms, Bobbitt acolytes gained a solid foothold in American education, making
relatively steady incremental gains over the decades. The 1994 passage
of Goals 2000, under the Clinton administration, ultimately cemented
standardized assessment in math and English as a federal mandate.[16]
This mandate not only accelerated when NCLB passed in 2001 under
the Bush administration, expanding the number of grades to be tested,
it also tied high stakes to the assessments.[17] Under RttT the mandate
burgeoned further still, raising the stakes for both teachers and students and stipulating testing for every grade through 11.[18] States that
do not comply with this regimen are threatened with the loss of federal
funding for failing schools and districts. In fact, the sticks and carrots
of federal funding are how all high-stakes testing mandates have been
achieved and enforced over the past several decades.

Standardized testing is but one of the scientific management spec-
ters that have come so thoroughly to haunt American education. By the
time of NCLB, Robert S. Kaplan's Balanced Scorecard approach to calculating performance in industry had triumphed as the latest efficiency
advance. Schools rushed to use it and similar approaches to show adequate yearly progress toward NCLB goals.[19] In complying with RttT,
many states have implemented the Danielson Framework for Teaching,[20] which ties teacher performance directly to that of students.[21] The
Danielson Framework's wide adoption accomplishes across most of the
nation exactly what Bobbitt had advocated nearly a century earlier.

Common Core's rise actually represents an interesting paradox. Embracing Bobbitt-style standardization, it also attempts to implement
ideas put forward by Dewey and his disciples. Common Core exemplar lessons, for example, routinely draw from constructivism, an educational philosophy with its genesis in Dewey's works. These underpinnings are especially noticeable in mathematics, where learning by
doing is routinely stressed, and in close reading and analysis exercises

on the English language arts (ELA) side.* While the Danielson Framework claims to be "grounded in a constructivist view of learning and teaching,"[22] it is routinely paired with standardized student test results for the purpose of teacher evaluation—amounting to VAM.

By marrying the thesis of standardization and test-based accountability with the anti-thesis of constructivist education theory, Common Core's architects have synthesized a standard that, at least initially, seems acceptable across a wide political spectrum. Most politicians can find something in the initiative that they can embrace, ensuring easy adoption. It's a clever use of Hegelian dialectic that has likewise enabled most states to adopt Common Core standards with little or no question.[23] In so doing, states have ceded most of their control to a handful of private organizations. Consider that just two consortia—the Smarter Balanced Assessment Consortium (SBAC) and the Partnership for Assessment of Readiness for College and Careers (PARCC)—now hold an oligopoly on standardized testing through grade 11. In turn, these two organizations have agreed to cede control over the standardization itself to the NGA and CCSSO, private trade associations, who have copyrighted the standards. Under that copyright states may not deviate from the standards by more than 15 percent, thereby guaranteeing the desired standardization and cross-state conformity.

While Bobbitt advocated placing control over educational processes solely in the hands of administrators, one wonders whether he would have been comfortable with the extent to which control has been removed from *local* school district managers. Yet, separation of planning from execution is a hallmark of Taylorism. Imbuing national-level experts in a far away city with full authority over what is to be taught clinches education's firm placement under scientific management. It ensures both centrally planned and approved standards (process) and assessments (enforcement). Only the execution of predefined learning tasks and the test administration is left to the teacher. Exemplar lessons

---

* EDITOR'S NOTE: While constructivism has potential value in the classroom, it is typically not developmentally appropriate for younger grades. Misapplied, it can also cause serious difficulties for children with learning differences. For more on this subject, see S. Wharton's essay, pp. 261-283.

contained within Common Core, along with aligned curricula, essentially serve as technical control over teachers, who, under the current circumstances, understandably want and need to have their students perform well on standardized tests. Adherence becomes paramount. Jabiri Mahiri, University of California at Berkeley, notes:

> Moment-to-moment, the curriculum controls teachers' and students' time and activities, and it does not require a trained and skilled teacher with disciplinary, pedagogical, and cultural knowledge to implement it as long as the students submit...Rigidly enforced and timed, piecemeal tasks are required of teachers and students, with few accommodations for diverse styles of learning or teaching. Administrators would be able to come into classrooms and check to see that their 'workers' are on the precise lesson, page, and the exact task prescribed for a given time slot.[24]

Standardization: Beyond Assessments

When education is reduced to test prep, rich curricula
and the craft of teaching are imperiled. The vapid classroom
of neoliberal school reform mirrors the vapid workplace of
Taylorism. Teach for America, which implicitly advances
the idea that the sparsely trained can out-teach veteran
educators, engenders deskilling and deprofessionalization.
Non-practitioners dictating to practitioners how they should
do their work mirrors management's disciplining of workers;
both militate against work as a creative activity.

– Shawn Gude[25]

The technical control exercised by the layout of the assembly line at the turn of the last century has been replaced by scripted curricula and performance metrics tied to aligned assessments.

By definition, Common Core aligned assessments serve as tools for marking deviance from the standardized norm, thereby distinguishing "winners" from "losers." As such, they function as a surveillance tool. Students either "pass" or "fail." Teachers "meet expectations" or "fall short." In this way, educational administrators and policymakers can efficiently monitor educational production, singling out for further analysis and action any students or teachers falling outside defined norms. A hierarchical system of authority and supervision is being imposed in which student performance and teacher scores are easily measured, increasingly visible, immediately available, and neatly individualized in order to facilitate convenient stigmatization. Over time, the managerial framework removes from the system those that fall outside assessment-established norms, thereby ensuring near total compliance.

The surveillance system provides a rapidly cycling feedback loop. It will detect as deviance from the norm the teacher willing to take even a small, calculated risk by trying something new. If the risk does not pay off with higher student assessment scores, management will take corrective action. In this Taylorist approach to education, risky behavior, such as tailoring a lesson to an individual, class, or community, is discouraged, both explicitly and as a natural consequence of the system. Safe behavior, such as using scripted, properly aligned curricula or an exemplar lesson, is reinforced.

In fact, Common Core provides a framework for fine-grained control over both the labor (teachers) and raw materials (students) involved in the education process. Formative and summative assessments, administered regularly via touch screens, can be scored almost immediately. Students can be easily tracked and managed, while teachers can be ranked, sorted, rewarded, and disciplined—all in real time. Comparisons can be made with teachers down the hall or across the country. Every day, teachers, schools and districts that fail to produce results can be identified and weeded out.

Common Core claims objectivity in measuring students against a standard. The word "common" implies this claim, that a student can be assessed universally, fairly, and objectively across differing populations and in different contexts. Yet, standardization demands decontextualization, thereby denying the existence of very real differences and variability. It embraces a fundamental assumption that a student is a student is a student…and how well any student does rests solely on how hard that student tries and how much value is added to that student by a teacher.

The problem is that students and teachers are, in fact, unique individuals, with widely varying interests, talents, and challenges. Moreover, they exist within contexts—personal, familial, local, regional, and beyond—that necessarily impact individual perspective, comprehension, passions, affinities, approaches, and many other aspects of personhood. Reducing students to a single score on a Common Core assessment objectifies students. Reducing teachers to a number based on their students' performance objectifies teachers. Grading schools based largely on standardized assessments potentially objectifies entire communities, despite rich histories and diverse populations.

The longitudinal data systems being deployed to track student progress on Common Core assessments provide quality control in the raw-material refinement process. These systems are entirely analogous to the CBS methods implemented by global corporations. The sole difference? The raw material being processed and tested for quality is our children, depersonalized and easily manipulated via standardized processes to produce desired outcomes.

Paid Piper, Called Tune

> And it's whispered that soon, if we all call the tune,
> Then the piper will lead us to reason.
>
> – Robert Plant[26]

> If you have 50 different plug types, appliances wouldn't
> be available and would be very expensive. But once an
> electric outlet becomes standardized, many companies
> can design appliances, and competition ensues, creating
> variety and better prices for consumers.
>
> – Bill Gates[27]

What outcomes are desired and by whom? Ostensibly, the $4 billion earmarked to the RttT program that embeds Common Core is intended to increase our nation's supply of students possessing science, technology, engineering, and mathematics (STEM) skills. Many states were seduced into adopting the Common Core standards by misleading claims that these standards would improve the flow through the critical STEM pipeline. Christopher Tienken has shattered this claim, noting that the United States already produces "more researchers and scientists and qualified engineers than our economy can employ, [has] even more in the pipeline, and [is] one of the most economically competitive nations on the globe."[28] Moreover, in both ELA and mathematics, Common Core is less ambitious than other available standards.* When asked in 2010 whether a Common Core aligned curriculum would prepare a student for STEM or for international competitiveness, Jason Zimba, a lead writer of the math standards, replied, "Not only not for STEM, it's also not for selective colleges. For example…whether you are going to be an engineer or not, you'd better have pre-calculus to get into UC Berkeley."[29] He admitted that under Common Core "college ready" is defined merely as someone who has passed Algebra 2.

If the United States does not truly need to strengthen the STEM pipeline to remain globally competitive, and if Common Core itself is not really designed to increase the flow of STEM graduates, then why are we pursuing this initiative at all?

Many major corporations and their associated foundations have donated millions of dollars to ensure Common Core's successful implementation. For some of these organizations, clear, direct profit motives exist. It's evident, for example, that companies like Pearson Education stand to profit on aligned tests, textbooks, and associated materials. In 2009, Bill Gates, the largest single funder of Common Core's development and advancement, acknowledged that the initiative would "unleash a *powerful market* of people providing services for teaching. For the first time there will be *a large uniform base of customers looking at using products* that can help every kid learn and every teacher get better."[30] (emphasis mine)

---

* EDITOR'S NOTE: For further information on the shortcomings of the Common Core standards themselves, see R. James Milgram and Ze'ev Wurman on the math standards (pp. 73-102) and Sandra Stotsky's analysis of the English language arts standards (pp. 103-122).

IBM, another major backer, clearly has an interest in providing solutions for the longitudinal data systems that states are installing to track students and monitor teachers. Cisco Systems, also a large investor, stands to profit in providing much of the network infrastructure needed to securely implement Common Core aligned assessments.

With many corporate donors, a profit motive is not as immediately obvious. These Common Core advocates are more interested in what our schools produce than in profiting directly from the unfolding realignment. Such companies include GE, State Farm, Prudential, and Boeing.

As already noted, Walmart and Amazon leverage CBS solutions heavily to monitor and control employees. Both the Walton Family Foundation and the Bezos Family Foundation provide major support to Education Reform Now, Teach For America, and the Knowledge Is Power Program (KIPP), each of which support Common Core standards, high-stakes standardized testing, and VAM-type accountability measures. In so doing, and in keeping with a Taylorist approach, they facilitate surveillance and foster student acceptance of it, all while objectifying students by equating them with their assessment scores.

Consider also that a 2013 Carnegie Corporation report projects an expected graduation rate under Common Core fully *15 percent lower* than today, with a *doubled* dropout rate.[31] Nothing in the report indicates that Carnegie finds these projections troubling.

Might these companies and foundations be seeking to use classrooms as a reliable source of low-cost, compliant, dependent workers?

GE Intelligence Platform is a major provider of CBS solutions. "Imagine that every worker is your best worker—and that every work process is a best practice...[R]educe the variation in performance, cost, quality and brand protection, achieving a new level of operational excellence," reads marketing for one of the company's chief workflow products.[32]

Prudential and State Farm have engaged in significant business-process reengineering projects to increase the efficiency of their customer service and claims processing. Both are major funders of Achieve, Inc., the organization that spearheaded development of the Common

Core for the NGA and the CCSSO.[33] Achieve, as noted, has long advocated for P-20 data systems to track people from pre-school into post-secondary education and the workforce. They likewise advocate assessment-based accountability for American education.

Boeing has had a long history of employee surveillance, much of which is due to the company's involvement in the defense industry.[34] Another important contributor to Achieve, Boeing also sponsored *Organizing Business Knowledge: The MIT Process Handbook*. Published in 2003, the *Process Handbook* gives a powerful sense that business-process reengineering is an enduring commitment in the corporate world.[35]

Cisco Systems has invested over $200 million in CBS upgrades to monitor all aspects of its operations.[36]

Microsoft, too, seems to have motivation to promote Common Core that is, at least in part, rooted in surveillance. In October 2012 Microsoft obtained a patent for enabling technology for use in workplace surveillance. The abstract of this patent states: "Approaches are provided for monitoring, analyzing, and influencing organizational behaviors through multi-modal communication systems. Desired and undesired behaviors and applicable organizational contexts are defined and action plans developed. The behaviors are then monitored through communication sessions between members and analyzed for comparison to the action plans such that feedback may be provided at individual and/or organizational levels to influence the behaviors"[37]

Another major study sponsored by the Bill and Melinda Gates Foundation is the Measures of Effective Teaching (MET) project.[38] Research partner Teachscape "developed 360-degree panoramic digital video cameras to capture over 23,000 classroom lessons in 3,000 classrooms." They "also worked with Charlotte Danielson and ETS to develop a rater training and assessment program to train over 500 evaluators to accurately and consistently score lessons captured on video."[39] This level of high-definition surveillance takes the motion studies done by Taylor at the turn of the last century to an unprecedented level. Every minute detail will now be recorded and used to rank and control educators.

Preparation for Stress and Boredom

> Our contemporary Western society, in spite of its
> material, intellectual and political progress, is increasingly
> less conducive to mental health, and tends to undermine the
> inner security, happiness, reason and the capacity for love
> in the individual; it tends to turn him into an automaton
> who pays for his human failure with increasing mental
> sickness, and with despair hidden under a frantic
> drive for work and so-called pleasure.
>
> – Erich Fromm[40]

In the 2013 U.S. Department of Education (DoED) report *Promoting Grit, Tenacity, and Perseverance: Critical Factors for Success in the 21st Century*, much mention is made of persevering in the face of boredom. In particular, the report found that "Students can develop psychological resources that promote grit, tenacity, and perseverance," including *"[e]ffortful control*," in which "[s]tudents are constantly faced with tasks that are important for long-term goals but that in the short-term may not feel desirable or intrinsically motivating. Successful students, by themselves or with the support of others, marshal willpower and regulate their attention in the face of distractions."[41] (emphasis theirs)

Another report, *A Framework for a Multi-State Human Capital Development Data System*, funded by the Gates Foundation, calls for the creation of a multi-state system for "[t]racking the stock and flow of the skills and abilities (represented by education and training) of various populations within a given state."[42] The stock of skills is simply the inventory of skills possessed by a given population. Flow refers to how well this inventory of skills in a population can be utilized as labor within an economy. The report continues:

> Reorienting accountability arrangements around longitudinal data
> acknowledges that developing productive citizens is a core goal of
> all levels of education. While workforce development is not the only
> goal of education, it is the one that is the most systematically mea-
> surable—through existing data collection activities undertaken by

state and federal agencies responsible for labor market information. Focusing on workforce development also acknowledges that students and families throughout the nation typically say that their principal reason for seeking a college education is to improve their employment prospects. Finally, this focus recognizes that many of the other benefits of education—including civic engagement, volunteerism, good health, and aesthetic appreciation—tend to accrue disproportionately to those who, by virtue of their employment, have a steady source of income.[43]

Its clear that support for standards, assessments, and related CBS solutions are to promote workforce development with public money.

Today employers are increasingly seeking employees willing to be surveilled and controlled via CBS management solutions. *Grit, Tenacity, and Perseverance* says that such non-cognitive skills can be measured, recorded, and developed: "Across the board in research, practice, policy, industry, and popular culture, there is an emerging and convergent recognition that the noncognitive factors—and particularly grit, tenacity, and perseverance—must play an essential role in evolving educational priorities. This view was echoed in an April 2012 address by John Easton, Director of the DoED's Institute of Educational Sciences, in which he stated that a concern of national importance is to bring noncognitive factors back to the front burner in education."[44]

In addition to the invasive monitoring, frustration, and boredom that students must endure themselves, what better way to promote perseverance than to present them with persevering role models? Over the course of an academic career in a Common Core, high-stakes environment, students cannot help but absorb that their teachers have persevered in presenting scripted curricula, continuing ever onward despite relentless surveillance and ranking. From this modeling, students learn that constant monitoring, or accountability as some would have it, is normal in school, workplace, and society and to be tolerated at increasingly invasive levels. They also learn that the purpose of this accountability—the shaping of their very lives and futures—is acceptable.

The "jobs of the future" share one thing in common. They all will come with an unprecedented amount of monitoring and control.

Considering the path we are on in today's global economy, nearly all jobs can and will be subject to reengineering by scientific management methods. Common Core requires that children develop deep perseverance skills so that they can combat the stress and boredom that will surely be required by work roles defined by experts and controlled by computers. The language of the Common Core State Standards Initiative's Standards Setting Criteria has a leviathan ring: "The standards intend to set forward thinking goals for student performance based on evidence about what is required for success. The standards developed will set the stage for US education not just beyond next year, but for the next decade, and they must ensure *all* American students are prepared for the global economic workplace."[45] (emphasis theirs) That workplace is increasingly dominated by CBS regimens that control every aspect of work life—an atmosphere for which, again, our children will have been thoroughly prepared.

During the rise of Taylorism at the turn of the last century, the trappings of scientific management were clearly visible. One could see and experience not only the assembly line but also the toll that the drudgery of repetitive tasks took on workers. Whatever one's opinion about them today, unions sprang up in Taylor's era to push back in favor of workers' rights.

However, the resurgence of Taylorism in the 21st century is much more difficult to detect and to resist. Far more pervasive than before, the trappings of scientific management today exist mainly in large computer systems that control our everyday lives. Modern Taylorism benefits from this obscurity. It touches not only blue collar, industrial jobs, but those in the service sector at ever-higher levels of management. Considering it as the norm, many of those newly affected by this phenomenon are not likely to organize against it as the labor movement did in the last century.

Ultimately, we must decide what it means to be human. Should we be managed through the careful construction of a system that alternately makes us slaves to reward and punishment or should human beings be free to determine their own way forward, based on individual interests, skills, and hard work?

Moreover, is the role of leadership to design efficient systems, monitor outcomes, and reward success? Or does true leadership instead inspire and enable us, setting us free to fulfill our individual potential? In advancing Common Core standards and aligned assessments, our government and industry leaders clearly would prefer that we choose a path where smart systems can monitor and control us as "dumb humans."[46]

Is it worth giving up our human freedom and dignity in pursuit of such efficiency?

And if it is not—whether surveillance and control are exercised in the name of streamlined education, corporate efficiency, or a better society—can we find the will to make an effective stand together against our own subjugation?

NOTES

1. Henri-Frédéric Amiel, *Amiel's Journal: The Journal Intime of Henri-Frederic Amiel*, translated by Mrs. Humphrey Ward (London: Macmillan & Company, 1889), 296. The specific entry from which the quote is drawn was penned on April 10, 1881.

2. Quoted in Darrell Fasching (ed.), *The Thought of Jacques Ellul: A Systematic Exposition* (Lewiston, NY: Edwin Mellen Press), 17.

3. Simon Head, *Mindless: Why Smarter Machines Are Making Dumber Humans* (New York: Basic Books, 2014), 35.

4. Sarah O'Connor, "Amazon Unpacked," *Financial Times*, Feb. 8, 2013, http://www.ft.com/cms/s/2/ed6a985c-70bd-11e2-85d0-00144feab49a.html#slide0; Hal Benton and Susan Kelleher, "Amazon Warehouse Jobs Push Workers to Physical Limit," *The Seattle Times*, Apr. 3, 2012, http://seattletimes.com/html/businesstechnology/2017901782_amazonwarehouse04.html; and Angelo Young, "Amazon.com's Workers Are Low-Paid, Overworked and Unhappy: Is This the New Employee Model for the Internet Age?" *International Business Times*, Dec. 19, 2013,

http://www.ibtimes.com/amazoncoms-workers-are-low-paid-overworked-unhappy-new-employee-model-internet-age-1514780.

5.   John Taylor Gatto, *The Underground History of American Education* (Oxford, NY: Oxford Village Press, 2006 revised edition), 43.

6.   Achieve, Inc., the National Governors Association (NGA), and the Council of Chief State School Officers (CCSSO), *Benchmarking for Success: Ensuring U.S. Students Receive a World Class Education.* Report prepared by Craig D. Jerald (Washington, D.C.: Authors, 2008), 6, http://www.achieve.org/BenchmarkingforSuccess.

7.   U.S. Dept. of Education (DoED), "Race to the Top Executive Summary," section (C)(1), Nov. 2009, https://www2.ed.gov/programs/racetothetop/executive-summary.pdf.

8.   Achieve, Inc., "Race to the Top: Accelerating College and Career Readiness in States: P-20 Longitudinal Data Systems." Information sheet, 1, http://www.achieve.org/files/RTTT-P20LongitudinalData.pdf.

9.   Quoted in Georges Friedmann, *The Anatomy of Work: Labor, Leisure and the Implications of Automation* (New York: Free Press of Glencoe, 1964 edition), 86.

10.   John Franklin Bobbitt, "The Elimination of Waste in Education," *The Elementary School Teacher* 12, no. 6 (1920), 260.

11.   John Franklin Bobbitt, "The Objectives of Secondary Education." In J. R. Gress (ed.), *Curriculum: Frameworks, Criticism, and Theory* (Richmond, CA: McCutchan Publishing Corporation, 2002), 142.

12.   John Franklin Bobbitt, *The Supervision of City Schools: The Twelfth Yearbook of the National Society for the Study of Education* (Bloomington, IL: Public School Publishers, 1913), 52-3.

13.   John Dewey, "Education as Engineering," *New Republic* XXXII, no. 407 (September 20, 1922), 91.

14.   The passage from Dewey cited above continues: "Education must measure its efficiency not in terms of so many promotions per dollar of expenditure, nor even in terms of so many student-hours per dollar of salary; it must measure its efficiency in terms of increased humanism, increased power to do, increased capacity to appreciate." The "increased power to do" is, in its own way, particularly troubling language because it still effectively ties human value to production. In so doing, it suggests education's role in reinforcing a worldview in which those who cannot or do not produce lack value.

15. Frederick Winslow Taylor, *The Principles of Scientific Management* (New York: Harper & Brothers Publishers, 1913), 7.

16. Goals 2000 mandated testing in grades 3, 8, and 11.

17. Under the No Child Left Behind Act, testing was mandated for grades 3-8 and 11. The high stakes tied to the assessments included school closures and teacher remediation and retention.

18. In grade 12, a Common Core aligned ACT or SAT test is subsequently administered to demonstrate "college and career readiness."

19. McKinsey & Company's 7-S rating system was another that saw significant adoption.

20. Developed by Charlotte Danielson, a former economist who also has teaching experience. Danielson bills herself as a teacher effectiveness expert, specializing in evaluation systems. Her framework can be explored on the Danielson Group's website, http://danielsongroup.org/framework/.

21. Alan Singer, "Who Is Charlotte Danielson and Why Does She Decide How Teachers Are Evaluated?" *Huffington Post*, June 10, 2013, http://www.huffingtonpost.com/alan-singer/who-is-charlotte-danielso_b_3415034.html.

22. "The Framework," The Danielson Group website.

23. Hegelian dialectic is a method of argument in which two opposing views are reconciled or synthesized into a more generally acceptable view.

24. Jabari Mahiri, "From 3 R's to 3 C's: Corporate Curriculum and Culture in Public Schools." *Social Justice* 32, no. 3 (2005), 82.

25. "The Industrial Classroom," *Jacobin Magazine* 10 (Apr. 2013), https://www.jacobinmag.com/2013/04/the-industrial-classroom/.

26. "Stairway to Heaven," *Led Zeppelin IV*, 1971.

27. Lindsey Layton, "Bill Gates Calls on Teachers to Defend Common Core," *The Washington Post*, Mar. 14, 2014, http://www.washingtonpost.com/local/education/bill-gates-calls-on-teachers-to-defend-common-core/2014/03/14/395b130a-aafa-11e3-98f6-8e3c562f9996_story.html.

28. Christopher H. Tienken, "Common Core: An Example of Dataless Decision Making," *AASA Journal of Scholarship and Practice* 7, no. 4 (Winter 2011), 4.

29. The meeting at which Zimba's remarks were made was video-recorded and is available to view on the Pioneer Institute's website,

http://pioneerinstitute.org/news/video-commoncore-lead-writer-jason-zimba/.

30. "Bill Gates at the National Council of State Legislators" (2009), *YouTube*, posted June 4, 2013, https://www.youtube.com/watch?v=323WQrPHslg.

31. Carnegie Corporation of New York, *Opportunity by Design: New High School Models for Student Success*. Report prepared by Leah Hamilton and Anne Mackinnon (New York: Carnegie Corporation, 2013), 10, http://carnegie.org/fileadmin/Media/Programs/Opportunity_by_design/Opportunity_By_Design_FINAL.pdf.

32. See GE's product page for Proficy Workflow, http://www.ge-ip.com/products/proficy-workflow/p2807.

33. Formed in 1996 at the National Education Summit with the blessing of the National Governors Association, a who's who of corporate leaders, and a number of other special interests, including Marc Tucker's National Center on Education and the Economy, Achieve essentially set out to realize Tucker's vision of a "new human resources development system for the United States," http://achieve.org/files/1996NationalEducationSummit.pdf. This vision was set forth in what has since become known as the "Dear Hillary" Letter, penned by Tucker to Hillary Clinton on November 11, 1992, on the occasion of her husband's election to the presidency. The letter is viewable in its entirety on the Eagle Forum website, http://www.eagleforum.org/educate/marc_tucker/. Through various reports and position papers over the past two decades, Tucker and his organization have continued to advocate for the same basic vision—the transformation of schools into labor fulfillment centers. The most notable of these publications include *America's Choice: High Skills or Low Wages!* (Washington, D.C.: National Center on Education and the Economy, 1990) and *Tough Choices or Tough Times: The Report of the New Commission on the Skills of the American Workforce* (Washington, D.C.: Jossey-Bass, 2006).

34. See Andrea James, "Boeing Bosses Spy on Workers," *Seattle PI*, Nov. 15, 2007, http://www.seattlepi.com/business/article/Boeing-bosses-spy-on-workers-1255840.php.

35. "Handbook Sponsors," Center for Coordination Science, MIT. List of sponsors of *Process Handbook* research from its 1992 inception, http://ccs.mit.edu/ph/sponsor.htm.

36. Andrew McAfee and Erik Brynjolfsson, "Investing in the IT That Makes a Competitive Difference," *Harvard Business Review*, July 2008,

http://hbr.org/2008/07/investing-in-the-it-that-makes-a-competitive-difference/ar/1.

37. Dan M. Bean, Sameer D. Bedekar, and Ross F. Smith, "Organizational Behavior Monitoring Analysis and Influence," U.S. Patent No. 8,301,475 B2, filed May 10, 2010, issued Oct. 30, 2012, http://pdfpiw. uspto.gov/.piw?Docid=08301475.

38. See the Measures of Effective Teaching website, http://metproject. org.

39. "Designing Effective Evaluation Systems: Emerging Findings," Teachscape, n.d., http://www.teachscape.com/products/reflect/research.

40. Erich Fromm, "The Contribution of the Social Sciences to Mental Hygiene," *Proceedings of the Fourth International Congress of Mental Hygiene*, edited by A. Millan (Mexico: La Prensa Medica Mexicana, 1952), 38.

41. DoED, Office of Educational Technology, *Promoting Grit, Tenacity, and Perseverance: Critical Factors for Success in the 21st Century*. Report prepared by Nicole Schechtman, Angela H. DeBarger, Carolyn Dornsife, Soren Rosier, and Louise Yarnall (Washington, D.C.: DoED, 2013), http://www. ed.gov/edblogs/technology/files/2013/02/OET-Draft-Grit-Report-2-17-13. pdf.

42. Brian T. Prescott and Peter Ewell, *A Framework for a Multi-State Human Capital Development Data System* (Boulder, CO: Western Interstate Commission for Higher Education, 2009), 3, http://www.wiche.edu/info/ publications/FrameworkForAMultistateHumanCapitalDevelopmentData System.pdf.

43. Ibid.

44. DoED, *Grit, Tenacity and Perseverance*, 22.

45. A copy of the Common Core State Standards Initiative Standards-Setting Criteria can be accessed at http://www.corestandards.org/assets/ Criteria.pdf.

46. Head, *Mindless*.

COMMON CORE AND AMERICA'S PEOPLE OF COLOR

CERESTA SMITH

Turning and turning in the widening gyre
The falcon cannot hear the falconer;
Things fall apart; the centre cannot hold;
Mere anarchy is loosed upon the world,
The blood-dimmed tide is loosed, and everywhere
The ceremony of innocence is drowned;
The best lack all conviction, while the worst
Are full of passionate intensity.

– William Butler Yeats, from "The Second Coming"

The renowned Irish modernist poet William Butler Yeats penned his apocalyptic poem "The Second Coming" just a year after World War I had ended.[1] Over four decades later, a line from the poem became the title for Nigerian writer Chinua Achebe's *Things Fall Apart*. Achebe's classic novel captures the misfortune and tremendous loss experienced by an African tribe victimized by colonialism. While coming from different time periods, cultural experiences, and literary genres; the two pieces of literature have much in common. Both manipulate language in rich ways that lend to multiple intellectual and emotional responses. Both have surface level meaning and a deeper allegorical sense, are rooted in historical reality and cultural clash, develop themes that characterize man's universal experience, and contain essential truths and lessons ignored both in the past and yet today. Moreover, both literary pieces could typically be found as anchor pieces for twelfth-grade language arts curriculum. However, nowadays, with the implementation of Common Core State Standards (Common Core), a close reading and analysis of either is rendered archaic and useless. Most high school language arts teachers will be hard pressed to fit either of them—or anything like them—into a language arts curriculum that places more emphasis on non-fiction text, is closely monitored by ongoing formative assessments, and culminates with an overarching standardized assessment that comes from outside the school community.

National standards in the form of Common Core are the best thing since sliced bread, according to: U.S. President Barack Obama; Secretary of Education Arne Duncan; former governor of Florida Jeb Bush; President-Elect of the National Educators Association Lilly Eskelsen-Garcia; President of the American Federation of Teachers Randi Weingarten; corporate philanthropists such as Bill Gates and Eli Broad; and many local, state, and federal elected and appointed officials, conservative and liberal. Even many educators, some very critical of the standards, accept them as a done deal; this despite the fact that those closest to the classroom had little say in the development of standards that emerged from a corporate, "market-based" consciousness with little knowledge of the art of pedagogy.

It is now clear that the standards:

- were never properly vetted through acceptable research and piloting channels;

- circumvent and possibly violate federal and state laws;

- are frequently developmentally inappropriate and unfeasibly or illogically sequenced;

- attach to costly formative assessments, summative assessments, and data mining that will ensure vise-like control over curricula, learning materials, and school spending;

- neglect the impact that factors such as second language, special needs, and poverty have on teaching and learning; and

- will negatively impact many teachers' careers.[2]

Turning and turning in the widening gyre
The falcon cannot hear the falconer

In *Things Fall Apart*, protagonist Okonkwo is a powerful man who achieves great wealth and status only to lose it all. Like most tragic heroes in classic literature, he constantly faces the struggle between fate and free will. However, in exercising his free will, Okonkwo fails to listen to cautionary words.

Limited by the fateful imposition of national standards, many people of color—inclusive of public education employees, students, union members, elected and appointed public officials, medical professionals, and taxpayers—are using their free will to question how national standards that were never fully vetted will impact non-white individuals and their communities. It remains to be seen whether the quiet rumble of their inquiry and protestations will turn to a loud roar. Regardless, the free will that drives their concern is genuine. They are right to be cautious and cautionary. To date, federal and state education policies—products of so-called market-based education reform that fully embrace outcome-based education—have not served communities of color well. Nor have the implementation of federal and state accountability polices, such as No Child Left Behind (NCLB), Race to the Top (RttT), Florida's A+ Plan, and other state initiatives, all of which have dispensed with teacher due process, netted positive results for non-whites. In fact it can be argued that they have caused a tremendous amount of loss and undue suffering. These negatives outweigh the modest claims of those that have benefitted from charter schools, vouchers, and improved test results for elementary math and middle school students—results apparently not maintained as students matriculate into high schools:

> Younger students' results on the 2013 NAEP were released in November and showed incremental progress, continuing a slow but upward long-term trend. Twelfth-grade performance, by contrast, has been stagnant in recent years, and senior achievement in reading has declined since the early 1990s. Moreover, despite more than a decade of federal policies intended to close achievement gaps, the margin between white and Latino 12th-graders in reading remains as large as

it was 15 years ago. The margin between black and white seniors has widened — not because white students have improved, but because black students' average reading scores have fallen.[3]

While graduation rates have improved in most school districts with the help of online courses, night school, summer school, and grade replacement; disparities persist, "[d]espite the high-water mark of 80 percent in the class of 2012. In many states, one-third of students from low-income families did not graduate. Black students had a 69 percent graduation rate and Hispanic students had a 73 percent rate, while 86 percent of white students and 88 percent of Asian students earned high school diplomas. English-language learners and special-education students had below-average rates of 59 and 61 percent, respectively."[4]

Intellectual development has similarly stagnated, as shown in the lack of preparedness of freshman students entering colleges and universities and those entering the labor force. The American College Testing service (ACT) reports that "[a]bout 69% of all 2013 ACT-tested high school graduates met at least one of the four ACT College Readiness Benchmarks in English, Reading, Mathematics, or Science. Fully 31% of all graduates did not meet any of the ACT College Readiness Benchmarks, while 43% met between 1 and 3 Benchmarks. Twenty-six percent of all 2013 ACT-tested high school graduates met all four ACT College Readiness Benchmarks, meaning that just over 1 in 4 were academically ready for college coursework in all four subject areas."[5]

Citing a study conducted by the Fordham Institute, Elaine Tuttle Hansen, executive director of the Johns Hopkins Center for Talented Youth, draws attention to evidence that school experience may specifically diminish, rather than develop, academic talent. The study found that among "young American students testing in the 90th percentile or above, roughly 30 to 50 percent of these advanced learners lost ground as they moved from elementary to middle school, or from middle to high school." The research further observed that "the focus on low-achieving students in public schools has disproportionately left more smart minority and low-income kids behind, creating a well-documented 'excellence gap.'"[6]

While the implementation of Common Core promises to create equity and close the opportunity and achievement gaps between students of color and their white counterparts, it fails to address the question: How will improved standards change the current realities faced by non-white students when standards, no matter how well written or implemented, never have before? Tom Loveless, former Harvard professor and education policy expert at the Brookings Institution pointedly observes that "[e]veryone who developed standards in the past has had a theory that standards will raise achievement, and that's not happened.[7] Basing this conclusion on his analysis of states' past experience with standards and several years of National Assessment for Educational Progress (NAEP) results, Loveless published *The 2012 Brown Center Report on American Education.*[8]

There are many issues negatively impacting non-white students:

- re-segregation of schools;
- cultural and racial biases in curricula and assessment;
- questionable oversight and appropriation of money to low-income urban schools;
- teacher quality;
- harsh zero-tolerance policies that facilitate a school-to-prison pipeline;
- indictments and cheating scandals involving non-white educators pressured to produce improved test score data amidst compromised circumstances;
- the negative impact of the closing of community schools; and
- the impact of poverty on academic achievement.

As an African-American educator in South Florida, I share all of these concerns. Yet, it took a foray into an urban school under sanction for low test-score performance and an exploration of how people of color have been impacted nationally to recognize all of the implications.

Miami Norland Senior High is a community school located in the township called Miami Gardens. It sits in the northwest corridor of

Miami-Dade County. It serves a predominantly black population. While black, it is diverse ethnically, as the students are native-born Miamian, Haitian, Jamaican, Bahamian, Trinidadian, and latino. A Title I school, based on its percentage of free or reduced lunch population, Miami Norland has a sizable second-language population. Many black professionals continue to live in Miami Gardens despite drops in property values. The surrounding community, mostly black, thus ranges from poverty to upper-middle class.

Five miles away is Dr. Michael Krop Senior High, which is not a Title I school. Krop is ethnically and racially diverse in its population of white, black, and brown students. Student socioeconomic status ranges from lower-middle to upper class. It houses the only high school arts magnet in the upper northwest section of the city and serves students living in North Miami Beach, Aventura, and Miami Beach. I worked at Krop for eleven years prior to answering the call to become the first National Board Certified Teacher (NBCT) on Norland's staff. Krop had well over twenty NBCTs. The differences between the schools, geographically just five miles apart, were stark. It took several months for me to adjust to the differences, though I never wholly accepted those reflecting unfair policies that it was difficult not to understand as racist.

In contrast to typically A- or B-rated Krop, Norland High was designated a D school and under sanction when I arrived in mid-October 2008. Over a ten-year period, Miami-Dade County's black populated community high schools rarely achieved grades above a C and usually flipped back and forth between D and F status. A shift occurred in 2012 when many non-white schools, including Norland, earned Bs and As. The grade increases were a result of a change in the State of Florida's grading policies, which placed less weight on reading and math test scores while including additional criteria such as the number of students enrolled in advanced academic classes. While the state-issued grades increased, reading scores remained stagnant or dropped in sanctioned schools, and math scores saw only small but steady increases. "Achievement gaps" remained pronounced.

"Underperforming" students, generally constituting two-thirds or more of the student population, take an English literature class, an intensive reading class, and a writing class, all of which have a mandated curriculum implemented by the state and the district. The students sit for many assessments, including:

- monthly assessments, evaluated in-house;
- two interim assessments for reading and math, evaluated by the district/state; and
- the state reading and math assessments, evaluated by the state and used as one factor for both school and teacher evaluations (weighted at 50 percent as of 2013).

In addition, other assessments are given at regular intervals:

- FAIR testing for reading;
- PERT testing for college readiness;
- PSAT; and
- state- and district-generated end-of-course exams (EOCs) for every enrolled course, beginning with the 2014 -2015 school year.

Some students are relegated to test prep pull-out during the course day and/or attend after-school and Saturday test prep. Sound like overkill? It is. And to date it has proven effective in closing neither achievement nor opportunity gaps between impoverished students and students of color and their white peers.

Things fall apart; the centre cannot hold;
Mere anarchy is loosed upon the world

Violating tribal law, Okonkwo engages in wife beating during The Week of Peace as well as both deliberate and unintentional killing of tribal members. He loses the respect of his tribal members and is forced out of his village into exile for seven years. During that time, his Igbo tribe is confronted with changes imposed on them by white, sometimes murderous colonizers and seemingly friendly missionaries. The result is chaos and a threatened traditional Igbo way of life.

Miami Norland Senior High, other predominantly black and brown high schools across this nation, and the communities in which they live face similar chaotic impositions analogous to the infringement of the Igbo tribe by colonizers. These impositions result in comparable threats to their autonomy and ability to survive and thrive. Without a firm foundation of quality leadership coming from visible and respected educators who are committed to the community, it is next to impossible to create a standard for academic excellence. Experienced educators are generally paid more than novices. However, there is a benefit to the cost. It ensures that knowledgeable and experienced principals and teachers remain long enough to establish a wholesome and nurturing traditional culture, in which consistent, productive communication facilitates autonomous decisions and solutions uniquely geared for their individual community. Similarly, adequate adjustments and modifications to changes in staff, finances, and student populations can more easily be made.

Unfortunately, "underperforming" schools are often filled with transient, inexperienced educators who lack vision, while more experienced educators often find their hands tied in terms of making meaningful changes. In fact, highly qualified and experienced educators are in many cases forced out via federal School Improvement Grants (SIGs) that allow for any school district in the nation to turn over staff. Alternatively, they choose to flee the frustrations of stress-filled communities in which staff, curricular, and textual mandates from outside of the school community have led to a lack of autonomy and students unprepared for academic and social success. Herbert Kohl has characterized such school environments as "educational panopticons":

> I mean a system in which teachers and students are under constant scrutiny, allowed no choice over what is learned or taught, evaluated continuously, and punished for what is considered inadequate performance. In this context students and teachers are forced to live in a constant state of anxiety, self-doubt, wariness, anomie, and even suppressed rage...The irony is that even with the imposition of so-called "teacher-proof" curriculum, teachers are evaluated on the effectiveness of their student's performance on tests relating to material they have no control over. It is the powerless "proofed" teachers who take the hit...People who insult and denigrate teachers by forcing scripted curriculum on them are perfectly aware that they are forcing teach-

ers to act against their conscience and students to close down their minds.[9]

Will the implementation of national standards facilitate an end to the practice of running experienced educators and administrators out of schools deemed "low-performing"?

"When students have teachers who are out of subject or lesser experienced, those types of teachers tend to correlate to lower achievement for students, and we see a higher concentration of those conditions within low-income communities and among kids of color," says Deborah Veney Robinson, vice president for government affairs and communications for the Education Trust.[10] In response to such criticism, the White House announced in July 2014 a three-pronged initiative, "Excellent Educators for All," administered by the U.S. Department of Education (DoED). By April 2015, states are asked to submit new plans in order to address the state-by-state distribution of effective teachers. DoED will also begin publishing "Educator Equity profiles" in Autumn 2014 to show how states fare on this front.[11] In conjunction with the equity initiative, the department will further spend $4.2 million to fund a technical assistance network, ostensibly to allow states and districts to share best practices.

Questions loom in the minds of many non-white people: Will this initiative be backed with the financial resources needed? What is the specific plan to make sure states and school districts comply? Will the definition of "highly qualified" be modified to exclude the wave of Teach for America (TFA) recruits, possessed of only five weeks of training but now disproportionately placed in urban schools?

The blood-dimmed tide is loosed, and everywhere
The ceremony of innocence is drowned

Okonkwo returns to his village after completing a seven-year exile. In his absence, white colonizers have infiltrated the core of Igbo life, engaging in economic exploitation and firmly entrenching western institutions—religious, educational, medical, and judicial. Okonkwo sees many of his tribal brothers and sisters adopting the traditions of their subjugators. Eventually, as a result of actions consequential to his desire both to gain prominence among his tribe and resist change, he ends up incarcerated in the white man's jail.

Like Okonkwo, resistors against state sanctions and mandates suffer punitive measures extolled by the state-controlled district administrative judges and jury. Administrators and teaching staff who resist or fail to meet harsh expectations undergo involuntary transfers or demotions. Disproportionately, these are people of color.[12] In Miami-Dade County, the contractual agreement between the United Teachers of Dade (UTD) and Miami-Dade County Public Schools (MDCPS) allows for superintendent involuntary transfer of teachers and administrators where such action is deemed necessary. This statute has frequently been misused to force out effective educators when they cross administrators who are complying with ineffective mandates—often because those administrators are visionless and powerless to effect productive change. Between 2009 and 2012, UTD leadership signed memorandums of understanding with MDCPS, rendering useless specific provisions in the union contract that had previously offered protection against such activity.

The best lack all conviction, while the worst
Are full of passionate intensity

Upon his release from jail, Okonkwo and other tribal members meet to discuss action against the colonizers. Five court messengers come to deliver the message that the white man has ordered this meeting stopped. Okonkwo reacts by beheading the lead messenger. The others are allowed to flee. Subsequently, the lack of inaction by his tribal members forces him to accept an unfortunate reality. Okonkwo realizes he has no backup for war against the white colonizer.

As, a parallel, teachers have had no back-up to fight and defeat the hands of a government-backed corporate colonizer that has destroyed the culture of public education in schools and communities. Certainly, in Miami-Dade County, black educators were those disproportionately drop-kicked out of sanctioned schools two days prior to reporting for a new school year. The *Miami Herald* reported that "[b]eginning in the fall of 2009 and ending in 2012, principals in 73 schools identified and transferred 375 low-performing teachers 'in the best interest' of the school district. The result: Test scores improved notably under new teachers who stepped in to replace those transferred.[13] The article went on to note that Pablo Ortiz, associate superintendent in charge of the district's Education Transformation Office, which oversees struggling schools, identified involuntary transfers as "step one" in the overhaul of failing schools. Miami Edison Senior High, where Ortiz served as principal in 2009, was cited as having replaced half its staff that year under a state mandate after receiving failing grades for years.

The *Miami Herald* article was, in fact, a response to a 2013 report, "Strategic Involuntary Teacher Transfers and Teacher Performance: Examining Equity and Efficiency."[14] In it, the researchers use "administrative data from MDCPS to investigate the implementation and effects of the district's involuntary transfer policy, including which schools transferred and received teachers, which teachers were transferred, what kinds of teachers replaced them in their former schools, and how their performance—as measured by their work absences and value-added in math and reading—compared before and after the transfer." The researchers found that, "[c]onsistent with an equity improvement… involuntarily transferred teachers were systematically moved to higher performing schools and generally were outperformed by the teachers who replaced them." The report also noted that educators transferred involuntarily were "more likely to be female and black than were teachers who stayed, voluntarily transferred, or left MDCPS."[15]

Was it—*is it*—really possible that somehow black, female educators are disproportionately bad or failed educators? What was going on under the surface of this report? A significant portion of the truth lies in the evaluation method the researchers applied to educators and schools—the "value added" noted in the passage above, more formally known as Value Added Models (VAMs).*

---

* EDITOR'S NOTE: Value Added Modeling, or VAM, is discussed in greater detail in at least two other essays in this collection. See, for example, Jeffrey Horn (pp. 147-170) and Kris Nielsen (pp. 209-223). Nielsen provides a relatively concise definition on p. 217.

Looking again at the particulars of the report, the researchers used VAM as a means of casting judgment on teacher quality: "Most centrally, the comparisons show that involuntarily transferred teachers tended to be less productive than other teachers. In math, involuntarily transferred teachers had statistically significantly lower value-added scores than stayers in the year of the transfer, based on a *value-added model* that includes school fixed effects (i.e., estimates are within school). They also had lower value-added scores in reading, though this difference is not statistically significant."[16] (emphasis my own)

> There was once a man who went to sell a goat. He led it on a thick rope which he tied around his wrist. But as he walked through the market he realized that people were pointing at him as they do a madman. He could not understand it until he looked back and saw that what he led at the end of the tether was not a goat but a heavy log of wood.[17]

On closer inspection, the report's researchers seem to be dragging, not a goat, but a heavy log of wood.

A sizable portion of the almost 400 relocated educators—my husband and I included—were transferred from six predominantly non-white high schools. Table 1 provides student scale scores for the Florida Comprehensive Assessment Test (FCAT) in reading and math, as well as grade 10 Algebra I end-of-course (EOC) scores, at six predominantly non-white high schools in Miami-Dade County from 2007 to 2014. In analyzing the scores, it becomes clear that the researchers' use of VAM to draw their conclusions is antithetical to the facts.[18] Prior to 2012, FCAT math testing included algebra and geometry concepts and was the required accountability test to meet the NCLB mandate. In 2012, FCAT Math was replaced with Algebra I EOC. Consequently, determining math score improvement that can be credited with certainty to the involuntary transfer process is difficult; however, it is clear that reading scores have not improved in any way that indicates teaching quality improvements attributable to the transfer of mostly veteran African-American female educators.

Likewise, the use of VAM to determine teacher effectiveness is erroneous at best. Many scholarly reports far more credible than the one above have proven VAM is not a valid measure for teacher effectiveness.[19] Moreover, in MDCPS, the VAM scores for the majority of teachers are taken not from students they taught but from scores based on *school-wide* reading, math, and science scores. Rather than providing greater transparency into teacher quality and effectiveness, accountability measures tied to Common Core are obfuscating the truth. Will Common Core, then, stop the mistruths?

The victimization of people of color, impacting first students and ul-

Table 1. FCAT Reading and Math and Algebra I End-of-Course scores at six predominantly non-white high schools in Miami-Dade County.

HIGH SCHOOL	TEST	YEAR							
		'07	'08	'09	'10	'11	'12	'13	'14
Miami Edison									
	FCAT Reading	235	246	260	248	254	229	230	229
	FCAT Math	284	302	301	311	294			
	Algebra 1 EOC						390	400	397
Miami Carol City									
	FCAT Reading	258	258	269	278	280	232	233	233
	FCAT Math	292	298	302	315	308			
	Algebra 1 EOC						339	392	389
Miami Jackson									
	FCAT Reading	248	264	262	265	272	230	232	230
	FCAT Math	283	303	296	307	307			
	Algebra 1 EOC						388	389	397
Miami Northwestern									
	FCAT Reading	256	263	271	280	271	233	233	235
	FCAT Math	289	299	307	311	310			
	Algebra 1 EOC						381	391	397
Miami Norland									
	FCAT Reading	267	276	271	271	270	232	234	234
	FCAT Math	298	306	307	308	306			
	Algebra 1 EOC						393	397	398
Booker T. Washington									
	FCAT Reading	252	255	256	260	267	227	230	230
	FCAT Math	295	300	305	308	311			
	Algebra 1 EOC						379	391	393

timately communities, goes beyond involuntary teacher transfers. The School Improvement Grants (SIG) program, part of NCLB, similarly attacked low test performance via a turnaround, restart, close, and transform model.[20] In Chicago, Philadelphia, Gary, New Orleans, Detroit, and other urban areas, entire communities, most of them already struggling, were further damaged economically by what was labeled poor academic performance on standardized tests. In doing so, it negatively impacted students and facilitated community destruction. Besides the stigma that comes with school grading and associated drops in property values, community schools have been shut down under SIG, often turned into exclusive, privately managed, and unregulated charters that do not and cannot provide quality education for the entire community. Often times such schools fail to provide quality education for those they do serve. Communities become increasingly destabilized, fodder for economic exploitation. Frequently, for example, people from outside the community will take advantage of these circumstances to buy up cheap land, making financial killings that have over time been removed from the reach of those within the community itself by the same or similar mechanisms. In a 2013 guest blog posted under Valerie Strauss' column at the *Washington Post*, Leslie T. Fenwick, dean of the Howard University School of Education and a professor of education policy, brought attention to this precise situation:

> In the most recent cases of Washington D.C. and Chicago, black parents and other community members point to school closings as verification of their distrust of school "reform" efforts…While mayoral control proposes to expand educational opportunities for black and poor students, more-often-than-not new schools are placed in upper-income, gentrifying white areas of town, while more schools *are closed* and fewer new schools are opened in lower-income, black areas thus increasing the level of educational inequity. Black inner-city residents are suspicious of school reform (particularly when it is attached to neighborhood revitalization) which they view as an imposition from external white elites who are exclusively committed to using schools to recalculate urban land values at the expense of black children, parents and communities….This kind of school reform is not about children; it's about the business elite gaining access to the nearly $600

billion that supports the nation's public schools. It's about money.[21] (emphasis my own)

Will the implementation of Common Core stop this corruption? Or will it only further facilitate the economic divide that clearly documented inequities in education have fostered?[22]

Establishing curricular and textual autonomy within each school building is a major component to building a tradition of academic excellence. Yet, the current trend in education reform is a one-size-fits-all blanket mandate in terms of curriculum and text; it drives instruction via "benchmarks" and has been an overall failure in fostering literacy, first and foremost in underperforming and non-white schools. Miami-Dade County serves as a classic example of the loss of and need to return to local control to avoid faulty and damaging pedagogy. Such educational instruction throws knowledge around randomly, with little foundation, or schema, to which new information can attach.[23] It ignores the reality that learners need a base for new information so it becomes available for automatic retrieval when new information is presented.

In lieu of these shortsighted and damaging mandates, schools must be allowed to provide documented curriculum-mapping that spirals and scaffolds instruction. Such enriched curriculum frontloads information and creates a strong knowledge base drawn from written and visual text, classroom discussion, and authentic experience in- and outside the classroom walls. Carefully crafting students' knowledge bases results in a subsequent reduction in the remediation population.[24]

Reading skills tests in and of themselves do little but test a student's knowledge base, assuming the guise of benchmark/skill assessors. Yet, in a 1988 study conducted by Recht and Leslie, the researchers found that students entering high school and labeled as low-performing readers often have untapped literacy skills that standardized tests don't reflect. In these cases, experienced educators must frequently reach beyond mere classroom expertise, drawing from their own rich knowledge base of experience and information to provide textual materials and experiences that tap into those students' "cultural backgrounds, language needs, intelligence level, and creative/intellectual aptitudes.

The prescribed curriculums and reading programs on the high school level," Recht and Leslie note, "are generally below the students' intellectual levels and fail to engage them due to their lack of creativity and cultural insensitivities. Using texts and activities that involve the student's cultural and background experience easily allows for fact and process acquisition...Stressors are reduced and resiliency is fostered."[25]

Common Core and the formative and summative assessments that accompany them make it imperative to use the textual materials that are produced by those commissioned to create the test. When Philadelphia Mayor Michael Nutter publicly distributed 200,000 donated books to K-3 students, Meredith Broussard, concerned mother and data journalism assistant professor at Temple University noted:

> Unfortunately, introducing children to classic works of literature won't raise their abysmal test scores. This is because standardized tests are not based on general knowledge. As I learned in the course of my investigation, they are based on specific knowledge contained in specific sets of books: the textbooks created by the test makers...Across the nation, standardized tests come from one of three companies: CTB McGraw-Hill, Houghton Mifflin Harcourt, or Pearson. These corporations write the tests, grade the tests, and publish the books that students use to prepare for the tests.[26]

It's a closed loop. Moreover, many schools lack funds to buy the books that ensure high test scores. Is it any wonder Broussard insists:

> Stop giving standardized tests that are inextricably tied to specific sets of books. At the very least, stop using test scores to evaluate teacher performance without providing the items each teacher needs to do his or her job. Most of all, avoid basing an entire education system on materials so costly that big, urban districts can't afford to buy them. Until these things change, it will be impossible to raise standardized test scores—despite the best efforts of the teachers and students who will return to school this fall and find no new books waiting for them.[27]

Schools under sanction for low performance are, in fact, often forced to use poorly developed curricula and materials that do not adequately prepare students for the assessments. At MDCPS's Krop Senior High, teachers were able to engage in "academic freedom," supposedly contractually guaranteed to all educators who teach in the district. However, teachers employed in sanctioned schools—and the sanctioned students forced into remediation as a result of low performance on mandated state assessments—are forced to use state selected curricula and materials for remediation. With limited monetary appropriations for public education, it is questionable if the State of Florida will, in fact, provide Common Core and assessment-aligned materials for remediation classes.[28]

There's more. In preparing teachers to provide Common Core-aligned "exemplar" lessons for "close and critical" reading of non-fiction texts, instructors were expected to engage students in cold reading, where excerpts from longer works are given to the student out of context. The student, with little to no support, is subsequently expected to be able to read, comprehend, and write analysis in response to the text. However, without prior knowledge of context, most students would be only able to parrot what is read with no true, critical response. In a recent op-ed, Henry Giroux observes that "[i]f we lose control of those spheres that cultivate the knowledge and skills necessary for rigorous analysis along with a culture of questioning, it will become more and more difficult for students and others to question authority, challenge commonsense assumptions, and hold power accountable."[29]

Clearly, emphasizing textual reading and analysis without reference to context or an encouragement of students' personal reactions leaves them void of developing an intellect that can turn outward to engage in critical thought that becomes the catalyst for social change or much of anything else of substance. The problem of "teaching to the test" will only further narrow curricular focus, failing to develop creative and critical intellect apart from the standards given priority on tests.

In Achebe's *Things Fall Apart*, Okonkwo, like most archetypal tragic heroes, ends up dead. He realizes the war is lost before it begins because his tribal members forget a proverb shared by the elders: "[T]he sun will shine on those who stand before it shines on those who kneel under them."[30] His warrior spirit is unable to live under the submissive and oppressive force of colonial rule. Consequently, he commits suicide. While viewing the body, one of the colonists decides to devote a couple of paragraphs to Okonkwo in a book he plans to write, *The Pacification of the Primitive Tribes of the Lower Niger.*

Unfortunately, many non-white people commit a symbolic suicide of self when they buckle under the pressure of a public school system that has a history of inequity, sublimation, and oppression. There is no strong evidence that the implementation of Common Core will not continue the history of institutionalized racism that has resulted in an increase in stressors and a consequential reduction in resiliency for non-whites, playing out as dysfunction and failure, often leading from school to prison for both students and adults. It seems contradictory that an institution that is supposed to nurture and build social skills, develop intellect, and prepare students for college and/or careers could somehow form a pipeline to prison; but, for non-whites, it does so disproportionately.[31]

The institution of "zero tolerance" policies that suspend and arrest students for very minor infractions (that would previously have been dealt with in-house), the trend of pushing out students with low standardized test scores that justify punitive accountability policies, and the failure of students to earn high school diplomas due to standardized exit exam requirements have facilitated an increase in student arrests and incarcerations.

Likewise, far too many non-white adult educators have faced indictments and possible prison sentences due to alleged cheating in relationship to standardized tests. "Wrong Answer," a compelling biographical narrative written by Rachael Aviv and published in the *New Yorker Magazine*, chronicles the Atlanta Public Schools test cheating scandal from the perspective of two individuals: Damany Lewis, a math teacher at Parks Middle School, first to be fired out of 178 accused educators; and Christopher Waller, a Methodist pastor who had worked in public schools for nine years before becoming principal at Parks.[32] While Lewis was initially hesitant to be involved in cheating, Waller was eventually able to recruit him to what was, by 2008, a team of nine educators. The cheating, as Waller phrases it, had become a "well-oiled machine."[33]

The test irregularities and improbabilities ultimately generated an investigation that included more than 2,000 interviews. The resulting report concluded that forty-four schools had cheated and that a "culture of fear, intimidation and retaliation [had] infested the district, allowing cheating—at all levels—to go unchecked for years."[34] The authors suggest that data had been, "used as an abusive and cruel weapon to embarrass and punish."[35] In the end, Waller, thirty-three other educators, and Superintendent Beverly Hall were brought up on charges. Waller agreed to act as a prosecution witness, serve five years probation, and pay financial restitution.

Atlanta is hardly an isolated case. In May of 2014, one principal and four teachers in Philadelphia, all women of color but one, were similarly arrested on charges inclusive of felony racketeering, records tampering, perjury, forgery, and criminal conspiracy.[36] In both Atlanta and Philadelphia, the educators taught in schools filled with impoverished students facing social conditions that wear on the ability to produce great results on high-stakes standardized tests. With the impossible demands increasingly placed on educators in similar communities, cheating has begun to occur all over the United States. One can only conclude that more "rigorous" national standards and their assessments will only increase the pressure on teachers in compromised teaching communities and exacerbate the teacher-to-prison pipeline.

National standards have to pack a very powerful punch to fight the problems that foster the opportunity and achievement gaps between students of color and their white counterparts. Additionally, they need a powerful punch to overcome the miseducation of *all* students as perpetuated by false reforms that have prioritized profit over quality teaching and learning. Facing reality, generated from a corporate mentality, national standards do not have the punch to do either as long as an oppressive control resulting in racism, poverty, and profit margins beats at the core of America's economic and social drum. Hence, they provide little hope for people of color—as with the Igbo people in *Things Fall Apart*, who are left with little hope in their fight against colonization.

Yeats' "Second Coming," on the other hand, does provide a sense of hope for humanity reflected in the beginning of the second stanza:

"Surely some revelation is at hand…" For all those that support unencumbered public education, likewise, "*some revelation is at hand*."

NOTES

1. *The Norton Anthology of English Literature: Twentieth Century and After*, edited by Stephen Greenblatt (New York: Norton, 2006), 2036-2037.

2. Implementation of the standards will also void many existing and wholly legal collective bargaining agreements.

3. Emma Brown, "Math, Reading Performance Is Stagnant among U.S. 12th-Graders," *The Washington Post*, May 7, 2014, http://www.washingtonpost.com/local/education/math-reading-performance-is-stagnant-among-us-12th-graders-assessment-finds/2014/05/07/6a5e743e-d47a-11e3-aae8-c2d44bd79778_story.html.

4. Lyndsey Layton, "National High School Graduation Rates at Historic High, but Disparities Still Exist," *The Washington Post*, April 28, 2014, http://www.washingtonpost.com/local/education/high-school-graduation-rates-at-historic-high/2014/04/28/84eb0122-cee0-11e3-937f-d3026234b51c_story.html.

5. ACT, Inc., *The Condition of College and Career Readiness* (Washington, D.C.: Author, 2013), http://www.act.org/research/policymakers/cccr13/pdf/CCCR13-NationalReadinessRpt.pdf.

6. Elaine Tuttle Hansen, "Top Students, Too, Aren't Always Ready for College," *The Chronicle of Higher Education*, March 11, 2013, http://chronicle.com/article/Top-Students-Too-Arent/137821/.

7. Tom Loveless, "Does the Common Core Matter?" *Education Week*, April 13, 2012, http://www.edweek.org/ew/articles/2012/04/18/28loveless_ep.h31.html.

8. Tom Loveless, *The 2012 Brown Center Report on American Education: How Well Are American Students Learning?* (Washington, D.C.: Brown Center on Education Policy at Brookings, 2012), http://www.brookings.edu/~/media/newsletters/0216_brown_education_loveless.

9. Herbert Kohl, "The Educational Panopticon," *Teachers College Record*, Jan 8, 2009. One must be a subscriber to access the digital version of this journal. However, Susan Ohanian has published the text of the article on her website with a fair use disclaimer, http://www.susanohanian.org/outrage_fetch.php?id=534.

10. Allie Bidwell, "Education Department Wants Better Teachers in Disadvantaged Schools," *U.S. News and World Report*, July 7, 2014, http://www.usnews.com/news/articles/2014/07/07/arne-duncan-education-department-want-better-teachers-in-disadvantaged-schools.

11. Ibid. See also the official press release issued when the plan was announced, U.S. Dept. of Education, "New Initiative to Provide All Students Access to Great Educators: U.S. Department of Education Launches 'Excellent Educators for All Initiative'," July 7, 2014, http://www.ed.gov/news/press-releases/new-initiative-provide-all-students-access-great-educators.

12. Jason Grissom, Susanna Loeb, and Nathaniel Nakashima, "Strategic Involuntary Teacher Transfers and Teacher Performance: Examining Equity and Efficiency," *Journal of Policy Analysis and Management* 33, no. 1 (Winter 2014), 112–140.

13. David Smiley, "Study: Struggling Miami-Dade Schools Benefited from Teacher Transfers," *Miami Herald*, November 11, 2013, http://www.miamiherald.com/2013/11/11/3746849/study-struggling-miami-dade-schools.html.

14. Grissom, Loeb, and Nakashima, "Strategic Involuntary Teacher Transfers."

15. Ibid., 112.

16. Ibid., 140.

17. Achebe, *Things Fall Apart*.

18. All scores were retrieved from Florida state records and made available by School Diggers, a website that provides an "easy way to evaluate schools," http://www.schooldigger.com/.

19. "Nonetheless, there is broad agreement among statisticians, psychometricians, and economists that student test scores alone are not sufficiently reliable and valid indicators of teacher effectiveness to be used in high-stakes personnel decisions, even when the most sophisticated statistical applications such as value-added modeling (VAM) are employed." A quote from Richard Rothstein, Helen F. Ladd, Diane Ravitch, Eva L. Baker, Paul E. Barton, Linda Darling-Hammond, Edward Haertel, Robert L. Linn,

Richard J. Shavelson, and Lorrie A. Shepard, *Problems with the Use of Student Test Scores to Evaluate Teachers*. Economic Policy Institute Briefing Paper #278 (Washington, D.C.: Economic Policy Institute, 2010), http://www.epi.org/publication/bp278/.

20. Eighty-one percent of the program was comprised primarily of student of color. Of that percentage, 44 percent were black, another 32 percent latino. "Our Communities Left Behind: An Analysis of the Administration's School Turnaround Policies," National Opportunity to Learn Campaign, July 28, 2010, http://www.otlcampaign.org/resources/our-communities-left-behind-analysis-administration%E2%80%99s-school-turnaround-policies.

21. Valerie Strauss, "Ed School Dean: Urban School Reform Is Really about Land Development (Not Kids)," *The Washington Post*, May 28, 2013, http://www.washingtonpost.com/blogs/answer-sheet/wp/2013/05/28/ed-school-dean-urban-school-reform-is-really-about-land-development-not-kids/. See also, Jeffrey R. Henig, Richard C. Hula, Marion Orr, Desiree S. Pedescleaux, and Leslie T. Fenwick, *The Color of School Reform: Race, Politics, and the Challenge of Urban Education* (Princeton NJ: Princeton University Press, 2001), from which Fenwick draws her evidence, and Valerie Strauss, "The Rev. John Thomas: No Act of God Caused Chicago Schools Closings," *The Washington Post*, May 23, 2013, http://www.washingtonpost.com/blogs/answer-sheet/wp/2013/05/23/the-rev-john-thomas-no-act-of-god-caused-chicago-schools-closings/, which she references in her guest column.

22. Tools such as SchoolDiggers (see note 18) not only publish and continually update school test scores, but also provide rankings, school and district boundaries, student/teacher ratios, ethnic makeup, property values, and other metrics and information for over 120,000 elementary, middle, and high schools in the United States. Such informational resources make it relatively easy to discover the problems for public schools in increasingly segregated communities, grasp the ways in which students of color are being isolated, and see how the deck is stacked against them in terms of preparation for college and career. Again, these realities have social and economic consequences. Recently, other researchers have clearly documented the same phenomenon. See, for example, Thomas Shapiro, Tatjana Meschede, and Sam Osoro, *The Roots of the Widening Racial Wealth Gap: Explaining the Black-White Economic Divide*. Policy brief of the Institute on Assets and Social Policy (Waltham, MA: Institute on Assets and Social Policy, Brandeis University, 2013), 5.

23. It also carries with it a blatant disregard for how short- and long-term memory banks function.

24. See Daniel T. Willingham, "How Knowledge Helps: It Speeds and Strengthens Reading Comprehension, Learning—and Thinking," *American Educator* (Spring 2006), http://www.aft.org/newspubs/periodicals/ae/spring2006/willingham.cfm.

25. Donna R. Recht and Lauren Leslie, "Effect of Prior Knowledge on Good and Poor Readers' Memory of Text," *Journal of Educational Psychology* 80, no. 1 (Mar. 1988), 16–20.

26. Meredith Broussard, "Why Poor Kids Can't Win at Standardized Testing," *The Atlantic*, July 15, 2014, http://www.theatlantic.com/features/archive/2014/07/why-poor-schools-can-t-win-at-standardized-testing/374287/.

27. Ibid. It's further important to recognize that many of the elementary language arts materials are far above the children's developmental levels. On both the elementary and secondary levels, the materials also narrow curricular choices and promote questionable teaching methodology.

28. If no new and aligned materials come through, eleventh- and twelfth-grade students who failed to earn passing reading scores will continue using a USA Today periodical and associated classroom activity materials. As a reading coach at Norland, I refused to build literacy with the use of the USA Today alone. I was criticized and reported to district administrators. Fortunately, I won that battle; but I had to fundraise to purchase alternative reading and writing materials. The school had none available besides those mandated by the state.

29. Henry A. Giroux, "Thinking Dangerously in an Age of Political Betrayal," *Truthout*, July 14, 2014, http://www.truth-out.org/opinion/item/24869-henry-a-giroux-thinking-dangerously-in-an-age-of-political-betrayal.

30. Achebe, *Things Fall Apart*, 5.

31. A Chicago youth-led participatory action research project, mounted collaboratively by the Rogers Park Young Women's Action Team and Project NIA, yielded an infographic in 2012 titled, "Are Our Children Being Pushed into Prison?" The piece is filled with startling statistics. It is worth citing some of those statistics here: 40 percent of students expelled from U.S. schools each year are black; 70 percent of students involved in-school arrests or referred to law enforcement are black or latino; black students are three and a half times more likely to be suspended than white students; black and latino students are twice as likely not to graduate from high school as whites; 68 percent of all males in state and federal prisons

do not have a high school diploma. In addition the infographic notes that while blacks and latinos make up only 30 percent of the U.S. population, they comprise approximately 61 percent of the incarcerated population. It goes on to note that one in three black males and one in six latino males will be incarcerated in their lifetime. The full infographic, including data sources, may be viewed on the Community Coalition website in a post titled identically to the infographic and dated June 14, 2012, http://www.cocomovement.org/2012/06/are-our-children-being-pushed-into-prison/.

32. Rachel Aviv, "Wrong Answer: In an Era of High-Stakes Testing, a Struggling School Made a Shocking Choice," *The New Yorker Magazine*, July 21, 2014, http://www.newyorker.com/magazine/2014/07/21/wrong-answer.

33. Ibid., 5.

34. Ibid., 7.

35. Ibid.

36. Maryclaire Dale, "5 Educators Charged in Philadelphia Test Cheating," *MSN News*, May 8, 2014, http://news.msn.com/crime-justice/5-educators-charged-in-philadelphia-test-cheating.

V. A DATA BONANZA
Exploiting Child and Family Privacy

COMMON CORE AND THE THREAT TO STUDENT PRIVACY

JANE ROBBINS

Several of the most prominent news stories of 2013 involved data privacy: the NSA scandal, IRS leaks of sensitive taxpayer information, the Target and Neiman-Marcus data breaches. "Big Data" is now a fact of life in the United States, for good or ill. The plans to employ Big Data in the realm of education are, to say the least, ambitious. They are also poorly understood by most Americans. Parents must realize that without new protections on student privacy, school will no longer be a safe place to send their children.

In K-12 education, parents are now beginning to understand the dangers of the Common Core national standards scheme (Common Core). A particularly troubling aspect of this scheme is the emphasis on massive data-collection on students and the sharing of that data for various purposes essentially unrelated to genuine education. U.S. Secretary of Education Arne Duncan has said:

> Hopefully, some day, we can track children from preschool to high school and from high school to college and college to career....We want to see more states build comprehensive systems that track students from pre-K through college and then link school data to workforce data. We want to know whether Johnny participated in an early learning program and then completed college on time and whether those things have any bearing on his earnings as an adult.[1]

To draw conclusions of this sort, of course, we have to know pretty much everything Johnny does, throughout his lifetime.

The underlying philosophy embraced by Secretary Duncan has roots in the early twentieth century.[2] At that time, progressives on both sides of the political aisle staked their philosophy on the belief that the modern world had become so much more complex than the world as it existed at the time of the American founding that the old principles of individual freedom and limited government were no longer sufficient. In the modern world, they asserted, experts would be needed to address increasingly complex challenges.*

Of course, expert administrators cannot plan and implement plans without data. As Sherlock Holmes once exclaimed: "Data! Data! Data!...I can't make bricks without clay."[3] An essential component of this "necessary" data is information that can be gleaned from the captive audience of public-school students (and preferably private and home-schooled students as well). Progressive** education reformers such as Marc Tucker, of the National Center on Education and the Economy, have long advocated the creation of massive student databases that can be used to track children from birth into the workforce. This is what Arne Duncan, quite openly, wants to do.

The problem, from Duncan's point of view, is that a federal statute prohibits maintaining a national student database.[4] What to do? What the federal government has chosen to do—and this predates the Obama Administration—is to incentivize the states to build identical databases so that the data can be not only collected but also easily shared. The result is a *de facto* national student database.

---

* EDITOR'S NOTE: In his essay (pp. 147-170), Jeffrey Horn examines in some depth the history of scientific management—also known as Taylorism—and its relationship to the U.S. educational system, a topic that has great bearing on what Robbins here discusses.

** EDITOR'S NOTE: In using the term progressive, Robbins here refers to a broad political philosophy based on the Idea of Progress, which asserts that advances in science, technology, economic development, and social organization can improve the human condition. She clarifies that, on whatever side of the political aisle, the philosophy has tended to assume that empowering trained "experts" to make policy is the best route to societal progress.

This massive initiative has been pursued through the power of the federal purse. In 2002 the federal government began something called the Statewide Longitudinal Data System grant program to offer grants to states that agreed to build their student data systems according to federal dictates.[5] The most recent iterations of this grant program were incorporated into the 2009 stimulus bill, which required the construction of particular data systems in exchange for money from the State Fiscal Stabilization Fund[6] and the Race to the Top (RttT) program. A successful RttT application required the state to adopt the Common Core standards, to also adopt an assessment aligned with Common Core, and to commit to expand its student database.[7]

What Kinds of Data Would Be Included in This Database?

The National Education Data Model (part of the National Center for Education Statistics) recommends inclusion of over 400 data points, including health history, disciplinary history, family income range, voting status, religious affiliation, and on and on.[8] While this is not a federal requirement (yet), states are urged to add as much data on each child as possible—all for the benefit of the child, of course.

What Is the Connection to Common Core?

The most direct connection is through the two national consortia that formed to create the Common Core-aligned assessments required of each state that applied for RttT funds: the Partnership for Assessment of Readiness for College and Careers (PARCC) and the Smarter Balanced Assessment Consortium (SBAC). Each of these consortia has signed a cooperative agreement with the U.S. Department of Education (DoED) in which DoED is allowed access to all *student-level data* the consortium receives through the testing. This access is to be allowed "on an ongoing basis" for purposes that include undefined "research."[9] The agreements further provide that the consortia will "provide timely and complete access to any and all data collected at the State level" to DoED.[10] Parents will not be allowed to object to this access; indeed, they won't even know it is happening.

We are told not to worry about this blank check to the testing consortia because any disclosure of data will comply with the Family Educational Rights and Privacy Act (FERPA). But as of January 2012, FERPA has been gutted and no longer protects our children's data from almost unlimited sharing.[11] Under the new regulatory interpretation, DoED (and in fact state departments of education, schools, etc.) may disclose personally identifiable student data to literally anyone in the world, as long as the disclosing entity uses the correct language to justify its action.[12]

Even for those states that have had the good sense to withdraw from the PARCC and Smarter Balanced assessments, the privacy threat remains. DoED is becoming increasingly aggressive about demanding personally identifiable student data in conjunction with all sorts of federal grants, as can be attested by the states that have not embraced Common Core. Moreover, the federal government is encouraging widespread sharing of student data within states, such as with departments of labor, public health, corrections, etc.[13] The idea is the State (upper case) should know everything there is to know about a student, so that he can be better directed toward his proper slot in the economic machine.

Whether Collected on the State or the Federal Level, Where Might This Private Student Data End Up?

One illustrative example (and an obvious one, in this workforce-development model) is the departments of labor. In fact, the federal Department of Labor and DoED have a joint venture called the Workforce Data Quality Initiative, the purpose of which is "developing or improving state workforce data systems with individual-level information and enabling workforce data to be matched with education data." Student education data are to be shared, to the extent possible, with labor agencies to promote the goal of workforce development.

Here, too, under the new regulations that gutted federal student-privacy law, data can now be shared with literally any agency if the correct enabling language is used: the Department of Health and Human Services, Homeland Security...the IRS.

DoED supports a plethora of other programs that encourage states to build ever bigger and more "useful" data systems on students. For example, it is funding the "Common Education Data Standards"[14] to help states develop a common vocabulary for their data—the better to enable interstate sharing. It is also funding the "Assessment Interoperability Framework" to "allow for the transfer of assessment-related data across applications within a district, between a district and a state agency, and across state lines."[15] These are just two of the myriad programs currently underway and designed to increase collection and sharing of student data.

So although the federal government assures us it is not building a *de facto* national student database, *everything* it is doing in the area of technology is designed to allow for just that end.

Both DoED and state education officials further insist that privacy concerns are overblown because student-level data will be anonymized. In the first place, the claim of anonymity is simply not true. The data coming from the Common Core assessment consortia, and the workforce tracking data showing which students participated in which education programs and then earned which salaries, are necessarily student-specific.

In the second place, in the era of Big Data, there really is no such thing as anonymization. With multiple, perhaps hundreds, of items in the database, the absence of a name or a Social Security number becomes a mere inconvenience, not an obstacle to student identification.

There are many examples of data re-identification, including some in education. In Kentucky in 1999, a researcher was able to match, with a 100 percent rate of accuracy, over 2,300 students who appeared on anonymized lists of test-takers.[16] That was almost fifteen years ago—long before education bureaucracies were collecting the myriad data they do now.

One scholar who has studied this problem has explained that "[u]tility and privacy [of data] are…two goals at war with one another…[A]t least for useful databases, perfect anonymization is impossible."[17] And DoED fully intends for student data to be enormously useful. Anonymization will be impossible.

Where Are These Big Data Plans Headed?

It is instructive to look at what DoED itself is working on and writing about.

Promoting Grit, Tenacity, and Perseverance: Critical Factors for Success in the 21st Century, a report appearing on the DoED's website last February, advances the thesis that education must inculcate these "noncognitive" qualities in students and that their presence or absence must be measured in some way. How? The report suggests assessment of physiological reactions that a student exhibits to stimuli such as stress, anxiety, or frustration. These reactions could be measured through posture analysis, skin-conductance sensors, EEG brain-wave patterns, and eye-tracking.[18] And the report barely mentions the appalling invasion of privacy this kind of physiological measurement would entail; rather, it focuses on the "problem" that this isn't practical for the classroom—yet.[19]

The *Grit, Tenacity, and Perseverance* authors also drew a direct line to the Common Core standards, noting that the math standards expressly require perseverance in struggling through problems.[20] If these noncognitive attributes are required by the standards, they reason, those qualities must be measured.

Another DoED report issued in the same month as *Grit, Tenacity, and Perseverance* focused on the enormous windfall of student data that will result from digital-learning technologies and digital assessment.[21] This report was authored primarily by Karen Cator, who now heads up a federally chartered nonprofit organization focused on development of education technology.[22] The type of digital learning that the Cator report promotes is not simply an alternative means of accessing text or lectures. Rather, it focuses on computerized products that work by stimulus-response; the student sees something on the screen and must choose a response, which leads to another prompt, and so on. This type of technological interplay generates enormous amounts of data on each student's behaviors and dispositions; the term for it is "data exhaust."

The Cator report urges that this data exhaust be leveraged to develop individual profiles on students, that it be shared with various institutions and other stakeholders who may have an interest, and that it become instrumental in "studying the noncognitive aspects of 21st-century skills, namely, interpersonal skills (e.g., communication, collaboration, and leadership) and intrapersonal skills (e.g., persistence and self-regulation)."[23] DoED also emphasizes that the gathering of this "extremely fine-grained information" on students will help with the implementation of the Common Core standards, which promote "deeper learning objectives" rather than acquisition of academic knowledge.[24]

In October 2013, DoED hosted a conference to explore the possibilities of implementing Common Core with the help of such types of intrusive digital learning. They marketed this conference as "Datapalooza." At this conference the CEO of one educational technology company waxed enthusiastic about the future. He said, "We are collecting billions of records of data…pulling data from everywhere… tens of thousands of places."[25] This data, he said, will help students develop the "21st-century skills" that the government has determined students will need.

And how are these "21st-century skills" being promoted in the classroom? Through Common Core. "Common Core," the same CEO said, "is the glue that ties everything together."[26]

Even disregarding the philosophical dangers of unlimited sharing of student data among government agencies and their "authorized representatives," and the sheer creepiness of science-fiction-style brain evaluation, there remains the garden-variety problem of protecting student data from hacking. The huge push for technologically enhanced, greatly enlarged, centrally located student databases is creating an enormously tempting target for identity thieves.[27] Already, according to the Privacy Rights Clearinghouse, 11,155,715 student records have been lost from 706 different security lapses between 2005 and November 6, 2013.[28] Malefactors in search of "pristine" Social Security numbers, as well as predators in search of student schedules and contact information, will be drawn to the treasure trove that now exists in our schools and education agencies.

The more personal information an education database contains, the greater is the threat to children's privacy and safety.

As serious as this problem of hacking is, the deeper problem is that the government has deemed our children little machines to be programmed, "human capital" to be exploited. Many—again, on both sides of the aisle—have yearned to achieve this end for at least 100 years. Now they have the technology to do it. And the Common Core Standards, which diminish academic knowledge in favor of the "21st-century skills" developed and measured by this technology, are their passport to the future. But is it a future the rest of us or our children would want?

NOTES

1.   Arne Duncan, remarks to the Fourth Annual IES Research Conference, June 8, 2009, http://www2.ed.gov/news/speeches/2009/06/06082009.html.

2.   See the section on administrative progressivism in the entry "Progressive Education – Philosophical Foundations, Pedagogical Progressivism, Administrative Progressivism, Life-Adjustment Progressivism" at StateUniversity.com, accessed July 6, 2014, http://education.stateuniversity.com/pages/2336/Progressive-Education.html.

3.   Sir Arthur Conan Doyle, "The Adventure of the Copper Beeches," *Sherlock Holmes: The Complete Novels and Stories*, Vol. I, Bantam Classic reissue (New York: Bantam Dell, 2003), p. 501.

4.   20 U.S.C § 7911.

5.   20 U.S.C. § 9501 et seq.

6.   "State Fiscal Stabilization Fund," U.S. Dept. of Education (DoED), Mar. 7, 2009, http://www2.ed.gov/policy/gen/leg/recovery/factsheet/stabilization-fund.html.

7.   "Race to the Top Program Executive Summary," DoED, Nov. 2009, http://www2.ed.gov/programs/racetothetop/executive-summary.pdf.

8.   National Education Data Model, National Center for Education

Statistics, http://nces.ed.gov/forum/datamodel/.

9. Cooperative Agreement Between the DoED and the Partnership for Assessment of Readiness for College and Careers (Jan. 7, 2011), http://www2.ed.gov/programs/racetothetop-assessment/parcc-cooperative-agreement.pdf; Cooperative Agreement Between the DoED and the Smarter Balanced Assessment Consortium (Jan. 7, 2011), http://www2.ed.gov/programs/racetothetop-assessment/sbac-cooperative-agreement.pdf.

10. Ibid., p. 10. The two cooperative agreements are essentially identical.

11. DoED, "34 CFR Part 99, Federal Educational Rights and Privacy; Final Rule," *Federal Register* 76, no. 232, Dec. 2, 2011, http://www.gpo.gov/fdsys/pkg/FR-2011-12-02/pdf/2011-30683.pdf.

12. Comments of American Association of Collegiate Registrars and Admissions Officers on the Apr. 8, 2011, Notice of Proposed Rulemaking in relationship to the Federal Education Rights and Privacy Act of 1974, as amended (May 23, 2011), http://www.nacua.org/documents/FERPA_AACRAOLetterMay2011.pdf.

13. See U. S. Dept. of Labor, "Workforce Data Quality Initiative," available at http://www.doleta.gov/performance/workforcedatagrant09.cfm; DoED, "Race to the Top Executive Summary," supra, at p. 4.

14. Common Education Data Standards Initiative, http://www.commondatastandards.org/.

15. Ibid., in particular, the "Assessment Interoperability Framework," https://ceds.ed.gov/aif.aspx.

16. Lauress Wise, "Impact of Exclusion Rates on NAEP 1994 to 1998 Grade 4 Reading Gains in Kentucky," *Human Resources Research Organization*, Sept. 27, 1999, http://nces.ed.gov/whatsnew/commissioner/remarks99/9_27_99pt2.asp.

17. Paul Ohm, "Broken Promises of Privacy: Responding to the Surprising Failure of Anonymization," *UCLA Law Review* 57 (2010), 1701, 1752.

18. DoED, Office of Educational Technology, *Promoting Grit, Tenacity, and Perseverance: Critical Factors for Success in the 21st Century*. Report prepared by Nicole Schechtman, Angela H. DeBarger, Carolyn Dornsife, Soren Rosier, and Louise Yarnall. (Washington, D.C.: DoED, 2013), 41-45, http://www.ed.gov/edblogs/technology/files/2013/02/OET-Draft-Grit-Report-2-17-13.pdf.

19. Ibid., 45.

20. Ibid., 6.

21. DoED, Office of Educational Technology, *Expanding Evidence Approaches for Learning in a Digital World*, (Washington, D.C.: DoED, 2013), http://www.ed.gov/edblogs/technology/files/2013/02/Expanding-Evidence-Approaches.pdf.

22. Cator is now the CEO of Digital Promise, a "public-private partnership" designed to bring together various stakeholders to enhance the use of technology in education. See Digital Promise, "Karen Cator Joins Digital Promise as CEO." Press release, Apr. 16, 2013, http://www.digitalpromise. org/karen-cator-joins-digital-promise-as-ceo/.

23. DoED, *Expanding Evidence Approaches*, (2013), xii.

24. Ibid., 11.

25. Christel Swasey, "White House Hosts 'Datapalooza' Built on Common Core Tests," *What Is Common Core? Blogsite*, Mar. 20, 2013, http://whatiscommoncore.wordpress.com/2013/03/20/white-house-hosts-datapalooza-built-on-common-core-tests/.

26. Ibid.

27. Gerry Smith, "In Push for Data, Schools Expose Students to Identity Theft," *Huffington Post*, Dec. 15, 2011, http://www.huffingtonpost. com/2011/12/15/students-identity-theft_n_1140119.html; "Prepared Statement of the Federal Trade Commission before the Subcommittee on Social Security of the House Committee on Ways and Means on Child Identity Theft." Field hearing, Plano, TX, (Sept. 1, 2011), http://education-newyork.com/files/110901identitythefttestimony.pdf.

28. "Chronology of Data Breaches: Security Breaches 2005-Present," *Privacy Rights Clearinghouse*, Nov. 6, 2013, http://www.privacyrights.org/ data-breach. The link is to the site's main page, which will contain entries for only the most recent data breaches. A quick search will yield the entry cited here.

VI. A CAREER SQUELCHER
Diminishing the Craft of Teaching

TEACHING THE COMMON CORE IS NOT TEACHING

Kris L. Nielsen

In 2010, I was teaching math in a very diverse middle school in Salem, Oregon. It was the kind of school that served as the hub of a community that relied on it for support in many ways. The school not only offered its students several different courses and opportunities to learn, but also their parents and families. In turn, the parents and families were always willing to offer their time and support to make sure the school had the resources it needed.

At 65 percent free and reduced lunch enrollment, it was not considered a low-income school, and certainly not a poverty school, although we did have a fair number of students who were not very well off. The staff was well-known in the city for being able to meet the needs of all students, regardless of background or socioeconomic status, and students felt at home there.

Our test scores always met with the district average and were always a little higher than the state's average. In other words, not exceptional, but not dismal. We never made adequate yearly progress, or AYP—that unreachable pie in the sky—and no other school in the district made it either. But, again, teachers and students were happy on a daily basis because we had the freedom to make learning real and to make sure that all were being served.

The second half of that year saw some interesting changes. In the spring of 2011, teachers started getting a kind of feedback from evaluations that they were perhaps not used to: We were told that we needed to start spending less time in the classroom on anything not directly related to standards or curriculum guides. We were required to start planting learning objectives conspicuously on our walls and to refer to them several times per lesson. Worst of all, we were increasingly required to "follow the script," as it's become known. Rather than listening to our students and their inquiries and needs, we were expected to follow prescribed steps to some magical program of learning.

This "new thing" coming down the pipe at meteor-like speed, was the Common Core State Standards (Common Core). No one knew what the standards were or what they meant. We just knew we'd better be ready. And, we knew that we didn't like what was happening.

The school resisted for as long as possible, only showing off for the occasional district visit. That strategy lasted for about a year before budget laid off over fifteen good teachers in that building alone, including me. While those cuts weren't directly related to the adoption of the standards, they did leave the need to apply for more funding through the Race to the Top program, which included the requirement of adopting college-and-career-ready standards. It felt like a set-up.

The good news for America is that there are still hundreds of thousands of amazing and caring teachers responsible for allowing our kids to learn naturally and wholly.

The bad news is that the American school system, since 2002, has increasingly been designed to punish teachers and students who attempt to take an authentic path to learning. The system has been taken over. Our kids have become commodities—traded and sold, ranked and filed by a wealthy corporate elite that now attempts to control their futures. Unfortunately, it doesn't seem to have been that difficult for this elite class to achieve these ends, and there's a reason for that.

My generation, and any generation before me, is trained to gauge success and learning through percentages and averages. My students today have parents who want to know what their children scored or how their work compares to the class average. We are so used to being competitive against each other and compared. This paradigm just won't work anymore, not in the rapidly changing times in which we live. The feedback on which we've long focused is, in fact, arbitrary and limited. We have to move away from it. Instead, I want to see students (and parents) move into more authentic, individualized feedback—the stuff that makes them part of the real world and really makes them proud.

I lacked a few critical things at the beginning of my career. Without them, I believe I was more successful in my efforts and my students felt not only greater pride and productivity, but also sensed they were part of something bigger. There was no Common Core. There were no benchmark tests every six weeks. There were no field tests that wasted my time or the precious learning time of my students. There were not yet the official one-size-fits-all models of teaching and learning, where every student in a grade level was expected to learn the exact same thing at the exact same time and was tested constantly for proficiency before moving on. My supervisor didn't have to tie student scores to my job performance; in fact, that would have been unscientific and unethical. Finally, our funding wasn't based on adhering to national standards and federal rules—our state and district were allowed to determine what was best for our local demographic. There *were* threats of sanctions against the schools for not making AYP, but at least we teachers and other school staff were able to band together to make a collaborative difference using our own collective expertise.

In the fall of 2012, due to health-related reasons that had begun to pile up, I resigned the position I then held as a science teacher with Union County Public Schools in North Carolina. When I left, I wrote a resignation letter that unexpectedly went viral worldwide in less than a week. The letter exposed hidden and serious circumstances that plague almost every teacher and every student—every day. My main message was: It shouldn't be this way; there is a better way; there are many better ways.

After the publicity and discussions started to wane, and with the help of my friends, I continued to feed the discussions that might move our schools back to being the academic community centers that we should expect them to be. I went from being a teacher to a parent activist. It was liberating as well as frightening. Over the next several months, I realized I wasn't alone. A growing network of us are trying our best to save what we know is the most important thing: a meaningful education for our kids.

Students: The Most Important Thing

A coworker of mine summed up perfectly the issue of classroom management in middle school: "If you treat them like babies, they will act like babies." Logic, then, dictates that if we treat them as people we respect and trust, students are far more likely to behave as respectful and trustworthy people.

In performing a Google search on "what makes a great teacher?" an exhausting list of articles from teachers, specialists, and academics pops up. Interspersed among them is the occasional article where a student survey was performed and analyzed. The differences between the two types of article are obvious right away. Almost every teacher or education specialist will point to "high expectations" as the most important characteristic of great teachers, and I tentatively agree. When you hold all students to the same high expectations to perform, they know where you want them to be and that you expect them to get there without accepting anything less. However, the number one aspect of a great teacher according to students is the ability to get to know them and make them feel important as individuals.

Teachers have to get to know their students—not just as data points in the manner fostered by Race to the Top (RttT) and related reforms—but also as individual human beings. We should know what they love, what they fear, what interests and bores them. We should get to know their social circles and their styles of interaction, and get to know their families and how we can work with parents to make sure there is a home-school connection. This sounds like a lot of work—and it is, particularly thanks to budget cuts that have ballooned many class sizes. But it's worth it when you realize the benefits that come from it for the rest of the year. When students feel that they have a positive relationship with their teacher, they will feel more engaged to meet challenges and share their successes and hardships.

These important relationships have taken a slide in priority with the growing focus on standardized testing achievement. There are more and more teachers who feel that building relationships with their students is a fringe duty that doesn't compete with the time needed to prep them for Common Core tests. These teachers end up seeing the blowback of this assumption with undesirable behavior and even negative impact on achievement.

In addition, most teacher evaluations look for the ability to create environments that are respectful of student differences and abilities—concern that standardization, with its unforgiving schedule and emphasis on sameness, essentially prohibits from being addressed. When students are reduced to scores and ranks, relationships become less important, and students notice. The ability to take the time to foster those relationships will cover all of those bases, and it will make teachers feel great about the things they're doing for our kids.

Encouragement is a powerful instrument in educator and parent toolkits. It doesn't always have to be praise and pats on the back; in fact, the most effective encouragement is usually of the "try one more time" variety. This means giving students meaningful feedback from which they can grow and continue to learn.

Percentages on tests and averages in class provide neither meaningful feedback nor encouragement—they deliver little more than a final message. The most heartbreaking experiences I've had over the years were when a few students who had achieved so highly and proudly all year were deflated after receiving their lower-than-expected scores on end-of-year standardized tests. Either you passed or you failed, neither of which will encourage a student to try harder or push their own limits. Why do we allow this? Imagine being the student who has been engaged, productive, motivated, and proud for an entire year, only to be downgraded by a percentile and a scale score.

No Teacher Voice in Policy

One of the popular social media memes circulating the Internet makes a poignant statement about how teachers and parents feel about our current educational policy: "Those who can, teach; those who can't, make laws about teaching." Another one shows a teacher standing by a blank whiteboard, explaining that it portrays the sum total of educational background of most legislators currently making educational policies. These are posted to break a smile, a snicker, and some head shaking.

Teachers know they are being forced to do things that have nothing to do with teaching or learning. It wasn't always this bad. Teachers and administrators seemed to have a foot in the door of education legislation for a long time, and when our place was threatened, we bargained collectively with districts and school boards. The whole idea behind teacher unions should be to lobby for practices and laws that make sense for educating kids.

At the same time, a massive and collective movement to take public education *away* from the public is on the rise. The corporate reform movement has benefited from the timing of the new millennium's Great Recession: it became very easy for business people, reducing education to the hard, cold numbers of return-on-investment, to point to excesses in public education budgets and the unimpressive results that were coming from that investment. Based on the bad science mentioned previously, reformers attacked teachers for being lazy, overpaid, underqualified, and even criminally spoiled by their unions. But what was the evidence of these charges? On what were they based? And were these accusations concerned with good teaching and real learning? Or was there another agenda?

The attacks on teachers and their pensions and the low scores received on standardized assessments, most particularly by underprivileged kids, led to a very fast and very clean takeover of educational policymaking. The reform movement discredited teachers' ability to lead and to be trusted. Then, when teachers and teacher groups spoke up to defend the schools and the kids that attend them, the reformers dismissed them as whiners and even as unpatriotic.

The Common Core State Standards Initiative is the glue that keeps this orchestrated attack together. Thanks to the standards, the government, the corporate charter managers, and the publishing companies can continue on with their collective agenda to create and maintain policymaking that is favorable to them. When teachers, universities, experts, or even parents speak up, the corporate reform propaganda machine kicks into high gear to bury, downplay, or divert any dissident action.

When teachers aren't allowed to decide what's best for the students who spend eight hours per day in their classrooms, and when teachers and parents can't decide together what the best practices for their children should be, then we have given our kids' futures to the corporate model that ranks and files them and places them into a constructed future before they can even graduate high school.

Common Core is the foundation of that system. All federal education policy is already being built on top of those standards. Think of the Common Core State Standards as a railroad track that leads to a predetermined destination ("college- and career-" readiness?). Riding those rails is everything that is being pushed to standardize learning. All student testing and tracking is done against those standards. Curriculum development is also riding those rails. And now, standardized testing is the focus and the law of all public school curricula, from Kindergarten through twelfth grade. The combination is going to limit and level-down classroom learning in public schools at the moment we most need it to be more open and limitless. In many cases, it already has been severely damaged.

Teaching to the Tests (or Else)

What Common Core is doing is not new. It's just an intensification of what has come before.

NCLB similarly mandated that students undergo end-of-year, summative exams. These exams have been completely useless to teachers and students. Tight security, threat of prosecution, and job loss due to any breach, keeps the test content completely private. During the test, teachers are not allowed to see what's on it. And afterwards, when it's all finished, teachers still can't see what's on the test until months to a year later, when the publishers and government officially release the used items. The tests are useless, in large part, precisely because we're not allowed to see them; they can't tell us anything that we can use to evaluate our programs, our teaching, our students, or our use of resources. We can't match our students' answers to the questions to find misunderstandings, discrepancies, or bad test items. We aren't allowed to see the test items to determine bias or language barriers until our students have left. We just have to trust that the Educational Testing Service, Pearson, and their kin know how to do this and that they have our kids' best interest at heart.

As you have certainly figured out by now, I have a problem with placing this kind of trust in the entities involved. I think the policymakers figured that a lot of us had a problem with it, so they came up with a new system to complement the summative requirements of NCLB. RttT puts the new plan into motion: a testing regime that's aligned with Common Core and ranks students against their peers regarding how well they perform on the standards.

Want to know one of the most beautiful points of pro-testing propaganda that is constantly regurgitated by Pearson, McGraw-Hill, and Arne Duncan? *Standardized tests are a tool for teachers to determine how well their students are performing in class and how well they master concepts.* But as I've already mentioned, summative standardized tests are worthless in that regard. The type of test to which they are actually referring in this context is called a "formative assessment." It's a tool in every teacher's kit, and good formative assessments are very valuable. They can be as simple as an observation, a single question, a short quiz, a dialogue, a debate, a conference, an essay, or any number of materials. Teachers use informal and formal methods of assessing their students every day, and sometimes more often than that.

However, the testing corporations saw another way to make money: create formative assessments for school districts, grade them, and send back score reports so that teachers can use the data to inform their instruction. It sounds magnificent. There are two, huge flaws with this system.

First, the tests—also called benchmarks because they try to measure if every student is where he or she should be in relation to the rest of the grade level—are based on Common Core, which means that students are tested against only content standards, rather than guidelines that help develop skills and academic ability. This narrow means of measuring success is very limiting to a good education, especially from the perspective of a good teacher, who laments the waste of time, resources, and money to make these tests happen. Second, teacher evaluations are now based, at least in large part, on the scores from these benchmarks.

Bullying Teachers with Statistics

The educational reform tool *du jour* is the highly-controversial "value-added measure" (VAM) of teacher effectiveness. What does this phrase, in fact, mean? Scores from student benchmark, or end-of-year, tests are factored into teacher evaluations. Standardized tests are designed to create a success versus failure scenario, where a child is compared to every other child his or her age. So you can see how adding "value" to them as an evaluation tool is also invalid. The tests are not designed to show individual progress, so it's impossible to know if a teacher is really doing good work. There will always be failure among the success, which makes VAM not just unscientific, but also unethical.

If you've been paying attention, you know that the evaluation focus for public education has moved quickly away from students and rapidly towards teachers and schools. The propaganda is everywhere, and too many people are convinced by the mantra that "the greatest factor of student success is the teacher in the classroom." I don't know who gets credit for that line, but I heard it first from Bill Gates. He actually changed it a little when he started calling it the greatest "in-school" factor, which gives the statement a little bit of a "duh" feeling.

I disagree with the mantra. The greatest determining factor of student success in school is…the student. But not just the student. It's the student's environment and support structure—home life, learning materials, exposure to learning opportunities, parent involvement, nutrition, health, social life, and the rest of the large, invisible bubble of influence that surrounds every child.

But we don't consider or deal with any of this other stuff. It's much quicker, easier, and more profitable to focus on creating failure inside entire districts than individual students, so reformers have chosen to focus on the strict evaluation of schools and teachers.

And, if you really believe that reformers have the best interests of children at heart, I'd like to direct you to my bridge-selling venture.

The doomsday scenarios that appear on the networks every so often are the public's only real windows into the world of education. And the measures that the public keeps hearing about—the ones on the news—are the test scores. Our kids are dumb, they say, and the schools and the teachers are to blame. Let's fix them! The reformers don't tell anyone how they'll fix what they've framed as the problem, they just say they will. And by "fix," they mean, "make money."

First of all, VAM is based on standardized test scores. It has been well established by researchers that standardized tests are not a good indicator of student abilities or capabilities at any grade level.[1] Along with many others, I have studied and written about this fact.[2] If, and only if, the standardized tests were a perfect way to gauge student success every year, would VAM work. However, because our kids are not computers or robots, standardized tests can do no such thing. VAM, then, is already based on a fallacy.

Second, VAM is being used in high-stakes decision-making, which statistics experts have plainly advised against. Study after study, for example, has found VAM scores entirely too unstable to use in personnel decisions or incentive schemes. At best, VAM is marginally valid and stable for 20 percent of evaluated teachers during any given study. It also inherently puts teachers into a competitive environment, which makes corporate reformers drool. But teachers tend not to work that way. We tend to be trusting and collaborative either by nature or by trade. When professionals are allowed to self-rule their environment, they weed out bad teachers and administrators naturally, while helping to develop those who are doing o.k. Other successful countries use this type of system in their schools and see great results. Unfortunately, schools have been messed with for so long, we've forgotten what self-rule looks like. The ranking system, in particular, tears that working approach apart. Unfortunately, it's already starting to happen.

Third, the entire purpose of VAM is to isolate teacher performance from other factors. It hides the effects of poverty, malnutrition, disability, language ability, and mobility. I'm no statistician, but I am a realist. It's not o.k. that we're permitting a statistics equation to effectively hide these problems for every student in every school—or that as the economy continues to founder, we'll also be hiding the *growth* of these same problems. Nor is it acceptable that instead of dealing with these significant problems as a community—as a country—we're going to hide them from constant public view and just put the heat on teachers.

There's a word for that: *scapegoating.*

Here's a list of factors that are controlled for in a typical VAM estimate:

1. Gender

2. Whether a student was present for a full academic year (FAY)

3. Language status

4. Economic status (free and reduced lunch, or FRL)

5. Disability

6. Race/ethnicity

7. Grade

8. School size

9. The students at the bottom quartile

If the sample isn't big enough, or if the error is too high, the school "borrows" data from the state average, which is somehow carefully inserted into the equation. Sounds fair.

Here's a list of significant factors that affect kids and impact their performance in the classroom on a daily basis:

1. Relationship problems

2. Parent education level

3. Parent work hours

4. Presence of both parents

5. Drug and alcohol use

6. Nutrition and health

7. Frequency and types of traumatic or violent events

8. Incidence of bullying

9. Depression, anxiety, or antisocial disorders

10. Self-esteem

11. Family events (e.g., death, divorce, marriage, birth of a sibling, etc.)

Teachers deal with these challenges every day of every school year. And they do so with compassion, poise, and care. But they can't change or control for them, just as VAM doesn't control for them. Yet, teachers are now misleadingly held accountable for all of these issues that naturally impact performance—and thus scores—on the same standardized assessments to which Common Core now ties teacher evaluations.

VAM has been explained to the public and to public officials as a way to reward the best and remove dead weight, It's a well marketed and even a persuasive-sounding plan for those who haven't spent more than 20 minutes in a school. But it doesn't work, because we are human beings caring for younger human beings. We are not a corporation of entry-level employees trying to meet a quota. Our motivation and vision of success rightly comes from somewhere else, and it translates into student success in more cases than VAM does.

VAM is a tool, just like testing. It should be used to watch trends and adjust the system slightly, as needed, with teachers doing the adjustments, in conjunction with parents wherever appropriate. Instead, VAM is being used to bully teachers and threaten schools.

Let Us Teach

When a teacher who is accustomed to seeing happy kids in his classroom suddenly realizes that he's not permitted to continue using proven methods, things can spiral downward quickly. If mandated new methods are not just unproven but also substandard, teachers are forced to watch as their students increasingly struggle to learn. The deficits only grow with time since one level of learning impacts the next. This is the effect of the Common Core and all of the things that accompany it.

A popular slogan of veteran public school teachers who know their practice leads their students to success is *"Just let me teach!"* They want to stop being quantified and objectified and watched under a microscope. They want to stop being evaluated by meaningless test scores and standardized lessons engineered by corporations that have lost sight of what leads students to real, substantive, and lasting learning.

It's long past time to give the teaching back to the teachers, the leadership of schools back to the principals (rather than state and district accountability offices, which should be restructured or dismantled), and the learning back to the students. Students should be given a voice and a choice in what they learn and how. This is not that hard, and we've done it before. If we can get our schools back in the hands of those who know what they're doing, and those who care about our kids, we may not make corporate reformers millions of dollars, but we will have successful kids and a better educated, more secure nation.

Teaching is a research-based yet heart-driven practice, based on many types of data, informal and formal, qualitative and quantitative. And it's getting more complex. However, the Common Core State Standards were designed to standardize both teaching and learning, measure that learning using very expensive low-level tests to derive only one type of data, then show the poor results as reason to hand public schools to private companies that wish to profit from their turnaround.

Unfortunately, "turnaround" is in this case a misnomer. Instead of investing in real student learning, the privatizers are fully invested merely in raising test scores to show so-called proficiency of students and schools, yielding more federal RttT funding. That's the deal. That's the plan. Nothing more.

American educators and administrators are stuck in the education power play being made by publishing and assessment companies, the politicians who enable them, and the corporate profiteers who wrote and are investing in the Common Core State Standards as the foundation of this corruption. These people aren't education specialists* and they aren't (usually) educators. Even the Common Core State Standards were authored by two policy wonks. Their friends are businesspeople

---

* EDITOR'S NOTE: Sandra Stotsky's essay on Common Core's invalid validation (pp. 55-72) strongly confirms this point.

who see an opportunity to make huge profits. It's all about getting their brands inside the classroom. There's a multibillion dollar prize behind the schoolhouse door if they can simply position their products and services in such a manner that it appears they have assisted in raising test scores. But as already noted, what appears to be success isn't actually success by any definition you or I would approve. In fact, the goal isn't real success at all. In many cases, its outright failure because replacing "failing" public schools with private charters is big money, just like Common Core-aligned testing and curricula are. Cronyism is alive and kicking in the arena of K-12 education.

Common Core advocates like to tell us that the initiative will benefit those who are challenged. But this is just another of the many falsehoods. Burying low-income and minority public schools, in particular, under the profiteering schemes will not prepare students for the future; it will have the opposite effect. And carving the country up by class will not bolster our economy or our society; it will bankrupt us and destroy our way of life, as we know it. The Common Core State Standards Initiative is the nationalization of public education that corporate-minded reformers need to make this happen.

There is, thankfully, a large team of specialists who have the energy, the drive, the ambition, and the experience to reform our schools the way they need to be reformed. That team should be moving us forward with the know-how that our students need and deserve. That team is made up of the millions of parents, students, and teachers in this country who are increasingly finding themselves in positions at the front lines of the battle to save our kids and their schools.

It's time to revisit our school policies to prepare our students for high school, for college, for work, and for life. Since we've seen that the "top-down" corporate model hasn't worked and will not work, let's start from the bottom up. It's important to realize that one person can't do this alone. Let's combine our tried-and-true expertise to make a real difference in the lives of our students. I and many others got into teaching for this reason.

My resignation and letter caused a wave to move through the system. Other brave educators followed suit by speaking up, speaking out, and pushing for change. People listened, but just listening isn't how the change is going to happen. It's going to take numbers. It's going to take a concerted effort among thousands—maybe millions—of citizens ready to defend our country and the promise of our kids' futures by refusing to participate in destructive policy and discourse.

Everybody in this country has a very real and very serious stake in what happens to education in this country. The future of our economy, our representative democracy, our national security, and our place in the global community depends on it. Parents have a particularly vital stake in this battle because these are our children—children we entrust every day to a system that has turned its back on them and their teachers.

It's time to stand up, take it all back, and make it count.

NOTES

1. Public Education Department of New Mexico, *Promoting Effective Teaching in New Mexico*. Report to the State Legislative Finance Committee (#12-12), Santa Fe, NM (Nov. 15, 2012), 29-34 and 49-50, http://www.nmlegis.gov/lcs/lfc/lfcdocs/perfaudit/Public%20Education%20 Department%20–%20Promoting%20Effective%20Teaching%20in%20 New%20Mexico.pdf.

2. Kris Nielsen, "Bullying by Numbers: Value-Added Measures," *@ the Chalkface*, Oct. 29, 2013, http://atthechalkface.com/2013/10/29/ bullying-by-numbers-value-added-measures/.

VII. A LEARNING KILLER
Stunting Students

IMPRESSIONABLE MINDS
UNDER PRESSURE

Mary Calamia

It is easier to build strong children than to repair broken ones.

– Frederick Douglass

"I'm never going to school again. I just can't do it anymore." The little girl sat on my couch, her feet barely reaching the floor. Arms folded, her chin determined, she was adamant. It was time to move on from elementary school and enter—well, whatever phase of life an 8-year-old might think she is ready for. Her mother sat next to her, clearly struggling to hold back the tears. "*Don't cry,*" I silently pleaded, "*whatever you do, please don't cry.*" I am not sure who I was more concerned about—the mother or myself.

My yellow lab, Jack, bless his furry little heart, chose this exact moment to climb up on the couch and rest his head on the little girl's lap, trying to nuzzle some joy into this very sad child. She remained stoic despite his best efforts.

"Why don't you want to go to school anymore?" I asked.

"Because I'm stupid. I'm the stupidest kid in the class."

***   ***   ***

I am a licensed clinical social worker in New York State and have been providing psychotherapy services here since 1995. I work with children, adolescents, and adults from all socioeconomic backgrounds

representing more than twenty different school districts on Long Island. Coincidentally, almost half of my caseload consists of teachers,
purely by virtue of my referral sources.

Over the years, I've worked with children growing up in the worst
conditions—some living in drug infested neighborhoods with parents
who were struggling with addiction, legal problems, and poverty. I
also worked in a juvenile corrections facility with girls who came from
equally horrific backgrounds, resorting to the most unspeakable acts
just to survive. I've even worked with kids who had every reason to
hate school and refuse to attend, like bullying victims, children with
separation anxiety, and kids who struggled with academics and never
seemed to "get it right."

Nothing prepared me for the Common Core.

Until this point in my career, school has been the one stabilizing
force I could offer to my young clients as they work through their psychosocial stressors. Even students who hate school because they do not
perform well have strengths that we can capitalize on; I could always
rely on the schools to help them to identify those strengths and give
the students with whom I've worked with the tools they need to build
their confidence. We could figure it out together, school personnel and
therapist, devising a plan to get food to a student who lives in poverty
and solace to a child who was experiencing emotional problems. I have
also always teamed closely with the schools to intervene with bullying
situations…

…but what do we do when the educational system has become the
bully?

Something's Rotten in the State of New York

My Common Core experience began in the summer of 2012, when
my elementary school teachers began to report increased anxiety over
having to learn two entirely new curricula for Math and ELA. They
were distinctly distressed about this "new way of teaching," many to the
point where they were obsessively calculating their time to retirement.

I discovered that school districts across the board were completely
dismantling the current math and ELA curricula and replacing them

with something more scripted; they were implementing a "one-size-fits-all" way of teaching that was taking any imagination and innovation out of the hands of the teachers. My teachers were reporting they would be working with modules and worksheets from which they were to read word-for-word. They were concerned that they would no longer be teaching—they would merely be reciting someone else's words.

I listened to their concerns and adopted a wait-and-see attitude. After all, this couldn't be right, could it?

Then came the fall of 2012, when I started to receive an inordinate number of student referrals from several different school districts. Honors students in large numbers—mostly eighth-graders—were suddenly streaming into my practice. These adolescents were self-mutilating—cutting themselves with sharp objects and burning themselves with cigarettes. I have treated self-mutilators in the past, but a sudden and drastic increase in referrals like this—and not from any one school or school district—certainly raises some questions.

What was prompting this increase in self-mutilating behavior? Why now? Why was I hearing about this in middle school aged children, but not so much their high school counterparts? Curious, I took as many of these new clients as I could into my single-provider practice.

The evaluation interviews with each teenager were almost identical in that every single one of them cited school problems as the source of their distress. Typical problems of adolescence, like problems at home, peer problems, or relationship issues were all secondary. I repeatedly heard statements like: "I can't handle the pressure," or "It's just too much work" where I would ordinarily hear, "I hate my parents," or "Nobody understands me." Anomalies always tweak the little part of me that grew up wanting to be a detective.

Then I started to receive more calls referring elementary school students who were refusing to go to school. They said they felt "stupid," and school was "too hard." They were throwing tantrums, begging to stay home, upset even to the point of vomiting. I had closed my practice to younger children several years ago after moving to a smaller office with no dedicated room in which to do play therapy. Despite my limited office space, I was intrigued and took some of these children in.

None of the presenting problems described by the children and their parents were unusual. Kids have issues. I've been treating them for years. What was so jarring was the sheer volume of calls I was receiving. The calls kept coming in—too many for one provider to manage. I had to keep referring these children out, so I never got to hear all of their stories. I am still referring several children a week to other practitioners.

In addition to the increased distress in children, I observed that my adult clients who had children were also becoming more distressed. There was a distinct shift in the issues they wanted to discuss in therapy. They had begun talking about their children bringing home indecipherable homework and were concerned that they couldn't help their children to complete it. I was alarmed to hear that in some cases there were no textbooks for the parents to peruse and they had no idea what their children were learning. Weekday afternoons had become a nightmare, consumed by 3-4 hour homework assignments that were unintelligible and laden with typographical errors. One parent complained, "How do you know if it's a typo or if you're just too stupid to figure out the right answer?"

Bedtimes and mornings were also becoming times to dread. Children were crawling into bed with their parents, afraid to sleep alone after years of doing so without incident. I heard about children who had begun wetting the bed again. Bellyaches were part of the daily routine, both day and night. More often than not, I was hearing about children who just did not want to go to school, doing everything from faking illness to throwing tantrums just to avoid going.

These parents felt powerless. They had become the enforcers—dragging their unwilling children out the door in the morning and making them go to school, then fighting the afternoon battle over homework day in and day out. Parent/child conflict was on the rise and most parents had no idea why. They questioned their parenting skills, thinking they were the only ones having these problems.

As the first quarter progressed, my teachers were reporting intensified levels of anxiety and depression. Teachers who were close to terminating their therapy were now asking for additional sessions.

I had heard about the Common Core months earlier, but what I was experiencing in my practice caused me to take a look at exactly what the Common Core is. I became fully awakened to a new set of standards that all schools were to adhere to—standards that, we began to say, "set the bar so high, anyone can walk right under it"—unattainable standards that, ironically, will produce students who are ill-prepared for college and career because they're too complex and too simplistic all at once. Standards that are, in my opinion, making everyone sick.

The Stakes Are High

After the winter holiday break, everyone began talking about "The Tests." As the school year progressed and "The Tests" loomed, my patients began to report increased self-mutilating behaviors, insomnia, panic attacks, loss of appetite, depressed mood, and in one case, suicidal thoughts that resulted in a 2-week hospital stay for an adolescent. I learned that these tests were being used to score teachers on their abilities, but that they would not be aware of what was on them. The material was going to be far more difficult than what the children were learning; the majority of New York State's students would likely fail the ELA and math exams. New York State Education Department (NYSED) Commissioner John King himself predicted a significant drop in student proficiency—significant enough that he asked school administrators to take this into account when performing teacher evaluations.[1]

Ultimately, nearly 70 percent of all New York State students failed those exams.[2] Instead of excoriating a process by which only about 30 percent of all children could succeed, NYSED Education Commissioner John King asserted that the new assessments were an accurate way to measure performance, calling the results "a new starting point on a roadmap to future success." The negative results of this assessment are two-fold. First, the needs of the children, apparently, are barely a consideration; at the same time, the teachers are acutely aware that their livelihoods are a pinpoint on this "roadmap."

The Common Core and high-stakes testing create a hostile working environment for teachers, thus becoming a hostile learning environment for students. The level of anxiety I am seeing in teachers can only trickle down to the students. No matter who I speak to—teachers, children, parents—they are all describing a palpable level of tension in the schools. Since I testified to the New York State Assembly in October 2013, more and more parents and teachers have reached out to me expressing concerns and asking for referrals and recommendations. Some of them just want to tell their story and to know that someone is listening.

Reality Bites

Much of the workplace stress is the result of teacher ratings being tied to student performance on high-stakes exams. When I first learned about New York's Annual Professional Performance Review (APPR) and the Common Core high-stakes testing, my first thought was, "Who is going to rate the *parents?*" How can teachers' livelihoods be held hostage by student performance when there are so many variables outside of their control?

Each day I see children and teenagers who are exhausted, running from activity to activity, living on fast food, then texting, using social media, and playing games well into the wee hours of the morning on school nights. Most of the children I see are getting less than adequate sleep. Some are up late doing homework, but quite frankly most of them are just socializing.

We also have children taking cell phones right into the classrooms, "tweeting" and texting each other throughout the day. According to the Pew Research Internet Project, 64 percent of teens with cell phones have texted in class; 25 percent have made or received a call during class time.[3]

We have parents—yes, *parents*—who are sending their children text messages during school hours. I once knew a teenager who was accused of cheating when he responded to a text message from his mother during a midterm exam.

Let's add in the bullying and cyberbullying that torments and preoccupies millions of school children even to the point of suicide. Bullying has been a problem for generations, but cyberbullying has raised the negative impact of bullying to a new level. Bullying victims tend to internalize their experiences; the resulting depression and anxiety, coupled with increased absences, is likely to have a detrimental effect on their schoolwork. When a child experiences bullying in a real-life setting, the home can at least be a safe haven, but when a child experiences cyberbullying, they can be victimized anywhere, anytime, and often anonymously. It is a far more pervasive means of inflicting harm on a victim. Moreover, while the effects of bullying are bad, the effects of cyberbullying tend to be more damaging because this type of bullying is limitless in its scope and duration. Cyberbullies follow their victims everywhere they go and can reach them at any time, day or night; a victim's attention span, ability to focus, and school performance all suffer as a result.[4]

Add to all of that the interminable drug problem we face in this country. We have kids whose minds are numbed by drugs sitting in classrooms, studying, taking tests…tests that can mean life or death to a classroom teacher's career.

These are only some of the variables affecting student performance that are outside of the teachers' control. Yet we hold teachers accountable, substituting innovation and individualism with cookie-cutter standards, believing this will fix our schools.

Something's Fishy

We also cannot regulate basic biology. Young children are simply not wired to engage in the thought processes for which the Common Core calls. That would require a fully developed prefrontal cortex, a part of the brain that is not fully functional until early adulthood. The prefrontal cortex is responsible for critical thinking, rational decision-making, and abstract thinking—all things the Common Core demands prematurely.

The misconception that children can think in the abstract can take a bad turn. For instance, I used to teach a "Stranger Danger" class to 6- to 8-year-olds. I would first show a film that depicted various ruses perpetrators might use to lure a child. In each vignette, the perpetrator was depicted as a man. After viewing the film, I would facilitate a discussion with the children, asking questions like, "If you're walking down the street and a man drives up to you and says your mom is in the hospital, and he is going to take you to see her, do you get into the car?" They all would scream, "No!" I would do this with several scenarios. After a short time, I would switch genders: "So if a woman drove up and said…"

Every single child I ever saw in my "Stranger Danger" class said they would get in the car if a woman asked them to do so. They could not transfer the knowledge they learned from the vignettes in the film to parallel situations with a gender twist. Children that young are literal thinkers and are simply not capable of making this type of leap.

I've discovered that I have something in common with Albert Einstein—we both like fish analogies. Einstein reputedly said, "Everybody is a genius. But if you judge a fish by its ability to climb a tree, it will live its whole life believing that it is stupid." Mr. Einstein? Allow me to introduce you to Common Core.

Asking a young child to engage in critical thinking is like asking a fish to fly. My little "fishes" come into my office blaming themselves for not sprouting wings. If we adhere to Common Core standards, then we are demanding that children do something they simply cannot. Without the ability to think rationally, a child will internalize their inability to perform as personal failure; this outcome has potential long-term—even lifelong—effects.

We teach children to succeed—even pressure them to do so—and then give them pre-assessments on material they have never seen before and tell them that it's okay to fail. Children are not equipped to resolve the mixed message this presents. Einstein himself might well have been undone at an early age by having to confront such conundrums.

In the Spring of 2013, a 6-year-old who encountered a multiplication sign on a first-grade standardized math assessment asked the teacher what it was. The teacher was not allowed to help him and told him just to do his best to answer. From that point on, the student's test performance went downhill. Not only couldn't the student shake off the unfamiliar symbol, he also couldn't believe his beloved teacher wouldn't help him.

Equally troubling from a developmental standpoint is that the Common Core requires children to read informational texts that are published by a handful of corporations and government agencies. What this amounts to, essentially, is a public-private partnership taking advantage of a captive audience that has limited ability to discriminate between biased, agenda-laden "information" and facts presented objectively and in full context. Lacking any filter to distinguish good information from bad, children will readily absorb whatever text is put in front of them as gospel. So, for example, when we give children a textbook that explains the Second Amendment in terms such as, "The people have a right to keep and bear arms in a state militia," they will look no further for clarification.

EngageNY.org is a website maintained by NYSED. It hosts a Common Core-aligned, module-based curriculum that is offered at no cost to all New York State school districts. The Grade 3 Module includes a "close reading" of *Nasreen's Secret School*, a story about a young girl in Afghanistan whose father is abducted by the Taliban and whose mother disappears to look for him, never to return.[5] After reading the story, my friend's 8-year-old son could no longer sleep alone and begged his parents to homeschool him. Another child read this same book and became extremely anxious, complaining of stomach aches and "feeling scared," particularly at bedtime. She eventually disclosed that she was afraid her mother was going to leave her and never come back. This book is supposed to teach children how to identify a story's message, how to describe a story's characters, and how a character's actions contribute to the story's plot. Is it really necessary to use literature depicting a child who is stripped of her right to an education and loses both of her parents as her country is invaded by "soldiers" just to teach these skills? I suspect there is less disturbing literature that could easily illustrate these very same skills without triggering anxiety.

Another story, part of EngageNY's Grade 7 Module, is *A Long Walk to Water*.[6] I have heard from a number of parents about 12-year-olds who are becoming extremely upset by the book's depiction of the main character's uncle being tied to a tree and shot dead (one parent said her son kept repeating over and over, "Mom…they shot him *three*

times…"). Others have openly wept in class while reading how the protagonist's 11-year-old friend is dragged off by a lion to a bloody death.
This book is used to teach concepts like how "individuals survive in
challenging environments" and "how writers use narrative techniques
to convey characters' perspectives." I learned these concepts in school
when I was growing up. I don't recall ever reading anything that had
me wanting to sleep in my parents' bed in junior high.

We are asking children to write critically, using emotionally charged
language to "persuade" rather than inform. Lacking a functional prefrontal cortex, a child will tap into their limbic system, a set of primitive brain structures involved in basic human emotions, fear and anger
being foremost. So when we are asking young children to use emotionally charged language, we are actually asking them to fuel their per-
suasiveness with fear and anger. They are not capable of the judgment
required to temper this with reason and logic.

So we have abandoned innovative teaching and instead "teach to
the tests," the dreaded exams that had students, parents, and teachers in a complete anxiety state last spring. These tests do not measure
learning—what they really measure is endurance and resilience. Only
a child who can sit and focus for 90 minutes can succeed. The child
who can bounce back after one grueling day of testing and do it all over
again the next day has an even better chance.

"Prove It!"

I am often asked to provide research to back up my assertions that
the Common Core is causing this increase in maladaptive behaviors.
I have two stock responses, depending on who is asking the question:

1. I never claim to have completed any research. I am only reporting *observations*. To design and implement a study, gather and
   analyze data, and then report research findings will take a great
   deal of money and time; and

2. Show me the research that proves Common Core works, and
   then we can talk about researching *my* hypothesis.

No, I do not know of any formal studies that connect these symptoms directly to the Common Core, but I do not think we need to sacrifice an entire generation of children just so we can find a correlation.

A recent Cornell University study revealed that students who were overly stressed while preparing for high-stakes exams performed worse than students who experienced less stress during the test preparation period. Their prefrontal cortexes—the same parts of the brain that we are prematurely trying to engage in our youngsters—were under-performing.[7]

Why do the "reformers" of our educational system continue to insist that inappropriate standards and undue stress will make children "college and career ready" when we have created college and career ready children for two centuries without the intervention of Bill Gates, Pearson, the Council of Chief State School Officers, and the National Governors Association? It doesn't take a genius to see that a system that believes all children can learn the same thing in the same way and at the same pace merits intense scrutiny.

Children will learn if they are given the opportunity to do so. Our country became an indisputable world power, with men and women who studied in one-room schoolhouses leading the way. It does not take a great deal of technology or corporate and government involvement for kids to succeed. We need to rethink the Common Core and the associated high-stakes testing and get back to the business of educating our children in a safe, healthy, and productive manner.

Understand why those of us in the trenches fight this fight day and night, working closely with parents, children, grassroots organizers, and legislators; learn why we organize forums, rallies, letter-writing drives, and phone banks. This is why we eat dinner no earlier than 10:00PM, if at all, and usually in front of a computer or with a phone in one hand. Now you know why "lunch" is sometimes just a spoonful of peanut butter and why we managed to work the words "Common Core" into every discussion we have, from close friends and family to the checkout clerk at the local supermarket.

We do this because Common Core is affecting real people, whose financial, educational, and emotional futures hang in the balance. Please get to know them as I have. Learn who they are and why this has become my passion. Even the smallest whisper is a voice, and they all deserve to be heard.

These are the faces of the Common Core:

…an entire third-grade class that spent the rest of the day sobbing after just one testing session,

…the second-grader who witnessed this event and, when she herself entered the third grade, was so afraid of the tests she had to be medicated just to go to school,

…a 6-year-old who came home crying because in September of the first grade, she did not know what a vertex was,

…two 8-year-olds who opted out of the 2013 ELA exam and were publicly denied cookies when the teacher gave them to the rest of her third grade class,

…the teacher who, under duress, felt compelled to shame two little boys in such a manner,

…a little girl who once loved everything about school and is now complaining of bellyaches and "homesickness,"

…a 10-year-old boy who says that Common Core is "sucking the fun out of school"; he has become discouraged because it's no longer "fun to learn,"

…a 9-year-old who says, "Common Core is the first worst thing to come into a child['s] life—especially for kids like me who have dyslexia and dysgraphia."

…a once very happy 6-year-old who, after only a month in the first grade, buckled at the knees and fell to the ground crying at the mere mention of starting the day's homework,

…an eighth-grade honors math student who, within the first month of taking Common Core algebra, started to call herself "dumb" and began self-mutilating. This once-confident young lady now constantly second-guesses herself and hates math,

…a 6-year-old boy who is scratching the skin off of his face, drawing blood every time he does his homework.

…a teenager who carved the word "stupid" into her wrist after failing the state exams.

…or the 13-year-old who will never realize her lifelong dream of studying engineering at MIT; her seventh-grade ELA exam score resulted in remedial course requirements, and it is now impossible for her to take AP math and science classes when she gets to high school.

*** *** ***

...and of course, my new little friend who is sitting with my 100-pound Labrador retriever on her lap, waiting for me to respond to her assertion that she is "the stupidest kid in the class."

I let her statement linger so I can gather my thoughts.

Here in New York, those in the anti-Common Core contingent refer to themselves as "warriors." But here we have these children—each and every day putting one foot in front of the other and going to school, facing their demons head on. Whether they feel stupid, inferior, anxious, depressed, alone, or angry, they go to the very place that validates those feelings because they are told that it's their job. They show up and keep trying despite the tears and the anguish, despite the fear of failure and the fear of ridicule, despite the fact that it feels pointless because they are certain they will never succeed. They show up despite feeling powerless and despite seeing no relief in sight. No folks, we are not the warriors. These children—they are the true warriors.

My little patient begins to rub Jack's ears. Canine therapy. The girl shows the slightest hint of a smile.

"No," I tell my newest little friend. "You're not stupid at all. You're just the bravest little girl I know.

NOTES

1. See New York State Education Department (NYSED), "State Education Department Releases Grades 3-8 Assessment Results." Press release, Aug. 7, 2013, http://www.oms.nysed.gov/press/grades-3-8-assessment-results-2013.html; John B. King, Jr., "Message from Commissioner King," NYSED, *News and Notes*, Mar. 2013, http://myemail.constantcontact.com/

Commissioner-King-on-Common-Core-Implementation.html?soid=1110 847617454&aid=h1uoXxbqV34; and Ben Chapman and Corinne Lestch, "State Test Scores Expected to Drop Dramatically from Tougher Reading and Math Exams," *Daily News*, Aug. 2, 2013, http://www.nydailynews.com/new-york/state-test-scores-expected-drop-dramatically-article-1.1416520.

2. NYSED, "Grades 3-8 Assessment Results."

3. Amanda Lenhart, Rich Ling, Scott Campbell, and Kristen Purcell, "Teens and Mobile Phones," Pew Research Internet Project, Apr. 20, 2010, http://www.pewinternet.org/2010/04/20/teens-and-mobile-phones/.

4. Christine Suniti Bhat, "Cyber Bullying: Overview and Strategies for School Counsellors, Guidance Officers, and All School Personnel," *Australian Journal of Guidance & Counselling* 18, no. 1 (2008), 53–66. See also Sheri Bauman, "Cyberbullying: A Virtual Menace." Paper presented at the National Coalition against Bullying National Conference, Melbourne, Australia, Nov. 2-4, 2007, http://www.academia.edu/3409628/Cyberbullying_a_virtual_menace/.

5. The reader can download this module by clicking on "Downloadable Resources" at EngageNY.org, http://www.engageny.org/resource/grade-3-ela-module-1-unit-1-lesson-6/.

6. This module, too, can be downloaded at EngageNY.org by clicking on "Module 1 Unit 2" under "Downloadable Resources" at http://www.engageny.org/resource/grade-7-ela-module-1/.

7. C. Liston, B. S. McEwen, and B. J. Casey, "Psychosocial Stress Reversibly Disrupts Prefrontal Processing and Attentional Control." *Proceedings of the National Academy of Sciences of the United States of America (PNAS) 2009* 106, no. 3 912-917. Published ahead of print, Jan. 12, 2009, doi:10.1073/pnas.0807041106 and online at http://www.pnas.org/content/106/3/912.full.pdf+html.

COMMON CORE HITS HOME

I wasn't looking for a cause. I definitely was not looking for a fight. My sons, David and Scott, were never brilliant students. I'd like to make that clear right away. They were typical boys; average students, full of energy and laughter. They played soccer, took karate, joined clubs, and participated in chorus and orchestra. Their favorite subjects were science and social studies, and they would often come home from school eager to share with me what they learned in those subjects.

In September 2010, David entered the fifth grade, his first year in a Long Island middle school, while Scott entered fourth grade, his last year as an elementary school student. It was an exciting year for both boys. David showed signs of maturity; at ten years old, he was proud to have a locker and change classes. Scott was happy to be in the graduating class in his school. The year was off to a great start. Things couldn't have been any better as far as we knew.

I was a working mother. Every day, David would take the bus, and Scott would be dropped off at a friend's house. Our routine worked well, and neither boy gave me a hard time. Absences were rare and, because a day home from school meant a day off from work for me, they were reserved for true illnesses. I made sure that my children ate, exercised, slept well, and had annual physicals. I encouraged family time, and friendships. I was a member of the PTA every year and signed up to volunteer at events throughout the year. By any standard, we had it good.

The Downward Spiral

As the school year progressed, I began to notice that schoolwork was intensifying. David was bringing home multiplication worksheets every night in addition to workbook and/or textbook pages in math. The worksheets were double-sided, sometimes with the same facts repeated, other times with mixed facts, always in a small font so that the page was packed with numbers. Test packets were also assigned for both boys—multiple-choice text packets in English language arts (ELA) as well as math from years past. The ELA packets were reading assignments followed by multiple-choice questions, and the math seemed to be an array of topics, all multiple-choice. Often I'd see a line or two in which the students had to explain "how" they got their answer. Although I had never seen homework like this before, I naïvely assumed it was because the packets covered what was being taught in class. As it turned out, they did not; instead the packets were just random test questions that did not touch upon most, if any, of the work the students were doing in class. I noticed David getting stressed out with the math, and both boys were asking me for help more than ever. Many times, I was confused by the ambiguous questions and answer choices in the packets. Often, we would sit up past ten o' clock before I would close the books, telling my boys they had done their best and that it was now time for bed.

I was in constant contact with the teachers. If extra help was available, my boys were there. Still, I was perplexed at why the work seemed so different from what I would have expected to see. Why were my boys being asked to explain how an answer in math was achieved when the work was right there for the teacher to see? Why were their teachers asking them to provide evidence when writing a paragraph about a reading assignment? In the past, writing the correct answer, or giving a meaningful perspective was evidence that a student comprehended the assignment. Many times, the boys would tell me they "just knew" what they wrote was right because it was. What was being asked seemed to be beyond their comprehension. The homework was certainly causing my boys stress, but I supported the teachers and pushed my boys to do what was required.

That spring, David began having stomachaches, often claiming he was too sick to go to school. Because he had always had very good attendance, never taking "free" days off, I kept him home, taking days off from work to take him to the pediatrician and care for him. However, when his feeling sick became a weekly occurrence, it raised a red flag for me. I wondered if he was trying to avoid something, and I spoke to him about it. I asked if anyone was bullying him or making him upset. He said no. I asked if anyone was mean to him, if something had happened to make him not want to go to school. Again, the answer was, "No."

I thought David was feeling his oats; maybe he just liked staying home with me. I spoke to the principal, assistant principal, his teachers, and the pediatrician. He had a clean bill of health, and with a wink, I would often be told he had a case of spring fever or school-itis. While everyone at school seemed to want the best for David, he began to think his teachers "hated" him. I couldn't imagine why he felt that way since they had not given me that impression. Yet David seemed convinced. My outgoing 10-year-old was becoming introverted. He was increasingly discouraged and unhappy with anything school-related at all. I obtained a list of therapists from the school psychologist and decided if David didn't "snap out of it," I'd start making phone calls.

Anxiety Whack-a-Mole

I can't remember the first time David had an anxiety attack. There were so many that followed that they all seem to meld together in my memory. What I do remember is my child, dressed for school, just minutes before the bus arrived, crumbling. He would fall to the floor, hyperventilating, sobbing, begging me to help him. Because I wasn't prepared for this—like so many other parents, I had another child to get off to school, a job to get to—my fear, frustration, and anger would overcome me. Here was my child, my little boy begging for help, and all I could do was contradict him. I would say things like, "Every kid is going to school, why can't you? You are no different than anyone else!" or "I have to get to work. You don't have a choice!" Thankfully,

Scott appeared unaffected. He would go to school every day without complaint, and would often get off the bus and ask if David had made it to school at all.

After a number of these episodes, I contacted a social worker who was able to see David every Friday at 5 p.m. I would rush home from work to get him to his appointment on time. Scott and I would wait for him for an hour. Because of a confidentiality agreement, I was not aware of anything specific said in the social worker's office. I did receive feedback, though; in the social worker's professional opinion, David seemed, for the most part, to be a well-adjusted 10-year-old. What never occurred to me until well after the appointments had ended was that on a Friday at five o' clock in the afternoon David was free. He had the weekend ahead of him, and looked forward to dinner with his family and plans with friends. The threat of school was lifted.

The school year finished, and we all sighed a huge breath of relief. The summer was fun and wonderful, full of good times, going to the beach, and trips to visit family and friends. Both boys were happy and active, often swimming and running around until dusk. It was truly a great feeling, knowing that whatever David was going through seemed to be over. We stopped seeing the social worker.

In August, we received the 2011 teacher assignments. Both boys would now be in middle school. I looked forward to them being to-gether in the same building, as David would be a good role model for his younger brother. When I opened the envelope for David, I realized the same teacher who had taught him in ELA and social studies the previous year had been assigned to him again. When I told him, his reaction surprised me. Three weeks before the first day of school, on a beautiful August day, my soon-to-be sixth-grade son fell onto his bed and began to cry. He claimed this particular teacher hated him, that he felt stupid in her class. I couldn't believe it. This teacher may have been strict, but from what I saw, she was kind and patient, and always had an open line of communication with me. I called the school to be sure they were aware of David's feelings, not because I agreed with him but because I didn't understand why his reaction was so negative. I was as-sured that he would be o.k. this year, and whatever it was he was feeling would be dealt with accordingly. The year began, and for the first few months, it seemed as if things were back to "normal."

Scott had a wonderful homeroom teacher that year. She was organized and very clear in her expectations. Scott thrived in her class. However, his math teacher seemed to think he was very far behind. Again, the test packets made their appearance in the form of homework, and the multiplication worksheets were a nightly assignment in addition to workbook and textbook pages. Around the holiday season, I began to see changes in Scott similar to those that I'd already seen in David during homework. I would try to have the boys put their homework away by ten o' clock, just as I had in years past, but that upset Scott. He would also get frustrated when I helped him with math because I couldn't do it the way his teacher did, yet he couldn't show me how she did it at all. After many phone calls and meetings, I was encouraged to have Scott tested for Attention Deficit Hyperactivity Disorder, or ADHD, by a school recommended psychiatrist.

The day of Scott's appointment, I took off from work. It was a beautiful, unseasonably warm spring day, and I told him we would get lunch when we were done. David had claimed he wasn't feeling well that day and stayed home. I was keeping a close eye on him because of the previous year's anxiety and absences, but when he fell asleep in the car on our way to the appointment, I felt he was being honest. Scott met with the psychiatrist while David and I waited. When it was time for me to meet with the doctor, I wasn't entirely surprised to learn Scott had been diagnosed with Attention Deficit Hyperactivity Disorder (ADHD). He had always had nervous energy, and I noticed him often fidgeting. Now that it was interfering with school, I was actually a little relieved to think that an individualized education program (IEP) would help as the work intensified. Scott's teacher was able to provide the school psychologist with her recommendations, and my feedback and observations were respectfully taken into account. Together, we were able to create goals for Scott as well as a plan on how to obtain the goal, including both criteria and expectations.

I attended my first Committee on Special Education (CSE) committee meeting soon after. Present at this meeting were the district superintendent for special education, Scott's classroom teacher, a special education teacher, a parent advocate, the school psychologist, and me. It was a little overwhelming to walk into a room of people who were about to make some pretty serious decisions about Scott's education. They were all experienced and had a lot more knowledge than me. I worried that I might not know what to ask—or what to accept. What did my son deserve? The members of the team quickly reassured me that they were on my side, on Scott's side, and truly wanted what was best for him. They knew him, and respected him. He was more than an IQ number, or a diagnosis. My mind was put at ease.

I was very pleased with the modifications put in place, such as extra time on tests, fewer questions on homework, redirection when needed, and strengthening of social skills. Scott had many friends, so the social skill goal was meant to give him confidence in the classroom for things like raising his hand and answering questions. It was a relief when his homework resumed being challenging but was no longer frustrating. For a while, things went back to being good; our family dynamic returned…until David fell apart again.

This time, the anxiety attacks were more frequent. I would tell David there were only three months left in the year and that all kids have bad days. I tried encouraging him. I tried punishing him. I tried rewarding him for the good days and eliciting why he felt so bad on the bad ones—all to no avail. I'm not sure what the experts would say, but when your 11-year-old son is squeezing your arms so tightly that he leaves marks, and begs through sobs to stay home, all the advice in the world means nothing.

One morning in particular, I was completely blindsided. It was a cold, rainy April morning. Scott made it onto the bus, and as I called for David to hurry up, he began crying. I lost my patience. I had already missed so many days of work to be home when David was "sick." I made him get in the car. We drove to the front of the school, where all the parents pulled in, dropped off, and pulled out as if in an assembly line. I stopped the car, but David wouldn't get out. I jumped out and opened his door as the cars began to pull around me. He refused to budge. Running late, and now growing more worried, I ran inside and asked for the school psychologist to meet me outside. Instead, the assistant principal and guidance counselor followed me out. My cell phone rang; it was a friend who was in the parking lot dropping off her son, asking if everything was o.k. With the assistant principal sitting in the backseat of my car and the guidance counselor nearby, I began to cry. I was soaked, late for work, and weeping in front of the school as I told my friend what was happening. She offered to help, but there *was* no "help." There was nothing that could be done, nothing anyone could say.

I hung up the phone and looked at the assistant principal's face as he got out of my car. It was a look of disappointment, his head shaking as he met my eyes. "What?" I asked, not believing that this man of authority couldn't coax my son into the building. "I'm very sorry, but he's not coming. He was very polite, but he won't come in. At this point, we will ask that you take him to an emergency room to be evaluated, and, unfortunately, he will not be allowed back into school without a doctor's note from the ER." My first instinct was to laugh. I'm sure if I had, the assistant principal probably would've suggested that I get an evaluation as well. The absurdity of the whole situation was just too much. How can an 11-year-old boy—how can my eleven year old boy need a psychiatric evaluation in order to be allowed into the school? He had not been harming himself, nor had he even threatened to harm himself or anyone else. He was upset, visibly, but no one knew why.

I admit that I was angry that the assistant principal couldn't force David to go to school. I was angry that the guidance counselor stood by idly, and I was angry that the school psychologist didn't have the time to come help. Mostly though, I was angry that my son was falling apart before my eyes and that I felt completely helpless in the face of that fact.

When I returned to work the following day, I was asked how my son was. I was running out of answers—or, more accurately, out of excuses. I was told that I should leave David home alone on days when he was sick so as to not miss any more work. I remember thinking, "Sure, I'll leave my crying child home alone," as if that was an option. I was so afraid that David's anxiety would lead to depression. I monitored him carefully, looking for signs, for triggers, and, most of all, for answers. Everything led straight back to school. At home, socially, and in public, he was happy, joking, energetic, and "himself." On school days, he was sad, crying, lethargic, and a shadow of himself.

I cautiously asked questions: "Is someone bullying you?" "Is someone threatening you?" "Is someone being mean?" And the most ominous, "Is someone touching you?" The answer to each of these questions was always the same: "No." What then? What could possibly cause my bright, happy, energetic child to become sad, lonely, and lethargic?

I found another social worker through the school, Laurie, who seemed more personable than the last. Every week, we would drive a half an hour to her office. David would go in alone some days; other days I would join; sometimes Scott would go in, too. The boys liked Laurie. She was easy to speak to and would engage in some really good conversations on their level. Of course, she wanted to see us all together to see how we interacted. It felt as though we were under a microscope, but I knew we had nothing to hide, and it was worth it to me to try to obtain help for my child. The only time David ever displayed his negative behavior was before school, so I knew Laurie was looking for anything that might help us in those one-hour visits. I would also speak to her on the phone. Twice, she insisted she couldn't find anything wrong with David, and she would not be able to continue with his therapy. Twice, I begged her not to let him go, pleading, "If you saw him in the mornings, if you saw how bad it is, you would understand!"

I resorted to taking video and pictures to prove to Laurie that David needed help. Yet, within hours, I would delete the evidence. Most moms have pictures of their children smiling, thriving, happy. I couldn't bear to look at and relive my son screaming, crying, and begging me to keep him home. I was often in contact with the school. I knew all of his teachers. I knew all of his friends and their parents. I knew I had to be missing something. I would ask Scott if he knew anything, saw anything, or if David had told him anything—again, to no avail.

One Monday morning in early spring, David had an anxiety attack. The windows were open. I was so afraid the neighbors would start to question what was happening. I had become disheartened with his behavior and the lack of response to therapy. I finally threw in the towel; I allowed him to stay home. It was too much of a battle to do otherwise, and I was losing.

The following day was a repeat. By nine o'clock that morning, I was too exhausted to try anymore. I wracked my brain, I begged God for an answer. I reached out to close friends and family for support, calling to give them the daily rundown, getting the same advice as the day before.

On Wednesday, I was able to get David and Scott both on the bus. I felt a bit of relief, yet I knew that one good day was just that: one good day. There was still no guarantee that I wouldn't receive a call from the nurse or that homework would be drama free. Although, over time, my kids had begun to do their homework independently, there were nights where David's work would be particularly frustrating.

I went to work, feeling ashamed that I'd not been there in two days. I completed everything without a word, including Monday and Tuesday's pile of paperwork. By afternoon I had caught up and sat down at my desk, my cell phone always in hand, just in case. My supervisor came into my office, which was unusual at that time of day. Her own supervisor was in the other room, she said, and had requested to see me. I walked in and sat down. "I want you to know that everything you do here is wonderful," her speech began, "You really have done so much for this office, and you're always willing to help out. But recently it has been brought up that we need to make cuts, and looking over all our employees…" I walked out of the office numb that day. I had never been fired before. Technically they referred to it as being "laid off," as if that would ease the shock. The fact remained—I had lost my job. My constant emergencies at home and the absences they necessitated had added up to this result.

In an attempt to think positively about the situation, I looked at it as a way to be there more for David and Scott. Unemployment was only a fraction of what I had been making, but it would do while I focused my energy and attention on David. My goal was to look for work in the summer, maybe something part-time. I knew that at a new job, I couldn't risk not being able to show up consistently.

The school year ended with a few more meltdowns. Some would end with David falling asleep, exhausting himself of all energy before ten o'clock in the morning. Other times, I wouldn't allow it to go that far, and I would take David for a drive. We'd go to a park or a store or just anywhere to remove ourselves physically from the situation.

I made frequent pediatrician appointments, as I wanted to be sure the behavior wasn't brought on by something physiological. At my request, Laurie referred us to a psychiatrist. I believed that if the anxiety attacks and school refusal were due to an underlying or emerging mental illness, a psychiatric professional may be able to diagnose it. Instead, he prescribed David Prozac and Xanax after asking both him and me a few questions. Although I filled the prescriptions, David never took them. I didn't feel confident that the doctor really knew what David needed. Besides, it was June and summer vacation had previously cured sadness and anxiety on it own.

The Eye of the Storm

The first couple of months of the 2012-2013 school year remained event free. In October Superstorm Sandy hit, leaving the school with no heat or lights for a week and a half and our neighborhood without power for over two weeks. It was all very exciting for the boys and gave them an unplanned break from school. With Thanksgiving and holiday breaks following quickly after, it made for an easy autumn into winter. Of course, the missed days from the storm had to be made up, so winter break was cancelled, and spring break was shortened. Still, the year flowed pretty well.

The boys were rarely home sick. Calls home from the nurse were even more rare. Homework was becoming more difficult for Scott, but he really pushed himself, and it paid off. He had a wonderful team of teachers. With his IEP still in place, he was showing his true colors. Many of his teachers would tell me how he was coming out of his shell, how artistic he was or funny—or just how proud they were of him. David seemed to have the most difficulty in social studies that year. In seventh grade, he was learning about early American history. It was a subject he really liked, yet the textbook seemed not to cover all the information; he had a 2-inch binder full of papers and booklets to supplement what he was learning.

Surprisingly, David was able to do his math homework mostly independently, except for the written responses, which had become more and more prevalent. His ELA homework was often comprised of multiple-choice questions that he had to answer after reading a passage. Some of the stories were strange in my opinion, yet I never thought to question anything. I did, however make notes about the answer choices. Many times, there seemed to be no right answer. The questions required one to make inferences in order to answer at all because the information being asked about simply wasn't there. I noticed very similar ELA homework coming home with Scott, but he was so easygoing that he didn't seem bothered by the ambiguity.

The Not-So-Merry-Go-Round

As spring approached, my husband and I discussed renovating our house to make more space for everyone. The boys were maturing and happy to be involved in the dialogue. They provided a lot of input. However, everything took a back seat when David had his first anxiety attack in almost a year. I didn't want anything to interfere with my taking care of him, nor did I want things to get as bad as they had in the past. I tried to call Laurie, who I had finally agreed David no longer needed to see because he had shown no signs of anxiety in the fall. However, she no longer worked for the office where we'd visited her, so I went online to find someone else who could help.

After three hours, I narrowed my search results and presented them to David. I wanted him to feel like he was in charge, and to be comfortable with his choice. We found a male therapist named Harold, just a few blocks from our house. Once again, each week we'd show up for an hour-long appointment. David would go in behind a closed door, and I would sit in the waiting room, wondering if the answers would be revealed this time. They weren't. One week, David walked out with a numbered list. He and his therapist had come up with affirmations to read when an anxiety attack loomed. Every one of them was related to school and teachers—ten reminders in total, authored by David, written out by Harold. We kept them in David's bedside drawer and referred to them almost daily.

That spring I was called in to my boys' school for a team meeting—all of David's teachers minus social studies. His guidance counselor, school psychologist, and I sat around a table in a conference room. One by one each person spoke. David's grades were faltering, and his absences were having a negative impact. I knew this to be true, but—just as I had in the past—I felt helpless and incompetent sitting there hearing it. About halfway through I stopped one of the teachers mid-sentence. "If I could," I stammered, "If I could just interrupt, and I am sorry because I don't want to sound like I am making excuses, but David is in therapy because something is wrong. And I don't know what it is, but there's something about school, and I know it's not any of you…" I looked around, my eyes welling up with tears. A few teachers diverted their glances, a few looked sincerely concerned, and one—his science teacher, who I know David adored—choked up. "Oh, I am so sorry, I had no idea," she said.

With my permission, the psychologist took over, and our meeting went from a discussion about grades to me crying, asking them if they knew what was happening. The door opened and the social studies teacher at last walked in, abruptly. She sat down next to me and proceeded to talk. The guidance counselor explained the situation I had just revealed to the rest of the team, to which the teacher replied, "Right, but he still needs to make up his work. I have here…" I tuned her out as she talked about the dates for which homework was missing, and what assignments needed to be made up. I made eye contact several times with the science teacher, who, after the meeting, told me not to worry about the assignments, that she would work closely with David, and make sure she kept communication lines open.

By now, the anxiety attacks were again routine. They came on without much rhyme or reason—most frequently on Mondays, but not always. I had gone back to school during the day, and was able to miss a few classes without any effect on my grades, which was a relief. Our discussion about renovating the house had now become a discussion about moving to another district. I felt David might benefit from a fresh start, and Scott was just so easygoing and happy all the time, he'd do great anywhere. We began house hunting, and it wasn't long before we found the home of our dreams, in a blue ribbon school district. We had family in the neighborhood, so the boys knew lots of the kids there. It seemed like a dream come true.

I believe the excitement kept David optimistic as the school year came to a close without much ado. We moved in the summer of 2013. Scott was able to stay in touch with many of his friends, and David kept in touch with his one best friend. The boys did all the typical fun activities: swimming, skateboarding, going to the beach, bike riding. As the school year approached, both boys looked forward to going clothes shopping, getting haircuts, and buying supplies.

Orientation was scheduled for late August. I was so concerned with David's past behavior and didn't want to pull any surprises on anyone at his new school. So I made sure the staff there were aware. Scott met with his guidance counselor one-on-one. I knew he'd be fine; he'd come such a long way from the shy child he'd once been. I had already visited the special education office with his IEP, and everything was in place.

On orientation day, the boys received their schedules, and based on their state assessment scores for the previous year, the school determined that both of them would need academic intervention services (AIS) for both math and ELA. I wasn't pleased, but I understood that a high percentage of students were in need of AIS, based on what I'd heard in passing, maybe on the news. Life had become so topsy-turvy that it escapes me now, how I knew anything then.

Because of the two AIS classes, and one resource-room class (where he was supposed to get organized and receive assistance with understanding the day's assignments), Scott had no room in his schedule for physical education (PE) during the regular school hours. Instead, he would have to go to school a half-hour earlier every other day for PE. Again, I wasn't thrilled, but we took the schedules home that day, and I must have told the boys at least twenty more times that they were going to have a great year.

The first and second days came and went as expected. There were a lot of stories. No one got lost. They saw kids they knew. Some teachers seemed nice. Others seemed mean. Overall, I was just relieved that they both seemed happy.

Then came day three.

Scott had PE but missed the early bus, as this schedule was still new. It really was early. I drove him to school, and he was able to get to class on time. The next early morning came, and despite trying to get Scott to hurry up and make the bus, he just couldn't seem to get it together. I drove him. Halfway to the school, he realized he had forgotten something important. I turned around to go home to get it. By the time we got back to the school, PE was about halfway over, but I encouraged him to get in and have a great day. This unassuming episode would turn out to be a telltale sign.

David was really making me proud. He was up, dressed, and ready on time every morning. He walked himself to the bus stop without a complaint, then came home and did his homework daily. I checked his work when he was done and was grateful that he didn't need help, as it looked really difficult. Scott on the other hand, was frustrated every night. The math was really stressful on both of us, and the other assignments seemed quite tedious. I encouraged and praised Scott for getting his work done, but I was exhausted just helping him.

The second week of school, Scott had an assignment that had to be completed with an adult. He was to interview someone about their job, their education, and whether or not they liked what they did. Scott had to decide if the job looked like something he might pursue. There were quite a few questions, and I thought it was strange but sort of fun for a change. Scott chose to interview his dad, and as they talked, they laughed at some of the answers. I reminded my husband that the teacher would be looking at the completed assignment, so he should keep the humor to a minimum. Deep inside, that assignment just didn't sit right with me. I wondered why it was such an in-depth interview, why so much detail was needed about personal matters. Still, I was happy to see Scott completing it enthusiastically.

By the third week, Scott was either late or missing PE altogether. He was "tired" and claimed the gym was cold, that he just wanted to sleep. I couldn't blame him, as the extended day was a long one, with no "specials," such as music or art, to break up the monotony. Nightly, he would come home and pass out on the couch, needing to be woken for dinner, homework, and a shower. He had never been big on napping, so this was something new. It was upsetting to me that he didn't have free time after school, but I figured he needed to sleep. I hoped that once he was fully adjusted to his new schedule, things would change.

The fourth week, Scott got sick and missed a few days of school. His work was sent home, and we completed as much of it as possible. When he returned, he was still behind, and I was concerned. I asked if we could have a team meeting. Scott had never fallen so far behind, and I wanted to see if there was something we could do. My husband and I sat down with all of Scott's teachers, each of whom seemed genuinely kind and concerned. At the end of the meeting, we called Scott in, and he walked over to me and gave me a hug first thing. It made an impact on his teachers, and I laughed because it didn't occur to me that a 12-year-old boy might not normally be so openly affectionate toward his mother. Scott was loved, and he was loving, and that showed. Scott realized we were all there for him. We wanted him to succeed, and in order for that to happen, we all had to work together. Scott agreed and said he would try to get all his work done on time.

About a week later, the school district scheduled a CSE meeting. We already had a great IEP in place from our old district. It seemed the meeting was just protocol to ensure things were still where they needed to be, so I intended to go. Scott had had a few rough mornings up to this point, but I chalked it up to simple adjustment. He'd always been o.k.; he would naturally be o.k. again.

The morning of the CSE, my husband and I woke the boys, but only David got up and off to school. Scott was lethargic. I hoped he wasn't sick. He had no fever, but he lay in bed, limp. I shook the bed a few times and called his name sternly before he would awake.

What happened next was something I had never dreamed possible. Scott began to cry, soft tears at first, then full-blown crying. It took both my husband and I to get him dressed and calmed down. I convinced him we just were going to the school for a meeting, and if he really didn't feel well, we'd take him home afterwards, but that for now he had to come with us. My husband was finally able to coax him into the car, and I snuck his backpack into the trunk.

I have to digress here. At the time I felt numb, yet I realize now that I was crying and shaking. I remember thinking over and over that Scott was my good kid! I don't have a favorite child, but it was undeniable that he had been the easy one. What was I doing wrong, I asked myself. Why was this happening to both of my kids? What was happening? I was beside myself, and I wondered if I had done something to make my boys feel this way. My mind raced as I drove to the school. Once I arrived, I tried to understand everything that was said, but really, nothing penetrated. I was too concerned about my crying son, brought through the side door into the guidance office. It completely went over my head that some modifications had been removed from Scott's IEP: He would no longer have extra class time or a modified amount of work in class. These two alterations had been meant to keep Scott focused, as "too much" work presented would lead to him shutting down. By giving him smaller increments of the same work as the class, he was able to stay on task and keep up. It was, in my opinion, one of the most important pieces of his IEP, and he no longer had it. In fact, he hadn't had it all year.

The meeting ended, at which point it was my turn to go home to cry. I pulled myself together afterwards and waited for the bus to pull up so I could say, "See, you had a good day, right? I told ya so!" But when Scott walked in the door, he was crushed. He wailed, "Why did you leave me there? I was crying, and people saw me!" He was beside himself. Guilt washed over me. Did I do the right thing? Why was Scott so upset in the first place? I spoke to one of his teachers and she claimed he was just fine after I left.

The Eureka Moment

The days that followed are a blur. Scott's homework backed up, and I would get calls telling me that he had to stay after school to make up missing assignments. He was tired every day, and he almost never laughed or even smiled anymore. One day after he arrived home, he fell asleep as I was in the middle of asking him about his day. He slumped over and just passed out. I went over to give him a pillow, and I noticed tears by his eyelids. I had had enough. And I knew my child had. I wanted answers.

I went into the kitchen, made a cup of coffee and turned on the TV. The commercials played as I opened my laptop to search "child anxiety" and "child depression." In the background, I heard, "Coming up at five…Commissioner King…cancelling forums…" and I thought, "What is that all about?" King is the New York State education commissioner. At the time, he was on a listening tour, looking for feedback on the Common Core.

In retrospect, I had heard plenty of bits and pieces about Common Core, the commissioner, the state board regents, the scores…but really never looked into it. Then, one day, I typed "Common Core anxiety" into the search field of my Web browser. What I saw next would change everything:

"rollout 2010" (David's fifth-grade year, when all the problems had started)

"anxiety and depression"

"developmentally inappropriate"

"rigor," "grit," and "scaffolding"

"cutting behavior"

"school refusal"

"disregard of IEPs"

"inBloom"

"400 data points"

"high stakes tests"

"cut score"

"refuse the tests"

All were phrases that I would see many more times over the next several months…and then some. A whole new world of information and understanding had just been opened to me.

I wrote my first letter that day, addressing it to the state commissioner of education and the governor. I sent them emails as well. Just for good measure, I cc'd the message to President Obama. I believed that maybe these officials were just unaware of what was happening, how bad this program was, and that if they heard my story they might be surprised to learn the truth. I wanted to connect the dots for them in the way the dots had just been connected for me, and I believed my story would speak to them.

It was now clear to me that David's anxiety attacks had been most heavily concentrated in the spring of each year since the rollout of Common Core, most particularly at the height of test-prep and test-taking season. Now my younger son was showing the same signs—signs just like the ones listed on my computer screen. I printed out refusal, or opt-out, letters for the Common Core tests that day as well.

I called David, now 13, into the kitchen and told him what I had found. I showed him a couple of web search results and explained to him that I believed I had finally figured out what was wrong—what had been wrong the whole time. The pressure on my sons to excel on the tests had been a huge part of the problem. Some of the techniques used to teach them—techniques embedded within the Common Core—had only compounded the problem. And, all this time, I had had no idea! David responded, "Oh my God, Mom, that was it!" As he hugged me, he said, "Don't feel bad, you didn't know. Don't be sorry."

It was a long journey I had to make to accept what is happening in our public schools. Even once I initially understood, I truly was naïve enough to think that if enough parents told their stories, Common Core, and the high-stakes tests would come to a screeching halt. As I learned more, however, I realized that, without knowing it, I had joined a growing movement of parents, grandparents, educators, politicians, leaders, and concerned taxpayers who know our students deserve better and are fighting to ensure that they get it—people who understand that, under Common Core and related programs, children are being used, and sold as data, to benefit others who could not care less about the lives and the homes they are ruining. The tests serve not only to enforce these controversial standards, they are also one of the chief ways that student data is being generated for those who want to acquire it and profit from it. The demand for high participation and high performance on the tests is yielding an unending stream of problems—for children and their parents alike. This situation will only get worse as full implementation of Common Core spreads beyond New York and a handful of other states that deployed it early.

Unfortunately, awareness of Common Core is still relatively low. In part this is because so many states haven't seen the full picture yet. Most parents still don't know—still don't understand—the pressures and risks to which their children are being exposed. For many parents, changes in their children's behavior as related to Common Core and associated high-stakes assessments are likely still as mysterious to them as my children's were to me. After discovering this reality for myself, how could I force my children to go back and be used—not taught, not educated, but used?

I raised these concerns on my next phone call with Scott's school psychologist, who not only dismissed my concerns but also corrected me when I called Common Core a curriculum as opposed to standards. My 12-year-old son was lying in bed hyperventilating because it was a school day, and I was being corrected on my terminology. She then suggested a really great inpatient mental hospital for children.

Needless to say, Scott is now home with me every day. We home-school him. We have tutors daily to keep up on academics. He sees a social worker weekly and doctors monthly to help him understand what he is feeling and why.

David actually chose to stay in school, despite my offer to home-school him as well. He has friends and finally feels confident there. He questions things he finds strange and does not give out personal information easily now that he is aware of the changes in curriculum and data collection. At his age, he knows that not everything he learns in school is fact, or even his teachers' opinions, and he knows businesses are looking to make money with his personal information. While this makes me proud, it also makes me sad. We have had some really great teachers over the years, who really care about and want to get to know their students. David should not have to decipher between that and corporate needs. I yearn for the days when a student could share something in school without the threat of it being misconstrued, recorded, inappropriately shared, and/or used against him. But the lack of transparency Common Core represents is worrisome, and while I do not like to cross into conspiracy theories, I do feel it is better to err on the side of caution. If I feel something needs to be shared with the school, I will share it at my discretion.

I do not know what the future holds for my children or for *their* children. I only know what is happening today. While I was not looking for a fight, I am now in the biggest one of my life. And while I was not looking for a cause, I cannot think of a better one for which to fight: our children.

CONSTRUCTING DISASTER:

Common Core, Constructivism, High-Stakes Testing, and Children with Learning Differences

S. WHARTON

A cross the United States today, students in public schoolrooms are being hindered in learning; teachers are being made unwitting or unwilling participants in this dysfunctional reality; and parents are having to shell out millions of dollars to have their kids tutored.[1] It's about to get worse.

What is happening? And why?

Out-of-touch "theorists" and corporations devoted to educational assessment are micromanaging both learning method and content, destroying education as we once knew it. At the heart of this debacle? The way stakeholders in the education establishment have increasingly redefined achievement. The new definition is incomplete, even backward—as is the associated definition of success that has been foisted not just on taxpayers and school districts but also, most troublingly, on the unsuspecting students that fill public schools. This not-so-subtle Newspeak, the embrace of ever-more-standardized approaches to education, and the negative results being reaped should cause us all alarm.

The Common Core State Standards (Common Core), the constructivist methodology in which they are steeped, and the high-stakes assessments designed to enforce them pose risks to any student in that they make little or no allowance for the unique learning needs and processes of each child. But for students with learning disorders (LD)—

perhaps better termed learning *differences*—the risks are even greater. Moreover, the developmental inappropriateness of the standards may well end up *producing* learning challenges for both LD students and those who learn in ways that have traditionally been considered more typical.

As a mother of two, one of whom has diagnosed learning differences, I was intent on understanding what my children were experiencing under Common Core. However, it's clear that the ramifications of what is unfolding within our education system reach well beyond my own family and into society at large.

Reading between the Lines: Standards or Method?

Common Core is marketed as "just a set of standards. We are told repeatedly that Common Core doesn't dictate method or curriculum. Why then, on close examination, are the "standards" filled with verbiage such as: "ask and answer," "collaborate," "participate," and "engage effectively"? Such language clearly suggests method, and method dictates how curriculum will be created. In particular, these terms indicate that Common Core embeds constructivism, an inquiry-based methodology, into the standards. Common Core's proponents fail to explain that to carry out the objectives of these standards, one must embrace constructivist teaching method.[2]

To be clear, I'm not against constructivism per se or other inquiry-based models that include collaborating and asking questions in a directed manner. Rather I am against *required standardization* of constructivism because it has led to inappropriate use; it's a methodology that doesn't work well with all age groups, in all settings, or with all populations.[3] It's particularly problematic for novice learners and kids with special needs.[4]

To understand my resistance to standardizing constructivism, in particular, some history and definition are valuable. Constructivism originated as a learning theory in the early twentieth century. Today's version postulates that humans learn through discovery and collaboration rather than by direct instruction. The theory suggests that new information is synthesized with prior knowledge, or schemas, in a self-directed manner. While this is one end of the learning "elephant," the other other end—ignored by many modern-day constructivists—consists of objective knowledge acquired by direct learning. For example, certain laws and rules of math or of phonics and grammar must establish concrete schemas in order for a child to have a solid foundation in which to ground their learning.[5]

Many constructivists discard guided instruction and repetition for multi-step reasoning and "real-world" problem solving. However, such tasks prove difficult for younger learners. According to Paul Kirchner, John Sweller, and Richard Clark:

> [F]or novices, studying worked examples seems invariably superior to discovering or constructing a solution to a problem. Problem solving only becomes relatively effective when learners are sufficiently experienced so that studying a worked example is, for them, a redundant activity that increases working memory load compared to generating a known solution.[6]

Many Common Core-aligned math assignments, steeped in constructivist theory, are, in fact, developmentally inappropriate, requiring young children to apply algebraic abstractions they have not yet learned.* Common Core-aligned elementary school math workbooks, such as Florida's "Go Math!", attempt to establish order and algorithms by beginning with difficult examples rather than simple ones. New concepts are introduced before any habit of form has been established with the previous concept. The ideal approach would instead be to provide enough opportunity for mastery of developmentally appropriate material, gradually increasing the difficulty to help students "stay in [their] 'sweet spot' of engagement, where the task is not so difficult as to be frustrating and not so easy as to be boring."[7]

These seeming attempts to create "rigor" will, in the early years, teach students only learned helplessness and anxiety. Unguided inquiry-based learning is especially difficult for kids with LD across the age

---

* EDITOR'S NOTE: To understand more about this reality, see R. James Milgram and Ze'ev Wurman on the Common Core mathematics standards, pp. 73-102.

spectrum. The requirement to create order and procedure, especially in math, puts a heavy reliance on the very skills with which many such children struggle the most. Inability to master skills via prescribed indirect forms of learning repeatedly sets these students up to feel inadequate. For LD students, repetition and practice—handled in a fun and colorful way—are frequently paramount to material comprehension.

More troubling still, because the approaches Common Core employs are so different from those used in the 1970s and '80s, most parents are now at a loss in helping their children with homework. This reality is creating a dilemma for parents, who are often left with no choice but to pay for additional tutoring.[8] The disparity in test scores between low- and high-income communities may, in large part, be explained by the fact that many financially challenged parents lack the means to afford additional assistance of this nature. With little support, many children in low-income communities, particularly those with LD, face compounded adversity in mastering material and passing standardized tests.[9]

Ironically, John Dewey, often cited as one of the first constructivist theorists, acknowledged that direct instruction of content by the teacher was also important.[10] Young children are concrete learners with large imaginations.[11] Constructivist learning, on the other hand, is most effective with children who have entered what developmental psychologist Jean Piaget has called the formal operational, or abstract reasoning, stage of development, typically around age 12. It is at that point, provided prior educational experience has allowed the acquisition of necessary schemas—that a child generally has the ability to begin reorganizing information into new constructions and viewpoints.[12]

It may be appropriate to employ constructivist method with elementary school students at the discretion of a highly educated teacher and with a high degree of guidance. Appropriate questions to engage students may be effective for conceptual topics.[13] However, it is incongruent and inappropriate to expect mastery using such an approach in early years or to test for mastery of conceptual understanding via three-hour blocks of highly detailed questions—the environment created by the high-stakes testing that enforces Common Core standards.[14]

Comprehending Learning Differences

As already suggested, constructivist methodology, used without adequate skill or guidance, is often ineffective for the average student. It will be a disaster of epic proportion for children with learning differences. Constructivism demands at least two things that children with learning differences often lack. First, it requires a high degree of executive function, the ability to sequence steps needed to solve practical problems. Second, it necessitates substantial reliance on "working memory," the capacity to focus and concentrate on material, manipulate it in one's mind, and come up with an answer.[15] Both of these abilities are regulated by the neurotransmitter dopamine. People with diagnosed attention challenges, for instance, typically have lower levels of dopamine and can only generate it through movement, sensory stimulation, high consumption of protein, caffeine, and/or stimulant medication. Dyslexia, which involves not only difficulty with interpreting symbolic language but also in regulating spatial skills and performing executive function skills, is also sensitive to dopamine levels. Dyspraxia, which involves difficulty with movement and coordination, likewise generally corresponds to an expression of low levels of dopamine in the motor cortex. The result of lower levels of dopamine in this region of the brain can affect muscle strength, coordination, fine motor skill, and motor planning, in turn impacting abstract planning and executive function skills in the prefrontal cortex. Dyspraxia and Dyslexia often overlap with ADHD.

While most of what are termed LDs have a genetic basis, including varieties of ADHD,[16] they can be affected positively or negatively by environmental factors such as amount of sleep, nutrition, and social stress levels. It's not simply about being easily distracted. Many of us distract easily, but we have adequately operating executive function capacity and working memory skills.

In fact, there is great misunderstanding of LD in its diverse forms. For many LD is synonymous with low intellectual capacity. Nothing could be further from the truth. In fact, I prefer the term "learning differences" exactly because such individuals simply learn differently than the norm. If we can understand intelligence as a set of varied skills and abilities, then defining intelligence at all is no easy task. As an example, Thomas Edison was unable to learn in a traditional 19th-century classroom because he could not sit still or keep quiet long enough to harness executive function and working memory capacities. However, no one could today accuse Edison of being intellectually inferior.

Evidence suggests that because many people with learning differences lack access to common forms of ordering the world, they instead rely on parts of the brain that are functioning more optimally such as aesthetic and artistic comprehension, divergent thinking, intuitive understanding, and emotional expression. In a recent study, individuals with ADHD were shown to score higher on tests of divergent thinking but scored lower on skills measuring convergent thinking.[17] Convergent thinking emphasizes higher executive function—such as analytical and deductive reasoning—toward the goal of arriving at a single right answer.[18]

People with ADHD and other learning differences do tend to be divergent and independent thinkers. They are frequently rebels against tradition, go-with-the flow explorers, risk takers. They often come up with solutions to problems not previously considered, despite having difficulty with some things that others grasp with relative ease. Describing his own experience with ADHD and dyslexia, Richard Branson, the highly successful CEO of Virgin Enterprises, notes:

> I had no understanding of school work whatsoever, and I certainly would have failed IQ tests. If I'm not interested in something I just don't grasp it…For example, I haven't been able to know the difference between net and gross.
>
> When I turned 50 somebody took me out of the boardroom and drew me a diagram and drew a net in the sea and the fish were pulled from the sea into the net and said that's the profits in the net. So I finally got it!"[19]

If teachers and schools are locked into a certain way of teaching that caters exclusively to convergent thinkers, we will undermine and lose people who think outside the box and, by nature of that fact, have the potential to make important contributions to our society. Without learning differences, Edison's celebrated insights and inventions aren't the only ones we'd be without. Leonardo da Vinci and Steven Spielberg are among many creatively minded innovators and artists who have struggled with dyslexia. Both Alexander Graham Bell and Walt Disney appear to have struggled with ADHD. The examples are plentiful.

Broaching the Common Core at My House

My two children currently attend public school in the state of Florida. Each child has a different way of learning and different gifts. My 6-year-old son, a kindergartner, attends a brick-and-mortar school. He is academically advanced for his years, able to read and perform mathematical operations at the second-grade level. He possesses the strong working memory and eye for detail required by constructivist method; his skills will be more "measurable" in the way that Common Core and related reform initiatives would demand.

My 11-year-old daughter, by contrast, has talents not championed by a one-size-fits-all system. She attended a brick-and-mortar school until recently. For the last year, she has been at home, enrolled in the Florida Virtual School middle-school program. She performs at the sixth-grade level. With the learning differences of Dyspraxia and ADHD-Inattentive Variety, she is not hyperactive or disruptive. She has difficulty with executive function skills such as citing details and concentrating on multiple pieces of information at one time.

As I write this essay, in 2014, Common Core is being implemented in our state in Kindergarten, first grade, and via the K-12 Florida Virtual School. The plan over the coming school year is to implement the initiative in all brick-and-mortar schools, K-12. Because of where my children are in school, I already have a window into what will unfold over the coming years for students across the state and the country. Particularly with my daughter, constructivist teaching methodology had already been an issue pre-Common Core. The issues are only growing with the implementation of the new standards.

MY SON

My kindergartener comes home from school with a math test that asks: "Think of an equation that you know. Write the equation. Draw a picture to represent the equation."He struggles with the question. The test, in fact, includes multiple vocabulary terms that are not easily interpreted by most 5- or 6-year-olds—even those like my son, who scores in the 92nd percentile for reading on the Stanford achievement test. Most young children have no experience reading, let alone applying, such vocabulary. Is my son's struggle to master higher-level "abstract thinking" assignments in elementary school reasonable? Is it likely to help, or will it more likely hinder in some manner, his later college and career success?

On Common Core-aligned homework, he is expected to "explain" on paper how he arrived at 7 after adding 5 + 2. On non-math assignments, he is asked to "identify the reasons an author gives to support points in a text."

At school, my son sits still all day and listens closely to the teacher's directions. He feels restrained all day. "I like my teacher," he says, "I just feel like I can't be free." He comes home not knowing what daily recess is.[20] Imaginative, or pretend, play is no longer permitted in my son's Kindergarten, leaving him little or no opportunity to further develop social skills. He recently told me he doesn't like math, because it makes his "hand hurt to have to draw all those circles," and it's "boring." This same child can tell me that two hours and twenty-five minutes have elapsed between 3:20 and 5:45 while he sits in his booster seat and ponders, looking out the car window. Clearly, it's not that he can't do the work. It's a question of whether the school experience he's having, and the work given to him there, are facilitating his desire to learn.

Other children in his classroom have greater difficulty sitting still all day without a daily outlet for free play. A mother of a boy with learning differences in my son's class tells me that the LD kids are often scolded, don't receive "tickets" for treasure box, and are losing the one 20-minute recess period permitted per week. Sometimes the nature of the system—accountability and performance pressure—creates a punitive environment despite a teacher's best intentions.

Despite my own son's good behavior and ideal academic performance, the teacher must follow the Common Core standards and cannot give him academic material beyond what is covered in the standards. There is no framework to provide him with academic growth at the pace he's ready to go. I go to the library or use online resources to build on his knowledge.

While my son will "fit" the academic system shaped by Common Core and related initiatives, I have become convinced that something has gone terribly wrong in the standard-creators' understanding of child development. Again, just because my son has what it takes to navigate Common Core and high-stakes testing doesn't mean it will provide an optimal learning experience for him.

MY DAUGHTER

After a long day at school, some recreation time, and a quick dinner, my pre-teen daughter settles into a dining room chair at a table carved by her great-grandfather to begin her sixth-grade math homework. The assignment requires her to complete fraction problems in three different ways. There are also complex word problems that demand multiple steps and high degrees of concentration. My daughter groans at the homework and tells me that it's stupid, that she cannot do it, doesn't want to do it, and has "other things to do in life." She gets up from the table. I firmly tell her, she needs to return. She rolls her eyes and slumps into the chair. This scene is probably repeated in millions of homes across the country, but in this case it is reflective of the ways in which my daughter's learning differences are being triggered.

Sitting down with her and studying her math book, I realize that I know a simpler way to teach her the algorithm being taught. When I show her my way, she says "Oh! That's so easy!" and tells me that math is actually kind of fun. I create columns for her, comparing decimals to fractions to percentages. We use concrete examples to practice the concepts over and over until they stick in her memory. Next, I must figure out how to help her take apart multi-step word problems that I don't remember studying in my own youth until the eighth grade.

***   ***   ***

My daughter writes creative fiction. Her stories are poignant, well-developed, humorous. She is a sprightly and confident speaker. She creates amazing Lego cities and environments, navigates computers and iPhones with the skill of an Apple employee, demonstrates perfect pitch, and can adeptly memorize musical rhythms. She excels at divergent thinking when given charades cues and can come up with more creative ideas than anyone else in the room. She gathers found objects and fashions interior design samples out of moving boxes. She is also skilled in reading the emotional dynamics of social interaction. She needs a place at school, a low-pressure setting, in which to share and grow these talents and strengthen those that cause her difficulty. Instead, she is constantly measured by standardized test scores that do not always reflect her true ability or allow her to reinforce the ways in which she can make meaningful contributions to the world.

The standardized methodology, convergent thinking, and constructivist methods that Common Core and high-stakes testing engender simply do not provide that adequate space for my daughter. I want for her to learn the skills she needs to operate effectively in the world, but the way in which this "one-size-fits-all" set of standards is being implemented is instead creating a sense of shame, learned helplessness, anxiety, and depression in her. These repercussions will only intensify the roadblocks toward future success. For these reasons, her father and I are in the process of placing her in a private school.

Last year, my daughter's fifth-grade class was paraded into the computer lab countless times for pre-tests and post-tests. The pressure on teachers and students to achieve high test scores created a toxic environment. Her teacher showed irritation if a child scored less than a B, and her brand of motivation was to shame children so that they might do better the next time. The teacher referred to this approach as "tough love." Constant positive regard for high scorers created a sense of preference and a competitive atmosphere in the classroom that lacked friendliness and dignity.[21] At the end of the year, my child averaged a B on overall quiz and test scores, but in her mind she only remembers the shame of her lower scores, due to the test-obsessed culture of her school environment.

Children with learning differences, such as my daughter, flourish much better by creating guided projects that can showcase their understanding. They need repetitive exercises, such as memorization, to find order and establish necessary schemas.

To her credit, my daughter's teacher listened when I explained what was needed. She began to guide my daughter in more specific ways. She recognized the strength and merit of my daughter's writing and speaking skills, even nominating her for best speech in the class when my daughter wrote a speech for a state competition. She was also helpful when she realized that the testing was not accurately assessing my daughter's knowledge. She saw how hard my child was working and came to understand the pain and learning debacles that the harsh competition was creating. However, the experience early on in that classroom affected my child's sense of competency so deeply that it contributed to her difficulty adjusting to middle-school.

Unfortunately, adaptations such as those my daughter's teacher implemented after we spoke—including the ability to veer away from inappropriate use of constructivist method—will become more difficult as Common Core and high-stakes testing are implemented more widely because, again, the method is implied in the standards and enforced by the tests.

The sixth-grade climate my daughter entered consisted of six classes, filled to capacity. Despite having As and Bs in grade 5, she earned a 2 on the math portion of the Florida Comprehensive Achievement Test, where 3 is passing and 5 is the top score.[22] She was consequently placed in all lower-level classes with low-achieving students and kids with behavior issues, despite her previous good performance in the classroom. The school wouldn't change her team, due to overcrowding.

In this new setting, my daughter's teachers were again using unguided inquiry-based methods. In Language Arts, she was required to keep an interactive notebook and to order her papers and assignments therein. It was her job to consult the classroom walls, find her assignments, and coordinate them to the journal's contents page. No guidance was provided on a daily or weekly basis. The notebook was to remain at school. Only at the end of the semester did the teacher check to see if her students were on task. When she saw that my daughter was disorganized and didn't understand the procedure, she provided no guidance, simply telling her to work on the notebook further at home. There was no direction on how the work should be accomplished. As a parent, I had no way to know what her progress—or lack thereof—was.

Math assignments have required my daughter to use multiple strategies to solve the same problems. As already illustrated in the example concerning fractions, decimals, and percentages, the approach prescribed at school and in her textbook caused her difficulty in mastering even one of these strategies due to lack of exercise, repetition, and time for practicing algorithms and mastering concepts. When consulted, her math teacher fully agreed that it was ridiculous to teach multiple strategies in a short duration of time, but her hands were tied—bound by the school and the county to teach math in this manner. It took hours of my own time to teach my daughter rather simple algorithms that she adequately comprehended. My daughter is highly teachable; her absorption of knowledge when taught in a way that accounted for her learning differences makes this fact plain. However, a standardized agenda meant to suffice for everyone—one tying the hands of my daughter's teachers—has been counterproductive, inhumane, and damaging.

While still attending a brick-and-mortar school, my daughter was more than once required to work in a group, reading a story or informational piece and then answering ten to fifteen "detail-finding" questions. The teacher sat at her desk while her students worked unguided. I don't know many adults—even those with masters or doctoral degrees—that would enjoy such tedious assignments, let alone a child with an attention challenge. Yet "inquiry" has increasingly come to be interpreted in this manner in new curricula—hyper-detailed, or close, reading of texts that requires a high tolerance for boredom and intense concentration. The Common Core standards seem to exacerbate the problem rather than ameliorating it.[23] It's further evidence of how constructivist method can go awry.

With all of the other pressures of middle school and the self-consciousness that pre-adolescence brings, my daughter simply crumbled in mid-October. She called me from the nurse's office, experiencing a panic attack. We attempted to take her back to school but she could not reign in her anxiety enough to return. Unguided inquiry-based learning models, large class sizes, and continual testing have wreaked havoc. She was ultimately clinically diagnosed with Irritable Bowel Syndrome, generalized anxiety with panic attacks, and "school phobia" just two months after starting middle school.

My daughter tells me that she doesn't trust that the public school environment will care for her or help her grow and learn. Given her circumstances and experience, she is right. Even the assignments she has received through the public Florida Virtual School program this past year have demonstrated heavy emphasis on constructivist method, making many of her assignments inappropriately difficult, even torturous, for her.

Evaluating the Evaluators

Recently, the New York Times published an interview with Google Senior Vice President of People Operations Laszlo Bock. Said Bock, "[Grade point averages] are worthless as a criteria for hiring, and test scores are worthless...We found that they don't predict anything."[24] It's a stunning statement, particularly coming from an executive at the world's pre-eminent data company, where measurement is everything.

Isn't "college and career readiness" supposed to be the chief selling point of the Common Core initiative? Yet, the emphasis of these "new" standards lies squarely in standardization and convergent thinking— precisely the things that grade points averages (GPAs) and high-stakes testing tend to measure. If the end game of a lucrative job is greater standard of living, and thus greater happiness and security, then the educational mindset inherent in the Common Core and attached to testing has lost its way and its purpose. It limits the freedom to grow intellectually and emotionally by limiting our children and our teachers.[25] Lessons must now align with a specific set of standards designed, in part, by testing corporations with monetary interests.

As attractive as it may seem to politicians, philanthropists, and academics to create lofty standards, quantify every person, and rate them at ages 8, 10, 13, and beyond, it is not possible. Too many variables exist in human nature, circumstance, and the world itself to derive a "number" for each child's potential for success. Numbers are potentially informative but are only one piece of a complex puzzle that requires parents and other sensitive, informed professionals to put together.

No Child Left Behind, Race to the Top, and Common Core have *all* focused quite heavily on evaluating a very narrow definition of student progress, one rooted in a standardized approach and constructivist methodology that cannot be ideal for all students—and, indeed, is *not* ideal for most. It seems a fair guess that education policy is created by convergent thinkers for convergent thinkers. Perhaps, that's at least in part why our 21st-century education system caters exclusively to this type of child—and why GPAs and high-stakes testing are structured to assess similar skills.

In education "reform"-speak, the message is clear: executive function skills and attention to details = "smart." Memory power is prized and test-taking skills will determine future academic success. But what if this formula is not correct? What if there are additional skills unaccounted for by formulaic educational initiatives and high-stakes standardized tests that determine "college and career success"?

By implementing this particular set of standards, focused only on a rigid set of convergent thinking skills and eschewing divergent thinking, we have failed to address the complexities and uniqueness of individual human abilities and potential. While students of all stripes will suffer under a system in which their individuality and specific needs are ignored, again, for students who learn differently, tears will abound as they attempt to "fit" an unworkable mold. Engagement and interest disappear. Stress rises. Confusion, frustration, and power struggles over homework permeate formerly peaceful family lives.

Exacerbating matters, teachers often end up using reward and punishment as motivators within the convergent system created by Common Core and its reform cousins. Yet, according to *Drive*, a recent book on motivation, engagement provides much greater motivation than compliance and leads to greater joy and purpose.[26]

What is the end game of convergent-type reform systems such as Common Core? Is this painful struggle necessary? I'm not convinced.

Where is our recognition, our remembrance, that it takes skills beyond those measured by tests of convergent thinking not just to make our world interesting, but to make it function? By inappropriately imposing indirect teaching methods and the pressures of high-stakes testing across every state, in every county, in every school, and upon every child, we are creating and, in fact, ensuring a less effective educational experience for everyone. Subjecting children with significant learning differences, specifically, to the kinds of judging and cataloging that Common Core demands is potentially inflicting permanent damage.

The current, popular constructivist math curriculum is failing our children. Common Core English language arts standards require "close reading" and detailed analyses that strike at the weaknesses of most children with "working memory" issues (e.g., dyslexia, dyspraxia, ADHD, auditory processing, visual processing, dyscalculia, etc.). Students that fall along the autism spectrum will, in middle school, be at great disadvantage in facing requirements to "explain character development in social contexts" and will also struggle with the standardized tests.[27] Moreover, constructivist learning methods are incongruent with the high-stakes tests being created to enforce the Common Core, rendering this system inherently flawed.

On examination, Common Core and the related assessments actually violate the Americans with Disabilities Act by automatically excluding an entire group of learners for whom teachers will not be allowed (or educated) to make adjustments. Thirteen percent of all children have some form of ADHD or LD.[28] Since the system is not designed for—or accommodating to—such children, instead of conveying academics, it will instead teach them that they are not "smart" or "good." Troublingly, the Common Core standards are so detailed and compliance is such a part of the initiative that a teacher will find it difficult to find the time or flexibility to adjust curriculum for different learning styles in the classroom.[29]

Other problems lie in the operational direction that standardized education is taking us. Students who struggle academically require more support and accommodations in order to reach their potential in myriad ways. Many large American schools already place one guidance counselor in charge of 500 students.[30] Guidance counselors oversee learning disability accommodations in the classroom. When they are overworked, the needs of LD and other special-need students cannot be adequately met.[31]

As class sizes similarly continue to expand,[32] testing and test preparation take up increasingly more classroom time. Meanwhile, technology infrastructure to support computer-based testing absorbs large percentages of district budgets; we will almost certainly see a significant decrease in the services needed to help struggling students navigate.[33] What will such circumstances mean for students who are already having difficulties? What will it mean for the students who begin to have difficulties specifically as a result of Common Core methodology or high-stakes assessment? What will the impact be on vulnerable populations, including those with learning differences? What is the logical outcome in inner cities or economically depressed regions where, again, parents may not have the financial resources to help their children navigate through the problems they are experiencing in the classroom? Is it reasonable to brand children, parents, teachers, or schools in such areas as "failing" when the system essentially sets them up not to be able to succeed?

Common Core bills itself as a way to ensure better and more uniform education for all. I would argue that it can't be both and that, in truth, Common Core potentially achieves only the latter. The question is, is uniform education true education? There is a natural series of follow-up questions: Do the high-stakes assessments that enforce standardized education have any true value to people like you and me? To our children? To teachers? And if they do not benefit us, *who do* they actually benefit?

What Should Education Be...Really?

Currently, educational freedom is being severely thwarted. Nothing good can come from the kinds of extreme control over other human beings that Common Core and high-stakes testing engender. We should halt these initiatives before more developmental and educational damage is done. A saner view of education is required, one that acknowledges, (1) that lucrative careers derive from *many* types of skills and talents and, (2) that preparation for a job is not the only or even the most important purpose of education. Creating conditions in which we can meet the needs of all of our students is, in fact, key to creating the kind of society we want.[34]

Zhao Yong, associate dean of global education at the University of Oregon, has written extensively about the problems with Common Core, noting, among other things, that we are idealizing authoritarian countries' models of education—particularly, China. Yet, says Yong on his online blog, 21st-century China "uses test scores as the primary or only criterion to evaluate students, hurting their motivation and enthusiasm, squelching their creativity, and impeding their overall development."[35] Stress levels run high in China, as do suicide rates.[36]

My own definition of education is Aristotelian. I believe that education is about coming to know ourselves, cultivating each person's unique abilities and gifts in order to discover the world's complexities, beauty, and truths—in large part so we can be free to experience "the pursuit of happiness." An education is also about mastering practical life skills that will allow one to have potency and ability in the world. Some skills that qualify? Balancing a checkbook, writing a letter, giving a speech.[37] Education gives us rich material to draw from in order to inform our lives with meaning and purpose. Public education—any education—should provide these basic launching pads; though, if it is to be effective, *how* that education happens will, by necessity, vary from one individual to the next.[38]

Self-esteem in children develops through experiences of competency. I am not talking about the artificial-sweetener version of "give-every-child-a-trophy" competency. Instead, I mean real mastery of skills that give human beings a sense of self-efficacy and personal power. Each child develops at a different rate and in response to different approaches, stimuli, and motivations. Children benefit cognitively and emotionally from activities that allow them to master concrete material, ask questions that interest them, develop their imaginations, inform them about themselves in relation to the world we live in, and take part in art, music, and games that embrace them with joy. Kids also need to experience lots of physical activity.[39] For the average child, it is healthy to take part in daily exercise; for a child with learning differences, it can actually be vital to academic success because exercise generates dopamine, the neurotransmitter so necessary to quiet concentration and the ability to engage in learning. Children need time to grow and develop. Learning to love *learning* is just as important to persistence in higher levels of education—and to a future life path, including career—as the academic material itself.

What would happen if, instead of putting children in a high-stakes pressure cooker, we gave them opportunities to grow their skills in each stage of development so that by the time they graduated high school, they would have a sense of their unique talents and abilities to take into the world? While this approach would certainly serve children with learning differences better, wouldn't it actually be more valuable for all children?

NOTES

1.   James Marshall Crotty, "Global Private Tutoring Market Will Surpass $102.8 Billion By 2018," *Forbes*, Oct. 30, 2012, http://www.forbes.com/sites/jamesmarshallcrotty/2012/10/30/global-private-tutoring-market-will-surpass-102-billion-by-2018/.

2.   A quick look at some of the Common Core training videos on the New York State Education Departments's website is all that's required to see the ways in which constructivist method is required to carry out the standards, https://www.engageny.org/video-library.

3.   Paul Bruno, "Bruno: Do The Common Core Standards Tell Teachers How To Teach?" Scholastic, *Alexander Russo's This Week In Education*, Mar. 25, 2013, http://scholasticadministrator.typepad.com/thisweekineducation/2013/03/bruno-do-the-common-core-standards-tell-teachers-how-to-teach.html#.UyW0VF5Vohttp.

4.   To be even more clear, I'm against standardizing or mandating *any* education methodology. Standards should point to the result of learning

alone, rather than enforcing any process by which to achieve learning. Specific learning methods belong to teachers, parents, and schools and should be determined in light of how each child is best served. Mandating methodology does not make for good public policy.

5. Education reformers have frequently complained that the direct learning necessary to establish such schemas amounts to "drill and kill" that will crush the desire to learn. Yet, many teachers over the centuries have used rhymes, songs, and even movement to teach knowledge basics. The ABC song or "Head, Shoulders, Knees, and Toes" serve as prominent examples.

6. Paul A. Kirschner, John Sweller, and Richard E. Clark, "Why Minimal Guidance During Instruction Does Not Work: An Analysis of the Failure of Constructivist, Discovery, Problem-Based, Experiential, and Inquiry-Based Teaching," *Educational Psychologist* 41, no. 2 (2006), 75–86, http://www.cogtech.usc.edu/publications/kirschner_Sweller_Clark.pdf.

7. Annie Murphy Paul, "What's the Sweet Spot of Difficulty for Learning?" *Mind Shift: How We Learn Blog*, Mar. 21, 2014, http://blogs. kqed.org/mindshift/2014/03/whats-the-sweet-spot-of-difficulty-for-learning/.

8. Just as troubling is the media's role in facilitating a mentality that parents shouldn't be assisting their children, regardless. See for example, Dana Goldstein, "Don't Help Your Kids with Their Homework and Other Insights from a Ground-breaking Study of How Parents Impact Children's Academic Achievement," *The Atlantic* (Apr. 2014), online posting dated Mar. 19, 2014, http://www.theatlantic.com/magazine/archive/2014/04/and-dont-help-your-kids-with-their-homework/358636/.

9. Formal surveys need to be conducted assessing the increase in tutoring in the U.S. The variable of access to tutoring has been left out of all testing results data.

10. Kirschner, Sweller, and Clark, "Minimal Guidance."

11. In the concrete-operational stage of cognitive development, children demonstrate concrete and logical reasoning but have difficulty applying abstract concepts with multiple variables. Dorothy Singer and Tracey Revensen, *A Piaget Primer: How a Child Thinks* (New York: Plume, 1996).

12. There are always exceptions. A handful of children will be able to grasp abstract concepts in the primary grades, but for the majority this is not the case.

13. Examples might include: "Can you think of an invention that might solve a problem?"; "Do you think the Browns will help Paddington find his way home?"; or "Do you think an ice cube will melt faster in the sun sitting on a black plate or a white plate?"

14. Standardized, high-stakes testing also turns out to be an unreliable measure of comprehension, particularly for those with learning differences, because scores depend on multiple uncontrollable factors. Was the child focused at that moment? Did the child have adequate sleep and nourishment? Such variables and numerous others affect concentration levels and impact test performance. Moreover, many kids with learning disabilities (LD) have sensory processing sensitivities that heighten stimuli in the surrounding environment; sounds are louder, smells stronger, touch more abrasive. All of these factors can significantly impact ability to concentrate. Yet, these sensitivities frequently make LD individuals better musicians, cooks, artists, and writers as well as more in tune to the feelings of other people. Standardized learning methods and high-stakes testing invalidate these attributes, again, championing only convergent thinking skills.

15. Rhonda Martinussen and Ashley Major, "Working Memory Weaknesses in Students with ADHD: Implications for Instruction," *Theory into Practice* 50, no. 1 (Jan. 2011), 68-75.

16. *The Diagnostic and Statistical Manual of Mental Disorders IV-TR* (Washington, DC: American Psychiatric Association, 2000) delineates three varieties of ADHD: inattentive type without hyperactivity, hyper-active and impulsive type, and combined hyperactivity/inattentive type.

17. Anne Abraham, Sabine Windmann, Ranier Siefen, Irene Daum, and Onur Güntürkün, "Creative Thinking in Adolescents with Attention Deficit Hyperactivity Disorder (ADHD)," *Child Neuropsychology* 12, no. 2 (April 2006): 111-123, http://www.tandfonline.com/doi/abs/10.1080/09297040500320691#.U8IL5VZZOYY.

18. *The Collins English Dictionary: Complete and Unabridged* (New York: HarperCollins, 2003), defines convergent as follows: (1) "(Psychology) analytical, usually deductive, thinking in which ideas are examined for their logical validity or in which a set of rules is followed; (2) thinking that brings together information focused on solving a problem (especially solving problems that have a single correct solution).

19. Richard Branson, "Classic TED: Richard Branson on How to Run a Business," Virgin, 2014, http://www.virgin.com/entrepreneur/classic-ted-richard-branson-on-how-to-run-a-business.

20. In fact, this sort of experience has become increasingly common as high-stakes testing has begun to drive school instruction. See "No Time for Recess, No Need for Nap," National Center for Fair and Open Testing, n.d., http://www.fairtest.org/no-time-recess-no-need-nap.

21. This sort of experience is, again, increasingly typical in the pressured environment that high-stakes testing creates for both teachers and students. Because teacher performance is now based heavily on student test scores, the scores become all. This sort of pressure was precisely the problem in my daughter's classroom. It wasn't so much a character-building approach as a need to drive test-scores. The teacher was, in fact, receiving high marks for the test results she was producing, but at what emotional price to the children in her classroom? Student-graded quizzes were an especially scary experience. My daughter was either relieved or heartbroken on the days such measures were administered. The way her peers graded her would vary significantly, depending on the day. One student called her stupid. Another, a friend labeled as gifted, told her she was "basic."

22. Classroom placements should not be based solely on one test. A significant problem with high-stakes testing is that merely administering a standardized test cannot fairly or equitably assess student learning. Various organizations have articulated wise principles of high-quality assessment that should be followed, including: (a) aiming at improving actual student learning, (b) being based on classroom performance and portfolios more than on high-stakes tests and aligning with local curricula, (c) emphasizing applied learning and thinking skills, rather than simply declarative knowledge and basic skills, (d) embodying the principle of multiple measures, incorporating a variety of formats such as writing, open response questions, and performance-based tasks, rather than just multiple choice, and (e) designing for accessibility by diverse learning styles, intelligence profiles, exceptionalities, and cultural backgrounds.

23. See, for example, grade 6 standards such as CCSS.ELA-Literacy. RI.6.1-5.

24. Thomas L. Friedman, "How to Get a Job at Google," *The New York Times*, Feb. 22, 2014, http://www.nytimes.com/2014/02/23/opinion/sunday/friedman-how-to-get-a-job-at-google.html?_r=0.

25. For additional information about the problems with standardized/high-stakes testing, see "What's Wrong with Standardized Tests," FairTest, May 22, 2012, http://www.fairtest.org/whats-wrong-standardized-tests.

26. Daniel H. Pink, *Drive* (New York: Riverhead Books, 2011).

27. Katharine Beals, "The Common Core Is Tough on Kids with Special Needs," *The Atlantic*, Mar. 14, 2014, http://www.theatlantic.com/education/print/2014/02/the-common-core-is-tough-on-kids-with-special-needs/283973/.

28. National Center for Education Statistics (NCES), Institute of Education Sciences, "Fast Facts: Students with Disabilities," 2013, http://nces.ed.gov/fastfacts/display.asp?id=64. The information is derived from chapter 2 of U.S. Dept. of Education, NCES, *Digest of Education Statistics, 2012* (NCES 2014-015).

29. When a third-grade teacher has over ninety benchmarks for ELA alone, are we actually creating a space in which teachers can operate with flexibility in the classroom? Also, see Katharine Beals, "Constructivism and Special Needs Students: Implications from Social Studies," *Out in Left Field*, Dec. 8, 2012, http://oilf.blogspot.com/2012/12/constructivism-and-special-needs.html and James Sheldon, "Mathematics Reform and Learning Disabilities," *James Sheldon Blog*, n.d., http://jamessheldon.com/mathematical-problem-solving/mathematics-reform-and-learning-disabilities/.

30. "State School Counseling Mandates and Legislation," American School Counselor Association, 2014, http://www.schoolcounselor.org/school-counselors-members/careers-roles/state-school-counseling-mandates-and-legislation.

31. Moreover, many states possess no mandate to have a guidance counselor on staff, and counselor hires are dependent on funding. My own state of Florida requires no knowledge or coursework in learning disabilities for counselors; and even many teaching programs require only one survey course on LD, providing little understanding of teaching practices needed to help students achieve effectively. Yet, guidance counselors play a key role in creating 504 and individualized education plans. This operational discrepancy poses a huge problem.

32. Sam Dillon, "Tight Budgets Mean Squeeze in Classrooms," *The New York Times*, Mar. 6, 2011, http://www.nytimes.com/2011/03/07/education/07classrooms.html?pagewanted=all&_r=0.

33. In Florida, and perhaps elsewhere, another problem will complicate matters for kids with what are termed specific learning disabilities. So-called professionals in charge of accommodating learning programs for LD students are not required by law to have a master's in counseling or proven knowledge and skill sets needed to accommodate each specific learning disability. Nor do they necessarily belong to professional counseling

organizations that aspire to specific ethical standards (i.e. beneficence, non-maleficence, justice, competence etc.). In addition, they are overburdened by too many students to give each one adequate service and attention. More worrisome still, many of these professionals work for the benefit of the school and not the child.

34. Eric Weiner, "Will Democracy Make You Happy?" *Foreign Policy Magazine*, Feb. 19. 2008, http://www.foreignpolicy.com/articles/2008/02/19/will_democracy_make_you_happy.

35. Zhao Yong, "Five Questions to Ask about the Common Core," *Yong Zhao Blog*, Jan. 2, 2013, http://zhaolearning.com/2013/01/02/five-questions-to-ask-about-the-common-core/.

36. Wang Hongyi, "Pressure Leaves Millions of Youth Exposed to Suicide Risk," *China Daily*, Feb.13, 2013, http://www.chinadaily.com.cn/china/2013-02/19/content_16234503.htm.

37. One might wryly add to this list, (1) thinking critically about education reform, and (2) analyzing faulty political agendas.

38. I often wonder why we haven't modeled our educational system to look more like Finland. Students are not expected to begin reading until age 7. Instead, play is emphasized in primary grades as if it is serious work—which it is. Short breaks are also taken every hour to allow kids to recharge their batteries and remain focused. With this approach, students still perform well in international assessments of achievement by grade 10. See Tim Walker, "How Finland Keeps Kids Focused through Free-Play," *The Atlantic*, June 30, 2014, http://www.theatlantic.com/education/archive/2014/06/how-finland-keeps-kids-focused/373544/, and Organization for Economic Co-operation and Development (OECD), "Finland: Slow and Steady Reform for Consistently High Results," chapter 5 of *Strong Performers and Successful Reformers in Education: Lessons from PISA for the United States* (Paris: OECD Publishing, 2010), http://www.oecd.org/pisa/pisaproducts/46581035.pdf.

39. Centers for Disease Control and Prevention, *The Association Between School Based Physical Activity, Including Physical Education, and Academic Performance* (Atlanta, GA: U.S. Dept. of Health and Human Services, 2012).

VIII. A FAMILY DESTROYER
Undermining Parental Rights

ANOTHER BRICK IN THE WALL:

Separating Parents from Their Children via Education Reforms and Technologies

KAREN LAMOREAUX

Amerncan education has arrived at a clear crossroads. Is the purpose of educating children to produce free minds and well-rounded individuals, or is it to produce global citizens subservient to social reforms and human capital for an industrial workforce? This debate over the territory of education, most particularly in public schools, is not a new one. And the reformations that we have been presented with over the last 40 years are simply rebranded versions of the same thing. It has been debated for generations.

In 1971, Robert H. Burke, a member of the California legislature, foreshadowed our current situation in commenting on the efforts of reformers of the 1960s. In a report titled, *Education: From The Acquisition of Knowledge to Programmed, Conditioned Responses*, Burke wrote: "[The various initiatives] were as parts in a puzzle—analyzed by themselves, each of these projects appeared to be either harmless or an expression of someone's 'dream.' When linked together with other 'harmless' programs, they were no longer formless but could be seen as an entire package of plans outlining methods of implementation, organization structures (including flow-charts), computerization, use of behavioral profile catalogs, and goals and objectives determination."[1]

A generation of separation later, and assumed forgetfulness on the part of the masses, the reformers are at it again, with the increasing power of the federal government and corporate "philanthropy" behind them. Indeed, the Common Core State Standards Initiative (Common Core) is the first of its kind to successfully combine nearly every facet of already-failed education reform into one nationwide package, making it nearly impossible for parents to avoid, undermining their rights all the while. Just as Burke described in 1971, Common Core contains many parts that, when examined independently, may seem relatively harmless. However, when combined into a single package and shackled to the U.S. government and powerful multinational corporations, the whole is clearly a violation of student and parent rights in a free society.

What follows is an account derived from my personal journals. It documents how my own experience with Common Core has unfolded—from my initial awareness and research of the initiative to my decision to take a strong stand against it. It is also an exposé of sorts that I hope will help others to understand how their rights as parents are being stripped away as well as how their relationships with their children are being undermined.

Spring 2011

School is almost over for the year. I am sitting in the school cafeteria for a typical Parent-Teacher Organization (PTO) meeting and listening to a PowerPoint presentation by the principal about a new, incoming set of standards called the Common Core. The presenter touts how wonderful the standards are because the states are working together for consistency. She says these standards will prepare students for college. I wonder to myself, "What were the current or previous standards doing? Weren't they supposed to be preparing kids for college, too?

The presenter also asks that we, as parents, be patient and flexible during the transition and expect the kind of hiccups that always occur in times of change. The standards will first roll out for the K-2 students this fall. Other grades will follow later.

My children won't be affected yet. I think nothing of it and, quite frankly, forget about it as the subject is not purposely brought to my attention again.

[Fast forward two years...]

September 2013: Macaroni Math

My fourth-grade son arrives home from school. We have a snack and get busy doing homework. He has a math worksheet that he can't figure out. In an instant he is crying in frustration, with his hands over his face.

"What's the matter? Did you have a bad day today?"

"I can't do this assignment, Mom! I think I need the tiles. The tiles are at school! Ugh!!!" He slides his work across the table in frustration.

"What tiles? What are you talking about?"

"The tiles! They're kept in a box at school. We line them up and count them. Or, I could use my hundreds chart. Where is my hundreds chart? Ugh! I can't find it anywhere. I think it's in my desk!" He continues to wail and is now pacing and kicking things across the floor.

I have never seen this behavior in my son over homework. He has always been a great student and scored in the above-average percentile in math on his standardized test last year. He has never before struggled academically. As I examine the assignment, I see that it includes word problems calling for simple multiplication, but it asks for drawings to support the answer. It looks ridiculous to me. I am not sure that I can figure it out, even with a college education. Have I forgotten elementary math?

I learned my multiplication tables in third grade. My son did not. I assumed he would memorize them this year. It is well into the first month of my son's fourth-grade year, but we have not yet seen any memorization of multiplication facts. I can't see how anyone can solve the problems at which I'm now staring without having memorized the tables.

I remember the dreaded hundreds chart that is he referring to from last year. I hated it. He carried a worn, wrinkled copy of it everywhere in order to complete math problems. In fact, we made multiple copies at home because I would find it shredded and soggy in his pockets when I did laundry or covered in mysterious sticky goo after he had left it on the kitchen counter. We would tangle during homework time when I tried to get him to do the math in his head. I recall feeling irritated that he was being taught to depend on a printed chart instead of doing mental math. When he is an adult years from now, making an important financial decision, is he supposed to pull a hundreds chart from his pocket? My daughter, just one year ahead of him, never used a hundreds chart; like me, she memorized her multiplication tables in third grade. What changed? Is it the teacher? I need to schedule a conference, I think to myself.

"Sweetheart, please don't be so upset. I think you are overreacting, here. We can do this together. Let's sit down and give it a try. "

My son can't tell me what 4 x 4 equals—or 2 x 3 or any single digit multiplication fact. He can skip count, though. This means he can count by twos or fives up to the answer. But even then he has to use his fingers. That works for some of the problems, but it presents another challenge for him because he has to show his work. This involves drawing lots of circles or squares to represent his answer. Anything beyond the number five is too overwhelming for him.

"I need something to count with! I can't do this mom! I hate math! I hate it! I'm never going to get it!" His response is visceral. This is coming from the same child who last year was quoted as saying math was his favorite subject.

"Okay, okay calm down, let's find something to use. "

I frantically scan around the kitchen while he sobs and pounds his fists on the table. I recall my first-grade teacher. She had used objects to help us learn math. I remember holding popsicle sticks in my hand and using blocks to learn place value and skip counting. Later I would learn from some teacher-friends that this was the Cognitively Guided Instruction, or CGI, method. CGI uses "manipulatives," such as blocks or tiles, to teach place value in primary grades. But that was first grade! This is fourth grade. What the heck is going on?

Whatever we choose to count with, there had to be a lot of them, at least 40 or 50. So we settle on a box of Kraft Macaroni and Cheese. He uses the raw noodles to perform the math. He keeps losing count of where he left off and has to start over. There is raw macaroni all over the table and on the floor. He keeps running out of room on his paper to draw his many circles, erasing, and rewriting. When I try to help him, he pushes my hand away in a panic and says, "NO! You are not allowed to write on my paper! It won't count if they know you helped me! Erase that!"

I am not allowed to help my son with his homework. To make matters worse, this nonsensical assignment sends a false message to my son that I am math illiterate and unable to assist.

Over two hours later, after drawing more than 100 circles and hash marks on his paper, the assignment is done. We are both exhausted and feeling defeated. No child in fourth grade should spend that much time on a math assignment after such a long day.

In the weeks to follow, more strange math assignments arrive. The math creates a divide between my son and me and makes homework time miserable.

I also start to notice some disturbing reading material coming home with my son—about social justice issues, focusing on racism, the proper role of the government, and global warming. The social justice issues alarm me. These are adult issues, the information provided is skewed, and in my opinion it's not appropriate for the classroom. I am anxious to find out why my son's teacher is using these materials. A parent-teacher conference is coming up, and I admire his teacher. She is professional, kind, and experienced. My son and I are very excited to learn he was going to be in her classroom this year because of her good reputation among the other parents and children. I believe I'll be able to have an open discussion with her about my concerns.

My conversation with the teacher reveals that the materials coming home with my son and the methods being used to teach him are a result of the Common Core standards implemented for grades 3-8 last year. I recall the PTO meeting held two years prior, but there was no mention of what we are now experiencing. She tells me she does not choose the topics, the materials, or the math methods. It is all provided to her. I express my disdain for what I am seeing and experiencing, including the fact that there is no call for rote memorization of multiplication. My son can't go through life as an adult drawing little circles on paper.

The teacher closes the door to her classroom and speaks softly. She explains to me that she has no choice but to teach these methods. She says my son is not the only one that did not memorize multiplication tables and that this fact will present a problem in the weeks to come when the class moves to fractions. She plans to start giving weekly fact quizzes on Fridays, but it will be up to the parents to catch their children up at home. She is swamped and overscheduled trying to keep up with the national Common Core timeline. She cannot stop and make sure the kids are caught up. She has to move according to the Common Core timeline, whether the kids grasp the information or not.

Right after this meeting, I have a scheduled conference with my older daughter's teacher, a veteran educator with over thirty years of experience. I asked her opinion of Common Core. She, too, rises from her desk, closes the door and lowers her voice. She hates it, she says, and gets pushback from administrators when she vocalizes her opinion of it. She tells me that teachers have little control over Common Core or what they teach. If I want to see Common Core go away, she says, I and other parents will have to take it up because the teachers have no voice. She is so upset by what she is experiencing that she has seriously considered early retirement. I am stunned and suddenly feel a strong urge to learn more about Common Core.

What I learn is heartbreaking. This is not just a set of standards, as is so frequently claimed. Rather, it is a comprehensive reform initiative with intentions that do not sit well with me. I find myself awake for hours at a time in the wee hours of the night, researching, trying to get my head around what I am finding.

November 2013: The Race to the Corporate Middle

My research continues.

In 2003, former President George W. Bush signed the United States into an agreement with the United Nations Education, Scientific and Cultural Organization (UNESCO). Our secretary of education makes a speech before UNESCO each year, updating the global organization on our reform efforts. Similarly, other member countries are in the midst of education reform with nearly identical goals and timelines.

In 2010, the same year in which the Common Core State Standards Initiative (CCSSI) was adopted by 45 states, U.S. Secretary of Education Arne Duncan outlined the education reform goals for our nation in his annual speech to UNESCO. He stated that the role of the federal government in education has always been limited and that the administration "seeks to *fundamentally shift* that role." (emphasis my own) He went on to outline a trajectory based on what he termed the Four Assurances of education reform. The Four Assurances include: the use of college and career-ready standards and assessments, cradle to career data collection and tracking, teacher accountability, and addressing low performing schools.

I note with concern that each of these four items was part of a binding commitment that states made with the U.S. Department of Education (DoED) in their 2009 Race to the Top (RttT) applications. In fact, each state's RttT application had to include a proposal on how the Four Assurances, among other things, would be addressed as part of an aggressive reform initiative. The Common Core standards not only shackle the states to the federal government via the RttT grant application* but also form the nucleus of the "assurance"-based reform Duncan described to UNESCO not long after the Common Core initiative had begun to ramp up.

As part of their agreement to embrace Common Core, states also entered into assessment agreements with one of two federally funded testing consortia. The assessments will measure adherence to the standards to ensure consistency of expectations and provide the reporting needed to conduct sound data analysis. The testing consortium memorandum of understanding (MOU) stipulates that the federal government and other education agencies or "researchers" have access to individual student data from the State Longitudinal Data System, or SLDS.

Duncan's Second Assurance is fulfilled in SLDS, which uses a P-20 model to mold and track what Duncan refers to in his UNESCO address and elsewhere as "human capital." These databases serve to collect and share data on students, creating a student profile from preschool through age 20—"from the cradle to career," as quoted by Arne Duncan in his 2010 UNESCO address.

---

* EDITOR'S NOTE: For more on the maneuvered adoption of Common Core and how it has shackled the states, see Shane Vander Hart's essay (pp. 3-28).

Unbeknownst to me and probably most other parents, the states have been establishing and expanding longitudinal data systems for years. Ostensibly, the idea has been to improve education using more accurate and comprehensive data on students, tracking them from pre-school to 20 years of age in order to tailor their education to meet the needs of the workforce. This vision mirrors the German model, which slots students into a career path by the time they are in high school. This data does not serve to enrich education academically or improve the achievement of students; rather, it sorts them, serving the agendas of multinational corporations and government entities.

This concept of determining the path of a student, rather than allowing them to determine their own course isn't new either. It was in the middle of just such a debate among parents back in the Netherlands of the 1600s that philosopher Baruch Spinoza said, "Academies that are founded at public expense are instituted not so much to cultivate men's natural abilities as to restrain them."*

Duncan's Third Assurance is seen in new teacher evaluation systems, now tied both to the results of the student assessments and new expectations set forth by corporations. Teachers are now keeping evaluation "portfolios" that require loads of bureaucratic paperwork to meet the demands of the evaluation systems.

The Fourth Assurance, addressing low-performing schools, turns out to be code for expanding corporate-owned, for-profit charter schools. The value of this initiative for those pushing Common Core lies not just in profit but in the fact that, in many states, for-profit charters do not have parent-elected boards and thus are not accountable to parents and voters. It amounts to taxation without representation.

THE PROPAGANDA MACHINE

I notice that the National Broadcasting Company (NBC) is now serving as a promoter for Common Core. The network's Education Nation initiative and NBC Learn video collection are chock full of

---

* EDITOR'S NOTE: Marsha Familaro Enright's essay (pp. 361-383) contains a discussion of some historic examples that would seem to confirm this point.

"support" for educators and parents in the transition to this reform. It brings to mind an MSNBC commercial from April, promoting Melissa Harris Perry's show. In the ad, expressing her thoughts on education funding and support, Harris-Perry said, "We've always had kind of a private notion of children. Your kid is yours, and your responsibility. We haven't had a very *collective* notion of 'These are our children.' So part of it is we have to break through our kind of private idea that 'kids belong to their parents' or 'kids belong to their families,' and recognize that *kids belong to whole communities*."[2] (emphasis my own)

Harris-Perry's words advanced a theme frequently detected among Common Core promoters, including the Center for American Progress: the mindset that our kids are better raised and educated by a wise and benevolent corporate elite than by the family.[3]

My ongoing exploration of Common Core reveals that, in addition to $4.35 billion in federal stimulus money, the Bill and Melinda Gates Foundation has held the purse strings to this reform. In essence, they bought the endorsement of every and any organization or state department that might push back against this effort, effectively silencing parents with would-be experts on education matters.

Expressing opposition to my own legislators has proven to be a challenge. I was countered with articles published by respected organizations such as the Fordham Institute—which received over $6.7 million in Gates funding. Fordham has, in fact, been a Common Core promoter extraordinaire.

GLOBAL PUBLIC-PRIVATE PARTNERSHIPS

Far too many published articles promoting Common Core can be linked directly to Gates grant money.[4] Yet promoters don't seem to see any conflict of interest in this reality. I find it interesting that the single largest financier of a reform initiative that supposedly promotes college- and career-readiness was a self-made man who dropped out of college.

I also learn that, like the United States, Gates entered into a cooperative agreement with UNESCO in 2004, in this case establishing Microsoft as a sanctioned non-governmental organization, or NGO.

Gates personally initialed each item of the document, to fund and create a global education system.[5]

In 2002, the UN announced the Decade of Education for Sustainable Development, 2005-2014. The goal of this initiative, according to
a variety of related materials, is "to integrate the values inherent in sustainable development into all aspects of learning to encourage changes
in behavior that will enable a more viable and fairer society for everyone." But what does fairer mean? And fairer to whom? It would seem
the answer is special interests, not least multinational corporations.

Between 2004 and 2008, other notables—among them Intel, Cisco,
Harvard University, and the World Bank—also entered into education
agreements with UNESCO. These contracts are part of a new era of
public-private partnership in education. The UNESCO agreements
give private multinational corporations a great deal of influence on
education policy worldwide, with little accountability to parents
or taxpayers, all the while tapping a global market worth trillions of
dollars.

November 24, 2013: Local Control Is Lost

I email a letter to my governor, sharing my concerns about the Common Core reform initiative. I promptly receive a boilerplate response
from his chief of staff. The letter thanks me personally for my "interest
in education" and asks to "please allow me to share some information with you about the Common Core." What follows this request
is nothing more than talking points lifted from the CCSSI web page.
The reply does not address my questions at all. I am certain that the
governor never even saw it. I ask other members of a coalition that I
have recently joined to send letters of their own. Over a dozen of us
receive the exact same boilerplate response, regardless of the concerns
any of us has posed.

I email the Arkansas State Board of Education, listing twelve concerns. Appointed by the governor, board members serve 7-year terms.
Only two of nine current members have an education background.
Regardless, it is the only recourse I have left. My own school district
has had no local elected board for the last five years.

The board chair and I exchange emails for two weeks. I am not satisfied with her responses. They are very condescending, and research reveals most of them to contain falsehoods or half-truths. Finally, I ask for placement on the agenda for public comment so that I can share my concerns in person and on the record. I am subsequently notified that I have been granted five minutes. Strangely, this notice comes from the same person that responded to my email to the governor—his chief of staff.

December 9, 2013: The Bully Pulpit

After weeks of preparing and rehearsing my testimony, I arrive at the Department of Education Building for the monthly meeting. The room is old, and small. There are pictures of cheerful children on the wall. The board members sit high on a platform in a formal area not accessible by the general public. Our seating area is beneath them, at least three feet lower and several feet away.

The board's chair, Brenda Gullett, opens the meeting by publicly making fun of parents that have emailed concerns about Common Core. Parents are referred to as hysterical conspiracy theorists that will believe anything they read on the Internet. I writhe in my seat. Three hours go by while charter schools beg for renewals and higher caps on enrollment. The assistant commissioner gives an update about how wonderfully the Common Core implementation is going and how great things are in the classrooms. When the chair asks her about parent complaints, Assistant Commissioner of Learning Services Megan Witonski, responds that some people just don't like change and will do anything to stop it, even when it is for good, and where were these people three years ago? The meeting adjourns for a 30-minute lunch.

When I return from lunch, the chair approaches me in a condescending manner and asks if I still plan to speak. When I confirm that I do, she apologizes that I will not get five minutes after all—rather just three minutes, assuming they do not run out of time. I politely ask her to use her authority as chair to keep it at five minutes since I had prepared accordingly. She cannot make any promises, she says, and proceeds to discourage me from speaking, saying it could be hours, that the "train has already left the station, the standards will not be rolled back" and that I am wasting my time.

I assure her that I intend to persist and get the legislature involved, if need be. She replies that she is a former Senator, and I will have to wait until the next session to get anything done anyway, so I may as well go home. This dialogue continues back and forth for a while. Ultimately, I tell her that there is no quicker way to get something done than to tell me I cannot do it. Funny, I think to myself, aren't these boards supposedly in place to serve as representation for the people? Instead, I have been sandbagged, intimidated, and publicly mocked. Who do they think they are? Who do our kids belong to?

After five and a half hours, my time to speak has finally arrived. As I stand before the board, the state education commissioner moves a cell phone in front of the chair, motioning her to keep track of my time. I give my testimony. Since my voice falls on deaf ears with the board, a fellow coalition member places a recording of my testimony on *YouTube*, where it promptly resonates with almost a million other parents over a 6-month period. I am flooded with letters from around the country. I am not alone.

December 2013: Unreasonable Search and Seizure

I read the new regulatory changes made by the DoED to the Family Education Rights and Privacy Act (FERPA). In the company of my fifth-grade daughter, I comment aloud on biometrics being added to the act's definition of personally identifiable information, wondering what such data could be used for in education circles. My daughter replies that the library at school has been using her fingerprint to check books out of the library since last year.

For a moment, I lose my breath. Certainly, I must have signed something at the beginning of the school year, giving permission to take my child's fingerprint, somehow missing the fine print in the stack of forms we are asked to complete. Or, perhaps a note was sent home, and I mistakenly threw it away. As I continue to read about the changes to FERPA, I realize the school didn't have to ask permission or send a note home. As of 2012, parent consent is no longer required to collect or share personally identifiable information. Some Internet searches reveal that other parents are reporting iris scans for bus transportation and fingerprint scanners in the cafeterias. I feel like the wind has been knocked out of me.

I make an appointment with the principal and the librarian at our elementary school to talk about the fact that they are using my children's fingerprint. They are very helpful and kind and share with me some information from the software vendor's web page. I even get a demonstration of how the software works and assurance that the system does not keep their fingerprint. It deletes the fingerprint, they tell me, and keeps only a template. They relate that this system is something the school had been asking to obtain for some time and that they were so excited to get it last year. Using the finger scanner, the checkout process is faster, they say. They no longer have to worry about kids losing their cards. No, they never requested a signed a consent form, and a note was never sent home to parents about the fact that fingerprints would be used.

I am still disturbed. There is a lack of consistency here. If my children wish to go on a field trip, I have to sign a permission slip. I have to sign a photo release for any school-related pictures of my children that will be used, a release for my children to be listed in the school directory. No consent is needed for fingerprints. If my friend wishes to serve as a substitute teacher at our school, she must be fingerprinted and sign a consent to allow that fingerprinting along with a background check. Yet, my children were fingerprinted without my knowledge or consent.

I return home and research the information the school has provided. The technology vendor, identiMetrics, explains that the fingerprint itself is not stored; rather a template is created, forming a binary number. That binary number is assigned to the student bar code and ID number. Therefore, says the vendor, no security risk is posed.

Other sources, including a government study disagree. The template itself is individually identifiable to the student. This binary code can be used to rapidly link different databases and create a personal profile without consent. According to The U.S. Government National Science and Technology Council, a user can reconstruct a fingerprint image from the template, and government security experts have successfully hacked the fingerprint scanners used in schools.

Kim Cameron, the chief architect of identity and access in Microsoft's Connected Systems Division disagrees with using this technology in schools, saying: "If you want to find out who owns a fingerprint, just convert the fingerprint to a template and do a search for the template in one of these databases. Call the template a binary number if you want to. The point is that all you need to save in the database is the number. Later, when you come across a 'fingerprint of interest' you just convert it to a number and search for it. Law enforcement can use this information—and so can criminals."[6]

I also find a 2011 report by the National Academy of Sciences, entitled *Biometric Recognition: Challenges and Opportunities*.[7] The report concludes that biometric recognition technologies are inherently probabilistic and inherently fallible. Sources of uncertainty in biometric systems include variation within persons, sensors, feature extraction, and matching algorithms, and data integrity.

Since 2012, identiMetrics has partnered with Pearson Education, one of Common Core's most prominent corporate partners.[8] Pearson is also America's largest single purveyor of textbooks and digital education media, dominating the market.[9] While the biometrics issue isn't Common Core per se, this association makes me even more uncomfortable, particularly given that Pearson develops the assessments that my children will now be taking under the Partnership of Assessment for Readiness of College and Careers (PARCC)

I call my superintendent about what I'm learning. He is aware the software is being used in our library and in the cafeterias of the entire district in a neighboring city. I share my research with him, asking why the district did not do similar investigation before implementation or ask parents about it. Did I miss a meeting? He responds that the vendor assured the district that the software was safe, and the decision was made on a state level, not with him. It's out of his hands. There's nothing he can do to change it. I hang up, flabbergasted and angry that the school district made a decision to violate my child's privacy based on a sales pitch and that parent input was never sought or involved.

I feel victimized, much like I did when my car was broken into a year earlier. At that time the creepy, violated, sick feeling that a stranger was prying into my personal life came over me like a wave. This time, it is much worse. Someone else, someone unknown, has my child's fingerprints. Controversial plans I found on the DoED website to study and shape personal traits using biometrics come to mind.[10] If the school can take biometric information from my children without my knowledge, what else will they collect? Where will that information go? Until my daughter happened to say something, I had no idea—nor did most of the parents of children attending our school—that fingerprint scanners were being used. Several teachers that worked there daily did not know either.

My child is subject to unreasonable search and seizure, without my consent or knowledge that it happened in the first place. Isn't this unconstitutional?

I immediately go back to the elementary school and request that my children be removed from the fingerprint scanner program. The librarian offers to create traditional library cards for my daughter and son with their student IDs incorporated so that they can continue to check books out of the library. They assure me that a few other parents have requested the same.

I am not alone. Rather, I am officially part of the conspiracy-theory "fringe," branded as paranoid by many because of our concerns about technology that is rapidly becoming part of our mainstream existence and facilitating intrusion into the privacy of our families. I watch as the librarian deletes my children's profiles and fingerprint templates. I insist that she restart the program and check to be sure the information is gone. I walk away uneasy that the template is likely still sitting on a server somewhere, waiting to be misused and forever violated.

March 2014: "Because I'm the Mom, and I Said So!"

Many state laws were changed between 2003-2013 to accommodate Common Core and related initiatives. For example, it is now mandated that students take new online high-stakes assessments. These new assessments support the Common Core initiative and are replacing all of the former tests our children took in my state, including third party norm-referenced tests. The assessments are brand new and have not been vetted. They include end-of-course assessments, literacy and math competency assessments, and career aptitude assessments. This last item bothers me most—that the government would mandate a career test. In Arkansas, there is no legal exception to opt out of these very intrusive assessments. How can the government mandate that my child take a test?

The organizations that develop and provide the new assessments have troubling connections to the people and organizations that devised the Common Core initiative itself. It seems to me that trusting these assessment providers is like asking the IRS to audit itself without any third-party input. What's more, the organizations that lead this initiative and own the copyright to the standards—the National Governors Association and the Council of Chief State School Officers—hold private closed-door meetings where parents or press are not welcome.

PARCC, the testing consortium to which my state belongs, is holding field tests this spring. They are testing the test. Our kids are already scheduled to sit through days of testing in the normal course of the school year, and now they are expected to sit through hours more in the name of corporate research.

A national opt-out movement has erupted as an unintended consequence of Common Core. As parents we have grown tired of the mega-testing culture that No Child Left Behind has created. Common Core expands on that culture and adds a disturbing amount of data collection to it. Opt-out forms are now flooding schools across the United States, not just because parents are in disagreement with excessive testing, but also as an act of civil disobedience against Common Core.

I have since withdrawn my children from public school. However, I am getting letters from parents all over the country with disturbing responses and reactions from school officials. They are being told that there is no opt-out provision, or that it is against district policy to avoid the test. They ask parents what our reasons are for refusing these tests and use intimidation tactics and a condescending tone. Perhaps the education departments around the nation misunderstand. As a parent,

I am not asking permission to waive the test. I am refusing to participate. Because my child belongs to me, and I said so.

It doesn't seem to matter how much research I do, how carefully I make connections, or how thoughtful I am in my communication about Common Core; a respectful response to my concerns is hard to find. Since Common Core is promoted as being "for the benefit of the children," any parent, such as me, that counters it is labeled misinformed or a victim of Internet hysteria. This attitude emanates from the top down. In November 2013 DoED Secretary Arne Duncan dismissed "white suburban mothers" for opposing Common Core because "our children aren't as smart as we thought they were." This bullying response trickles down into the states as well. In Wyoming, a legislator referred to concerned parents as "Political Pundits sitting behind their computers late at night in their underwear!."[11] In Missouri, State Representative Mike Lair officially added $8.00 to the state budget for tin foil, accusing parents opposed to Common Core of being black-helicopter-chasing conspiracy theorists.[12]

In my own state of Arkansas, in a public Joint Education Committee meeting, one representative asked Assistant Commissioner of Education Dr. Megan Witonski how to respond to the many email concerns she was receiving about Common Core. Witonski's response: "Only wet babies like to be changed." She doesn't get it. Parents aren't simply resistant to change. The truth is, we know more about Common Core then she does.

Too many see Common Core as just the latest educational idea or fad rather than as the final phase in a long progression of false reforms. Game-changing laws like Goals 2000 and the Federal School-to-Work Opportunities Act of 1994, for example, have contributed substantially to the achievement of the fundamental shift we see in K-12 education today. Education is no longer about the development of well-rounded, free-thinking individuals. Rather it is about producing mere "human capital"—as Arne Duncan has so frankly and inelegantly put it—for the workforce. Big Government and Big Business, working hand-in-hand, have bypassed the people, gradually making education into something it should never be.

Few legislators are willing to stick their neck out on Common Core, considering that, in my state, as well as most others, the State Department of Education accounts for the highest budget and the heaviest lobby. The few lawmakers that do support parents' rights in opposing this false reform do so at risk. For example, they may lose the support of their leadership or other legislative colleagues on separate legislation they're attempting to advance. They also tend to face a great deal of pressure from their respective governors as well as local industries and corporations that have vowed to support the effort.

The voice of corporate totalitarian America is one of the loudest in favor of Common Core. The U.S. Chamber of Commerce, arguably one of the most powerful lobbying organizations in the nation, has received approximately $1.3 million from the Gates Foundation to date for the purpose of promoting Common Core. Local chambers are now promoting the standards in luncheon presentations. State chamber presidents are doing interviews with local newspapers and radio stations, bragging about how Common Core will prepare little worker bees for the twenty-first century.

Sadly, upon confronting our own state chamber about the initiative, it turns out that they have no idea what they are furthering. They know nothing about the testing, the privacy invasion, or the system of teacher evaluations. They firmly believe that Common Core is "just a set of standards." The top businesses in the states also promote it. Here in Arkansas, The Walton Family Foundation and Tyson Chicken are advocates of the reform. In Pennsylvania, the CEO of Exxon sent a threatening letter to the governor when he asked to pause the reforms.[13] How can parents be heard over all of this money and political influence, especially when our boards are shackled to the state? Our children belong to us, not multinational corporations.

The Problem with Apathy

The problem with apathy is that it gets us the government—and the education—that we deserve. Over the years, small initiatives that seemed harmless on their own are, in hindsight, now revealed as bricks laid into a wall designed to separate children from their families, gradually denying parents the liberty to raise and educate their children as they see fit. The Common Core initiative brings what Sir Michael Barber of Pearson education heralds as "sustainable reform" and "irreversible reform." He suggests that reformers "work on the culture and the minds of teachers and parents" so that they can "never go back to the way it was before."[14] It's not just any brick wall we've been building, then; it's one designed to ensure that parents cannot break through it—to leave them no choice but to bend to another's will and give up their educational freedom.

One might suggest that if a parent does not agree with the changes being proposed in the public school system, the parent should simply withdraw the child and turn to private or home school. There are two flaws in these suggestions. The first is that private school and homeschool students will still be impacted by Common Core because the GED, ACT, SAT, and educational materials are all aligning to it.* Second, not every family in America realistically has either of these options. Since they pay for the public school system with their property taxes, they shouldn't have to make a change in the first place, and they have a right to representation.

I am fortunate. I have been able to make my own way in life. I own a small business and am not dependent on any assistance to raise my family. While I do not feel I make enough money to afford private school for all three of my children, I do have the schedule flexibility to homeschool them. I am also fortunate to live in a state with very loose homeschool regulations. However, I come from a single-parent household in an inner city, full of gang and drug violence. I know that side of life, too. While I have options, what about the parents who do not?

The media continues irresponsibly to further the myth that homeschool families are unsocialized, radical, religious hermits. In so doing, they create fear and doubt in the minds of parents that might otherwise consider this reasonable option to what Common Core and related reforms are now foisting upon children in the classroom. Moreover,

---

* EDITOR'S NOTE: William Estrada's essay contains additional information about the alignment of well-known national standardized assessments to Common Core (pp. 125-146).

reformers and their media acolytes regurgitate propaganda aimed at convincing parents that they do not have what it takes to raise their children without some form of government intervention. But at this point can any of us deny the wisdom of Sir Walter Scott: "All men who have turned out worth anything have had the chief hand in their own education."[15] How is it that humanity has turned out so many educated success stories without government? Seems to me that education has only diminished since the DoED's creation in 1979.

We cannot have it both ways in America—a constitutional republic *and* education reform dominated by Big Government and Big Business—because to do so requires that parents and students give up their unalienable rights to educational freedom and privacy. Reform math in grades K-5 renders parents unable to help our children with their homework and does not work for the majority of concrete thinkers. The lack of transparency silences parental intervention when it comes to the concepts, worldviews, and even the mindsets our children are being taught. The longitudinal data systems impose unreasonable search and seizure, providing the government and multinational organizations access to our children without our consent. Attempts to expand charter schools lacking parent-elected boards remove the parent's voice regarding policy and curricula selection. State laws mandating high stakes assessments force the parent's hand to government obedience and sweep out from under the feet of their children the American Dream—the ability not just to pursue opportunity but to create it. Each one of these items serves as a brick in a wall built between parents and their children. Government and its corporate partners are constructing this wall, assuming a generation for their own in the name of social reform and human economic capital. Will we stop them before the wall is complete?

NOTES

1. The paper was prepared by Burke's office during his time as representative of California's 70th Assembly District. This quote is pulled from the first page of the introduction.

2. Harris-Perry's comments can be easily found on *YouTube*. See, for example, http://youtu.be/N3qtpdSQox0.

3. "Panelist at Podesta's Think Tank on Common Core: 'The Children Belong to All of Us'," *MRCTV*, posted Jan. 31, 2014, http://www.mrctv.org/videos/panelist-podestas-think-tank-common-core-children-belong-all-us.

4. To see who the Gates Foundation has funded to implement, research, or promote Common Core, a simple search of the foundation's grants database will reveal much: http://www.gatesfoundation.org/How-We-Work/Quick-Links/Grants-Database.

5. The agreement, signed on November 17, 2004, was still retrievable via UNESCO's website as of July 30, 2014, http://www.unesco.org/new/fileadmin/MULTIMEDIA/HQ/CI/CI/pdf/strategy_microsoft_agreement.pdf.

6. Kim Cameron, "Just Lie So You Can Sell Your Product," *Kim Cameron's Identity Weblog*, May 9, 2007, http://www.identityblog.com/?p=775.

7. Whither Biometrics, *Biometric Recognition: Challenges and Opportunities*, edited by Joseph N. Pato and Lynette I. Millett (Washington, D.C.: National Research Coucil), http://dataprivacylab.org/TIP/2011sept/Biometric.pdf.

8. The partnership appears to be run through PowerSchool. The PowerSchool information sheet dated 2011 and accessible at the following link, in fact, bears the identiMetrics logo, http://www.fccsc.k12.in.us/fccsc/PSU_Docs/3%20Pearson%20ISV%20Partners/identimetrics/pearson-partner-identimetrics.pdf.

9. Reuters entry for Pearson PLC (PSO), http://www.reuters.com/finance/stocks/companyProfile?symbol=PSO.

10. Nicole Schectman, Angela H. DeBarger, Carolyn Dornsife, Soren Rosier, and Louise Yarnall, *Promoting Grit, Tenacity, and Perseverance: Critical Factors for Success in the 21st Century*. Draft of a paper prepared for the U.S. Department of Education, Office of Educational Technology (Wash-

ington, D.C.: U.S. Department of Education, 2013), http://www.ed.gov/edblogs/technology/files/2013/02/OET-Draft-Grit-Report-2-17-13.pdf.

11. Kristy Tyrney, "Whose Knickers Are in a Knot Now," *Adventures of an Inspired Housewife Blog*, Jan. 28, 2014, http://adventuresofaninspiredhousewife.blogspot.com/2014/01/letstake-stroll-down-memory-lane-shall.html.

12. Anne Gassel, "Missouri Budget Amendment: $8 For Tinfoil Hats," *Missouri Education Watchdog*, Feb. 19, 2014, http://missourieducationwatchdog.com/missouri-budget-amendment-8-for-tinfoil-hats/.

13. Diane Ravitch, Truth in American Education, Breitbart, and numerous other sites that track education covered the letter from Exxon to Pennsylvania's governor in December 2013.

14. Oak Norton, "Who Is Sir Michael Barber," *Utahns Against Common Core Blog*, Oct. 16, 2012, http://www.utahnsagainstcommoncore.com/who-is-sir-michael-barber/.

15. Letter to J. G. Lockhart, 1830.

IX. THE WAY OUT

Saying No to False Reform

THE SLIPPERY SLOPE
OF EDUCATION REFORM:
Confusion, Complexities, and Concerns

Morna McDermott

The American Legislative Exchange Council...

Though it's a powerful and highly effective organization, the American Legislative Exchange Council, or ALEC, is an organization about which most people remain unaware. What is ALEC, exactly, and what does it have to do with education reform?

In a 2003 *Governing* article, Scott Pruitt, then an Oklahoma state representative and chair of an ALEC task force, explained ALEC's basic operations succinctly: "ALEC...puts legislators and companies together and they create policy collectively."[1] In essence, ALEC provides a forum in which special interests can work directly with state law makers to "craft" model legislation favorable to ALEC's corporate members and benefactors. The model bills are subsequently made available to legislators to carry back for sponsorship in their own states.

Quite simply, then, ALEC is public-private partnership at work—government and special interests holding hands to advance mutually beneficial agendas. However, in so doing, public-private partnership short-circuits proper representation in the legislative process, tending to trammel the voices, rights, and livelihoods of average citizens.

Discussed below are several ALEC model education bills that demonstrate precisely this self-interested behavior, some of which have already been approved by ALEC's board of directors for potential advancement in states across the nation.

...And Why You Should Worry About Them

THE STUDENT ACHIEVEMENT BACKPACK ACT

An ALEC model bill crafted in 2013, the Student Achievement Backpack Act certainly sounds innocuous enough—if all you pay attention to is the title. But the description should raise eyebrows: "This bill provides access by a student's parent or guardian or an authorized LEA user to the learning profile of a student from kindergarten through grade 12 in an electronic format known as a Student Achievement Backpack."[2]

"Learning profiles? Access? What the heck is an LEA? And what exactly is this bill aiming at?" you're now hopefully asking yourself. LEA stands for local education agency, but language within the same model legislation indicates that "local" doesn't necessarily mean local anymore:

> Section 2. {Definitions} (A) As used in this act: (1) "Authorized LEA user" means a teacher or other person who is: (a) *employed by an LEA* that provides instruction to a student; and (b) authorized to access data in a Student Achievement Backpack through the *Student Record Store*. (2) "LEA" means (a) a school district organized and existing pursuant to law; (b) a board of cooperative services or intermediate school district; (c) a publicly funded agency established by the state for the express purpose of authorizing charter schools; (d) a public charter school authorized pursuant to state statutes; or *other local education agency in the State that has administrative control of public education*. (emphasis my own)

Honestly, I have no issue with my child's records or data being shared with his school or teachers. But when the Student Achievement Backpack Act and related legislation come to your state, remember this phrasing: *"or other education agency...that has administrative control of public education."* Through this legislation corporations and other private entities, once employed or contracted by a school district, will now have legal cover as LEA users and, very likely, full access to your child's personal records.

The Backpack legislation adds: "The [State Department of Education] shall use *the robust, comprehensive data collection system* maintained by the [State Department of Education], which collects longitudinal student transcript data from LEAs and the unique student identifiers to allow the following to access a student's Student Achievement Backpack: (1) the student's parent or guardian; (2) *each LEA that provides instruction to the student.*" (emphasis my own)

Backpack is just one of several model bills presented at ALEC's 2013 annual meeting that would facilitate the violation of student privacy and make children and their families increasingly vulnerable to data collection and data mining—not just by state and federal governments but also third parties, including corporations with strong profit motives. Backpack was approved by ALEC's board of directors early in January 2014.

Despite potential abuses of such information sharing, not to mention massive threats to data security, ALEC seems to have no qualms about making student data widely accessible or storing it in the cloud. In fact, their model legislation varies very little from—and actually appears to leverage—the massive data collection we are currently seeing under federal imposition of Race to the Top (RttT). Many of us didn't imagine it could get any worse, but ALEC's legislation will facilitate the further collection of data and potentially track as much if not more information than RttT:

> Section 3(E). No later than June 30, [20XX], an authorized LEA user shall be able to securely access student data in a Student Achievement Backpack, which shall include, at a minimum, the following data, or request the data be transferred from one LEA to another: (1) *student demographics*; (2) course grades; (3) course history; and (4) results for any state-mandated assessments
>
> (F) No later than June 30, [20XX], an authorized LEA user shall be able to access student data in a Student Achievement Backpack, which shall include the data listed in Subsections (E)(1) through (4) and the following data, or request the data be transferred from

one LEA to another: (1) *section attendance*; (2) *the name of a student's teacher for classes or courses the student takes*; (3) teacher qualifications for a student's teacher, including years of experience, degree, license, and endorsement; (4) results of formative, interim, and summative computer adaptive assessments; (5) *detailed data* demonstrating a student's mastery of core standards and objectives as measured by *computer adaptive assessments*; (6) a student's writing sample written for an online writing assessment; (7) a school's grade {or equivalent, based on the state's accountability system}; (8) results of benchmark assessments of reading; (9) *a student's reading level at the end of grade 3*; and (10) *any teacher comments, recommendations, or notes applicable to an individual student, as determined useful for inclusion*;...(12) Federal Free or Reduced-Price Lunch Program eligibility. (emphasis my own)

Interestingly, section G of the approved draft also appears to ensure that "[n]o non-academic centric data can be gathered and leveraged." It provides a long list of data types suggested as out of bounds, from information pertaining to religion and politics to psychometric, biometric, and medical data. It stipulates that parents are to be notified in the event that the district does maintain any such information on the student. Yet, close inspection reveals that section 3(E)(1) of the model legislation nevertheless requires the gathering of "student demographics"—and demographics can potentially mean whatever those gathering the information wish. Depending on how the required demographics are defined in any given state, a vast amount of personal and intrusive data could be collected, bypassing parent notification entirely.

Also troubling is section 3(F)(11), which asserts that "[n]othing in this act shall require any state agency to collect new data fields or categories for a student than the data categories used in the 2012-2013 school year." If the data being collected in the 2012-2013 school year was already problematic, Backpack will do nothing to stop it. Moreover, not requiring new data fields or categories to be collected is a far cry from forbidding new data fields or categories. Legal phrasing matters.

Rather than closing the data spigot, Backpack, as structured, seems instead to allow the data to keep flowing.

Think federal student privacy laws protect you and your children from the passage of Backpack in your state? Think again. With the Federal Education Rights and Privacy Act, or FERPA, now gutted, your child's data can be handed to just about anyone who says they "need" it.* Whether it's federally, state, or privately managed, all of this data potentially flows to the same places and for the same dubious reasons.

At least two additional model education bills introduced at the 2013 ALEC meeting pose just as great a threat to students and their families.

STUDENT FUTURES PROGRAM ACT

An additional passage in Backpack promises "a complete learner history for postsecondary planning."[3] This language would essentially pave the way for the Student Futures Program Act, another bill submitted to ALEC for consideration in November 2013, though not yet listed as approved on the organization's website.[4] In shorthand, Student Futures provides private corporations and education delivery systems with access to personal student data in order to market and promote products to those students. It's like Web "cookies" via K-12 education. Companies can track those students who they think will be interested in their products, making every classroom a finely honed profit center. The act would:

> [a]llow an education provider to (a) *research and find student users* who are interested in various educational outcomes; (b) *promote the education provider's programs and schools to student users*; and (c) *connect with student users* within the Student Futures website; (3) allow a {insert state} business to: (a) *research and find student users* who are pursuing educational outcomes that are consistent with jobs the {insert state} business is trying to fill now or in the future; and (b) *market jobs and communicate with student users* through the Student Futures website as allowed by law. (emphasis my own)

Just as insidiously, Student Futures would involve skiing down the slippery slope of leveraging student data for education and career tracking. Most states are too far down this slope already, but Student Fu-

---

* EDITOR'S NOTE: See Jane Robbins' essay in this volume, which deals specifically with the data collection and data mining on students (pp. 195-204).

tures would "allow the Department of Workforce Services to analyze and report on student user interests, education paths, and behaviors within the education system so as *to predictively determine appropriate career and educational outcomes and results.*" Using data collection systems under the guise of "career and college ready," children can be steered into particular programs or career opportunities.

I am all for vocational education. I am all for providing information to students about career possibilities. I am all for encouraging children early on to dream about what they want to be when they grow up and helping them to get there. To be blunt: The Student Futures Act ain't that program. Instead, it is Big Brother's Big Corporate Sister rearing her ugly head. Without so much as a second thought, public-private partnership is facilitating the prediction and shaping of children's futures before those children have had a chance to determine a future for themselves.

Just because this model bill does not yet appear to have attained approval from ALEC's board of directors, does not mean that citizens are safe. It may yet gain approval. If it doesn't make it through ALEC, those keen on advancing the agenda it contains may well find other ways to move the ball forward.

COURSE CHOICE PROGRAM ACT

ALEC has still more to offer in the form of the Course Choice Program Act, approved by its board of directors on the same day as Backpack. Interested ALEC stakeholders have evidently realized that while they may not fully be able to take the public out of public education, they can bring the private into the public sphere. Meet the new education LEAs—corporations and edutech companies "privatizing" public education:

> The Course Choice Program created by this Act would allow students in public schools and public charter schools to enroll in online, blended, and face-to-face courses not offered by the student's school, and would allow a portion of that student's funding to flow to the course provider. This Act creates an authorization process for providers and identifies provider and course eligibility criteria. *This Act*

requires course providers and the State Department of Education to regularly report on the key measurements of student success and enrollment. This Act gives the State Department of Education authority to enter into an interstate course reciprocity agreement, allowing students within the state to take courses from providers domiciled in other states.[5] (emphasis my own)

Who are the course providers referenced in this language? Again, quoted directly from the model legislation: "'Course Provider' shall mean: (A)n entity that offers individual courses in person or online, including but not limited to online or virtual education providers, public or private elementary and secondary education institutions, education service agencies, private or nonprofit providers, postsecondary education institutions, and vocational or technical course providers, and have been authorized to provide such courses by the State Department of Education."

Disturbingly, then, the Course Choice bill would further encourage educational providers to gather data on students, share it, and leverage it. Moreover, the Course Choice model language includes monetary incentive to feed this data stream; it allows for a portion of student funding to flow to course providers, essentially in exchange for regular data reporting and sharing with a state department of education. Public schools, private schools, virtual schools, non-profits, and for-profit corporations—as providers of instruction, everybody will now have access to data collection 2.0.

The Course Choice bill accomplishes its mission, in part, by opening the way for public education courses taught by public education teachers in physical public education settings to be parsed out, course-by-course, to private providers. These private providers will subsequently receive public moneys and access to student data. As indicated above, the course providers defined in the Course Choice language fit the parameters for the not-necessarily-local LEAs described in Backpack.

Deployed, all three ALEC model bills would facilitate each other. In the case of the Course Choice bill, the increasing marginalization of local teachers becomes yet another troubling mechanism for compromising student privacy and freedom.

Swapping in For-Profit Charters

As becomes apparent when one starts to dig into current education policy trends, it's not just Common Core that needs to be fought. It's a bundled package of so-called reforms, of which Common Core is just one important component. As discussed above, data collection and the data mining of students is part of that package. So is the corporate takeover of public education and attempts to "privatize" it. While privatization may sound good on the surface, we're already getting a strong indication through key model legislation that the approach to—and goals of—privatization envisioned by many of the heavyweights pushing such policy is not all it's cracked up to be and will come at a heavy price.

In addition to data collection and data mining, ALEC model legislation has also facilitated a process whereby public schools judged to be "underperforming" or "failing" can subsequently be replaced, managed, or even owned by private corporate interests as for-profit charter schools[6]—all legally sanctioned by state governments and quietly blessed by the federal government.

At least until May 2012, when it beat a hasty public retreat, the National Association of Charter School Authorizors (NACSA) was a member of ALEC, serving as a member of the organization's Education Task Force in 2009.[7] According to its website, NACSA receives funding from the Walton Family Foundation, the Michael and Susan Dell Foundation, the Bill and Melinda Gates Foundation, and the Robertson Foundation, among others.[8] Valerie Strauss reports that the Walton Family Foundation gave NACSA $1,874,274 in 2010, while also doling out money to those who, in turn, fund NACSA.[9]

But wait…There's more! Sourcewatch reports that NACSA has ties with the Obama administration. Race to the Top included a $5 billion stipend to push for charter schools on a state-by-state basis. NACSA has cozied up to all sides—conservative-minded ALEC as well as key liberal progressives. They're all patting one another's backs, while the rest of us have been cajoled into blind infighting.

It's all a manipulative game. Not only has the very definition of what it means to be educated shifted, so have the methods and criteria by which the performance of students, teachers, schools, and districts are evaluated. Race to the Top (RttT), Common Core, school "turn-around" policies, new teacher evaluations, high-stakes testing, and increased funding for charter schools work in tandem to ensure that public schools, public school students, and public school teachers ultimately fail. For example, FairTest, a watchdog organization for fair and open testing, has suggested that "race, class and gender biases give White, affluent, and male test-takers an unfair edge."[10] Creating circumstances under which large numbers of public schools (especially those populated by poor black and brown children) can't succeed provides a subsequent convenient justification for closing them and flipping them into private charters.

Unlike the original conception of community-based charter schools envisioned in the 1970s—creative spaces to try "out-of-the-box" ways of teaching and learning—the charter school movement in the last decade has been almost wholly co-opted. Private business figured out that charter schools can reap them enormous profits. In very frank terms, they are using Common Core and related initiatives to create a public, national factory to churn out student widgets, only to close down those plants that don't measure up to their bizarre expectations. They then install *private* widget plants instead, accountable to all of the same questionable Common Core standards and compliant with all of the same data collection and data mining stipulations. The only real difference is that these shiny new McCharters, with all of the educational value of a fast food operation, are for-profit. The Success Academy chain of charter schools in New York, owned by Eva Moskowitz, stands as a classic example.[11] Success Academy has moved to colonize public school spaces, receiving public tax dollars as part of the opportunity, then picking and choosing which children they will even serve.

Revised tax law has made these new charter schools the investment darling of hedge fund corporations because of maximized investment returns:

> Thanks to a little discussed law passed in 2000, at the end of Bill Clinton's presidency, banks and equity funds that invest in charter schools and other projects in underserved areas can take advantage

of a very generous tax credit—as much as 39%—to help offset their expenditure in such projects. In essence, that credit amounts to doubling the amount of money they have invested within just seven years. Moreover, they are allowed to combine that tax credit with job creation credits and other types of credit, as well collect interest payments on the money they are lending out – all of which can add up to far more than double in returns. This is, no doubt, why many big banks and equity funds are so invested in the expansion of charter schools. There is big money being made here—because investment is nearly a sure thing.[12]

In many states, legislation is being passed to privatize public education on a nearly statewide level. See Michigan for example where new supposed reforms not only open the door to who can create charters and instructional delivery models (i.e. online education), but also whether they can charge fees and who charters can choose to accept (or not) as students. Privatized or not, charters will still receive public money.[13]

Is what I'm describing any sane person's idea of real educational reform?

In 2008, Naomi Klein wrote about "manufactured crisis," including the education reform narratives that "our nation is lagging behind" and "we are a nation at risk."[14] These narratives create a constantly renewable sense of instability and panic. Reformers use language like "status quo" in attacking the teachers and parents who are simply attempting to defend what they believe to be good and right for their children and their schools. The chaotic, untested, and forced implementation of Common Core and the rest of the current reform package is certainly keeping public school teachers, parents, and children off balance, just as Klein describes. Ultimately, it is facilitating a level of government oversight and intrusion that allows unconstitutional levels of federal involvement in education and undemocratic levels of corporate interest.

Ins and Outs of Bridge-Building

Those of us who critique a one-size-fits-all model for education are not seeking a one-size-fits-all solution. If we're going to navigate through or around the false reforms that are constantly being shoved at us, we need to be talking and listening to each other. There's an ideology of greed and control that spans both sides of the aisle when it comes to education. The people and the traditional signposts in which we all used to place trust are being turned upside-down and, in many senses, leveraged to fool us. In fact, when it comes to education, most of us have been duped. A fresh perspective, along with a lot of communication and cooperation, is required.

The question is how do we get there?

Despite the collective willingness of some of us—Left, Right, and middle—to embrace dialogic, shifting, and even contradictory approaches to creating what we could consider real reform, there are real and often substantive differences that we will need to acknowledge, negotiate, and—where possible—bridge. What are the advantages and the limitations of working together toward the goal of real and substantive education reforms?

I believe in, and I have seen, successful alliances in opposition to the Common Core between groups or individuals from all over the political spectrum. In fact, I must state emphatically that I believe that collaborative efforts between groups that normally don't mesh is both possible and necessary. Of course alliances can be formed across the political aisle! Our differences need not be an obstacle to our efforts. If Teach for America advocate and StudentsFirst founder Michelle Rhee and former Florida governor Jeb Bush can make strange bedfellows, then why can't we?

Yet, as a "progressive"—whatever that means these days—I struggle with the over-generalized notion held by some that any collaborative resistance is good resistance. I do not agree with the idea that in order to collaborate and be effective we must put aside all differences. Incidentally, I am not talking about differences in our labeling. Terms like Democrat or Republican, "the Left" and "the Right," mean very little in identifying one's personal values either for or against so-called reform in education these days. In fact, such labels can be defined in a myriad of ways, making them entirely unreliable as a means of determining where alliances can and can't be forged. No movement, Left or Right, can be defined as monolithic. Just as groups that identify on the Left are not all one set of anything, neither are those on the Right.

For those who are "liberally" minded, the notion of democracy for marginalized voices is important. For people who are more "Right"-leaning, the idea of representative republicanism is important. And yet, all semantics aside, can we agree that the voices of people, not corporations, must have the central role in public education?

Here are six key items that would help me, for example, abandon defunct political labels or other differences and forge working alliances:

1. Protecting children's privacy rights from the "data pirates" (a phrase coined by Leonie Haimson on Twitter);

2. Opposing the developmentally inappropriate and harmful effects of the Common Core on our children's learning;

3. Desiring to fight for the possibility of far reaching, self-directed, and meaningful public education for *all* children by supporting the rights of communities, parents, teachers, and children in forging that vision;

4. Advocating for greater state and local control; opposing the gross over-reach of the Federal Department of Education in state and local education policies;

5. Protecting our democracy from corporate-controlled decision making; and

6. Fighting for fairness and restorative justice for all children, especially those historically marginalized, underserved, or confronted with oppressive circumstances.

While groups from the far Left and far Right both share an opposition, it is still uncertain whether or not they share a solution. By now the reasons to critique and outright oppose Common Core are not just many and varied; they are painfully clear. What remains to be seen is what will take the place of Common Core once it has been ended. In part, possible answers to this dilemma rest with local sociopolitical influences that vary from state to state, even from community to community. Rather than casting aside our differences in order to defeat Common Core, only to face each other as ostensible opponents once it is eliminated, I'd rather forge sustainable and transparent alliances now that can not only defeat our joint foes but also help us mutually to agree upon "what happens next" and work toward any such goals more amicably. In fact, whether or not we can cast aside our "differences" depends on what those differences *are* and involves critical conversations over whether or not we are fighting *for* the same things. If we are not fighting for the same things, then we need to discern together whether there are ways for our separate goals to co-exist peacefully. It's a dialogue worth having.

To that end, it's also become vital that we begin to distinguish between individual/personal differences and true ideological differences. One of the best ways to do that is to stop drawing dividing lines according to labels and start talking to each other about ideas, values, principles, and issues. No one political ideology can or should own the narrative. The party of "greed" has no problem crossing the aisles, and so long as we have some shared vision for solutions, why shouldn't we?

Few human beings can actually be summarized in totality by any over- arching system, whether it be the Democratic Party or the Catholic Church. Each of us constructs personal meaning and individual purpose within or around these larger systems. There are persons who happen to self-identify as both conservatives and progressives who share common values about public education—their political labels notwithstanding. There are also persons or organizations opposed only to Common Core based on a distinct set of ideological values, and who likely conflict on principle with their collaborative counterparts in regard to other, even related, educational matters. For example, a group opposed to Common Core might also support other initiatives that they perceive as leading to the dismantling of public education, such as vouchers, union busting, and charter schools.

If you are a "progressive" like me—not to be confused or associated with "progressives" like Bill Gates)—and opposed to Common Core, I wonder: how can we, *or should we*, negotiate differences in relationship to voice and motive?

VOICE

What often gets ignored in media coverage about Common Core opposition is that numerous *Left-leaning* voices have been vocally opposed to top-down, federally mandated policies, forewarning us back in the 1990s of what was going to happen if we didn't fight to stop them. I'm pleased that opposition to the Common Core has finally been addressed more publicly in the mainstream media, but largely it is presumed that opposition to it is merely something "conservative" or of "the Tea Party." Efforts from "the Left" have been vocalizing and mobilizing as well.

There are myriad reasons for this lopsided reporting, beyond the scope of this chapter. Two possible reasons might be, first, that the U.S. Department of Education (DoED) thinks it can shore up Common Core support among moderates by associating opposition with the Tea Party; and, second, that radical-Left scholars have failed to reach the general public, spending too much time in the ivory tower using impenetrable language and not enough with their boots on the ground.

Yet, again, many "progressive" social justice scholars were vocally opposed to a federally mandated curriculum and corporate partnerships long before the Tea Party ever existed. Just a handful of such scholars and educators include Henry Giroux, Alfie Kohn, Maxine Greene, bell hooks, Bill Ayers, and Peter Taubman—some of whom are now ironically implicated in creating Common Core.[15] For example, in 2007, Taubman warned about corporate and governmental interests hijacking a "liberal" narrative, noting that "[p]rogressive educational projects are transformed by translating them into rationales for greater accountability and by reconfiguring pressing social issues and political issues as the responsibility of teachers who can only meet that responsibility by surrendering to disciplinary technologies and audit practices, such as those required by [the National Council for the Accreditation of Teacher Education or No Child Left Behind]...or state and local regulatory agencies."[16] In fact, it wasn't just progressive educational projects that were being hijacked; it was education itself.

Many of us "liberal" scholars have even been critical of other "liberal" scholars who have endorsed such government-corporate partnerships. Taubman rightly illustrates how, "even so-called progressive educators seem to feel compelled to qualify any critique of this new order with 'but of course we support accountability and standards.'" I agree with him that such examples "reveal the support voiced along the educational spectrum for the transformation that is occurring" and share his mystification in wondering "why educators would willingly collude in what many view as an education nightmare."[17]

To my conservative readers, please understand this: *We've been framed!* While you and I may differ about the roles or values of social justice, diversity and equity in public education, Left-leaning progressives neither wrote nor endorsed the usage of those terms to promote Common Core and related initiatives. Rather, sell-outs, corporate interests, and non-profits, such as Achieve, inserted faux social justice and other misleading language in an effort to attract liberal support. By and large, we have not taken the bait. In fact, on the whole we have been against a nationalized curriculum or system of testing from the beginning. Critical cultural scholar Michael Apple forewarned in 1996: "While proponents of a national curriculum may see it as a means to provide social cohesion and to give us the capacity to improve our schools by measuring them against 'objective' criteria, the effects will be the opposite...Rather than leading to cultural and social cohesion, differences between 'we' and the 'others' will be produced even more strongly, and the attendant social antagonisms and cultural and economic destruction will worsen."[18]

MOTIVE

Can I work with anyone who refers to Common Core as "ObamaCore"? Perhaps. The initiative is driven by President Obama's administration. But what of the original idea for a nationalized curriculum documented in the meetings of the National Business Roundtable as far back as 1989 under George H. W. Bush? What about Common Core pimps like former Florida governor Jeb Bush, the supposedly free-market loving Walton Foundation, the Eli Broad Foundation, and Fox News mogul Rupert Murdoch?[19] As this list attests, any alliance must be grounded in a shared set of facts and the concession that Common Core and other schemes to nationalize education have been and are promoted by *both* Democrats and Republicans, liberals and conservatives.

My fight against Common Core is not an attempt to discredit the entire Republican party nor to gain influence for my own party—of which, by the way, I have none. My fight is against what education activist Susan Ohanian refers to as *"the corporate party."*[20] Corporate investments, including well-funded lobbying efforts, in what have been termed public school "alternatives" will permit the swaying of curricular and instructional decisions favorable to those corporations' interests in future U.S. and global labor markets. This is the true meaning of "college and career ready."

Full Circle

It is precisely a concern with how public-private partnership is facilitating false education reform that brings us back to where this essay began: ALEC.

While some folks might believe that ALEC's model bills could hold some benefits for the public, the very nature of the organization and its operational framework contain an inherent threat of corruption and essentially undermine both the voice of the people and transparency in government. When an organization that solicits the membership of public servants is heavily funded by private interests, citizens should remain watchful. Private organizations, such as ALEC, are not obligated to share their membership lists. Nor must they reveal which of their members or corporate stakeholders have had a hand in crafting the legislation that they ultimately work to advance. To be clear, ALEC is far from alone, though it is easily one of the best funded and most powerful organizations of its kind. Many entities and individuals on both sides of the political spectrum seek to influence policy in similar ways—which is why we would all be wise to delve beyond the talking points surrounding any proposed legislation in order to understand where it came from and who most truly benefits from it.

Interestingly, a schism seems to exist within ALEC in regard to Common Core and related policy initiatives. Though they're facing a very uphill battle, particularly due to the financial influence of pro-Common Core special interests, some members within ALEC do appear to oppose false educational reform. In December 2011, not only did ALEC's Education Task Force pass a strong anti-Common Core resolution, it also voted through a comprehensive legislative package opposing Common Core.[21] Both items were intended for use as model state legislation.

Unfortunately, at the same meeting during which these items passed, minutes reveal that three new members were accepted onto the task force. One of them was Wireless Generation—since renamed Amplify Education—a subsidiary of the Rupert Murdoch-owned News Corp. As education watchdog and blogger Mercedes Schneider and others have noted, Wireless Generation had a substantial monetary stake in the student data machine that Common Core helps to feed, in that it "built the data storage system for the controversial data cloud, in-Bloom."[22] A year later, ALEC had done an abrupt about-face on the issue, publicly adopting a neutral stance on Common Core and allowing the initiative to roll forward unhindered. Connections Academy, the country's largest for-profit provider of online education, also holds membership in ALEC and currently sits on the ALEC Education subcommittee. As such, the content of the Backpack and Course Choice bills, in particular, should come as no surprise.

It should be noted that just because a legislator works to advance an ALEC model bill in his or her state does not mean that it will ultimately pass or that it will pass in the same form in which it was originally structured by the ALEC stakeholders involved in its development. Proposed bill language is still subject to any given state's legislative process, during which it may be altered significantly or fail to pass in any form.

Nevertheless, there are additional reasons to be watchful of any education-related policy originating from within ALEC, in particular. A number of ALEC's known corporate stakeholders also played a large part in creating and advancing Common Core, not least by funding Achieve, Inc., which was involved from early on in Common Core's development. A short list of donors[23] who have given to both ALEC and Achieve includes:

- DuPont

- IBM Corporation

- Nationwide Insurance

- State Farm Insurance Companies

- The Bill and Melinda Gates Foundation

- The GE Foundation

- AT&T Foundation

- Lumina Foundation

Conclusion

Then Common Core tsunami has everything to do with the other facets of corporate-style reform discussed in this chapter. It's a wave we all hold a stake in resisting. Some conservative groups, such as the Heritage Foundation, have ideological reasons for opposing Common Core but continue to promote charters and vouchers because they value what they understand as a privatized model of education. Many libertarian-minded individuals and organizations reject charters and vouchers along with Common Core for a variety of reasons, not least because they see them as detrimental to a truly free marketplace in education. Opponents coming from a progressive social justice perspective see Common Core as part of plan to collect and manage the data used to close schools and re-open them as charters, to re-segregate schools, and to use poor black and brown children as widgets in the plan for profits. In this sense, Common Core is much like a work of (bad) modern art. Each of us interprets it according to our subjective set of values, what offends us, and what it is we believe should happen.

So here we are, all staring at the same God-awful work of modern art (metaphorically speaking). What does it mean? What is the purpose of it? How can we change it? And most importantly, can people across the political spectrum work together in this regard? We have all the findings and information one might need to launch a resistance. We know what's wrong with these reforms. We know who's lying and who's selling out. What we need now is a different, more emotional/social skill set: Can we listen to one another? Can we be open? When we disagree can we do so respectfully? Can we be humble when needed? Can we come from a place of love rather than anger? Can we care about ourselves and our individual needs while empathizing with others?

I'm a "glass half full" kind of person. And I have hope in human beings. Or maybe I'm just whistling in the dark, convincing myself of this because, quite honestly, the alternative is too unimaginable. So let's hope…

NOTES

1.   Alan Greenblatt, "What's Smart about ALEC?" *Governing*, Oct. 2003, http://www.governing.com/topics/politics/What-Makes-Alec-Smart.html.

2.   ALEC, Student Achievement Backpack Act, approved by the ALEC Board of Directors Jan. 9, 2014, http://www.alec.org/model-legislation/student-achievement-backpack-act/. It is worth observing changes to the language of this approved draft from that initially submitted and included in ALEC's November 2013 meeting agenda packet, http://alec.org/docs/ED_2013_SNPS_35_Day.pdf.

3.   See section 3(A)(2)(b) of the approved language at the link referenced in note 2.

4.   See the November 2013 meeting agenda cited in note 2 for draft language of the Student Futures Program Act.

5.   The draft language for what was then titled the Student Course Choice Program Act was submitted for initial consideration in November 2013 and is contained in the meeting agenda cited in note 2. The language as approved in January 2014 can be found on ALEC's website, http://www.alec.org/model-legislation/course-choice-program-act/.

6.   For example, see ALEC model bill "Next Generation Charter Schools," http://alecexposed.org/w/images/5/57/2D4-Next_Generation_Charter_Schools_Act_Exposed.pdf.

7. Sourcewatch, Entry on the National Association of Charter School Authorizors (NACSA), last updated July 2012, http://www.sourcewatch. org/index.php/National_Association_of_Charter_School_Authorizers.

8. See the organization's "Funders" page, http://www.qualitycharters. org/about-nacsa/funders.html.

9. Sourcewatch, "NACSA."

10. "The ACT: Biased, Inaccurate, and Misused," FairTest, Aug. 20, 2007, http://fairtest.org/facts/act.html. See, specifically, paragraph 4 of the article.

11. Celeste Katz, "Ex-CM Eva Moskowitz Expanding Charter Empire?" *New York Daily News*, Jan. 25, 2012, http://www.nydailynews.com/ blogs/dailypolitics/ex-cm-eva-moskowitz-expanding-charter-empire-blog-entry-1.1688698.

12. Kristin Rawls, "Corporations Advise School Closings, While Private Charters Suck Public Schools Away," *AlterNet*, Feb. 15, 2013, http://www. alternet.org/education/corporations-advise-school-closings-while-private-charters-suck-schools-away?akid=10062.34521.o_lD0E&rd=1&src= newsletter795084&t=5.

13. Bob Kefgen, "New Oxford Memo Outlines Sweeping Rewrite," Michigan Association of Secondary School Principles, Nov. 12, 2012, http://mymassp.com/content/new_oxford_memo_outlines_sweeping_ rewrite.

14. Naomi Klein, *The Shock Doctrine: The Rise of Disaster Capitalism* (New York: Picador Press, 2008).

15. See, for example, Henry Giroux, *Theory and Resistance in Education: A Pedagogy for the Opposition* (New York: Bergin & Garvey, 1983); Aflie Kohn, *The Case Against Standardized Testing: Raising the Scores, Ruining the Schools* (Portsmouth, NH: Heinemann, 2000); Maxine Green, *The Dialectic of Freedom* (New York: Teachers College Press, 1988); bell hooks, *Teaching to Transgress: Education as the Practice of Freedom* (New York: Routledge,1994); William Ayers, *Teaching Toward Freedom: Moral Commitment and Ethical Action in the Classroom* (Boston, MA: Beacon Press, 2004); Peter Taubman, "The Tie That Binds: Learning and Teaching in the New Educational Order." *Journal of Curriculum and Pedagogy* 4, no. 2 (Winter 2008), 150-60.

16. Taubman, "The Ties That Bind" (2008), 157.

17. Ibid., 153.

18. Michael W. Apple, *Cultural Politics and Education* (New York: Teachers College Press, 1996).

19. Bruce Anthony Jones and Susan Otterbourg, "School Change Business and the Private Push" in Bruce Anthony Jones (ed.) *Educational Leadership: Policy Dimensions in the 21st Century* (Stamford, CT: Ablex Publishing Corporation, 2000), 123-37.

20. Susan Ohanian, "Data Warehousing Will Destroy Your Soul," *Susan Ohanian.org*, Mar. 17, 2010, http://www.susanohanian.org/show_commentary.php?id=786, excerpted from "Our Schools/Our Selves," *Canadian Centre for Policy Alternatives* 19, no. 2 (#98, Winter 2010).

21. For more on this occurrence, see "The Time That ALEC Got It Right." *Deutsch29: Mercedes Schneider's Edublog*, July 29, 2013, http://deutsch29.wordpress.com/2013/07/29/the-time-that-alec-got-it-right/.

22. Ibid. inBloom announced in April 2014 that it would be shutting down operations due to a firestorm of concern about the privacy of student data. See, Natasha Singer, "InBloom Student Data Repository to Close," *The New York Times*, Apr. 21, 2014, http://bits.blogs.nytimes.com/2014/04/21/inbloom-student-data-repository-to-close/?_php=true&_type=blogs&_r=0. While it was a bit of good news, no one should rest easy yet.

23. On several of the entities included in this list, see the following articles on the *Deutsch29* edublog: "The Common Core Memorandum of Understanding: What a Story," Oct. 14, 2013, http://deutsch29.wordpress.com/2013/10/14/the-common-core-memorandum-of-understanding-what-a-story/, and "More on the Common Core: Achieve, Inc., and Then Some," Dec. 2, 2013, http://deutsch29.wordpress.com/2013/12/02/more-on-the-common-core-achieve-inc-and-then-some/. For those interested in exploring other corporate and public-private connections in education "reform," Schneider's blog is highly searchable.

JUST SAY NO:
Cutting the Core

BRIAN MEDVED

I am fairly confident that very few readers will know my name or who I am. A handful may be familiar with my role in what has so far been a successful fight against Common Core in Wisconsin's Germantown School District. Our success is all the more remarkable because, as of this writing, we are one of the only districts in this state to have waged a concerted battle against Common Core.

I'll share with you how we got there and my role in that process. But I also want to share with you something of the convictions I've developed as a result of my research on Common Core and my battle against it, in particular, how imperative it is not just for parents but for all citizens to be engaged on education matters.

As a disclaimer, I must mention that, even though I sit on the board, I am writing as a dad and a private citizen. While I have perspective to offer as a board member, I speak only for myself—my beliefs and my opinions—and not as a representative of the board or any other body.

The Creation of a Common Core Activist

Because I have been interested and involved in the education of my boys, I have always watched the activities of our school district and the Germantown Board of Education. As is the case in many families with young children, I did not pay as close attention as maybe I should have. However, when in 2009 the school board put a referendum for a new pool on the ballot, things began to change. I was in touch with a group of concerned parents in the district that were closely following local politics, and my interest and involvement began to grow. In 2012, I decided it was time for me to try to get elected to the board of education and see if I could make a difference.

As I was preparing for my run for school board, I kept coming across this issue called Common Core State Standards (Common Core). In doing my homework I found that it had already been accepted by our board in 2010 and was in the process of being implemented. At that time no one could tell me what it was or why we were implementing it in our district. So, out of curiosity, I started to look into the standards on the website of the Wisconsin Department of Public Instruction (DPI). I read through the standards and DPI's talking points.

At first blush, Common Core seemed like a good idea. I liked the idea of rigor, internationally benchmarked standards, and accountability—all claims the Common Core proponents boldly made. How could anyone *not* like these things? Better still, DPI explained that these were "just standards" and would not take away local control; districts would be able to develop their own curricula.

Yet, at some point in my investigation process, the wheels came off. I began to understand that Common Core wasn't what it appeared to be on the surface—that there was a lot going on behind-the-scenes—and that Common Core architects and proponents had reasons for keeping some things hidden. This reality is not necessarily easy to explain or understand succinctly, which immediately put a concerned citizen and school board candidate such as me at a disadvantage. What's more, Common Core proponents had done an outstanding job of pushing the initiative through quickly in forty-seven states, with little or no fanfare and no public debate. It made it look to the uninformed citizen or elected official as though the initiative had broad-based support nationwide. I would argue that this illusion was fostered by design.

I will not go into all the issues with Common Core. I will leave that task to others in this book. But I will share with you a few of those that I had from the perspective of a parent and, ultimately, as a school board member.

I think the best description of Common Core that I could offer would be to identify it as the insidious union of Big Business and Big Government. Those who identify on the political Left tend not to like big business. Those on the Right instead tend not to like big government, so their issues with Common Core have in many cases focused on the Big Government, or federal control, angle. But in order to understand the full truth of Common Core, it's important to recognize that it really is a partnership between the two, to the detriment of most citizens, our teachers, and especially our children.

The issues for me started with discovering the fact that the Common Core standards were created and approved by just a small handful of people, none of whom had ever taught in a K-12 classroom. Two of the architects had had no standards experience whatsoever.

My concerns grew in learning that the only two content experts brought on to validate the standards, along with three other of the twenty-four Common Core validation committee members, refused to sign off on them.[1]

I then further learned that the teachers the Common Core authors claim to have brought in to provide opinions and input were completely shut out of the process and had no indication if their ideas were implemented or even considered.

I dug further.

I found that the curriculum aligned to the Common Core was frequently very political in nature and not fact-based. Wisconsin belongs to the Smarter Balanced Assessment Consortium (SBAC), so I also took a look at the sample assessments on the consortium's website. What I found there was even more politically charged. It made me very uncomfortable to think that the materials in our classrooms or the questions on the assessments were being used to advance a political agenda, regardless of who was pushing it; such material does not belong in our classrooms. Many parents are getting upset— justifiably so, I would argue—in learning that Common Core is more about teaching kids what to think and not how to think.

Just as troublingly, I began to understand that the high-stakes SBAC tests would be aligned to the Common Core standards at the same time curricula were aligned to the test. Once again, we will be teaching to the test. We all saw how well this method worked with No Child Left Behind (NCLB). Never mind that parents aren't allowed to see what's on these tests without an act of Congress or that, if by some miracle you do gain access to them, you're forbidden to disclose what you saw.

My findings continued, raising even more questions and concerns. ACT college entrance exams, it turns out, are currently being aligned to Common Core. I had previously understood that the ACT was intended to assess content knowledge. Unless we are drastically changing the content of learning, why would such an alignment be needed?

The final straw for me as a school board member was that I had taken an oath to uphold the U.S. Constitution—and thus the Tenth Amendment, which reinforces that policy areas, such as education, not specifically within the purview of the federal government remain under the sovereign authority of the states and the people. My oath also bound me to the Wisconsin State Constitution and our state statutes on the general operation of schools, which affirm local control of education. Common Core made it impossible for me to fulfill my sworn oath or to obey the spirit of state law. I could not sit by and accept changes to Germantown's standards and curriculum that would violate the rules by which we, as citizens, are guided.

Coming down from the U.S. Department of Education (DoED), Common Core was adopted immediately, unilaterally, and sight-unseen by Wisconsin State Superintendent of Schools Tony Evers on the first day the standards were offered. In fact, Evers made Wisconsin the first state to sign on to the Common Core standards, unilaterally adopting them for Wisconsin literally within hours of the standards becoming available and well before they were actually drafted and available for inspection. Evers made this commitment in exchange for the mere opportunity to apply for Race to the Top funding. He did so without any substantive public discussion or debate.

Both the standards and the assessments remain untested and without scientific validity. Together, they amount to an expensive, risky, experiment on our children. Even Bill Gates, whose foundation is the largest financial contributor to the development of the Common Core standards stated that it would be at least ten years before we would know if the standards would produce the desired results. In states such as New York and Kentucky, where full implementation of Common Core and aligned standardized assessments occurred early, disastrous results are already being felt.

Fifty million children will be affected by Common Core on its current path—a million plus in Wisconsin alone. The potential cost of losing a generation of kids is incomprehensible and irreversible.

At this writing, the State of Wisconsin continues to move forward with full implementation of the Common Core standards and SBAC assessments for the 2014-2015 school year. Despite the fact that we are a local-control state, so far most communities and school administrations are embracing the initiative. In large measure, this fact stems from the reality that Wisconsin's official accountability measure will be the Common Core-aligned SBAC assessments. Schools and districts—who will be judged based on the performance of their students on the SBAC assessments—likely see the adoption of an alternative set of standards as too risky

Germantown thought differently about the problem.

The Germantown Way

On December 9th, 2013, in a seven to zero vote, and with the support of our administration, the Germantown Board of Education voted to drop the Common Core standards in favor of creating the Germantown Model for Academic Achievement. As part of the motion we will make our unique standards and curricula available online for all to view—and review. This decision will be the beginning of a long process that should continue indefinitely. Particularly with the rapid changes in technology and the world around us, we should always be evaluating new ways to innovate, including refining our curricula and delivery methods. There are many tested, proven ways to educate; we will find ways to implement these methods and techniques into our standards and curricula.

Rejecting the Common Core standards was a bold move for the district and will come at some cost. We are fully aware of the scope and magnitude of this decision and are willing to accept the challenge. It is a price we are willing to pay in the best interests of our students and community. The costs will most likely be the investment in time, and not necessarily financial. We have a budget for developing and revising curricula, as all districts should. We will be redirecting this money to provide materials that align with our own standards; we will find ways to fit this initiative within our budget. We have been in contact with several content and standards experts, and many are more than willing to help us with our standards creation and implementation at little or no additional cost to Germantown School District.

We are the first district in the state of Wisconsin to make such a move. We were told by the Wisconsin Department of Public Instruction that we could proceed without loss of funding, which made for an easier decision. Now we begin the work of developing the Germantown Standards to educate our students.

How did we get to this point? It did not happen overnight. It took the dedication of many people over the course of several years. The successes we've had happened only because of the engagement and support of dedicated parents, educators, and the community.

The Right People, the Right Conditions, the Right Results

I can't stress enough how important it is to have the right people represent your community on your school board. This will make all the difference as you attempt to gain local control and make the move away from Common Core.

Germantown is a fairly small district with four elementary schools, one middle school and one high school. At the same time we are not so small that we can't dream big. We currently have an enrollment of approximately 4 thousand students and a staff of just over 400, including administration. Our high school ranked sixth in the state last year.

As I stated earlier, back in 2009 when I was considering a run for school board, I was approached by a group of concerned parents that were very active in the community. I became part of this group, which was working behind the scenes to get solid candidates elected to the board. We wanted fiscally responsible, actively engaged candidates, individuals dedicated to making Germantown the best school district in the state. We fully understood this was no small task.

In a way, from a timing and personnel perspective, the stars aligned in Germantown. Just prior to my election, our superintendent had resigned to go to another district. Common Core was already on the radar screen as we began to search for a replacement, giving the members of the Germantown Board of Education a unique opportunity to hire someone that had a shared vision and the dedication and resolve to accomplish the big things we were looking to achieve. The person we selected, Jeff Holmes, fit the criteria we established, is a visionary, and has worked tirelessly for our students and teachers since coming on board. There are people in the state capital and in the district that have been resistant to change and, in particular, our move away from Common Core. Mr. Holmes understands what it takes to educate children and is willing to step on a few toes to get our district on the right path.

At around this same time, we were also looking to hire a replacement curriculum director. Here again, we were able to find someone that fit our needs to a T. Our new curriculum hire has a vision, understands the direction we are heading, and is up to the task of getting us to the next level.

Both of these individuals fully understand the benefits and the challenges of establishing our own education standards and are willing to collaborate with and motivate others to realize this goal; doing so will enable us to make Germantown the premier district in the state. I anticipate hurdles along the way, but none will ultimately stop us.

In February 2014, the Germantown board voted to form an ad hoc committee to create our new standards and curricula. I am honored to serve as that committee's chair. Developing our own standards will most likely be a multiyear project. We will be requesting input from all stakeholders, parents, teachers, and community who were shut out of the Common Core standards development process. We also are including local businesses that may be able to help, offer input, and possibly provide facility or financial support. No one will be barred from the process if they are willing to offer ideas and their support. I truly believe that this is what making schools local was intended to look like.

Germantown has—and I believe will continue to have—one of the hardest working school boards in the state. We are not a rubber stamp for anything or anyone. We do our homework and get to the heart of the matter to make the best decision for our stakeholders. We are pushing our vision forward with a collaborative approach. I have no interest in micromanaging the district. It's not our role to oversee day-to-day operations such as classroom homework assignments. Rather, it's our job to put the right people in place and establish the right conditions and parameters to make our vision a reality, and we are well on our way.

As we create our new standards we will be bringing in the best people in their areas of expertise to provide direction and advice so that we can create the best possible standards for our community. Over the course of this project, we hope to become a great model for any district to follow. We've even developed a website that will show our progress and lay out our standards and curricula. It went live in April 2014. Anyone can follow what we're doing.[2]

The elephant in the room continues to be the coming Smarter Balanced assessments. At this point we do not have a good exit strategy in place. We are looking for a waiver for a couple of years as we develop our own standards and curricula. Ideally we would like to create our own testing as well. We are not sure this will be an option, but is one path we are pursuing.

There is a small but growing opt-out movement in Wisconsin. We may end up at the point where we join this movement and encourage parents to opt their children out of the tests. We will be sure to share how we accomplish this goal as it becomes a reality.

A Way Forward for Others

"That's all great," you're saying to yourself…"but how do we escape Common Core?" There are several things I would recommend.

EDUCATE YOURSELF

Take the time to find out what is going on in your state, your town, your community. I will be the first to admit that I was not paying close enough attention. I was involved, an avid reader, and followed the news every day. It was not enough—even when I was considering running for school board and thought I was paying close attention. It wasn't until I really started digging that I made necessary discoveries.

One great way to inform yourself is to get involved with a group of engaged citizens in your area. If you can't find one, start one. It can be as simple as meeting at a local restaurant, library, or in someone's home to determine what's happening, where the gaps are in your information, and what you may need to work together to find or do. Most parents with children of school age are already in several groups, be it sports, Scouts, PTA, or any number of other groups. Get to know those other families. If you're already a leader or a coach, you'll have a good headstart on building a helpful network.

Many hands make light work. Once you've got some people together, divide up research and other information-gathering tasks in order to establish a list of local 'go-to' experts. To facilitate research efforts, you can start an information-sharing Facebook page, a Google group, or an email distribution list; it just takes a little creativity.

EDUCATE OTHERS

We cannot win the battle against false education reform or any number of related issues unless we share the truth with others. Talk to your family, friends, neighbors—anyone that will listen. I have yet to meet anyone that is not appalled by Common Core once they have deeper knowledge and understanding of what it is and the direction in which it is taking our schools. You now know a lot more than most from reading this book. Don't keep it to yourself.

There are lots of ways to communicate and spread the word. Social media is a great way not only to share but also learn vast amounts of information in a short amount of time. For some people technology may seem intimidating, but most of what I'm recommending is actually very easy to learn. Find someone to show you or take a quick Facebook or Twitter tutorial online. You'll be amazed at what a *powerful tool* social media can be for you.

In my own efforts to get the word out, I put together a website to share what I have learned. I've made it a one-stop shop for all things

Common Core.[3] Feel free to share my site with your email list or on Facebook or Twitter. Or create your own. With just a bit of multitasking, I am able to manage my website and stay up to the minute in a couple of hours a day.

Another way to communicate is to stage educational events for groups or the general public. Since Germantown has made the decision to move away from the Common Core, I have been invited to speak to several groups. I was recently invited to talk at a friend's home on Common Core standards. It was a small 'coffee and conversation' a local mom had put together for concerned parents. Over fifty parents showed up, including the principal of a local elementary school. This was a great opportunity for them to address their concerns, and now good information continues to flow out to the community.

There are plenty of other articulate activists who have done their homework on this issue and who would be more than happy to come help people in your community understand what's at stake—even providing suggestions on action items or next steps. Many of them are willing to speak for free or for just their travel expenses. Take advantage of these resources.

CHOOSE TO ENGAGE LOCALLY

It's easy to use the excuse that we're too busy. As someone once said, "Don't sweat the small stuff." The question is: Is the education of our children small stuff? What are our priorities?

It is not enough to just show up at the polls on Election Day and say we did our part. It is up to every citizen to hold local officials accountable. Make it a point to show up to at least one school board meeting a year, more if at all possible. Let your board know you care and are paying attention. Common Core was adopted almost by default in countless communities simply because no one showed up to school board meetings. People didn't hear the words "Common Core" until long after the local school board had already rubber-stamped it. As opaque as the adoption process was, it could have been stopped in more districts if people had simply been at the meetings and asked themselves earlier: "What is this Common Core thing they're talking about?"

Every school district that I know of has a website with a plethora of information for you to leverage in your research. An increasing number even have a video archive of all board meetings for anyone to review, in case you could not make a meeting. As noted, Germantown plans to put its standards and curricula online for all to see. These are all great resources. But none of them do any good if no one ever goes and looks to see what the heck we or other school boards are doing. It is up to all citizens, and especially parents, to hold schools accountable and keep them transparent in all they do. Again, you don't have to do it all. Working with friends and neighbors will facilitate accountability with very little effort on any one person's part.

In particular, get to know the curricula being used in your schools. Whether or not you are in one of the states that signed on to Common Core—and even if you're a charter school, a private school, or you home school—this awareness is still necessary. With most educational materials and assessments now being aligned to the Common Core, you will, at the very least, have to deal with the curricula issues associated with it. It's best to start figuring out how to limit or prevent damage to the greatest degree possible. I never thought some of the curriculum issues that I was reading about would come to my district, only to find they already had.[4]

It's true that the systems used to develop curricula had already been corrupted and politicized long before Common Core. We trusted "the experts" to filter things and look out for our kids, but it has not been happening as we thought. However good you think your school district is, I would wager that Common Core-aligned curricula and materials are in your school as I write this. In many cases, these curricula are developmentally or age-inappropriate, opening children to a range of problems, from stress and depression all the way to long-term disadvantages in their ability to read, write, or do math.*

At the local level, fostering communication between parents, teachers, and administrators is another important area to keep your hand in.

---

* EDITOR'S NOTE: Numerous contributors to this volume confront the negative impact of Common Core on students. See, in particular, the essays in section 7, "A Learning Killer: Stunting Students."

The people in this education triangle can be some of your best allies and sources of information. Most will welcome your help and support.

Parents should never be shut out of the process; they need to be brought in as much as possible. Whatever you do, if you're a parent, don't shut yourself out. Go on field trips. Volunteer for any activity where helpers are needed. Spend time in the schools. Familiarity is a big part of what will provide you with needed awareness of what is going on in the classroom so that you will know if something is wrong—whether with standards, curricula, teaching methods, or testing.

Websites are an outstanding way to communicate with parents and keep them involved. One of my favorite teachers in the Germantown School District was my son's fifth-grade teacher. He had a website that he kept up-to-date and shared with the parents of all his students. It had links for the kids and included all of his curricula and assignments for the week. As a parent, I found the site to be a great tool to see what was going on in the classroom. If my son forgot a homework assignment, it was there for me to print out. I was able to review his assignments and learning goals and help him study for tests.

If you are retired and have some extra time on your hands, check with your local school. Our school district has a Senior Tax Exchange Program (STEP); program seniors are paid to come into our schools and 'volunteer' to help our students. The more that people engage and observe firsthand in our schools, the better off everyone will be—students, teachers, and the community as a whole.

If you are hitting a brick wall with your local school board, it's probably time to get new leadership on your school board. Make a run yourself or encourage and support other informed candidates.

FAMILIARIZE YOURSELF WITH STATE AND LOCAL LAWS

Getting to know the laws in your community and in your state will be crucial to any effort to defeat false reforms and enhance local control and education options. We are using the laws and statutes of Wisconsin to help in our local efforts. When they are not in our favor, we will work to change them. Education in Wisconsin is primarily guided by the state DPI; in many states you have a state board of education that guides your districts. You need to develop an understanding of the laws and statutes in your state. This will help you to know the directions in which you will need to move to get the best results in your area. I know there are many groups and organizations in each state that can help you in this effort, reach out to them and join their efforts.

WORK TO IMPACT STATE POLICY

Local control is one of the primary reasons that we have historically had some great school districts in this country. Education needs to start in the home. Local control and more and better options are the only answers to save our education system.

Yet, even in local-control states such as Wisconsin, impacting state policy is a crucial fight—whether to increase or bolster local control; enhance protection of student data; or prevent future unilateral adoption of state standards.

Get to know the cast of characters in your state legislature. Figure out who would be most open or amenable to advancing the kind of legislation you have in mind and make an appointment to begin a conversation. In the event that it's not *your* legislator, do your best to have someone from the individual's district with you, as it will likely make a difference in his or her receptiveness to your thoughts and ideas.

In Wisconsin, during the last legislative session, several bills were drafted that would have improved our situation. Yet, because we have not seen full implementation here in Wisconsin, many legislators on both sides of the aisle still don't fully understand the risks Common Core poses. Some have been hesitant to take up the fight, while others have actively worked to keep Common Core in place and marginalize those fighting against it. Every helpful bill that was put forward unfortunately died at the end of the session, but we are hopeful something will advance in 2015. We will have more support and louder voices the next go-round. We refuse to be shut out of the process.

OPT OUT OF THE ASSESSMENTS

You may not be able to get your state or district to move away from the Common Core anytime soon. But in most states you still have the right to opt your children out of the standardized testing, or assessments. Forms are available online for such a purpose.[5]

Understand that state and local education officials may not like you choosing this option, and you may meet some resistance. However, in one New York school, 80 percent of the parents opted out of the assessments, and they were eventually canceled.[6]

We all know there is strength in numbers. If you decide to opt out, don't go it alone. Get as many other parents as possible with you.

GIVE PARENTS THE FINAL SAY

A state legislature will exercise power over schools in any manner consistent with its state constitution. Many state legislatures delegate power over the school system to a state board of education or similar body.[7] Regardless, it should still be up to parents how that education is accomplished.

Common Core takes away the options that we should have—both within and without the public school system—by making all school settings virtually the same. Many of us cannot afford any other option besides a public education and don't have the time or knowledge to home school. As already noted, we need more alternatives, not fewer. Ultimately, though, if Common Core prevails, even current alternatives will be compromised and homogenized.

It's not just the parents of public school students that should be concerned. All parents have a stake in this fight and will need to work to ensure that they do not lose their right to determine what and how their children learn.

The Place of Technology in Our Schools

I am an advocate for technology; I firmly believe it has a place in our schools. I would argue that it needs the right approach. Technology does not replace the basics of math, reading, and writing.

Common Core does nothing to address how to implement standards with the use of technology. What's more, it necessitates spending a lot of money on technology for the ability to deliver online assessments. It's is a huge waste of money to create computer labs that will be used only for testing and not for learning. In our school district in the 2014-2015 school year, our computer labs will be used for Measure of Academic Progress testing, or MAP, a computerized adaptive test that ostensibly helps teachers, parents, and administrators get a snapshot of a students' performance level for a specific point in time. MAP will take up ninety school days, and that's *without* the Smarter Balanced assessments coming online in the same academic year. This focus on testing needs to stop—and stop now.

Technology should instead be used to enhance actual learning opportunities for students and simplify life for parents, and teachers. Several teachers in Germantown use Google Apps for Education. They are able to receive all assignments from their students electronically, also saving a few trees. After reviewing an assignment, they can enter a grade and give instant feedback to the student via voice message. Similar to voicemail, the student can listen at their convenience. There are many more ways to use technology that can streamline workloads and make the life of the teachers, parents, and administrators less complicated. It should never be used to make things more complicated or tedious.

Cradle-to-Career Data Collection

I do have some significant concerns about technology that relate to—and arose around the same time as—my initial investigations into the Common Core. Many states were given money from the American Recovery and Reinvestment Act (ARRA) to set up massive databases to track everything that our students do in school. Some states will be tracking as many as four hundred or more data points. If this data were kept anonymous, I am not sure I would have much of a problem, provided the data is used to track progress and make our schools more accountable to the public. But that is not the path we currently seem to be going down. Attention is increasingly being drawn to the fact that the student data being collected, stored, and mined is, in fact, personally identifiable.[8]

Just as troubling, parents can no longer opt out of the data tracking. Nor can they any longer control who sees the data, due to significant changes to the federal Family Education Rights and Privacy Act of 1974 (FERPA), which was supposedly written to protect students and their families. FERPA was gutted around the same time Common Core was rolled out, obliterating crucial restrictions on who can gain access to students' personal data.[9]

We have seen what happened in recent years when data got into the wrong hands, and we have also seen that no database is safe. Data collection and mining poses a huge risk to your kids. There is a reason that the courts seal juvenile records. Kids should not be held to the same standard as adults. They will inevitably struggle, make mistakes, and even commit errors in judgment. Parents should not have to be concerned that if their child makes one mistake, has a bad attitude for a few years, or has trouble mastering certain academic subjects that these matters will be leveraged unfairly and haunt them for the rest of their lives.

Final Thoughts

After spending billions of dollars for studies on education and how to improve teaching methods, we are not, in general, in a better place today than we were one hundred years ago. Some would say we have taken many steps back.

I believe education is simple if we stick to the basics, but that's different than the increasing trend toward standardized "reforms" we've been seeing in recent decades. We know that no child is "common"— that each one is unique. We need to find more ways to individualize learning for each student. Administration and bureaucrats need to get out of the way—no more initiative-of-the-month; no more teaching to the test and holding children back to be more successful on the assessments. Our core subjects need to be our focus. We need to teach with some breadth and let kids dig into the topics that interest them. Teach kids to read and then let them read to learn. We need to teach children *how* to learn, not *what* to learn.

Part of ensuring this end is to find, explore, and facilitate many different, effective ways to educate children. I am a firm believer in school choice, as long as choice does not mean replacing public standardization factories with private ones that will still make widgets out of our kids. There is a reason that our colleges offer so many different degree options and that each college has different choices as well.

Never be afraid to do the right thing. Even if the results you want don't happen right away, your efforts and persistence will be rewarded in the end. We are talking about the future of our children, our communities, and our country. There are many forces working against us, so we need all hands on deck. An hour a day, or a few hours a week, is all it takes. Make the fight against the destruction of real education a priority. I promise you that when you do get involved—when you take the time to do your part—there is a sense of camaraderie, enjoyment, and accomplishment that comes from it.

NOTES

1. Both content experts—Dr. Sandra Stotsky in English language arts (ELA) and Dr. R. James Milgram in mathematics—have taken issue not only with the quality of the standards but also with claims made by the standards' architects concerning international benchmarking. They were among five original members of the committee who refused to sign off on the standards. For more detail surrounding the Common Core validation process, see Sandra Stotsky's essay on the topic in this volume.

2. Visit the Germantown School District's site at https://sites.google.com/a/germantownschools.org/germantown-standards-and-curriculum-development/.

3. See http://www.brianmedved.com.

4. Social studies and science standards are now also coming down the pipe. Among the individuals, organizations, and processes being leveraged to create and advance them, there appears to be a significant degree of overlap with those involved in the creation of the Common Core. If we are already seeing problems with the current ELA and mathematics standards, as well as aligned curricula, I can only imagine the problems that will develop with these new standards. Of course those marketing these new social studies and science standards are not stupid. They are called "Next Generation

Standards" to avoid any association with the already problem- and scandal-ridden Common Core standards.

5.　More on opting out, including forms, can be found, for instance, at the websites of United Opt Out National, http://unitedoptout.com/, and Truth in American Education, http://truthinamericaneducation.com/uncategorized/ccss-parent-opt-out-form/.

6.　Rachel Monahan, "Forget Teaching to the Test—At This Washington Heights Elementary School, Parents Canceled It!" *New York Daily News*, Oct. 21, 2013, http://www.nydailynews.com/new-york/uptown/parents-opt-city-test-article-1.1492127#ixzz2iOhMVv90.

7.　See Legal Information Institute, "Education Law: An Overview," Cornell University, WEX, http://www.law.cornell.edu/wex/Education.

8.　For more on the troubling trends in relationship to student data, see the essays within this volume by both Jane Robbins and Morna McDermott. See also Alex Newman, "Orwellian Nightmare: Data Mining Your Kids," *The New American*, Aug. 8, 2013, http://www.thenewamerican.com/culture/education/item/16193-orwellian-nightmare-data-mining-your-kids.

9.　Here again, see Robbins.

NAYSAYING, EMPTY DISCOURSE, AND TALKING TO YOUR NEIGHBOR

Jed Hopkins and Tim Slekar

We are colleagues working in the School of Education at a small liberal arts college in Madison, Wisconsin. In addition to our main focus of educating future educators, we also see the importance of establishing public spaces where informed discussions about the meaning of education and the implications of so-called education reform can take place. In addition to coordinating and creating public forums, we have spent many hours discussing reform issues. When asked to write a contribution to this volume, our first thought was to try and capture one of these dialogues. What resulted was the following text, which developed as a series of email exchanges.

*** *** ***

JED: I'd like to just start by saying how privileged we feel to do the work of providing educational opportunity to existing and would-be teachers who serve the public education system of this country. What great work it is to provide educational opportunity for people who are themselves dedicated to doing the same for the children and communities that make us who we are. We like to think of ourselves as being in the possibility business. In fact, education is about opening up human possibility, a process whereby people can flourish and ultimately dedicate themselves to worthwhile pursuits and attitudes that make for promising and humane futures.

But, these days, we've become increasingly uneasy with this work. Uneasy not with our commitment to what has just been said about the meaning and purpose of education but rather with the way reform efforts and policy trends are affecting our nation's public education system—or threatening to—and seem so out of whack with the meaning of education itself. Uneasy, too, with even uttering what was just said in that last statement. We are in an ethical crisis where it is difficult to even discuss real problems without sounding weak or facing accusations that one is just a member of the naysayers clan, full of fancy talk and critique but with no hard practical solutions. Does that sound like the situation we're in, Tim?

TIM: The "naysayer" situation. That resonates and it does communicate the problem associated with standing against something—anything for that matter. In a sense it is easy to oppose something. It is also easy simply to label the opposition as naysayers. But here is the problem that "naysayers" like us must learn to communicate: arriving at a point of opposition is not a mere reflexive action, devoid of deep thought and meaningful consideration of the topic, concept, or issue—in this case the Common Core standards (Common Core). In fact, it is by looking very closely and having authentic deliberative debates that the opposition to the Common Core has developed for me. In other words I didn't wake up one morning, hear about the Common Core, and think to myself, "I think I'll oppose that." The opposite is actually true. As an educator who has spent the last twenty-five years engaged in some form of professional education—second-grade teacher, fifth-grade teacher, eighth-grade teacher mentor, adjunct teacher education faculty, tenured teacher-education faculty, and teacher-education administrator—the roll out of the Common Core simply was an item of news with implications for my profession. I decided, and was responsible as a professional, to educate myself about it.

So, yes, Jed, when you ask if the situation we're in is one in which an opposing view is discounted as a non-thinking, reflexive action, it does make having conversations about "education" a challenge. I would say this realization may be one of the hardest I have had to admit to myself. The idea that simply thinking deeply and openly discussing education policy critically was being dismissed as simple naysaying was hard to understand. Think about it. We are educators. Something that was going to be implemented in educational settings was being proposed— Common Core. An educator with any sense of deliberative process would take the step of engaging intellectually, theorizing, and working to understand the many directions a full-scale adoption of Common Core might take. That type of rational exercise is quite a different process than naysaying.

JED: Engaging in a process that truly inquires into how something like the Common Core might look and be implemented is *not* just naysaying—yet we're made to feel that that is what we're doing. Or worse.

I want to say that there is a challenge for educators even to be heard in the right way these days, and it has something to do with a monopoly of sorts that has developed in relationship to how we're permitted to think and talk about educational reform. I'll call it Educational Mainstream Public Discourse, or EMPD (pronounced "empty"). And what is EMPD? Overtly, it's a way of understanding the improvement of public education as essentially a public accounting management exercise and, more covertly, with the added "bonus" of commercial potential. EMPD discourse is hard to challenge. In critiquing these standards, however valid the reason, we risk sounding like we endorse the substandard. For example, to point out that teaching teachers to become educators might be more than a technical exercise in transmitting a set of scientifically proven skills and techniques is to risk sounding like we don't have a firm grip on our profession; and to suggest that reforms relying so heavily on creating more and more accountability mechanisms might be dangerously compromising the ethos in which educational possibility can take flight is to risk sounding wishy-washy or, most certainly, as if we're trying to evade our responsibility. When we talk about public schooling, I wish words and phrases such as "authentic experience," "culturally relevant," "play," "child-centeredness," and "school ethos" were as common as "performance," "competency," "standards," "closing the gap," and "achievement" seem to be.

As I observed above, educators are in the possibility business. One of the communication challenges for us is to show our commitment to how taking that responsibility seriously means opposing any kind of thinking that separates means from ends. Yet, that is exactly what EMPD is having us do. Accounting and management is mostly concerned with measurable outcomes, not the qualities of the means by which they were achieved. As I say to my students, if a reading program enabled students to read at or above their reading level (according to a standardized test) but also managed to make the act of reading an onerous and unrewarding task, it wouldn't be educational—no matter what "scientific" endorsements it was purported to have. In a moral realm like education, concern with effectiveness is not a substitute for wisdom.

TIM: The EMPD, or empty, discourse in public education really helps explain what so many of us are trying to communicate in critiquing the Common Core. Although we are simply pushed aside as naysayers, it is really Common Core's supporters who have nothing substantial to communicate. In the real world of teaching and learning, the simple approach of writing standards and then using tests to measure the acquisition of those standards has been a dismal failure. Since 1983, Americans have been engaged in the process of writing standards and testing students. The results are always the same: Zip code predicts test scores. So when a proponent of the Common Core simply dismisses me as a naysayer, it is now evident that it is just a rhetorical tactic used to hide behind the fact that Common Core is an EMPD promise.

The mainstream public discourse around education reform remains committed to a failed or failing public school system viewed as in need of reforms that simply look at curriculum and instruction. These tactics employ only a technical business plan with technocratic thinking at its root supposedly to disrupt the failed public school system. That thinking goes like this: "Schools are failing. How do we know? Standardized test scores. How do we fix schools? Bring up standardized test scores. How do we bring up standardized test scores? With simple adjustments to standards, curriculum and assessments." This is the true empty vision of real education, and it is an assault on the attempt by us "naysayers" to create, as you say, Jed, an ethos committed to understanding and exploring education. So, it is Common Core proponents that should actually be offering a deep and evidence-based argument for why this package of initiatives comprise an equitable reform that will help all public-school students deeply engage in learning. In fact, they can't, and this is where we should shift the EMPD discourse. Common Core and the high-stakes testing designed to enforce it lack the soul of transformational education. Simply writing standards and testing children *is* an empty promise; it will never create an ethos around the deep needs and conditions that must be explored to truly help us build relationships with students.

JED: Yes, it's an empty promise. But, it sounds so rational:

1. Assess the situation by measuring performance outcomes.

2. Find a failed system.

3. Identify mechanisms that will fix the failed system.

4. Require accountability in order to demonstrate to "the powers that be" an unwavering commitment to these mechanisms.

5. Jettison the fat and weak, those who would resist this commitment, while rewarding the lean, compliant, technically proficient workforce of the future—perhaps by not closing down their schools.

Doesn't this sound strongly responsible, scientific, and miles from the ideologically messy? To change EMPD and truly attend to the ethos of education—the conditions that make for flourishing humans who can ultimately dedicate themselves to worthwhile pursuits and attitudes for humane futures—is quite a challenge in a cultural climate that has bought into this kind of EMPD thinking.

Without sounding too much like a conspiracy theorist—which these days is basically admitting that you're either a troublemaker or a misguided crank—I'd also like to say that there is a subtext to each of the five moves I just mentioned. The subtexts go something like this:

1. Assess the situation by measuring performance outcomes.

    Subtext: When we say, "Reduce educational assessment to the measurable," we really mean what can be frequently, quantifiably measured by a standardized tool that will have little or no diagnostic value for the teacher.

2. Find a failed system.

   Subtext: The finding will not be surprising and will not tell us anything really new; but its frequent publication will show that we are in a crisis, that we care about this crisis—because we're brave enough to admit it exists—and that teachers and school administration will be kept busy, scrambling to change future results.

3. Identify mechanisms that will fix the failed system.

   Subtext: We want educational administration to focus on systems of intervention that can be scaled, managed, and monitored across schools. By doing so, we'll reduce the professional autonomy of teachers as well as further reinforce the managerial and compliance-monitoring role of administration. We will also open up new—or bolster existing—revenue streams in the textbook, software, and testing industries.

4. Require accountability in order to demonstrate to "the powers that be" unwavering commitment to these mechanisms.

   Subtext: Fashion an understanding of the professional teacher as someone who has to put matters of compliance and the role of curriculum technician before any expectation that they become members of a community of teacher-scholars attuned to such things as the local cultural resources in which they teach.

5. Jettison the fat and weak, those who would resist this commitment, while rewarding the lean, compliant, technically proficient workforce of the future—perhaps by not closing down their schools.

   Subtext: Closing schools and firing teachers makes for dramatic press coverage, reinforcing the idea that a system in crisis requires extreme measures by a strong leadership. Measures such as hiring poorly trained young teachers—who typically give two or three years to teaching before burning out[1]—will ensure the continual poor performance of some of our neediest schools. Bottom line? We want to ensure that the public education system will be reformed in name only, that the iniquity of the system will remain unaddressed, and that administrative control will be difficult, if not impossible, to challenge.

TIM: Jed, I believe we have addressed Common Core implementation as an empty attempt to leverage the over-simplifying rhetoric of failure or crisis—what Naomi Kline would call "shock doctrine."[2] However, all of the scholarly thinking and deep reflection on our part to understand this state of affairs—while intellectually rewarding—doesn't help my "neighbor" understand the important subtext of your five points above. That understanding is crucial if there is ever to be a true public dialogue about education outside of the simplistic "standards rule" rhetoric. The most important step we have left to take is to talk to our neighbors about the subtext you point out. We must do so in a way that communicates the folly of first "shocking" the public and then disrupting those that should be leading the discussion around how to restore education as the goal of public schooling.

As Marion Brady recently pointed out, we don't need standards to enhance learning; rather, we need *standards!*[3] Standards that insist on treating students, teachers, and parents with dignity. Standards that ask the community to value the learning process and to be a part of it. Standards that elevate teaching and learning. Standards that recognize the process of education in a public system as anything but "common." As Brady puts it, "standards for the qualities of mind, emotion, character, and the spirit the young must be helped to develop if they're to cope with the world they're inheriting."

The so-called debate—these standards are better than those standards—around the Common Core is nothing more than a planned distraction. If powerful teaching and learning in an ethos that values educational discourse is our standard, then we go forward not as naysayers, perpetually forced to explain our criticism of the Common Core; rather, we must reclaim the crisis conversation and take back ownership of educational discourse. The "standard" must be simply a devotion to an equitable public education that prepares students to participate in authentically democratic practices. Of course, the relationship between education and democracy would be worth a bipartisan discussion in itself. The Common Core is merely a disruptive distraction. It is now time for us to disrupt the anti-intellectual ethos that has been assigned to the entire idea of equitable public education.

JED: Yes—disrupt the anti-intellectual ethos and establish a moral and an authentically educational one. To do this, I think we should indeed be having conversations with our neighbors about what might be the educational way with a host of things. You mentioned democracy: For me the educational way with that concept is less about the ballot box and its mechanisms—mechanisms that many of us know can be strategically exploited, resulting in democracy being reduced to something like mob-rule—and more to do with nurturing our sensibilities. The word sensibility has an old-fashioned ring to it. That's too bad because it's a great educational word. Authentic democracy relies on individuals not only knowing what's going on but also developing the skill of attuning, in caring and creative ways, to possibilities afforded by situations. Let's strive for a discourse that puts a concern with an educational ethos on the table.

TIM: Amen to that!

NOTES

1.   The Teach for America program, specifically, was founded by Wendy Kopp, based on her 1989 Princeton University undergraduate thesis. Its mission is to "eliminate educational inequity by enlisting high-achieving recent college graduates and professionals to teach" for at least two years in low-income communities throughout the nation. These unlicensed/uncertified corps members receive alternative certification through coursework taken as part of the program, via an intensive five-week summer training.

2. Naomi Klein, *The Shock Doctrine: The Rise of Disaster Capitalism* (New York: Picador, 2008).

3. The specific remarks to which Tim refers were published on Diane Ravitch's blog on July 24, 2014, in a post titled: "We Need the Right Kind of Standards, Not CCSS," http://dianeravitch.net/2014/07/24/marion-brady-we-need-the-right-kind-of-standards-not-ccss/. Brady has also made these remarks available as a downloadable document under the same date and title via the Op-Ed page of his *Reality-Based Learning* site, http://www.marionbrady.com/Op-Eds.asp.

LIBERATING EDUCATION

Marsha Familaro Enright

> Discipline must come through liberty. . . . We do not consider
> an individual disciplined only when he has been rendered as
> artificially silent as a mute and as immovable as a paralytic.
> He is an individual annihilated, not disciplined.
>
> – Maria Montessori[1]

If you're familiar with 2- to 5-year-old children, then you understand what Aristotle meant when he said "All men, by nature, desire to know." Very little will stop the young child from exploring the world and trying to learn.

The young child who carries into adulthood his restless eagerness to learn, create, and achieve is the fountainhead of human progress. Michelangelo, Leonardo da Vinci, Isaac Newton, Benjamin Franklin, Emily Dickinson, Richard Branson—these are people that never lost the 2-year-old's passionate, internally generated drive to know and, consequently, change the world. These are the types of people who made Ancient Greece, Renaissance Florence, Enlightenment England, Revolutionary America, and our current technology-abundant culture possible. *This* is the state of mind that education *should* strive to achieve if we want a flourishing free society.

By nurturing this state of mind, a society would create a self-perpetuating future of creative ideas, science, technology, liberty, and art in the renaissance of a New Enlightenment. This is what real education reform should aim for if we want happy children and a bright future.

Creative autonomy is the crucial, common element among the innovators mentioned above. "'Autonomy' suggests, strictly speaking, that one gives or has given laws to oneself; that one is self-governing; that in essentials one obeys one's own imperatives," said philosopher Walter Kaufmann.[2] "Giving oneself imperatives" is a very active state, that of someone who knows how to take rational risk—exactly the state of the entrepreneur, no matter in what field of endeavor.

In thinking about the best form of education for a free future, consider this: The classroom is a micro-society in which the social order emerges through the exchange of ideas and values, explicit and implicit, and from the way in which participants interact with each other according to the classroom principles.

Is an autonomous mindset nurtured in most of today's classrooms?

From grade school to graduate school, U.S. classrooms have historically relied heavily on a single arbiter of knowledge, often in the position of lecturer, discussion leader, knowledge authority, and director of learning. The teacher is often considered the repository of truth, and the student taught limited lines of reasoning about the subject matter. Directed group lessons in traditional grade school and lectures in higher education are favored methodologies. Students listen to the directions or lectures of their teachers and receive assignments and, increasingly, standardized assessments that they must complete to prove they have learned those facts and ideas that the authorities deem valuable.

Students are expected to be filled with knowledge by the academic authority. The teaching paradigm encourages an authority to convey the "right answers" to the waiting student-receptacles. The student is the receiver of learning, not an initiator or active agent in the learning process. "Learning" is measured by the amount of instructor-proffered information that the student is able to reiterate on tests and in papers.

Can we tell if the student has deeply incorporated the information and ideas into his or her thinking? Whether the student can use this information in his or her life? Whether the student has an understanding of the information's relevance to living at all?

Consider the psychological effects of the traditional methods of teaching in this paradigm. How does the student:

- learn how to arrive at truth himself?
- discern that there are multiple ways of approaching a problem?
- discover subjects of interest to himself, individually?
- engage the process of learning new material?
- develop skills for fruitful collaboration with others?

If students have no skills in these processes, how can they grow into independent actors, arriving at their own conclusions, discovering new ideas and processes, and navigating all the choices and opportunities needed to create new endeavors?

How shall a young person become an autonomous individual if he is treated merely as an empty vessel to be filled? What opportunities are students given to practice the skills of a self-reliant, independent, and self-responsible person? Where is the student's agency in this process?

This top-down environment is counter-productive to conveying the ideas, values, and virtues of autonomy and a free society.

How did we arrive at this state of education?

From Freedom to Factories

> Above all things I hope the education of the common people
> will be attended to; convinced that on their good sense
> we may rely with the most security for the
> preservation of a due degree of liberty.
>
> – Thomas Jefferson[3]

Prior to the era of mass education, children were "homeschooled," ironically, something many look upon skeptically today. Yet the early American populace was remarkably literate and numerate for the times. Consider alone the fact that *The Federalist Papers* were published in common newspapers, fodder for debate in homes, local taverns, and church gatherings.

According to Jack Lynch, "[l]iteracy had been an American obsession since the beginning. As early as 1642, Massachusetts passed a law ordering the selectmen to monitor children's ability 'to read & under-

stand the principles of religion & the capitall lawes of this country.'"[4]
Ninety percent of the white male population was literate by the end
of the 18th century; nearly 100 percent of white women born in 1810
were literate. About 20 percent of late-18th-century American colonists were African-American, 8 percent of them free.[5] While slave states
kept their African-American slaves illiterate, by 1860 less than 8 percent of black Bostonians were illiterate.[6]

This obsession with literacy owes something, no doubt, to the legacy
of the highly educated, principled, middle class Pilgrims who colonized
New England in the quest for freedom of conscience. Harvard was established in 1636 as the first college—a seminary—with nine students,
one of myriad educational institutions to follow in New England.

Except for Massachusetts, education was private and mostly at home
in the first colonies until the late 1700s. But Jefferson wasn't alone in
his concern that the new republic have an educated populace; our publicly funded school systems arose in response to this goal.[7] In 1647,
the Massachusetts Bay Colony required the establishment of public
schools in all communities over 100 persons.[8] The next were created in
New England towns in the 1770s.

Later, public schools became state-run bureaucracies; today they're
over-lorded by the Federal Department of Education.

Barry Dean Simpson has pointed out the perverse economic incentives in government-funded education:

> Between 1900 and 1949, teacher salaries rose 709% while per-capita
> income rose by only 513%…One benefit of compulsion to teach-
> ers was…to increase their salaries. An increase in demand leads to an
> increase in price, ceteris paribus…And since the education system is
> being funded by tax dollars rather than by the demanders themselves,
> it becomes much easier to increase salaries (regardless of competence).
> …[B]y making the school system public rather than private, teach-
> ers and administrators also insulate themselves from the wishes of
> students and parents—the ultimate consumers of education. This
> insulation from market forces solidifies the power of the elite group
> of educationists for years to come. The suppliers, not the demanders,
> choose the curricula, the textbooks, decide the certification process
> for teachers, etc. They run the whole show, and only have bureaucrats

to please rather than consumers. Not only are bureaucrats easier to please since they don't spend their own money, but if the politician/ bureaucrat needs information to placate angry demanders, to whom do they turn? The educationists, in the positions of power, have all of the "relevant" information.

...Public education, with the added feature of compulsion, reduces the cost to politicians of making wealth transfers. The cost of making transfers is diminished by reducing the opposition to transfers. If politicians can reduce the cost of transferring wealth by reducing... opposition...then they can continue to authorize transfers to interested parties for a price.

Public education reduces opposition to wealth transfers by teaching students that redistribution, public works, and democracy are the American way...Public education tells us we need government all the time. Public education introduces the mantras of democracy to the young. Democracy keeps the two major parties in power, keeps their spoils flowing in, and tells us that intervention is okay because the majority voted for it.

The conclusion is that public schools and compulsory attendance laws benefit educators, administrators, and politicians more than citizens or their children."[9]

It is difficult not to infer that the pecuniary benefits of public education are its venial sins; worse is its purpose to conform students to specific values and habits in order to make them compliant to authority.

Compulsory schooling is often couched in terms of insuring that poor children have the opportunity to be educated, even if their parents can't afford it or are too irresponsible to send them to school. Today, the attendance requirements vary in the United States by state, but the average compulsory age range is 7 to 16.[10] However, there's a pile of evidence that the deeper motive of compulsion has always been to inculcate obedience.

Martin Luther instigated the modern practice of compulsory education in 1542, persuading the German state to institute it in order to "drive out the devil."[11] John Calvin likewise demanded compulsory schooling to inculcate religious values—and obedience. The Calvinist Puritans of the Massachusetts Bay Colony followed suit, becoming the first to require education of all citizens in 1642.

Horace Mann, who imported the Prussian education system in the formation of both the Massachusetts and U.S. public school systems,[12] admitted "the whole plan of education in Prussia, as being not only designed to produce, but as actually producing, a spirit of blind acquiescence to arbitrary power, in things spiritual as well as temporal, as being, in fine, a system of education adapted to enslave, and not to enfranchise, the human mind."[13] Regardless of any motive to use this system for good, such an effort was doomed to failure at the outset because it mitigated so deeply against the needs of free human beings.

One of many who followed the Prussian system, Archibald D. Murphey, architect of public schools in North Carolina, summed it up: "[A]ll the children will be taught in them....In these schools the precepts of morality and religion should be inculcated, and habits of subordination and obedience be formed....Their parents know not how to instruct them....The state, in the warmth of her affection and solicitude for their welfare, must take charge of those children, and place them in school where their minds can be enlightened and their hearts can be trained to virtue."[14]

Obedience to the State is far removed from Jefferson's original motive for public education—that free men be sufficiently knowledgeable and capable of thinking so as to be able to *govern themselves.*

And what has been the effect of this shift in motive on education itself? In *Anti-Intellectualism in American Life,* Richard Hofstadter observes that, while serving as secretary of the Massachusetts Board of Education after 1837, Horace Mann had cause to criticize one of the nation's best school systems, noting "'obvious want of intelligence in the reading classes'; 'the schools have retrograded within the last generation or half generation in regard to orthography'; 'more than eleven-twelfths of all the children in the reading-classes in our schools do not understand the meaning of the words they read.'"[15]

Further, in 1870, "William Franklin Phelps, then head of a normal school in Winona, Minnesota, and later president of the National Education Association, declared: 'children are fed upon the mere husks of knowledge. They leave school for the broad theater of life without discipline; without mental power or moral stamina...Hundreds of our

American schools are little less than undisciplined juvenile mobs.'"[16]

Do these criticisms seem familiar—as if you've heard them today? Hofstadter goes on quoting the same kinds of criticisms, decade after decade from 1837 on. Doesn't this show that the problems we see today are inherent in public education? And isn't it possible—even likely—that these problems are inherent because public education is a bureaucracy beholden to administrators, not businesses aiming to please customers? Think of the difference between dealing with the IRS or with H & R Block. Which tries to please you? Finds ways to serve you better? Is efficient?

At root, the bureaucracy of government-run schools has been a permanent detriment to their functioning.[17] Recent, laudable attempts to leverage charter schools and vouchers to reform the public education system cannot overcome the fundamental problems inherent in government-run bureaucracies. Furthermore, many school reform advocates do not recognize the dangers of vouchers: once instituted, only the wealthiest private schools can avoid accepting them and remain economically competitive. Moreover, as in all government-run programs, corruption is inevitable. What will be the consequence? Government oversight and regulation of private schools that accept voucher dollars, with the institution of government-mandated teacher certification and curricular programs. The result: the wiping out of independent schools and choices for students.

Returning to our history of public education: In the early twentieth century, psychologists and educators decided to apply principles of scientific management to education, focusing on exact measurements to assess outcomes.[18] According to a respected resource of the day: "Our schools are, in a sense, factories in which the raw products (children) are to be shaped and fashioned into products to meet the various demands of life. The specifications for manufacturing come from the demands of twentieth century civilization and is [sic] the business of the school to build its pupils according to the specifications laid down."[19]

Can we expect much else from this approach than dull and obedient students? Pawns of the state and its cronies? Cogs of the exact same width, length, and breadth as John Taylor Gatto argues in *Dumbing*

Us Down: The Hidden History of Compulsory Schooling?[20] Gatto sees schools as factories turning out compliant corporate robots. William Derescewicz argues powerfully that the elite colleges are similarly turning out "excellent sheep."[21]

The long result of this methodology, combined with failed education theories and approaches, faulty "self-esteem" ideology, and false reforms, such as No Child Left Behind, leaves our schools, at best, far from ideal environments for young minds and spirits, at worst, "soul-wrenching, mind-numbing, drugged-out catastrophes," in the words of a friend who endured and barely escaped with his mind and ambition intact. Common Core is just the latest in a long string of such fads, drawing on the same failed experiments of past decades.

In a free society, children need to learn the virtues of independent judgment, self-reliance, justice, self-initiated productiveness, honesty, and hard work—all virtues needed to navigate a bustling cooperative and innovative culture. Can the rigidities of factory-style education develop these qualities?

Let's first consider another point Hofstadter makes. He insists that the American emphasis on utility of knowledge has continuously caused a problem with its quality as students, parents, and administrators demand that learning be of practical use. What's a bit paradoxical is: learning *should* be of practical use—to live well—but not in the now common but narrow sense of obtaining a specific job. Life and circumstances change too frequently for that.

This context is *especially* true of American society. The very innovations that provide us with an ever-improving life—creative destruction—prevent us from knowing the most useful knowledge for the future. Anne Neal, president of the American Council of Trustees and Alumni, commented at a recent seminar that Americans will change jobs eleven times between the ages of 18 and 45, either between or within companies.[22]

In a fully free society with an even more innovation-driven culture, students and parents would demand a very different type of education than we see today. But, in order to imagine what shape education would take, we must first define what we mean by "free society."

The Shape of a Free Society—Voluntary Cooperation

Freedom, or liberty, is the ability of an individual to make his own judgments and choices, and implement them in action, as long as he does not use force or fraud against another.[23]

Humans survive and flourish by the use and judgment of reason. Our ability to reason enables us to create what we need and adapt the world to our needs, rather than merely adapting to the world. In order to be able to live as well as possible, each person must remain free to decide what he needs and wants, what to do in his or her life, and with whom and how to interact, as long as no force or fraud is involved. These fundamental facts not only permit human flourishing, they are the foundation for insisting that societies should be organized to allow each person as much freedom as possible.[24] Their essence is a society of voluntary cooperation.

To those who object that many humans cannot manage their own affairs properly but need to be overseen and directed by a higher authority, most generally government, a question: If individuals cannot manage their own individual affairs, how can we suppose that they could manage ours? Why should we suppose someone else could do a better job?

In a society of voluntary cooperation, law ensures only enough government oversight to protect individual rights. Economic transactions between private parties are free from government restrictions, tariffs, and subsidies. In the English-speaking world, Adam Smith was the first to reach a wide audience with the remarkable fact that the choices and actions each person takes in rational self-interest result in the greatest benefit to everyone—flourishing, cooperative, and peaceful societies of spontaneous order.[25] An examination of history demonstrates that governments limited to protecting individual rights via the courts, the police, and the military result in the most freedom; the more limited, the better in terms of economic growth and human flourishing.[26]

We have yet to see a government so limited as to have a strict separation of government and economics; yet, given the evidence since the industrial revolution, the results would be astonishing. Opportunities would abound; individuals, no matter how poor, would have the chance to rise through hard work and ingenuity, as they did by the millions in 19th-century America, one of the freest moments in world history. Free-trade colony Hong Kong's development from the 1950s to the '90s or a simple comparison of East and West Germany or North and South Korea strikingly demonstrates the remarkable power of freedom to improve lives.

But such a society would only be possible if its most influential ideas, and the consequent attitudes and practices of the people, were significantly different from today. A revitalized vision of the independent-minded individualism of previous eras would need to pervade the culture, along with a richer understanding of how to protect individual rights from those who inevitably want to use government power for personal gain.[27] A large minority of people would have to value reason, self-reliance, hard work, honesty, and fairness in their dealings with others and eschew the use of government for cultural change, personal gain, or power.

In other words, autonomy would be highly valued *and* needed in a free society.

Let's explore what might happen to education in *that* society.

The Shape of Education in a Free Society

> To consider the school as the place where instruction is
> given is one point of view. But to consider the school as
> a preparation for life is another. In the latter case,
> the school must satisfy all the needs of life.
>
> – Maria Montessori[28]

A free society requires not serfs to the state or "company men," but capable individuals, entrepreneurs of their own lives, able to peacefully collaborate with others while creating remarkable and new solutions to human needs and problems. In a voluntary, cooperative society, responsibility for educating children would fall clearly to the parents. As part of the ideas and values that would form such a society, parents would largely tend to value and foster individualism and independence as needed characteristics to flourish in freedom. Many would recognize that their responsibility as nurturers would be to help their children develop into achieving, passionate individuals, whatever path they might choose. Constant, upward striving—*real* progress—would be the social bellwether.

Old WASP families in the United States historically imparted an ethic of responsibility and achievement in their progeny. Rather than becoming dissolute ne'er-do-wells who hadn't a clue about how to live up to or surpass previous generations, such heirs were encouraged to find their passion and use the family resources to achieve it. Children interested in the family business frequently became thoughtful stewards, adding to the family's achievements, including the delivery of products and services, the creation of businesses and jobs—even extraordinary philanthropic endeavors. On an episode of the popular TV show *Undercover Boss*, Dave Rife, head of the family-owned White Castle Corporation, expressed something of this attitude in his desire to improve the business his grandfather had started and make him proud. This ethic of achievement and pride is fostered not by dependence but by independence. It comes out of the opportunity to take risks and meet challenges—to use one's individual nature, perspective, intellect, and drive to do so.

Rather than protecting children by giving them everything, many parents would teach their children the joy of responsibility and work. A 2007 documentary, *The Call of the Entrepreneur*, includes a valuable example. Frank Hanna, one of the individuals featured in the film, is the son of an investment banker. Instead of taking his two sons to Little League, Hanna's father provided opportunities for the boys to work at various family businesses. The boys experienced achievement early—not a mere taste for making money but the analytic knowledge to understand how businesses work. After a brief stint as a lawyer, Frank joined his brother in opening their own investment banking firm, reveling in the joy of developing great, productive businesses by providing capital to fund their growth.

Having lived with tax-supported, government-provided education as a major supplier for 200 years, many people can't imagine how most children could be educated otherwise. But in a cooperative, voluntary society, all education would necessarily be entirely private, mostly supported by tuition income, with help from a vast array of private philanthropies. There would be no "privatization" in which for-profit businesses could take public money while remaining beholden to government-dictated standards, curricula, testing—and data-mining.

The United States already leads the world in philanthropy,[29] especially for education, and has the most private schools, colleges, and universities. Imagine what people would do for those families and children struggling to get a good education if everyone could keep the lion's share of their income.[30] Voluntary help would dispense with both the problem and the fear that the poor could not afford education.

A long-voiced motivation for compulsory public schools has been to ensure that irresponsible parents educate their children. Yet, we know that carrots work better than sticks—that positive persuasion and incentives motivate people far better than punishment. In a free, cooperative society, concerned volunteers could form organizations to ingeniously motivate undependable parents to educate their children—with money, games, prizes, honors, opportunities. Who can tell what ambitious, free people might invent? Likewise, those concerned with the acculturation of children and new immigrants to a voluntary cooperative society would form educational and immigrant aid organizations and other philanthropic endeavors to convey the ideas, knowledge, and values important to freedom.[31]

Another initial motive of compulsory public education was the equalization of opportunity for all citizens. Today, many continue to advocate the idea that, *somehow*, a society can enact laws and practices that will equalize differences in wealth, inborn talent, skills, family connections, and other advantages. Yet, the only way to "equalize" what people are born with is to handicap those with more talent and skill, bringing everyone down to the lowest level. Ironically, in "equalized" societies, the most disadvantaged are worse off because the talented are not permitted to create and build. Think Soviet Russia or North Korea.

Putting aside the injustice of forcibly taking from some to give to others by the decree of government bureaucrats, realistically, there is no way to give everyone equal advantages, no matter how much money is spent—even if it were entirely private money. Human beings are individuals with hugely varying talents, abilities and interests.[32]

Human beings enjoy changing the world for the better; helping others is a large part of that enjoyment. This was recognized at least as long ago as ancient Greece. Aristotle, for instance, described the Great Souled man who delights in using his wealth and ability to help others. In a voluntary and cooperative society, private individuals and organizations could find ways to help those with less talent, skills, wealth, and family advantages—and they'd have much more of their own money to do it with than today. The government's only role would be to insure the equal protection of each individual's freedom to act on his own judgment, leaving him able to pursue all the opportunities he could create or that others would offer.

The Shape of Schools in a Free Society

Based on the principles by which cooperative societies operate, and upon my years of experience in psychology and Montessori education, here is a picture of how I think schools might be affected by a freer society.

While public schools, by their very nature, are not in a position to respond nimbly to differing needs and wishes, market competition would provide a myriad of choices, with a buffet of prices, quality, environments, methodology, and locations sensitive to the real customers for education, parents and students. This would include a significant offering of schools for all circumstances and income levels. The large and growing number of inexpensive private schools in remote and poor areas of India illustrates how the market could fulfill parental demands.[33] Parents and students would be treated more like customers of a service business, with schools competing to do the best job possible for each individual. Everything could be run more efficiently with little or no bureaucracy—actually *responsive* to those customers.

Let's compare the market for education to the lively and innovative market for smart phones or computers, one of the least regulated markets in the nation. Smart phones are ingeniously customizable to suit the needs, purposes, and tastes of the individual. The companies that make them furiously scramble to offer the latest and greatest innovations to keep their customers. Entrepreneurs likewise race to create more and better application for these tools: apps that find you the cheapest gas; that scan a bar code on a "home for sale" sign and yield all the information you could want about that property; that keep track of your health data and teach you the latest, scientifically-validated preventative measures to take; all on top of the phone's function as a phone, camera, calculator, internet browser, and library of online books. The list is practically endless.

Can we imagine what people might invent for schooling, if it were free and fueled by competition? What life-changing differences for children, parents, and teachers might follow?

VARIETY AND CHOICE

The staid rigidity of traditional education would be overturned. Schools of every ideology and methodology could pop up around the country in response to the needs, desires, and interests of parents and their children. Big, medium and small schools, urban and rural, could offer a variety of programs, from "unschooling" arrangements, which have no curriculum but many opportunities to explore, all the way to strict programs with carefully selected and implemented curricula that every student was required to follow—along with everything in between. Some schools could offer only classic books to study, others faith-based programs or modern studies; some could emphasize science and technology, others business, the fine arts, or crafts and the trades. Entrepreneurs could also find new ways to help children with special physical conditions, specific learning differences and difficulties, or talents, physical and mental.

The possibilities would be as numerous as the individual attendees.

Rather than constantly adapting to bureaucratic wishes, piles of paperwork, and mandated yet unworthy experimental approaches that they know fail or even damage their students, teachers would be free to practice their craft. Overfull classrooms would disappear as education entrepreneurs responded to the desires of parents and teachers.

Like innovative technology businesses of today, many, many schools would give staff a wide platform for their creativity, leaving them much discretion for implementing curricula, programs, and school goals. Currently, this happens in private schools, which is one of their allures to teachers, despite much lower pay and benefits. In a voluntarist co-operative society in which people retained most of their earnings, the market could reward teachers more powerfully, as it is doing today in South Korea: "Kim Ki-hoon earns $4 million a year in South Korea, where he is known as a rock-star teacher—a combination of words not typically heard in the rest of the world. Mr. Kim has been teaching for over 20 years, all of them in the country's *hagwons*, private, after-school tutoring academies. Unlike most teachers across the globe, he is paid according to the demand for his skills—and he is in high demand."[34] Of course, not everyone would earn $4 million, but compensation in a free market would closely reflect ability, creativity, hard work, and perseverance, like it does in today's technology labor market.

PHYSICAL ENVIRONMENT

School buildings could be of every shape, size, and location, to fit each school's outlook and purposes, with one school building more beautiful and luxurious than the next, even for the most inexpensive schools. Doubt it? Just think how much more attractive Dunkin' Do-nuts stores have become since the spread of Starbucks; how many more offerings your local grocer boasts since Whole Foods came to town.

Schools could be exciting, attractive environments in which to explore the world and oneself. In many schools, students would not be confined, since the classroom can't provide enough experience of the world to become sufficiently educated. Because knowledge is practical, students could go out to explore the places in which they live, learning to shop for themselves, camping, and working in local businesses. Their responsibility and independence would grow with their age.

Creative building designs, such as those used by Apple or Google or Pixar to foster innovation and collaboration, could abound. The playful intermixing of students and staff, along with the freedom to work by oneself or together—at a table or desk, lying down, standing up, walking around, taking breaks to play games—would allow individuals to follow their own needs and paths to learning, creating, and problem-solving.

Schools could be well-integrated into natural landscapes or cleverly designed in highly urban environments to keep children in touch with nature and spontaneous opportunities to observe and experiment. The layout would make it easier to incorporate physical activity into every day, aiding the connection between mind and body.

ASSESSMENT

Monolithic testing regimes would be dead. Entrepreneurs would compete to discover tools of *authentic assessment*—whether a student has mastered knowledge and can implement it in his life. Tools such as optimal-experience researcher Mihalyi Csikszentmihalyi's Experiential Sampling methodology could be adapted to determine the actual attention and engagement students give to various ways of teaching, thereby testing the teaching's effectiveness.[35] New tools of psychological evaluation and growth derived from the discoveries of researchers in the psychology of high functioning, happy individuals would also be used to craft better in-class processes.[36] Rich use of data analytics would aid this entire process, as it is doing for some of the most innovative educational programs today.[37]

TECHNOLOGY

Technology could be used for information delivery and rich simulations through which to practice all kinds of skills, from sports to governance to running a business.

We have a little taste of the innovations possible with the recent rise of online learning tools and games, programs such as Khan Academy, and crowd-sourced information universally available on Wikipedia and other Internet sites. Another example is MIT's physics program, which uses hand-held devices. The teacher broadcasts mini-quizzes during class to discover how well the students grasp the concepts he is teaching. When many students fail the quizzes, the teacher adjusts his pace, explains his concepts differently, and/or presents more illustrations.[38]

HIGHER EDUCATION

There would be no government-generated push for "everyone" to attend college, a goal that has resulted only in the increase of unnecessary degrees and punishing debt. Rather, high school education could be far more challenging and deep than it is today—so rich and thorough that students could be knowledgeable, engaged citizens without college.

With the emphasis on individualization, many students would be interested and skilled in non-academic areas such as crafts, trades, the arts, and business. Detailed, targeted technical education post-high school could flourish. People without an advanced degree would not feel like second-class citizens as they often do today, as the importance of non-college work would be honored for its excellence and importance.

Colleges would also be free from government interference or help. The U.S. higher-education market would be a hotbed of competition, as it was up to the last forty or fifty years. Many more small colleges could arise to give personalized guidance and service, allowing students more easily to know and connect to each other and their teachers.

Higher education could undergo a liberation and renaissance of striking proportions too.

PARENTING AND CHILD DEVELOPMENT

Many parents would desire the best means to educate their children, fostering their autonomy, creativity, and ambition. They would seek programs and curricula well-grounded in the science of human needs and developmental processes.

Competition could fuel exact scientific research and understanding of what human beings need to develop well. And *within* an institution, careful scientific observation and experimentation about the best means of learning would be *de rigeur*.

Montessori as a Resource for Liberated Education

The ingeniously designed, developmentally appropriate physical and psychological learning environments of Montessori schools point to the kinds of transformative, scientifically based changes that could sweep education. Researcher Angeline Lillard summarizes their starkly different results in *Montessori: The Science Behind the Genius.*[39]

Business as well as Academia are beginning to take note. A study released in 2009 examined the way business executives think. Surveying 3 thousand business executives over six years and incorporating interviews with 500 participants, the study uncovered that an unusual number of leading innovators had been Montessori students.[40] "A number of the innovative entrepreneurs also went to Montessori schools, where they learned to follow their curiosity...To paraphrase the famous Apple ad campaign, innovators not only learned early on to think different, they act different (and even talk different)," says Hal Gregersen, one of the lead researchers. Such luminaries included Amazon's Jeff Bezos, Wikipedia founder Jimmy Wales, Google founders Sergey Brin and Larry Page, and French cuisine guru Julia Child.

At root, the Montessori program nurtures autonomy and creativity *par excellence.* Imagine if students and teachers alike were able to leverage these crucial advantages, unencumbered by the control of overweening bureaucrats and "experts" who set themselves up through the force of government as the authorities and tell the rest of us what to do.

It sounds fantastic to us now, perhaps, because we are off the mark. But ultimately, the education practices of the free society would result in an unimaginable outpouring of excellence, energy, and creativity, far beyond even the imagination of science fiction writers. Because these practices would nurture the best within each individual, maximizing them would set the stage for a future of higher human fulfillment, amazing technology, inspiring art, and a host of other positive outcomes. Let us work our mightiest to see the creation of such a society in real life.

> The greatest [obstacle for] an attempt to give freedom
> to the child and to bring its powers to light does not lie
> in finding a form of education which realizes these aims.
> It lies rather in overcoming the prejudices which
> the adult has formed in this regard.
>
> – Maria Montessori[41]

NOTES

1. *The Montessori Method*, translated by Anne Everett George (New York: Frederick A. Stokes Company, 1912), 86.

2. Walter Kaufmann, *Discovering the Mind* (New York: McGraw Hill, 1980), 15.

3. Letter to James Madison, Paris, Dec. 20, 1787. The letter can be read in its entirety online at American History: From Revolution to Reconstruction and Beyond, http://www.let.rug.nl/usa/presidents/thomas-jefferson/letters-of-thomas-jefferson/jefl66.php.

4. Jack Lynch, "Every Man Able to Read: Literacy in Early America," *Colonial Williamsburg Journal* (Winter 2011), http://www.history.org/Foundation/journal/Winter11/literacy.cfm.

5. Edgar A. Toppin. "Blacks in the American Revolution." Published essay, Virginia State University (1976), 1, http://www.history.org/almanack/people/african/aaintro.cfm.

6. Kimberly Sambol-Tosco, "The Slave Experience: Education, Arts, & Culture," *Slavery and the Making of America*, Wisconsin Public Television, (2004), http://www.pbs.org/wnet/slavery/experience/education/history2.html.

7. *School: The Story of American Public Education*. Four-part PBS documentary series (2001), https://www.facinghistory.org/for-educators/educator-resources/resources/school-story-american-public-education.

8. John William Perrin, *The History of Compulsory Education in New England*. Doctoral thesis, University of Chicago (1896), 19-20, https://archive.org/details/historycompulso00perrgoog.

9. Barry Dean Simpson, "The Common School Movement and Compulsory Education," Ludwig Von Mises Institute, *Mises Daily Blogs*, Nov. 29, 2004, https://mises.org/daily/1679. In his article, Simpson cites George Stigler, *Employment and Compensation in Education*, (National Bureau of Economic Research, 1950), appendix B; and William M. Landes and Lewis C. Solmon, "Compulsory Schooling and Legislation: An Economic Analysis of Law and Social Change in the Nineteenth Century," *Journal of Economic History* 32, no. 1 (Mar. 1972).

10. National Center for Education Statistics, Table 197: "Age Range for Compulsory School Attendance and Special Education Services, and Poli-

cies on Year-Round Schools and Kindergarten Programs, by State: Selected Years, 2000 through 2011," *Digest of Education Statistics*, 2012, http://nces. ed.gov/programs/digest/d12/tables/dt12_197.asp.

11. Perrin, *History of Compulsory Education*, 7-8.

12. Yehudi Meshchaninov, "The Prussian-Industrial History of Public Schooling." Paper produced for the New American Academy, Apr. 2012, http://www.thenewamericanacademy.org/images/the-prussian-industrial-history-of-public-schooling1.pdf.

13. Ellwood P. Cubberley, *Readings in the History of Education: A Collection of Sources and Readings to Illustrate the Development of Educational Practice, Theory, and Organization* (Boston: Houghton Mifflin, 1920), 488.

14. Archibald Murphey, *The Papers of Archibald D. Murphey* (Raleigh, N.C.: University of North Carolina Press, 1914), 53-54.

15. Richard Hofstadter, *Anti-Intellectualism in American Life* (New York: Vintage Books, 1963), 302.

16. Ibid., 303.

17. For a brilliant and thorough examination of the fundamental mismatch between bureaucracy and education, see Jerry Kirkpatrick, *Montessori, Dewey, and Capitalism: Education Theory for a Free Market in Education* (Claremont, CA: TLJ Books, 2008).

18. Robert J. Marzano, Tony Frontier, and David Livingston, "A Brief History of Supervision and Evaluation," chapter 2 in *Effective Supervision: Supporting the Art and Science of Teaching* (Alexandria, VA: ASCD, 2011), http://www.ascd.org/publications/books/110019/chapters/A-Brief-History-of-Supervision-and-Evaluation.aspx.

19. Cubberley, *Readings* (1920), 338.

20. John Taylor Gatto, *Dumbing Us Down: The Hidden Curriculum of Compulsory Schooling* (Gabriola Island, BC: New Society Publishers, 2002).

21. William Derescewicz, *Excellent Sheep: Thinking for Yourself, Inventing Your Life, and Other Things the Ivy League Won't Teach You* (New York: Simon & Schuster: New York, 2014). It is also worth listening to Derescewicz discuss "The Disadvantages of an Elite Education," *American Scholar*, June 2008, http://theamericanscholar.org/the-disadvantages-of-an-elite-education/#.U7kD6xZZOYY) the essay that ultimately led to that book. See the video "Bill Derescewicz: 'Are Stanford Students Just (Really Excellent) Sheep?'" recorded April 12, 2011, and available on *YouTube*,

https://www.youtube.com/watch?v=DKVLf7X4zSQ.

22. "Number of Jobs, Labor Market Experience, and Earnings Growth: Results from a National Longitudinal Survey News Release," Bureau of Labor Statistics, July 25, 2012, http://www.bls.gov/news.release/nlsoy.htm.

23. Force and fraud are the only ways someone can make another act against his own judgment and will.

24. Historically, this point of view has been called classical liberalism, and now, often, libertarianism.

25. See Smith's *The Wealth of Nations*. For a modern formulation of the philosophical justification for voluntary, cooperative societies, see Ayn Rand's essays "Man's Rights" and "The Nature of Government" in *Capitalism: The Unknown Ideal*. For massive and detailed information and analysis of the economics of voluntary societies, their history and consequences, see the work of thinkers such as Carl Menger, *The Principles of Economics*; Frédéric Bastiat, *The Law*; Eugene Bohm-Bawerk, *Capital and Interest*; Murray Rothbard, *The Mystery of Banking*; Frederic Hayek, *The Road to Serfdom*; and especially Ludwig Von Mises, *Human Action*. Henry Hazlitt's *Economics in One Lesson* is a powerful and informative summary of economic principles for the layman. These thinkers have, in turn, influenced other contemporary economists. Some of the most compelling belong to what is known as the Austrian School of thought, concentrated at George Mason University but also spread across the country and the world today.

26. These are the principles outlined in political philosopher John Locke's *Second Treatise on Government*, which was the philosophical basis for the Declaration of Independence and the American Constitution. The Fraser Institute's Freedom Indexes summarize the evidence for freedom's superior ability to produce human flourishing. The indexes are available on the institutes website, http://www.fraserinstitute.org/programs-initiatives/economic-freedom.aspx. Current nighttime satellite maps of North and South Korea starkly dramatize the difference between freedom and control. While South Korea is far from a fully free society, it is yet ablaze with light—and activity. In contrast, the North is black but for a tiny point of light in Pyongyang.

27. In her 1964 work, *The Virtue of Selfishness: A New Concept of Egoism* (New York: New American Library, 1964), Ayn Rand argued (p. 129): "Individualism regards man—every man—as an independent, sovereign entity who possesses an inalienable right to his own life, a right derived from his nature as a rational being. Individualism holds that a civilized society, or any

form of association, cooperation or peaceful coexistence among men, can be achieved only on the basis of the recognition of individual rights—and that a group, as such, has no rights other than the individual rights of its members…An individualist is a man who says: 'I will not run anyone's life—nor let anyone run mine. I will not rule nor be ruled. I will not be a master nor a slave. I will not sacrifice myself to anyone—nor sacrifice anyone to myself.'"

28. Maria Montessori, *From Childhood to Adolescence* (Oxford, UK: Clio Press, 1994; orig. pub. 1948).

29. Elisabeth Eaves, "Who Gives the Most?" *Forbes*, Dec. 26, 2008. http://www.forbes.com/2008/12/24/america-philanthropy-income-oped-cx_ee_1226eaves.html.

30. Right now, combined federal, state, real estate, and sales taxes take more than 50 percent of the average person's income. If every individual in the United States were able to keep all but perhaps 3 percent, we'd all be more than twice as well-off. What would we be able to do with that money and the free choices that would accompany it, not least in the realm of educating our children?

31. The fictional society in Kurt Vonnegut's *Harrison Bergeron* paints a clear picture of how this formula works. Of course, such scenarios aren't pure fiction: Soviet Russia, Communist China, and Pol Pot's Cambodia all illustrate the results of attempts to equalize individuals.

32. Individuality is the source of the advantages of a division-of-labor economy.

33. Vikas Bajaj and Jim Yardley, "Many of India's Poor Turn to Private Schools," *The New York Times*, Dec. 30, 2011, http://www.nytimes.com/2011/12/31/world/asia/for-indias-poor-private-schools-help-fill-a-growing-demand.html?pagewanted=all&_r=0.

34. Amanda Ripley, "The $4 Million Teacher," *The Wall Street Journal*, Aug. 3, 2013, http://online.wsj.com/news/articles/SB10001424127887324635904578639780253571520.

35. Mihalyi, Csikszentmihalyi, *Flow: The Psychology of Optimal Experience* (New York: Harper Perennial, 1991).

36. In a free society, all such research would be transparent and voluntary; students would not be captive subjects of psychological, psychometric, or biometric data-mining as they are sometimes today. The latter would be a violation of rights and therefore prohibited.

37. Doug Guthrie, "The Real Disrupters: The Innovators Who Are Truly Transforming Education," *Forbes*, Mar. 18, 2014, http://www.forbes.com/sites/dougguthrie/2014/03/18/the-real-disrupters-the-innovators-who-are-truly-transforming-education/.

38. Here, the technology is used to facilitate both better teaching and surer absorption of knowledge rather than measure "accountability" to the state, which places stress on students and teachers alike.

39. Updated edition by Oxford University Press (2008).

40. Jeff Dyer, Hal Gregersen, and Clayton Christiansen, "The Innovator's DNA," *Harvard Business Review* 87, no. 12 (Dec. 2009), 60-7 and 128, http://www.ncbi.nlm.nih.gov/pubmed/19968057. See also, Peter Sims, "The Montessori Mafia," *Harvard Review Blogs*, Apr. 5, 2011, http://blogs.wsj.com/ideas-market/2011/04/05/the-montessori-mafia/.

41. Maria Montessori, *The Formation of Man* (Oxford: Clio Press, 1989; orig. pub. 1955), 48.

APPENDIX A:
The Review Form for English Language Arts Standards

A. READING PEDAGOGY AND INDEPENDENT READING

1. The document expects explicit and systematic instruction in decoding skills in the primary grades as well as use of meaningful reading materials and an emphasis on comprehension.

    0   Phonics or decoding skills are not mentioned at all.

    1   Phonics or decoding skills are mentioned only in the context of other strategies so that it is unlikely they are addressed independently or systematically.

    3   Phonics or decoding skills are given a separate bullet or statement but there is nothing to suggest explicit and systematic teaching and independence from contextual approaches.

    4   Explicit and systematic instruction in decoding skills, both independent of context and in context, is clearly suggested or spelled out.

2. The standards make clear that interpretations of written texts should be supported by logical reasoning, accurate facts, and adequate evidence.

    0   The standards imply that all points of view or interpretations are equally valid regardless of the logic, accuracy, and adequacy of supporting evidence.

    1   The standards imply that all literary texts are susceptible of many equally valid interpretations.

    3   The standards indicate that interpretations of texts must be in part on what is in the texts.

    4   The standards indicate that interpretations of any text must accord with what the author wrote.

3. The document expects students to read independently through the grades and provides guidance about quality and difficulty.

0 Independent reading isn't mentioned at all.

1 Regular independent reading is recommended but not quality, quantity, or difficulty.

3 Quality, quantity, or difficulty of independent reading is indicated in some way (e.g., by a list of recommended books or by a recommended number of words or books per grade).

4 Quality, quantity, and difficulty are indicated in some way.

B. VALUE ACCORDED LITERARY STUDY

1. The document expects and enables teachers to stress literary study at the secondary level.

   0 Literary standards are not distinguishable from non-literary standards.

   1 Literary reading is stressed about equally with non-literary reading throughout the grades.

   3 Literary reading is stressed more than non-literary reading in the ELA class only at lower grade levels.

   4 Literary reading is emphasized throughout the grades.

2. The document and the standards indicate that assigned texts should be chosen on the basis of literary quality, cultural and historical significance.

   0 The document says little or nothing about literary quality and historical significance.

   1 The document expects assigned texts to be chosen on the basis of literary quality and historical significance but offers no criteria for selection, no recommended lists of authors or works, and few or no standards to guide selection based on quality and significance.

   3 The document expects assigned texts to be chosen on the basis of literary quality and historical significance and provides some standards and examples to guide selection.

   4 The standards clearly require assigned texts to be selected on the basis of literary quality and/or historical significance.

3. The standards promote study of American literature.

   0 American literature is not mentioned as such in any way.

   1 American literature is mentioned, but no more than that.

3   American literature is mentioned in an inclusive way.

4   American literature is described in an inclusive way and is to be studied
     in depth from a historical perspective.

C. ORGANIZATION AND DISCIPLINARY COVERAGE OF THE STANDARDS

1. They are grouped in categories and subcategories reflecting
    coherent bodies of scholarship or research in reading and the
    English language arts.

    0   They are mostly grouped in unique or incoherent categories or
         subcategories (e.g., categories reflect pedagogical strategies).

    1   Some categories or subcategories reflect coherent bodies of scholarship
         or research.

    3   Most but not all categories and subcategories reflect coherent bodies of
         scholarship or research.

    4   All categories and subcategories reflect coherent bodies of scholarship or
         research.

2. The standards clearly address listening and speaking. They
    include use of various discussion purposes and roles, how to
    participate in discussion, desirable qualities in formal speaking,
    and use of established and peer-generated criteria for evaluat-
    ing formal and informal speech.

    0   Standards for listening and speaking are not included.

    1   Some of the above areas for coverage are addressed adequately.

    3   Most but not all of the above areas are addressed adequately.

    4   All of the above areas are adequately covered.

3. The standards clearly address reading to understand and use
    information through the grades. They include progressive
    development of reading skills, knowledge and use of a variety
    of textual features, genres, and reading strategies for academic,
    occupational, and civic purposes.

    0   Standards for informational reading are not distinguished as such.

    1   Some of the above areas for coverage are addressed adequately.

3 Most of the above areas for coverage are addressed adequately.

4 All of the above areas are adequately covered.

4. **The standards clearly seek to develop strong vocabulary knowledge and dictionary skills.**

   0 Vocabulary standards are not in a distinct strand or category for instruction.

   1 Vocabulary standards emphasize use of context throughout the grades.

   3 Vocabulary standards highlight specific figures of speech and rhetorical devices but are limited in the categories of words they highlight and stress contextual approaches.

   4 Vocabulary standards teach dictionary skills, use of glossaries for discipline- specific terms, ways to use context, and all useful categories of phrases, words, or word parts (e.g., foreign words, idioms, proverbs).

5. **The standards clearly address the reading, interpretation, and critical evaluation of literature. They include knowledge of diverse literary elements and genres, different kinds of literary responses, and use of a variety of interpretive lenses. They also specify the key authors, works, and literary traditions in American literature and in the literary and civic heritage of English-speaking people that should be studied for their literary quality and cultural significance.**

   0 Standards for literary study are not distinguished as such.

   1 Some of the above areas for coverage are addressed adequately.

   3 Most of the above areas for coverage are addressed adequately.

   4 All of the above areas are adequately covered.

6. **The standards clearly address writing for communication and expression. They include use of writing processed, established as well as peer- generated or personal evaluation criteria, and various rhetorical elements, strategies, genres, and modes of organization.**

   0 Standards for writing for communication and expression are not distinguished as such.

   1 Some of the above areas for coverage are addressed adequately.

3   Most of the above areas for coverage are addressed adequately.

4   All of the above areas are adequately covered.

7. The standards clearly address oral and written language conventions. They include standard English conventions for sentence structure, spelling, usage, penmanship, capitalization, and punctuation.

   0   Standards for oral and written language conventions are not distinguished as such.

   1   Some of the above areas for coverage are addressed adequately.

   3   Most of the above areas for coverage are addressed adequately.

   4   All of the above areas are adequately covered.

8. The standards clearly address the nature, dynamics, and history of the English language. They include the origin of its vocabulary, its structure (grammar), the evolution of its oral and written forms, and the distinction between its oral and written forms today.

   0   Standards for this area are not distinguished as such.

   1   Some of the above areas for coverage are addressed adequately.

   3   Most of the above areas for coverage are addressed adequately.

   4   All of the above areas are adequately covered.

9. The standards clearly address research processes, including developing questions and locating, understanding, evaluating, synthesizing, and using various sources of information for reading, writing, and speaking assignments. These sources include dictionaries, thesauruses, other reference materials, observations of empirical phenomena, interviews with informants, and computer databases.

   0   Standards for the research processes are not distinguished as such.

   1   Some of the above areas for coverage are addressed adequately.

   3   Most of the above areas for coverage are addressed adequately.

   4   All of the above areas are adequately covered.

D. QUALITY OF THE STANDARDS

1. **They are clear, specific, and measurable.**

   0 They are vague, filled with jargon, and/or expressed in ways that are not measurable (e.g., use unmeasurable verbs like "explore," "investigate," "inquire," or ask for personal experience).

   1 To some extent, clear, specific, teachable, measurable, and reliably rated.

   3 For the most part, clear, jargon-free, teachable, and measurable, and reliably rated.

   4 Overall, they are clear, jargon-free, teachable, measurable, and reliably rated.

2. **They are of increasing intellectual difficulty at each higher educational level and cover all important aspects of learning in the area they address.**

   0 For the most part, they show little change in difficulty over the grades, or are frequently repeated for many grades at a time.

   1 Increases in difficulty may sometimes be reflected in the wording of a standard.

   3 Most of the standards show meaningful increases in difficulty over the grades and address the important aspects of learning in the area.

   4 Overall, the standards show educationally appropriate and meaningful increases in difficulty over the grades and cover all imporant aspects of learning in the area.

3. **They index or illustrate growth through the grades for reading by referring to specific reading levels or titles/authors of specific literary or academic works as examples of a reading level, or by spelling out the nature of the intellectual task required by the standard.**

   0 The reading standards contain no clue as to reading level other than something like "using texts at the appropriate grade level."

   1 The reading standards are sometimes accompanied by examples of specific texts or authors.

   3 The reading standards are frequently accompanied by examples of specific texts or authors or spell out more advanced content.

4   The reading standards are almost always accompanied by examples of specific texts and/or authors, or spell out the advanced content required by the standard.

4. They illustrate growth expected through the grades for writing with reference to examples and rating criteria, in the standards document or in other documents.

0   The document provides no criteria or samples for the quality of writing at assessed grades.

1   The document provides criteria or examples for the quality of writing at some but not all assessed grades through high school.

3   The document provides criteria or examples for the quality of writing at all assessed grades through high school.

4   The document provides examples and criteria for the quality of writing at all assessed grades, including high school.

5. Their overall contents are sufficiently specific, comprehensive, and demanding to lead to a common core of high academic expectations for all students.

0   No. They cannot lead to a common core of high academic expectations.

1   To some extent only.

3   For the most part.

4   Yes.

MAR - - 2015